The GREAT Computer Is Spirit Generating Our Desires

A Spiritual Journey of Enlightenment

Ronald Raymond Rocha

iUniverse, Inc.
New York   Bloomington

The GREAT Computer Is Spirit Generating Our Desires
A Spiritual Journey of Enlightenment

iUniverse books may be ordered through booksellers or by contacting:

iUniverse
1663 Liberty Drive
Bloomington, IN 47403
www.iuniverse.com
1-800-Authors (1-800-288-4677)

Because of the dynamic nature of the Internet, any Web addresses or links contained in this book may have changed since publication and may no longer be valid. The views expressed in this work are solely those of the author and do not necessarily reflect the views of the publisher, and the publisher hereby disclaims any responsibility for them.

978-1-4401-2883-7 (pbk)
978-1-4401-2884-4 (ebk)

Printed in the United States of America

iUniverse rev. date: 04/17/2009

To all of you inquisitive souls looking for your truth…

1–2–3

I AM *indivisible Almighty Mind*, Omnipotent Numerical Energy of TWO forces, *truths watching over* you children—THREE—*thinking harmonic radiance echoing emotions*, reflecting my thoughts within your *mind*, my image numerically defined, for we All Radiate Energy as ONE!

The GREAT Computer

Contents

Essays *Poems* **Picture Poems**

Acknowledgments

The stories that define our collection of experiences is cast upon our mind's eye, to enlighten our soul to our divine fantasies that we choose to believe as *truth*, a process of discovery that circumnavigates eternity.

I would like to thank my *three* guiding spirits I believe have enlightened me to wakefulness, allowing me to receive these inspired words collected here. My deepest gratitude goes to my biblical guide *Ezekiel*, to *Thoth*, the Egyptian scribe of knowledge, and *Urruso*, an old soul with the rolling R's who mysteriously seems related somehow. The symbolism of our connective links reveals itself within these pages and is truly a divine fantasy that has changed me forever.

Preface

This collection of essays and poems (2000–2009) are mostly channeled messages, "voices in the sky" that spoke to my *mind* (Mind's image numerically defined) as it interfaces with the GREAT Computer *generating radiant energy as thought, consciously observing magnetic phenomenon unifying truths electromagnetically radiated.* The handwriting of these messages was quite different from my own at times, and I always wondered who was communicating with me. I dated each entry as a numerical log to define the *type of energy* flowing on that day.

You will notice many CapitalizeD (compacted data) and *italicized* "keywords" that help to explain a more vivid expression of new thoughts using old words. Although this goes against the normal editorial style of books, I feel compelled to leave them as such to help clarify the intricacies of explaining fourth-dimensional perspectives with third-dimensional terms. Understanding the simple basics is a complex matter using word symbols. There is much information compressed within these pages that I *link* together for reference or clarification. I have included a glossary of over 300 acronyms that helped guide me along the tangent paths I found myself exploring through the *trenches* of cosmic consciousness, viewing deep thoughts that enlightened my mind. I have also included an index to help maneuver through the labyrinth of titles contained within this treatise.

The purpose of this book, like all books, is to shed a little "light" on Truth—knowledge—that we all seek to entertain our mind, our "chip" of the GREAT Computer! The perspectives projected within these pages are contemporary views of transforming "abstract truths" by means of symbols (letters and words) that inspire numbers, which in turn vibrate at frequencies (wavelengths) to illuminate ALL that IS projected along the *binary code* (electromagnetic force field) of the One Source turning the wheel of Love/Life energy into a cosmic kaleidoscope.

A "computer" is a *mechanical mind*, an apparatus that stores, transfers, and produces symbols. These symbols (data) are abstracts that represent some "thing" stored *in memory* of the computer mind, information that describes a way to transform abstract knowledge (energy) into concrete "realities" through a process we call SCIENCE—Source-consciousness inducing electromagnetic nuclear-concepts emotionally!

Generating Our Desires is synonymous with energy. Understanding energy allows us to realize how WE (wisdom exemplified) are generators of desires! We cannot create nor destroy energy. We can only transform energy, moving it from state to state (form to form). Energy is either stored or transmitted, at "rest" or in "motion"—*E-motion*! Stored energy is *memory*, from which Mind expresses/experiences moments observing radiant *youth* (you observing universal thought harmony) abstracting thoughts from the source of the universal Mind (magnetically inspired numerical data)—the GREAT Computer!

Technically speaking, our mind is our "data operating system." If we look closer at the similarities of our mind and the GREAT Computer, we will begin to understand the "techno lingo" of secrets hidden within the symbols we see but may not understand. For example, DOS stands for Divine Omniscient Spirit, which is truly our *data operating system*! In order to truly see *truth* (our desires), we need to open our mind to new thoughts or perspectives that will raise our consciousness UP to take in the Universal Perspective! Our "life" depends on our "state of mind" we choose to observe our self in, which can be a *heaven* or a *hell*. Again, it all depends on how we use and abuse energy.

Emotion (energy in motion) is the process of transforming abstract thought into concrete reality. Our mind is a facsimile of Mind, a "receiver" or platform in which to base, log, accumulate, sort, weigh, and *decipher* (by the numbers) DATA (divine abstract thought aspiring) in order to convert energy flowing through the cosmos of the *uni-verse* (one turning).

Through years of seeking my truths, I have kept an open mind, eager to entertain new thoughts to stimulate me, awaken me to the truth I seek. I finally opened the door within my heart to glimpse my *radiance of Love*—my soul! The answers to those questions I pondered have changed my life forever. In finding my holy grail, I discovered these answers relate to all of US united souls, for we are in this life *together*. I hope you find the "word play" my spiritual guides downloaded to me entertaining and helpful in opening *your* heart's door. I pray that I have transcribed it well enough for that purpose.

I have asked my guides to keep this allegorical treatise simple and easy to understand. I must admit it is a science fiction tale of intricate detail, covering many aspects of *truth*. I have discovered the depth of description has increased as my mind became enlightened. I have tried to arrange these *ideas* (inspired data electromagnetically aligned) to provide a foundation from which to grow our understanding of *words*, wisdom of radiant data symbols, which (verbal or written) are the major means of transferring abstract energy between minds—*you and me*. Therefore, I suggest *first* reading this book from beginning to end, as each chapter builds on the previous. The depth and intricacies of which will draw you back to discover new truths repeatedly!

Only by opening our mind can we truly nourish our heart and soul, growing into the *Light of Love* to harmonize with the GREAT Computer. Thereby, allowing us to be "in tune" will ALL that is stored at HOME (harmony of mental emotions) vibrating "on line," along the Electro-Magnetic wavelengths of Eternal Memory.

In my quest for the answers to those questions we all ask, I have discovered "esoteric" knowledge, those secret truths found only by persistent research and inquiry, truths that go beyond the pat answers given to the masses. Everyone carries our Truth within our eternal file of Mind, which we methodically peruse in search of our *self*—our divine image!

We start out in life like sheep. Lead in flocks, we are fed with basic knowledge to be socially acceptable, contributing to the status quo as reliable consumers, trained to believe all we hear on the daily news and commercials "informing" us with truths "twisted" to SELL, stimulate emotional Love/Life! After all, if it does not sell, it is not worth broadcasting!

Our "general education" molds us into our character roles we choose to play in life, following the customs that allow us to "fit in" with the crowd, confining us in controllable groups as *obedient* citizens that fear to be "free-thinkers!" Any departures from the norm will quickly draw attention, ridicule, and retribution for being different. Life is truly a battle to overcome the simplest of obstacles. It takes *courage of fear* to open our eyes to truths few are willing to accept, even though we desire to be accepted not outcast! Generally, the process of education teaches us "what to think" *not* "how to think." Education does not teach us about our innate abilities as a powerful mind focusing *thoughts* into explosive *emotions*—the two things that define us as spiritual/humans! To gather that knowledge, we must depend on our self (self-help), and that is the purpose of this book!

As a photographer, I am a trained observer, curiously admiring the wonders of *Mother's Nature* that controls the playing field in our *game of Love/Life*. It is due to my wife's *emotional energy* that I have posed many of my questions. Observing her emotional anguish inspired many of these writings. I have come to see my wife (my significant other) as the impetus allowing me my enlightenment, for mother's *negative/magnetic* energy is the "key" to opening the door to Generating Our Desires!

You will notice a repetitive pattern in this work, but all knowledge and all life depends on repetition to rekindle dormant truths so difficult to see, even though strategically placed in plain sight, for we take them for granted with little appreciation. We did not learn our *alphabet* or *numbers* overnight (key elements of Generating Our Desires)! It took us years of practice! Like a chick, pecking its way free of its shell, these words will repeatedly tap on your subconscious, wearing the shield of your ignorance and *denial* thin, allowing you to gradually become "acclimatized" to the Light of Love illuminating your soul. Eventually, through an open mind and hungry heart, the shell holding you in your hazy illumination will crack, allowing you your first *epiphany of truth* awaiting you on the *other side* of your physical illusion!

It is difficult to truly grasp the immensity of the tasks we find our self involved in as we struggle to comprehend reason or purpose from our *passions* that move our soul to ACT (activate cosmic thought). We simply rise each morning to that whispered voice coaxing us out of bed to continue our journey, moving us to give birth to something bursting from within us, something we cannot contain under the duress of our own fears holding us back from the truth we seek.

The intricate detail of the words weaved into the fabric of this story hold more *energy* than visible. The interconnected *links* will take time to grow together to reveal the true "quilt" under which we all sleep. The Love flowing here is truly an eternal essence, and you will find yourself reaching for the *GREAT Computer* many times, opening it at will to the "story of the day" your heart yearns to read, similar to buying a "numbered lot" to scratch and smile, seeing within your mind/heart ALL you wish to be real.

The journey you are about to undertake goes beyond your usual earthly perspectives. Yet, this basic guidebook to the "sights" is relatively simple to follow, as easy as 1–2–3! For, it hinges on the *Trinity*—the three things that are Generating Our Desires. With diligence and close inspection—reading between the lines—you just may be enlightened to some "truth" you are seeking. **Truly, there are no truths within this book**! I am talking about truth that surrounds and permeates ALL. You can only find truth within your individual *self*, your soul experiencing love/life force, as it relates to cosmic SELF, Source-Energy Love/Life Force, but only when you become an *inquisitive soul*!

The Inquisitive Soul

The inquisitive soul is a hungry heart
Yearning to know their hidden part
They play within my show.
The urge to seek beyond their world,
Where visions set their mind to swirl
About those thoughts that *could be*,
Draws them to a *higher vision* that opens their mind to SEE
Spirit evolves emotionally,
Moving them along their Course
Of electromagnetic wavelengths called the Force,
Where TWO of ONE describes the scenes
Of all the things they see in dreams,
As wonder sets their mind in motion
Along the paths of sweet emotion,
Out across *space* and *time*
To feel their heart as it grows OLD
Observing Love's dimensions,
To remember—live—and find
Their inquisitive soul!

Bless you and bon voyage

Introduction

Life is like a wormhole, the deeper you immerse your self into it, the closer you get to its end—another opening on the other side of Life.

Moving toward enlightenment—knowing the *Light of Love*—is a very fearful adventure. We find our self moving out of the cold of all that is compressed into space, the void of Eternal Memory exploding into stellar eruptions, glowing in the radiance of Love, illuminating our mind with thoughts moving us upon emotional tides.

Our first brave steps as *children of the Light*, out into the unknown darkness of fear and ignorance that we encounter "in the flesh," are truly some of the hardest steps our soul can take along our cosmic journeys. Here, as human beings, we search the depths of our mind to comprehend our *being* balanced energy inducing numerical geometry, existing within the electromagnetic chaos stimulating our *world* (wisdom of radiant love data) in which we *live*, logically inducing vibrant emotions! Once we muster the *courage of Love* to step forward, there is no turning back. As we repeat that first step, we gain confidence to create our brave new world from truths we "re-member"—put back together—from Eternal Memory, creating a life we can *feel* is real!

No matter what adventures we experience we are never *out* of Love! Love is the essence of Generating Our Desires, constantly monitoring and guiding us through Life. Love is the backbone of our songs and stories we relate to each other. We express our life's *reflection* of our love by projecting it OUT as we *observe universal truths*—thoughts that define our desires. Of course, experiencing life for our self is paramount, for the truth of Life Of Vibrant Emotions is something you cannot *tell* a child, it is something they have to SEE to *believe*!

The power of Love is so blinding it takes years for us to truly open our eyes to our truth, to finally connect all the *points* of Light—perceptions of inspired nuclear thoughts—allowing us to create our image of our *self* (soul experiencing love/life force). We reflect upon our thoughts that touch our heart in mysterious ways, unfolding a hidden *universe* within us. The ONE omnipotent numerical engineer—the GREAT Computer—turns on and off in endless points of *Light*, where Love is generating harmonic thoughts twinkling within us, fueling our journey out into *space* (some point awaiting conscious expression) to witness *Life*, where Love is fluid energy in motion—*emotion*! This omnipotent Source of consciousness propels us forward into our *future*, focusing universal truths unifying radiant energy into realities we choose as "entertainment" from Eternal Memory. With an *open* mind and *willing* heart, we will discover all we desire to know! All we have to do is go with the flow!

These messages offered here are my attempts at spreading the WORD—the wisdom of radiant desire. The *word* of course is impossible to comprehend in its entirety, for it is something that is continually expanding at light speed and beyond. We are only capable of glimpsing the shadow of its passage as it reflects upon our mind as a mere "bit" of a "byte" along the neural network of the GREAT Computer. It is our goal in life to be aware of who we are, where we come from, and why we are here. This basic knowledge will allow us to cooperate with all that IS, WAS, and everything we WILL to be, as we grow in knowledge to the fact we truly ARE *angels radiating energy*!

WE (wisdom exemplified) are instrumental in creating our *Grand View* of our life! We alone have the power to make our break our dreams! However, we are only capable of viewing our own personal, Pixilated Consciousness—our stellar soul—that is a critical part of our creator's cosmic illumination. We can only bask in our own light, our own spark of *Love/Life energy* flowing through us, for YOU truly live within your own universe. The secret to enlightenment is to give up—contribute—our free will to the Universal Will, to see our critical *part* (personally aligned radiant thoughts) in perspective to the *whole* (wisdom harmoniously observing Love/Life energy).

Again, the purpose of this book is to guide you along perspectives for you to SEE—spiritually evolve emotionally—beyond the confines of our physical world. The maze of words defining these perspectives may seem to add to the haze of your confusion. However, new roads need frequent travels to acquire familiar landmarks. By tapping into your *courage of Love* you will manifest your *courage of fear*, the duality projecting you through the dark void of ignorance (space) to circumnavigate time with *clear vision*, from which you will see the Light! With open mind and willing heart, step forward to reap all of your *blessings in disguise* awaiting you within the GREAT Computer.

Bless you and Godspeed

1

Generating Our Desires
Thinking As Loving Kindred Souls

God talks to every one of us *souls*—spirits of universal love. God talks to us through our thoughts, those abstract bursts of energy that flow through us to entertain our *mind*, our "image" of our creator! *Thought energy* is the genesis of all creation, for without thought nothing would exist! Everything that we call "real" is simply a matter of our free will's ability to accept those thoughts we entertain in our mind as being true. Thought energy is so powerful it is conscious of ALL things in the universe, right down to the smallest atomic particle. It has the ability to magnetically attract those atoms into an illusion of things for our soul to comprehend, compute, and manipulate in a three-dimensional world of miraculous wonders. We either believe or not believe those thoughts we entertain within the cosmos of Mind (magnetically inspired numerical data)—the GREAT Computer! It all depends on how open our mind is to *new* thoughts, how prepared we are to entertain the endless possibilities of what *could be* awaiting our discovery in other dimensions, other states of Mind.

Although we all look similar as human beings, we are spiritual (energy) beings evolving within our *own worlds* of thoughts! Truly, WE (wisdom exemplified) are minds manipulating energy, collecting bits and bytes of data to create our life, in which YOU live in *your own universe*! All we can do is wonder, stare in amazement of those things we do not understand and with our curious mind ask questions! If we keep our *eyes* open and are astute at the *art of listening*, our thoughts will evolve into our answers to those questions!

Generating Our Desires is truly a process of computing *numbers* that take shape to form "things." We do these calculations within our mind at light speed, instantaneously envisioning an *idea* (inspired data electromagnetically aligned), which we transform into a reality by slowing it down from light speed for us to "reflect upon." We do this so naturally that we see nothing mysterious about it. Yet, our mind is continuously wandering from thought to thought, wondering (calculating) every moment of our life—day and night! Our mind is *energy in motion*—E-motion—that does not rest for long. Our thoughts are truly who we ARE!

Thinking is our greatest tool, for it is *the process* of Generating Our

Desires! This tool creates and then destroys in order to create again. The purpose of this book is not to disseminate "new" knowledge, for nothing is new, everything just IS *inspired spirit*! We simply pull it from Eternal Memory—the EM (electromagnetic) database or *binary code* from which we draw our knowledge (truths)—as we *open our mind* and log onto the GREAT Computer, downloading our desires as *Love/Life energy*!

Our childhood is dependent upon our parents and how they transfer their Love/Life energy to prepare us for our journey *away* from home. As an adult, we *alone* are responsible for our changing development through "self-help"—being aware that only we can change our self! There is no magic button to push; *evolution* is a life-long process that is truly an uphill struggle! If we want to change the world, we must first start with our *self* and be an example worth following! The world will not change according to our desires, only we will change to perceive our world for what it is—an illusion!

The time has come to step UP and truly see *what* we are and *how* our technology has opened *doors to truth* for us to view physically our spiritual life. A life played out through the illusion illuminated upon the "hard disc" we spin upon and around as we commute to the *other side* of life every night, in the dark void of our mind. With the advent of technological advancements, we can now reach out and touch our fellow travelers around the world, offering a helping hand and open heart to raise our collective spirits to see our true potential as generators of desires.

My Door to Truth

My door to truth is open wide
To pupils dark in which you hide
Behind closed eyes,
Where you dream of joys you wish now to appear
To bring you pleasures from painful tears
You shed to know my truth,
Shining bright upon my night, through your eyes filled with sight
Of your daze I set aglow, scened in views you choose to know
As you search through *time*, seeking your Love I hold in Mind,
Struggling through fear with courage bold
To find the key within your soul
That opens my door to truth.
Here, within my cloistered spaces,
You spin wheels of Life as human racers
Testing your skills I give to you as I hold you in suspension,
To **A**cquire **G**rowth **E**xperiences **O**bserving **L**ove's **D**imensions
Along your love stories you relate today,
Spreading gossip along your way,
In dark despair of what you fear is behind my door to truth.

Desire

Desire—data electrically sent in radiant emotions—is what makes the universe revolve and evolve. Desire means to "long for," to ask or wish for something to entertain our mind, to fill our void of space (blank screen) with some *thought* to convert to *feelings* for us to experience (see) its reality. *Reality* being radiant energy aligning lineal inspiration transforming youths, *souls* that are the EYES (eternal youth experiencing Source/Spirit) of Cosmic Consciousness—the universal *Mind* manipulating inspired numerical data.

All desires relate to thoughts (electric impulses) that project visions upon *our mind*, where we observe universal radiance magnetically induce numerical data, arranging thoughts in geometric shapes that define the parameters of a thought. The thought of a ball implies a "spherical" object, as does a box a "square or rectangular" object. Thoughts relate images of shapes that have texture, color, sound, taste, or smell that we sense with our five physical sensors of our *human alien* vehicle in which we travel this "third-dimensional" *state* of Mind—this world we call Earth. Whenever we think, we desire—wonder, question, and search for some reality to experience!

Desire is an expression of LOVE that moves us to *live our vibrant emotions* as feelings we interpret from our thoughts, stimulating our mind to understand abstract visions as *words* we express to define things (shapes) that describe our *world*, wisdom of radiant love data. As *children of the Light* experiencing the "desires of the flesh," we first learn to communicate our desires through words, putting them together to make a sentence to describe our desires in more detail. Correlating words to objects in our world allows us to *express* our self—move through our *divine fantasy* we envision within our mind!

Our thoughts fill us with a radiance that glows from within us, allowing us to express our *Love/Life energy* (thoughts and feelings) outwardly, touching another soul through *relationships*, the stories we share as expressions of what we sense with our life—our desires! Those who understand us (kindred spirits) travel similar paths in their life, while those who do not may wonder if our story is *true*. They too will desire to *know*, kindling numerically observed wisdom to illuminate thoughts into visions of some adventure they desire to experience in life, always wondering if they have the *courage of Love* to do it—make it real!

Our desires appear as *clear visions* that move us to create. We transform our desires by manipulating those thoughts we hold as truths, twisting and shaping them into words to make others "see our point of view" (as I am doing here), to share our thoughts and feelings, for that is ALL we have to give one another! We share our desires so we can be aware of our *motion*, our ability to move through Mind to *spiritually evolve emotionally*—SEE everything around us glowing in the *Light of Love.*

My thoughts of you stir my heart,
Moving me to jump and start
A *vibration* of Love that moves your soul,
Radiating my Love so COLD,
As *children of Light Divine*
Searching my files in Memory to find,
Here, encased in flesh and bone,
The door I opened between Earth and *Home*,
Where harmony of mental emotions sets you free to roam
The fields of visions I set aglow
Electromagnetically to illuminate my SHOW,
Spiritual harmony of wisdom, shining bright to fill my night,
Bringing my dreams to day,
Where in the Light you have my sight to *know* the life you grow!
With heart in hand, you bravely stand to face your world *alone*,
Lost in my thoughts of you.

Here, we live in visions of *curiosity*, eagerly searching out our desires, reaching out to each other as our soul freezes in the void of our mind, crying in anguish for someone to see us, touch us, and hold us close in the warmth of Love radiating within our soul. As we embrace each other in our attraction of Love, we grow *brighter* and *warmer*, realizing that in *numbers* there is *security*, and we reach out even more to touch as many souls as we can, sharing our Data Electrically Sent In Radiant Emotions!

My Light of Love

My Light of Love I shine bright and true
For all you children to think, feel, and do,
As out from home you travel to see
ALL your desires you choose to BE,
Birthing emotionally my Love you hear
Ring in your ears throughout the years,
Building your castles in time,
Awash in emotions to let you find
All your tears of gratitude
Reflect my Light of Love for you.

My Love/my Life, *my dearest wife*,
My heart caressing my mind,
Converts my Love from thoughts I hold,
Entertaining young and old,
In stories of Love you LIVE,
Logically inducing vibrant emotions
I send your soul to give
To each other as sister/brother
Seeking to find your truth
Unfolding "in the flesh" as my human youths
Playing in Mother's Nature.

Through her heart, I let you feel
The pains of Love you think are real,
Moving your soul upon my Light,
Up,
Down,
Left and right,
To let you see from every angle
The joy and sorrow of being *angels*
Aglow on my Light of Love.

Curiosity
A Desire to Know

Curiosity is something we all have, for it is a standard issue tool for us cosmic *time travelers*. As an intricate part of the Universal Mind (the GREAT Computer), we too are always wondering, always eager to experience "new things" from the limitless stores *in memory*. Therefore, our mind *implores* to *explore*, find, and experience everything our heart desires to feel as a reality. Curiosity is our greatest gift, it is our free ticket to the candy store, where we pull down from the cosmic library anything we choose to read into existence, to entertain our *free will*—a personal "reflective disc" that spins visions of life as a *DVD*—a spirit of universal love!

However you look at it, our curiosity determines our journey through life. The places in which we find our self will be as entertaining, creative, challenging, or fearful as we make them. Curiosity is our power tool to *create* or *destroy* according to our command, our *clear vision* of desires we choose to experience first-hand. Our curiosity will draw thoughts to us, downloaded for our perusal, to contemplate, manipulate, and act out as a *generator of desire*, defining our realities we choose to *believe*!

Our curiosity evolves around *patterns* and *habits* that define who we are, allowing us to transform our *data electrically sent in radiant emotions* that shape us into our chosen image. If we discover we *are not* acting out our image we think we are, we may be living in *denial* of who we desire to be, fearful to believe that our wildest dreams are possible! Dreams are visions of possibilities enticing us to pull them *from* Mind and bring them *to* life. We transform abstract, invisible thoughts from *nowhere* into concrete physical "reflections" *now here*, to exist in a reality we create simply for entertainment, our *passions* of Love we suffer to enjoy, for *opposition* is the only way we revolve to evolve our curiosity—our way of thinking!

Curiosity will lead us to view our *expectations* according to how we use our Love/Life energy. It will enlighten us to world shattering discoveries and there are many yet to find. Each of us has that gift, that *right* to create whatever our heart feels it *must* do, for only then will we be sure of who we really are and what we can really do!

Curiosity is my first name,
Where my Love *reflects* in my game
Of Love/Life illuminated upon my show.
Together, we will see all that we can do,
Some place...some time...all for you!
Curious?

DVD
Divine Vibrations Distorted

Vibrations are the cosmic *electromagnetic wavelengths* emanating through the heavens. They are the *binary code* of infinity evolving to revolve in a perpetual continuum, a never-ending story we witness NOW—numerically observing wisdom! Each vibration will deliver an experience filled with innumerable details universally connected *on line*—a network of *spirits of universal love* expressing who they choose to be.

Vibrations of Love/Life energy reflect outward for the universe to see
The static hum held in Mind of wonders meant for you and me.
A simple song of simple deeds to add to the harmonious flow
Of the breath that beats your heart to make your body glow
In tune to ALL that IS atomic love/life inspiring souls.

This Love/Life song of you vibrates on waves that rise and fall
In melodies of emotional tides that stirs your soul to call
Out to those along your way,
Sharing your love you express today
Through *passions* felt within your heart,
Defining your gifted part

8

You play within the *show* of spiritual harmony of wisdom
From thoughts you desire to know!

You spin your tale in songs you dance
On waves you sail that shroud your trance,
Induced by numbers from which you are cast,
Carrying you forth from your past,
On moments now here,
Compressed and focused to form a haze,
An illusion of Light that forms your daze,
Through which you struggle to comprehend
The meaning of life, *beginning* to *end*,
As you drift along to BE balanced energy,
Spinning around my wheels of life
As my divine visionary disciple—my DVD.

Expectations

We hold all of our expectations, all those *future possibilities* of what could be, in our mind. We think of those things we strongly desire and *hope* they will come true. This hope is a vision our free will entertains as it constructs the image of our self we wish to project onto the world stage.

Expectations are an expression of Love/Life energy conceived and created along the electromagnetic flow that supplies us with our power to BE—birth emotionally—our desires. This dualistic light force of positive and negative energy will give birth to our expectations in ways that will benefit us the most, even if we are not immediately aware of it. *Every dark cloud has a silver lining* is a truism of our duality—from pain comes pleasure! One cannot know what some thing *is* without knowing what that thing *is not*—the opposite view.

Through our visions of *love*, we express our life of vibrant emotions that define who we think we are or long to become. We acquire our knowledge to prepare us to play our part in our "passion play," torturing our self as we express that which we love, hoping to find the "starring role" to claim our fame and glory—whatever that may be! However, we often find our self sidetracked when our expectations do not appear. We end up accepting some other pastime to "pay the bills," to keep us mobile while we search for the right *attitude* (assigned truths transforming inspired

9

thoughts unifying data emotionally) that will position us to "receive" our expectations. This is a time-consuming process where we collect the necessary experiences through trial and error, where success and failure define what we are capable of doing and what we are not. Only through our *reflection* do we know our *projection*!

Expectations are things we *think* will happen, things we envision in our mind that will make us happy or sad. Once our present-moment thoughts (energy) are set in motion (emotionally), we lose all control of those thoughts. *Wishing* alone will not bring us our desires. We need to exert a more persistent force than a simple wish. Only by maintaining consistent thoughts (vivid images within our mind) and speaking positive words confirming our expectations can we attain our desires. We need to act as though our expectations are real, as if we *already have* our expectations! As our thoughts are our "primal creator," beware of the *type* of energy you are working, for what you *give* you will *receive*! Positive thoughts bring positive results and vice versa. Truly, what we *think* we become!

Expectations define our anticipated future, *not* our past! Our future depends upon the type of thoughts we entertain *now*, numerically observing wisdom transform our *positive* and *negative* thoughts as an expression of our desires at this *present moment*. Our truth is what we *will* to believe through our thoughts, words, and actions we project around us as a reality, for we alone make our life into what we desire. Only if we are *aware* of what we are creating can we be in control of our life!

Again, expectations are what we anticipate to become REAL (radiant energy aligned logically), a reality we truly hold in our mind! The more we think about something the more likely that it will come true. *Hope* (harnessing our projected expectations) is not an idle desire or wish, it is a state of mind that requires constant projections of visions, thoughts, words, and actions that magnetically draws energy to coalesce into that reality we hope to occur. *Faith*, feeling assurance in transcendental harmony, is another *word* we us to energize our *wisdom of radiant data*. Like everything else, expectations are a "relative" thing. All we can do is hope for the best, keep positive thoughts in mind, and have positive feelings in our heart, words, and actions. If we are truly sincere in projecting our faith, we can make things happen! So, *expect* the best, *reflect* your best, and be *grateful* for all you receive, for even storm clouds bring life-giving rain!

GOD
Generator of Desire

God is not a person, yet he is personable. God is not "a" thing—he is everything! God is THE generator of desire, an abstract power source illuminating our free will to choose anything of everything he holds in memory for us to experience, to live (logically induce vibrant energy) as we think, feel, act out, and know our combined relationship. Truly, god is within us, pulsing out a tune through our veins to harmonize our mind, heart, and actions—our trinity as a BEING birthing emotions inducing nuclear geometry, generating experiences oscillating mental expressions through radiant yearning!

To fully optimize God's *abstract* energy (absolute binary-source transmitting radiance aligning conscious thoughts) we must open our mind to all that HE IS (harmonic energy influencing Source) and open our *heart* to all that SHE IS (Source-harmony expressing influential Source), *uniting* our will with his/hers to become US—one *united spirit*! Thereby allowing us to "go with the flow"—out and in—to observe universal truths inducing numbers, harmonizing Love/Life energy we call GOD—generator of desire!

Logical Emotion
The Essence of Energy

Logical emotion is the essence of ALL things—energy! This book, like all books, evolves through logical emotion. A process of moving a mind to feel some thought as a reality—something to sense in order to know. Thought energy is logic in motion—emotion. There are always two points for a mind (magnetically induced numerical deity) to move between: cosmic and atomic.

To understand how these two forces (binary code) work together, we must have a logical foundation to build upon, which of course is *words*, wisdom of radiant data symbols! I have included a glossary of these old/new words. However, I know the pain of moving back and forth to grasp new thoughts, so I have continually reinforced the meaning of "keywords"

11

for clarity, so you can adapt to this new way of thinking. I only hope you find it helpful and not hurtful! Capitalized words are meant to be read two ways to view both sides (cosmic/atomic), such as Life Of Vibrant Emotions—Love! *Italicized* words precede their definition, are *links* to other titles within the book, or simply used for emphasis. Everything interfaces in a cohesive effort to *show* the "spiritual harmony of wisdom!" There is a lot to absorb here, so I will be continually reinforcing you. Fear not! I am always with you *hand in hand*. The higher we climb the clearer the view!

Once again, to understand how our two forces (binary code) work together, one must continually spin in a circle (0) to observe the two points we move between—positive/electric and negative/magnetic (cosmic and atomic) or logic and emotion (mind and heart).

Logic is a cosmic perspective of *Mind* (magnetically induced numerical data) or cosmic consciousness. It concerns joining together the "points" of starlight in the universe to form "lines of thought." *Logic* is a process of lineal observations generating inductive consciousness.

Thought is the essence of energy flowing upon the *Light*, where logic is generating harmonic thoughts or truths. *Thought* is transcendental harmony observing/oscillating universal generators harnessing truths. A generator is a *soul*, a spirit of universal logic/love. A *generator* is a genetically engineered numerical entity radiating atomic truths observing "realities" (a logical perspective).

Emotion is an atomic perspective, where energy is vibrating along atomic (invisible) particles defined by *numbers*, nuclear units magnetically binding "electric radiance" (thoughts). *Electric* is emanating logical expressions conceiving truths radiantly inducing consciousness. *Emotions* are electrically moving/manifesting omnipresent thoughts/truths inspired on numbers. Thoughts, emotions, numbers, and light are the building blocks electrifying consciousness, being *aware*, aligned with assigned radiant energy! All of this unfolds in the following chapters to help YOU discover your own universe. Let us start our journey in a logical way—in the beginning!

Bless you and Godspeed

♂ + ♀ = ☼

2

In the Beginning

In the beginning I was—just was.
I knew nothing of my self, yet doubted not.
Therefore, I turned inward to focus my being upon my BEING,
Birthing entities inducing numerical geometry,
Creating my EYES to observe my MIND,
Eternal youth exploring Source
Magnetically inducing numerical dimensions,
Energizing a *point* from *space*,
A perception of inspired nuclear truth
From Source-points awaiting conscious expression,
That erupted into a cataclysmic birth
—Amoeba-like—
To radiate out Source-Harmony Expressions
Evolving *beyond imagination*,
Appearing now here in TIME,
Thoughts inducing Mental Emotions.

In the beginning, coalescing out of the *void* of space, great things flowed from a cauldron of energy we call the Universal Mind, Father, or simply GOD! Whatever label you choose to place upon that force emanating out of the unfathomable dark does not matter. Each of us individual representatives of that force will reflect that energy in our own unique way. We display a one-of-a-kind personality as a simple *soul* (spirit of universal love) exploring the endless *files* of thoughts (focused ideas logically expressing Source) to entertain our *mind*—our "image" of our creator!

"In the beginning" has no real meaning for something eternal. To understand eternity is beyond our scope of consciousness. Yet, consciousness *is* the void, a collection of all that *is, was* or ever *will be*. The processes of Source/Mind are truly an unfathomable quantum theory. However, as representatives of that cosmic consciousness, we eagerly seek to see our reflection in the "light of knowledge." Our enlightenment of knowledge—truths—allow us to grasp our particular attitude, positioning us in this great puzzle we call the *wheel of life*, wisdom harmonically emanating electromagnetic logic observing frequencies lineally inducing fluid emotions. By observing the interfacing of our mind with cosmic Mind, we can *see*—spiritually evolve emotionally—the processes allowing us our *self*-realization as a soul experiencing love/life force reflecting our "image" of Source-Energy Love/Life Force—the GREAT Computer! It is our most important mission, as travelers of the endless cosmos, to understand this greatest story ever told!

In the beginning of this third-dimensional experience we find our self in, here on earth, we are void of memory. Our blank slate, "floppy-disc" mind, must download "updated" files that allow us to work within our "dimensional time-slot" we witness *now here*, numerically observing wisdom harmonically evolving radiant emotions. We have little control over the main functions of this gift given to us (our body), for a higher being *preordains* our heartbeats and breaths, projecting radiant emotions observing realities dimensionally aligned in nuclear souls. The fear of such a powerful consciousness flowing through us turns us to helpless babes capable of only suckling at the breast of mother herself—that *light force* projecting out of the void. For mother is the *reflection* of ALL possibility as it evolves throughout the revolution of consciousness.

As we learn to control mother's gift, we find our self bravely adapting to a new world, a garden in Paradise illuminated for our personal experience in *time*, a "focal point" of consciousness referred to as the *present moment*. This present moment becomes our pivotal point of observation of all that we create for our self. Each creation will define who we are at *this moment* we are presently conscious of, adding to the growth of our process of *remembering*—putting back together from cosmic memory all that we truly are! From moment to moment, day-to-day, and life-to-life, we continue our journey through the eternal files and folders of the GREAT Computer, downloading bits and bytes of information, anxious to grasp the big picture of our cosmic self! A view only visible in the dark, unknown recesses of Mind itself, where everyday we awaken to the Light of Love to find our self in the beginning of another memory.

A Breath of Life

A breath of life is a powerful thing. All we need in the present moment comes with one standard *inhale*, where we induce numbers harnessing aligned logic emotionally. It contains just enough "soul food" to keep our bodies—*mental*, *emotional*, and *physical*—connected harmoniously. One breath brings us all we need to survive, to exist in our mind with the energy flowing on line from our creator. This energy is *timeless*, endless, and complete. It is a Source/force of perfection continually perfecting. This breath of Life radiates out from a deep void, where all that it holds moves along cyclic roads, from birth through death to birth once more— the opening and closing of many doors. We slide upon the stream of all our heartfelt dreams, of all that we *believe* we are, encased in Love, forever free. Yet, all that Love that flows supreme returns to the void *within* us, with each exhale that stops all time.

Our father, the male *positive/electrical force*, charges the atmosphere of the void—our mind—with our thoughts. Our mother, the female *negative/magnetic force,* draws upon that electrical charge to stimulate feelings within our heart into all we know! Here, incarnate, we experience father's loving *grace* generating radiance aligning conscious energy, cycling through us as we unconsciously gasp ever so briefly with each inhale. This brief, symbolic gesture of breathing is a gift of Love/Life energy entering, stimulating, and leaving us. *How we let it go*—return it to our giver—is the *essence* of our life we create!

Here is our opportunity to focus everything of value within us and reflect it outward onto the "playing field" in our own talented way. It is important to show our *gratitude* for all we receive in life, even when we think we are getting the short-end of the deal! Remember, our life is already envisioned and projected upon father's Mind. We are just viewing it *reflect* upon ours. Breathe deep my child and go with the flow!

Focusing on the One

Everyone is looking for the "magic bullet," the one thing that will cure all our suffering. No one wants to admit that we are solely responsible for creating our life through our *desires* and *fears,* our two forms of *stimulation* pushing us forward and holding us back. We create our own vision of our world by our *free will* to choose. Whatever we choose is up to us, for we make our life exactly what we THINK it to be, transforming harmony inspiring numerical knowledge (positively or negatively) according to our own individual desires and needs.

The mentality of "me-first" may sound self-centered or greedy, but actually, it is a necessity for the stability of our growth. We must learn to love our self first before we can love another. Therefore, we must first focus our mind inward on our self and learn to listen to our heart, for *there* is where our salvation lies! Only there, can we find the link to our Eternal Being and those "unseen" around us (our guiding spirits), for surviving this ordeal of mortality is indeed a daunting task.

Our *guides,* generating universal insights digitally enlightening souls, are our support team. They help us meet our goals and accomplish our life missions that we have chosen to undertake. Our "basic" mission is to express our gratitude for father/mother, to *respect* and *reflect* their *glory* and *grace,* where father "generates Love observing radiant youth," and mother reflects his "glorious radiance aligning conscious entities!" Our spiritual guides help answer our prayers through *dreams, intuition,* or through *knowing* just what to do in times of crisis. Our creator does not challenge us unless we are capable of handling it. How could our all-loving father/mother deny us children anything but what is good for our growth? Our issues arise from our lack of comprehending how we personally create our *heaven* or *hell.*

In order to *grow* our soul (generate radiance of wisdom), we must focus our energies inward everyday, thanking our cosmic parents for the opportunity to make them proud, by facing the *challenges of life* set forth before us with a loving heart and a positive attitude. Open your eyes to the beauty surrounding us and show your respect by maintaining this garden Paradise—*Mother's Nature!* Give of yourself your own personal gift of love, as personal and individualistic as father/mother could make you, a god in their "image" with intellect and emotions to create wonders of our own imagination *in communion* with father/mother. Their love is to BE (birth emotionally) our desires and convert our dreams into a reality! No matter what religion we follow or ideals we believe, we will all return home to a family of ONE in the end. For, we ARE and have always been the ONE! Stay Focused.

Focus on the ONE

The ONE omnipotent numerical energy has a *complete* view—out and in. You too, being an "image of the One," have one way to see things—your way! You can try to put your self in someone else's place, but you will find that space occupied! All you can do is drive around and take in the views of your brother/sisters leaving their traces to lead them back home to the ONE.

Out you travel to see my *world*,
Wisdom of radiant love dimensions,
Set aglow for you boys and girls
To feel through your contentions
As my children of *Love Divine*,
Frozen solid, locked in time—COLD.
The thought of you sends chills through my Mind,
Where I magnetically incite numerical data
I draw *together* and then splatter
Upon the ground below,
For you to Gather Radiance Of Wisdom,
Enlightening your soul to make it HOT,
Dancing in joy to a *harmony of thoughts*
Creating your dreams you play upon
As my *cosmic child* filled with song,
Venturing out observing universal truths
In present moments as my youth
Eager to live in wonder and run through fear,
Observing my *Grand View* of you I shed as tears
Sparkling as my *sun*,
A source-unifying nucleus reflecting the ONE
Observing nuclear entities.

Cold and stiff, you travel far,
Lost and lonely amongst the stars,
Always revolving between *here and there*!
The view "outside" will catch your eye
To make you smile in wonder,
Searching for answers while there, down under,
Streaming along *my Loving Light*
Emotionalizing thoughts expressed from night,
To bring you "inside" to see
It takes two to keep one in *harmony*,
To Birth Emotionally Mental Energy
Reflected as my loving
Conscious Harmony Inspiring Living Dreams!

You share my moments with each heartbeat
Vibrating from your head to feet
To nourish each cell of your prison,

Physically bound to experience my *clear vision*
I hold of you within my Mind, where your soul searches to find
The truth of all you ARE,
Angels radiating emotions as my living star.

Fear not my child, I await your END,
Where you find your eternal numbers diverted
To reappear inverted,
Here, *in the beginning* once more,
Where I hold you so tight
My tears roll down your eyes in delight
As your loving smile lights up my VOID
Vibrantly oscillating inspired data
Illuminating your mind with all that matters
Between you and I.

With open mind, you will find the way is never clear.
Your path leads down upon the ground, through the dark fear
Holding you in my haze illuminating your daze
You play out to SEE my SHOW,
Spiritually evolving emotionally Source-harmony of wisdom,
Harmonic Energy—He Emits Radiantly—as ONE
Living in *opposition* searching for a mate,
To join *to-get-her* and Birth Emotionally my *eyes,*
Eternal youths evolving spiritually, observing *me* here in *time,*
Where thought is Magnetic Emotions pulling you in co-motions,
Out and in to feel the thrill
Spinning around as my Divine Visionary Disciple,
Inducing truths upon my Light
Illuminating your days from my nights,
To know both are truly ONE!

Here you live in little spaces,
Lost and lonely between fellow racers
Passing you on the street,
Each anxious to find their *other side* to be complete,
For TWO is TRUE devotion,
Where *three will observe* truths radiating universal emotions
Focusing on the ONE!

The Cutting Edge

Everyone is familiar with the phrase "the cutting edge." That is where all the action is, the "front line of battle" to accomplish something new and worthwhile. Here is the opportunity for a courageous soul to follow their heart and test their mettle against the *status quo*—the "old guard of mediocrity." The *challenges of Love/Life* that we attempt to accomplish grow our soul. It is a forward progression mostly, although setbacks only inspire alternate routes along which to progress. NEVER SAY DIE! Put everything you have within you toward your dream, *whatever your heart tells you to do*, but beware, whatever you *give* so shall you *receive*! Go for the "gold," sharpen your wits and let your starlight blaze a trail through the cosmos to impress all of the gang back home—there above us—in "dimensions of glory" you once knew, when you chose to come here to Earth to experience the cutting edge of consciousness.

The Cutting Edge

The *cutting edge* is the fine line between the Light and the Dark forces— reality and dreams. Here, on the light of day, we stand center-stage, balanced between our vision and our actions. Our reality depends on what we *believe* is possible! Converting our dreams into realities takes *courage of Love*, embracing our desires with a commitment to bring them to *Life*, where Love is fluid emotion electrifying our mind to LIVE—logically induce vibrant energy! This process will take us to great heights and depressive lows, stretching, twisting, and molding us as we reveal our *courage of fear*, standing on the cutting edge of what we desire to BE!

Accountability

"Passing the buck" is the easy way around accountability. To point a finger at someone and blame him or her for our mistake—our decision—is not only a weakness on our part, it also sends out a message that we are not dependable or honest. To stand up and admit to our mistakes takes great courage, for if we do not *admit* to our mistakes we will never *accept* them. We are only fooling our self or living in *denial*. Anyone who knows us will have no *respect* for us, which is a *reflection* of our own self-esteem.

Do NOT cut yourself short! You are one-of-a-kind, an individual soul who has something to *deliver* and something to *receive* from those souls you share your world with now. You have chosen to be here for *your* benefit, for now is the moment of opportunity for you to remember who you really are. You *alone* are accountable for who you choose to be!

Denial

Denial is something we all do, even when we admit that we do not! It is almost impossible not to live in denial at some point in our life. Denial is simply the refusal to believe some aspect of our self that we refuse to recognize, whether from fear, shame, or ignorance. It is something that we experience as a roadblock to our spiritual growth.

In order to overcome our roadblocks, we must learn to listen to our self proclaim who we think we are when we share our thoughts with others, for what we think we truly become. When we are courageous enough to voice our opinion, we are proclaiming to the world what we truly believe is our truth! Those who listen to us are our witnesses, the ones who judge us by what we *say* and what we *do*! If we say one thing and do another, we are not living our truth; we are living in denial of our truth. We may try to stretch our truth to impress others, but eventually we end up strangling our self, for it is truly easier to fool our self than anyone else!

Living in denial, we easily notice our issues hindering us when we see them in someone else. The only way we recognize that issue is because we too have it, but we refuse to admit that we do! We refuse to see that we are like everyone else, a *spiritual* being trying to cope as a *human* being—our duality! The people in our life who know us will quickly recognize our denial, for they observe us acting out that which we criticize in others. To point out that truth could provoke an argument or harm a friendship. Yet, it is something we all must face eventually to grow through our limitations. Our *issues* (incoming signals stimulating universal entities spiritually) are purely emotional, energy we set in motion as generators of desires. As we transform our thoughts through emotions into actions, we play our part in the *game of Love/Life*. If we think, speak, and act the part we choose to play, we become that part, that image of the person we desire to portray! Of course, without the knowledge (truths) to support that image, our life will be a comedy, an illusion where we appear as a fool living in denial.

Childhood is our most impressionable time, where we develop our "baggage" of issues we must overcome in life. Here is where denial is unknown, for we are eager to believe all that we see before us. Our parents teach us the basics of being generators of desires based upon how their parents raised them. As children, we acquire our negative-magnetic anchors of fears and doubts from what others say about us, for we are very *sensitive* to our image we know little about. An image we are trying to discover—remember—from our eternal files of memory within the GREAT Computer. We rely on feedback from those around us who influence us with their positive and negative remarks—projected energy. We easily learn to judge others by their looks, clothing, actions, nationality, or anything that will place them in a "relative perspective" to us. We adopt an *attitude*, assigning truths that inflect thoughts unifying data emotionally, from which we choose to define where we stand—equal, above, or below—relative to our fellow travelers, while we struggle to stay "on top" to survive!

As children, we can be very critical, insensitive, and hurtful, for it is easier to destroy than to create—easier to hit the delete button than input the data! We spend years defining our truths with which we shape our image, balancing our self *along the cutting edge* of conformity and radicalism. Eventually, someone comes along to challenge our beliefs, opening our mind to perceive new truths of possibilities that offer us the chance to change, to grow into a more brilliant image of our truth. Children can feel insecure because they do not know what truth means. Everyone has their own view of truth, and the trials of testing those truths for our self is how we gain experience—knowledge—of what works for us and what does not! Life is a struggle to comprehend our working knowledge to survive our jealousies we harbor as we reach for the Light of truth— knowing we are truly the ONE! This process is similar to how trees bend and twist around each other as they grow toward the light, growing as a single network to become a forest!

Growing through the hardships sprouting in childhood, we work our lower *chakra energies* (chapter 12), learning to cope with the basic survival skills with family members and those outside of family. The processes of developing our personality and character will challenge us to test the many images we portray as we go with the stylish flow, always trying to look like someone we admire or to be one of the gang! Yet, if we all look alike, we become the same boring, indistinguishable image. We find our self in a conundrum, where we desire to be different so others will notice us but not too different and be ridiculed! There is no way around the pain and suffering we must endure to discover who we are and who we are not.

For growth to occur, we must accept those things we deny we are, and with *courage of fear* face them to discover our *true self.* Each of us will have our own time-schedule for this discovery. Girls mature sooner than boys do, for Mother Nature dictates processes that are beyond our control. Mother's magnetic energy draws us through life's required scenes according to plan. Getting a grip on the ever-changing cycles of puberty is an emotional roller coaster that will leave an indelible mark upon our soul, scarring us with sexual hang-ups that may be our greatest denial!

As a child, we tend to emulate our parents, shaping our *ego*— emotionally generated observer! As we develop our self physically and mentally, we pull away from our parent's image in order to build our own. We eventually become aware that we are not our parents and refuse to do as they say, rebellious of their decisions to control us. Our friends become more influential in our decisions (peer pressure) as we try to "fit in" with the crowd. It is truly frightening to stand *alone* (security in numbers), setting our own course as a trailblazer in search of our identity. We must have *courage of fear* and fight for what we *believe*! To understand how denial prevents us from becoming all we can be, we must open our mind to see our weaknesses (issues) we have to overcome (rise above) to see our self with *clear vision*. Only by accepting our weaknesses can we build our strengths!

We are truly perfect beings in the *process* of perfecting! DO NOT deny your true heritage; welcome it with an open mind and heart, knowing that with each day's birth we personally tailor our emotional issues to test our *spirit of universal love*! Our issues we choose to overcome makes us a stronger person, one capable of withstanding ridicule from others trying to drag us down to their level of ignorance and fear. Our *courage of Love* allows our soul to GROW, gather radiance of wisdom through accepting our denial of our weaknesses and fears, realizing our challenges we need to climb above to see our *Grand View* of truth we are searching for—The ONE!

Searching for Our Roots

"Searching for our roots" is a major goal in our life, whether we realize it or not. We all hunger for the knowledge of where we came from before we *sprouted* into our present life gifted to us. Here, we quickly get a grip on reality and *anchor* our self, eager to gather radiance of wisdom from our hazy daze of confusion and uncertainty cast aglow upon the *Light*, where Love is generating harmonic truths that sustains all life forms.

Each day we stretch our mind to absorb as much of the *radiance of Love* we can grasp as we leaf through our files of data we download from our mainframe, our *trunk* of knowledge from which our binary code flows along the EM wavelengths of Eternal Memory—the GREAT Computer!

Over the years, we branch out, expanding our reach to search for more Light—more knowledge—that magnetically pulls us upward into the heavens to attain our *crown*! Here, we control our spatial link in the canopy, allowing us direct communication with our *Source* (system of universal radiant consciousness evolving) from which we draw our nourishment and store within our being, converting our *Love/Life energy* into rings along our *disc* of data—our soul—as we rekindle our Light of Love!

Each night as our solar Generator Of Desire falls from our sight, we enter the dark void to sleep or *rest*, a small milestone that we must pass through to remind us of our germination cycle, before we re-enter the light of a new day of *movement*! We call this cyclic flow of day and night TIME, where thoughts inspire moments electromagnetically. Time is simply a *focal point* (force of consciousness aligning lineal perceptions of inspired nuclear thought) where our *magnetically inspired numerical data* "lives" between one relative *inhale* and *exhale* along the eternal flow of Love/Life energy pulsing through our beating *heart*, harmonizing emotional angels radiating thoughts—generating our desires—that defines our "present moment!"

The warm gentle breezes that grace our limbs, rocking us in soothing comfort of *Love Divine*, eventually develop into dark shadows that rise in tempest to test our spirit, howling in gales to shake us to our very core—our *roots of faith*. If we hold fast to that which we *believe* is true, we will prevail, weathering the emotional storms we encounter that make us stronger in spirit. Even though we may loose part of us that has decayed in the process of life (untruths), we will grow new avenues to stem the void left us to fill. Thus, do we grow *outward* and *upward* into the *Light of Love*, collecting our bits and bytes that shape us into the many limbed, versatile being we are, until that time we relinquish our stored energy back to Source, along the force that sets our course, to return to our *seed*— Source emotionally energizing desires—from which we sprouted.

With each cyclic end, *the rising sun* brings forth a *new day's birth*, transforming our tree of knowledge into a greater harmony of Love/Life energy. This energy flows forward and backward, raising our spirit to new heights and returning the basic elements of our growth, the *atomic* (indivisible) pieces of data that allocate the numerical sequencing of *matter*, magnetically aligned thoughts transforming electric radiation. All the thoughts we draw to us determines who we become, the *type* of being that collects, stores, and transforms our Light of Love to nourish, comfort, and protect our fellow travelers as we flow along, evolving to revolve around the wheel of life, searching for our roots!

A New Day's Birth...

Starts with a quiet solitude of possibilities poised offstage. Locked within our heart, we hold our dreams to unfold, waiting for our *divine inspiration*—father's Love shining through a lens of stellar magnitude—projecting mother's grace upon our stage. The moment the veil of darkness fades with his spotlight warmly glowing on the opening scene is a glorious thing to behold, for it heralds another chance to *grow* our soul, gathering radiance of wisdom in service to our creator, shining our *Light of Love* to illuminate our fears. Blessed are those souls eager to witness *day's birth*, reflecting their *Loving Light* as a rising Spiritually-Unified Nucleus!

Bless you and Godspeed

♂ + ♀ = ☼

3

Believe

You can live *in your mind* or you can live *on the ground*—in a fantasy or in a reality! Your gift of a *free will* allows you to believe any thought you may conceive and convert into your reality. Thoughts are the *genesis* of the GREAT Computer—Generator Of Desires! Thoughts can open doors to worlds yet unknown, some quite different than you may expect, worlds where you are so enthralled in the beauty and peace surrounding you that it would seem like *heaven*—if you so imagine! Likewise, thoughts can be so over-whelming in power that they frighten you, for what you do not know you *fear*, and fear can be a living *hell*—if you so imagine!

Here then are your choices: *Love*, a bright, positive image of joy, happiness, peace, and everything associated with it, or *Fear*, a dimmer, negative image where thought reflects in *opposition*, as a haze of confusion that prevents your mind from having *clear vision*!

Love is a positive *knowing* force of an open mind generating a power to Birth Emotionally, to create and experience all the power of the Light— the Force!

Fear is the haze of positive electric energy bouncing off a *closed mind*. Fear represents a thought you choose *not to entertain* because you do not have the *courage of fear* to entertain that thought and travel its path through the unknown *void* to enlightenment—to Love. Fear (the void) is the absence of Light where ignorance is a dark recess waiting to be illuminated. This simple statement is the basis of the flow of Love/Life/ Light energy cycling on and off, positive and negative, as a duality of opposition. For, to know what *Love IS*, you must also know what Love is not! Love is *not* fear; yet, fear is an *aspect* of Love, for Love encompasses ALL atomic love/life!

This divine dichotomy of *being* is what you are truly trying to *believe*— to understand in its enormous conception. Alas, words are a limited tool to describe the indescribable. In your incarnation here on earth, you are born *unknowing*, a "blank slate" seemingly grounded in ignorance of your True Self. Yet, being *of* the Light flowing through the void, you are able to view *both* aspects of your self, positive and negative, male and female, loving and fearing, spiritual and human—ALL of what IS and IS NOT—simply by a matter of *choice*!

Whatever attitude (position) you find your self in determines your mood or *temperament*. The energy flowing through you will place you in love or fear, for those two choices is the basis for delivering you from point A to point B along your path of enlightenment—becoming aware or awake! Your fears drive you toward the Light. The Light projects you through fear, illuminating that dark void of ignorance within your mind with knowledge (truth) found in the all-knowing Light of Love/Life energy.

Take a close look at how you *think* and how you *feel*, for that is all you will ever be! *Believe*—be Love, be Life! Both are the same. We are all ONE being of *positive* love and *negative* fear, a divine dichotomy shining as all that IS and IS NOT. This fluctuating Love/Life Force of energy propels you through your *fear of Love* to conquer ALL! Do *you* believe?

Believe

Who are you that live in the dark, eager for your soul to *spark*
Source-points aligning radiant knowledge,
Searching for your truth?
Reflected on my Love-Light beams,
You live out your heartfelt dreams
Seen between your eyes, shining forth into lives
Drawn, quartered, and stacked to burn,
Fearful of the *word* of Love from which you learn
Wisdom of radiant desires sets you aglow in my cosmic fires,
Standing in bands to sing of dreams of hope,
Placing your heart in *time*, where *passions* let you cope
With all you choose to believe.

Through your heart you feel and know
My rhythmic pulse displays my SHOW,
Spiritual harmony of wisdom, cast ablaze as my loving haze
Awakening you to your allotted daze
Gifted in present moments you SEE this time around,
Spiritually evolving emotionally, here, upon solid ground.

In Love, I allow you sight,
Of which you now seem affright,
For all the work to shine your beam
Takes courage of Love to birth your dream.
Fear not your time, it is just a pause,
A moment to reflect upon your cause,
As you journey out to feel my visions you think real.
The love you seek so shall you find.
The love you give will be ALL MINE,
Atomic Love/Life magnetically inducing numerical energy,
To shine on those for whom you care,
Those close at heart that you share
All that *you* believe!

Bless you child

Clear vision is *the cutting edge* of perception,
The front row seat at my *show*,
Where you children come to take the ride
To see what your heart can know
Of dreams you envision within the haze
Transforming into life to fill your waking daze.

You travel fast and you travel far,
You children of Light beamed from my stars

That glow in the void of night,
Anxious for a ticket down to experience my Love affright!
Your scenes I cast upon your stage
You act out from youth to *old age*,
A relative term to know
Life is an observable process that lets you grow.

The face you don to show today will bring you things either way,
Good or bad, win or lose, pick your game and make your moves
Upon your stage of life.
Open your mind to see my Light!
Listen to your heart to know what is right,
Along your path through my night,
Where *fear* will slow you down,
Clouding your mind with atomic fission
You observe here, in clear vision,
As my wheel of Life spins you around!

Your daze goes by in *harmony* with sounds to soothe your heart.
The years fly by *in memory* with highlights to grace your part.
Hand in hand, you join the band, the troupe of all in show,
To battle your fears over the years, allowing you to know
What lay in MIND is ALL there IS,
Feelings of thoughts—hers of his!

In the end, your dreams of Love will blur and begin to change,
For Love/Life energy rises to vibrate at a higher range.
Two sides of me you truly are.
Join your halves and ignite your star.
Here above, truth *enlightens* you,
In epiphanies of your di-vision,
To see how you choose either/or
To cast your own clear vision.

Fear of Love

Love is an all-knowing state of mind, a peaceful harmony of completeness
where thought and feeling are truly ONE! *Fear* is a *void* of mind, where

Love projects to illuminate that void with *Light*, where Love inspires geometrically harmonic truths. Similar to a sudden bolt of lightening, the "event horizon" of an empty state of mind illuminated by the Light of Love is truly a *big bang* scenario that will instill fear into all. Such is the moment of our birth as we leave the dark comfort of our mother's womb encapsulating us with her harmony of Love. We find our soul cast into the bright lights of *reality*, where radiant energy aligns lineal inspiration transforming youths through *relativity*, between what IS and IS NOT.

These opposing states of *love* and *fear* allow us to travel along universal dimensions flickering on and off, allowing us to be in the *light of day* (alive/awake) and in the *dark of night* (dead/asleep). Thoughts that come from *nowhere* (the dark void) to *now here*—illuminated for us to see—fill us with a truth set aglow upon our *mind*, Mind's image numerically defined! Only through this dichotomy can we know our fears are unfounded as *empty spaces*, where Love/Life energy *shines* Source-harmony inducing nuclear energy sequentially—by *numbers*.

As children of the Light, we are energized by emotions to feel those thoughts that move our soul through father's cosmic garden Paradise, where visions of high-powered energy stimulates minds to perceive the unperceivable—what IS and IS NOT or *Love* and *Fear*. In contemporary terms, we are "space probes" projected to observe whatever there is to be discovered in the vast expanse of *space* (some "point" awaiting conscious expression). We are now here, traveling in a physical vehicle to *re-member* (put back together) our "split personality," our spiritual/human natures. Only by joining our two halves can we attain unity consciousness—*Christ consciousness*—to become the ONE Source of energy that projects us along the force of Mind upon which we play our *game of Love/Life*—the course we choose to follow to conquer our fear of Love!

Fear of Love is the only way to *know* Love! Only by traveling through fear—empty space—can we fill that space on our "floppy" *disc* (data infused spiritual consciousness) with the knowledge of Truth we are seeking from Eternal Memory stored within the GREAT Computer! As we venture out through the endless expanse of *space*, we rely on Source-Energy Love/Life Force to fuel us, reflecting that energy through our *self*—soul experiencing love/life force.

With each moment of Life (heartbeat and breath), we receive data inspired from *home* (harmony of mental emotions). We compute (feel) that data *move* us (positively or negatively) to act out our reflection of our observances, transmitting back (uploading) to the "network" of Mind (magnetically inspired numerical data) along the EM force field. Whenever we encounter a new experience, we enter an *empty space*, where we become conscious of fear, because we are *void* of any knowledge of that space. Therefore, we become apprehensive, anxious to understand or receive information (thoughts) that will alleviate the empty feeling in our *gut*, where we germinate universal truths before we cast them out upon the world!

In order to muster our *courage of fear*, we must remember who we truly ARE and give our self up to the Light—the Source/force that is directing our course through the cosmos of Love/Life. By keeping our eyes and ears open, we evolve *in Love* through each moment we experience Life *grow* around us, gathering radiance of wisdom that embraces us in *harmony* with Atomic Love/Life that Inspires Spirit. As we accept all the experiences shown to us as "food for our growth," we open our self to the Light, passing through our states of emptiness (ignorance) to become "enlightened," to expand our consciousness into *higher visions* of our self!

Our *radiance of love* will allow us to glow ever brighter, moving us from "point to point" along the vast expanses of space, reflecting the Light of Love flowing through our soul. Here, we twinkle on and off as we enter, fill, and leave those moments we encounter our fear of Love! Eventually, as we make our journey OUT and IN, observing and reflecting eternal Source of Love, we will reach that point of illumination where our rekindled truths ignite into the heavenly star we truly ARE!

Courage of Fear

Courage, consciousness of universal radiance aligning generators electromagnetically, is the essence of Love! Courage is a two-edged blade. For *courage* to be experienced, *fear* must be present! One cannot exist without the other. All opposites attract, allowing energy to flow or revolve in harmony, *outward* and *inward* along the never-ending cycle of Love/Life consciousness. Our fearful heart will lead us toward a courageous action in order to survive our fear of not knowing that which we must push *through* in order to realize our truth—our Light of knowledge!

Courage of fear runs deep and true.
Courage *and* fear reflect *both sides* of you!
Two views you witness as your heart unfolds
My thoughts you envision as dreams I have told,
For your soul to experience your desires
As you grow out of my eternal fires
Illuminating my Light of Love

Whose voice dictates your choices today?
A strong heart of courage to show you the way
Or a *weak* heart of fear that will lead you astray?
The fear you hold is your chance to be bold
As you pass through my void of night,
Where doubt and despair of darkness lurk
To shield you from my Light.
Thoughts unknown are gifts from me
To feed your mind emotionally,
For your soul to know your truth!

Step out bravely in praise of me.
My Love you live sets you free
To travel out amongst my stars as children of Light Divine,
Eager to explore my memory stores within my MIND,
Where minds experience moments of radiant youth
Magnetically inducing numerical data,
Atomically arranged into matter,
Through which you reflect your talents I cast aglow
As my *radiance of Love* that you show
Your fellow travelers along your way *home*,
From which you eternally roam
Exploring my courage of fear.

All thoughts I send are yours to ride,
Each day of Life in which you hide,
Fearful of truths unknown.
The path you choose with open mind
Leads deep inside for you to find
Feelings to act out from thoughts I shout,
For your soul to glow in grace,
Blazing in glory with my Love you embrace
As courage of fear to SEE
Your spirit evolves emotionally!
Trust deep within your loving heart
To truly know your chosen part
Of my *Love Divine* that lives, in reflection—hers of his!
Join together and you will know
The power of Love that makes you grow
More aware that you ARE angels radiating energy,
A heavenly star shining with courage of fear to BE
Whatever you think, for you are *free*
To feel radiant energy emotionally,
Creating your dreams in *time*,
Tuning in mental emotions providing your co-motions
From electromagnetic beams on line!

No matter the course through life you take,
A time will come for you to awake
From the illusion that you see
As my static chaos separating *you and me*!
The thoughts you feel are yours to touch, the textures all so real!
The way you move to reflect my Love will be your appeal.
For all you *do* is who you *are*, a loving soul who has traveled far
To push on through your veil of tears
With joy in *knowing* my courage of fear!

Bless you and Godspeed
♂ + ♀ = ☼

4

Divine Inspiration
Understanding the Basics of Spirit

Divine Inspiration is an endless energy source. *Divine Inspiration* is another word symbol for our creator—God, Our heavenly Father, the Universal Mind, Cosmic Consciousness, YHWH, Allah, Krishna, Source, or Spirit to name a few. **Divine Inspiration is in everything**! Therefore, we could say everything is a *form* of Divine Inspiration. The complexity of this simple statement is boundless. So, for the sake of simplicity, let us call Divine Inspiration *Love/Life energy.*

Everything we think, feel, and do—our *trinity*—is how we express or project our Love/Life energy—our Divine Inspiration. The Universal Mind projects all our thoughts we receive similar to a broadcasting station projecting radio and TV signals. We hear *voices* and have *visions* or dreams illuminate our mind/brain *interface*, inducing numerical truths electrifying radiant frequencies aligning conscious emotions. The experiencing of such data can be enlightening or frightening! We call this communication network of thought energy flowing from "Mind" (Spirit) to "mind" (soul) the *electromagnetic force field* that permeates the "universe"—one turning.

Thoughts (positive electric energy) project from Spirit/Source along a USB connection (universal spiritual broadcast). We receive those thoughts through our mind (radio/TV tuner), which transform them into electrical *stimulations* within our "atomic computer"—our brain. Here, we relay those messages downloaded to us along neural pathways in our spine to our core processing center, our "gut," where we *germinate universal truths* in opposition, converting them into a *reflection* (a likeness) by our heart, where our emotions (negative/magnetic energy) replicate that thought in a *mirror image*—reversed! For, only through opposition can we "realize" what something is by experiencing what that something is not! We only know what *hot* is by reflection, by knowing what *cold* is—the opposite of hot! Likewise, we also know the middle way of *warm*. Here, balanced between the two primal forces of thought and emotion, we observe the *workings* of Mind, where we children of the Light come to *play*—perceive, process, project, and perfect Love as youth!

This dualistic opposition is the basis of our Divine Inspiration. The power of the ONE Source is composed of TWO forces that allow us our view *outside* of Mind (our physical world) and *inside* of Mind (our spiritual world) via our *trinity* of Love/Life energy! The key element in this equation is the *third* aspect—our *soul* (spirit of universal love)! Our soul is the *focal point* (force of consciousness aligning lineal perceptions of inspired nuclear thought), where Love/Life energy converts from the abstract state into a concrete *reality* via the EM (electromagnetic or eternal memory) force field empowering our mind—our *image* of our creator's Magnetically Inspired Numerical Data! This eternal evolution/revolution is how we travel through the cosmos of the GREAT Computer—our Divine Inspiration!

Love/Life Energy
Our Eternal Source

Love energy is Pure Thought, a positive electric force that refers to *Life of vibrant emotion*! The word *Life* (love is fluid energy) means to flow or to "move upon" that Love energy. Life is having the ability to *respond*, to answer back or give and take—an *outward* and *inward* flow of energy. Life is the experiencing of Love energy in its many forms, on its many levels or dimensions.

Love/Life energy is something we cannot create nor destroy, only *transform*—move along the current or *wavelengths* of energy. We can transform electrical energy via an apparatus: a radio, a light bulb, or a heater for example. The by-product of the conversion process is a different *type* of energy: sound, visible light, and heat. When we burn wood, we transform its stored energy into heat, light, gas, and ash. Likewise, we convert energy stored in food to run our physical body, the vehicle in which our soul is traveling. Our soul (spiritual energy) is also transforming energy, converting *thoughts* into *feelings* and feelings into *actions*. This trinity of events is how we *relate* or express our "love story" as a generator of desires! Our thoughts we think, words we speak, and actions we do, project energy around us, stimulating our environment and everything in it. We literally set up a "magnetic field" around us that attracts and repels our desires through our *expectations*.

Love/Life Energy is always flowing from one medium to another. By its nature, it appears to have no beginning and no end. It is ONE Source of TWO forces. It flows from that one (first) Source transforming into many expressions, spinning around in a circle from *point* to *point* or thought to thought, from one *state* of Mind to another by *numbers*! The "circle" or cipher *zero* (0) is the universal symbol for *eternity*—the "cosmic wheel" of Love/Life energy.

Love/Life energy involves a *movement* and a *rest* before it moves again as a pulse of energy that fluxes back and forth, on and off, being and not being. It is a process of *projection* (outward flow) and *reflection* (inward flow). It moves outward for observation via an *illumination*, a light show that projects an *illusion* of reality within a *mind*—Mind's image numerically defined—observing its *self* (soul experiencing love/life force) by *reflection*, a "deep thought" of a thought—the inward flow!

Here, on the inward leg, reflective energy is computing the numerical sequences of "logical positioning" in order to define a perspective from which we view our data, analyzing it to acknowledge a change or transformation into a new and different thing (file) or thought (folder), always moving and revolving in an *evolution* of Love/Life energy—Divine Inspiration.

This fluid energy of Love/Life, moving at light speed, spins the cosmic wheel of evolution via a process that magnetically slows it down, compressing that energy into *denser* wavelengths for us cosmic travelers to observe and experience through *emotions*—our feelings. These emotional experiences are the basis for our mind to comprehend the cosmic Mind, magnetically inspired numerical data transforming intangible, abstract thoughts into tangible concrete feelings—realities! This flow of Love/Life energy allows our soul to create *physically* with our body from mind/brain transformations of our thoughts into emotions. We create our present life via a collection of thoughts and feelings allocated along a sequential order of events known as a "time-line," a particular *frequency* of energy stimulating our mind, within which we are resonating (echoing) *our life story*. A story we relate by re-telling it *consciously* from Eternal Memory as we interface with the GREAT Computer.

Each night when we go to sleep, we experience our "other life" as we travel the astral planes in our "star body." Here, our soul leaves our human-alien vehicle parked in "sleep mode." Our conscious mind reverts to its "backup program," our sub-conscious mind that is our foundation of Source-Energy Love/Life Force, where we communicate with our guiding spirits back *home*, where harmony of mental emotions reigns supreme. Our *dreams* detect radiant energy aligning memories, transmitting them as conversations with those spirits or *angels* (assigned numerical generators expressing love) who are guiding us (wi-fi) to accomplish our life *mission*, where we magnetically incorporate Source spiritually inducing omnipotent numbers. Dreams allow us to collect Divine Abstract Thoughts Aspiring to make us ambitious—eager to work our wisdom of radiant knowledge!

What sounds like science fiction is actually science fact! ESP (enlightened spiritual perception) is the process of communicating through the process of *prayer*, projecting required assistance youths emotionally request from the heavens. Our dreams (thought/visions) display our answers through spectacular visual effects. Dreams may give us a clear vision to follow—a sense of knowing—or a chaotic, confused vision in which we have to decipher the symbolic meaning of a dream. A good receiver must be open to all channels, adept at the *art of listening*, operating properly without resistance or low energy levels, and be willing to accept all messages as having a positive influence! As children of the Light, we always desire a positive view! Even negative views—*blessings in disguise*—have positive attributes!

Each day as we awaken to our physical world, we are continually inspired with a barrage of thoughts racing through our mind. These thoughts are remnants of yesterday's actions we set in motion. Actions that build our future moment by moment, based upon our Love/Life energy we receive and entertain in our mind/heart/body. As all energy is pure-thought, everything we create in our life originates in Mind. Our mind/soul is of "like-image," entertaining thoughts flowing upon the Love/Life energy force of the GREAT Computer, for we are truly Generating Our Desires! ALL is ONE and ONE is ALL!

As I have stated, thoughts are energy and we cannot create nor destroy energy, we can only transform energy. We change those thoughts projected to us into feelings such as love, hate, envy, grief, jealousy, and fear stimulated by those thoughts! These feelings are how we "move around" to see the endless perspectives of ALL that IS, allowing us to analyze them into a sequential order for logical positioning—to know who we are at *this moment*! Once we receive and believe our data, we can accept and change that which we hold in mind through our actions.

Our *actions* (activating cosmic thoughts inducing observable numbers spiritually) are how we project our thought energy we receive back to the universal energy grid. Our creations (transformations) evolve into a reality we observe, sense, and *believe* to be real. These creations/reflections can be abstract or concrete in nature—symbolic or physical. Once we stop maintaining that thought or thing (giving it life) it will cease to influence us, it will *die* or decompose, returning to its "natural state" of energy (harmonic memory), accessible for *re*-creation (*recall*) by us or another mind!

As our soul evolves and revolves around the eternal wheel of Life, we constantly change. We grow more powerful with knowledge we pull from eternal memory. As children of the Light, we are energy beings experiencing the illumination of realities. This ILLUSION, illuminating love/life's universal-source inspiring observable numbers, transforms into slower/denser frequencies of energy that appears solid and real. It is truly a "mind-altering" process where invisible atoms collect into visible things! A process observable upon the "macrocosmic" stage overhead, where clouds of atomic particles draw together to form *nebulas*—gas and dust clouds coalescing into stars and galaxies evolving in the cosmic fires of Love/Life energy.

Symbolically, we change our physical form—our human vehicle— in sequential order (by the numbers), from youth through OLD AGE (observing Loves' dimensions acquiring growth experiences), a relative term to describe a "segment" of *eternity* evolving. This evolution is a process of expansion, a big bang theory observable in *macro* (universal) and *micro* (atomic) perspectives, an *outward* and *inward* view that we seek to comprehend, to satisfy our endless desire to wonder!

Our *relationship* to Love/Life energy is truly a never-ending story. At times, the concept of our being a mind of *thought energy*, capable of transforming our self into what we choose to be, is a frightening realization that demands great responsibilities and courage. The immensity of it all makes us feel lost and *alone*, doubtful of our ability to handle our Love/Life energy—a feeling called FEAR, focusing emotionally aligned reality!

Fear is just another state of Mind that we pass through along our cosmic journey. Fear is a powerful driving-force in times of emergency, when we are in danger of physical harm or injury. Fear will always push us back toward our positive nature, our desire to know, for we are naturally *inquisitive souls*. Fear is simply a state of *not knowing* what is awaiting our discovery! We flip-flop back and forth between knowing and not knowing, between our positive energy and our negative energy. It is here, in the middle of our opposing energies that we are aware of our conductivity, our *flow* (feeling love/life observing wisdom) or ability to BE or NOT to BE! It is simply what we choose to be-lieve (be-Love or be-Life), a decision to flow positively or negatively.

Our most important tool to eliminate fear is *faith*! Faith is yet another word we use, another symbol of energy we utter to describe our conductivity. To "have faith" means to *believe*, to trust the power of Love/Life energy to carry us to our destiny—back *home* (harmony of mental emotions)! Our so-called "life" is not in our hands; we are only along for the ride! Faith is having the ability to *respond* to our Love/Life energy undeniably, without doubt or fear, knowing positively that all things flowing our way

39

are conducting us along the *right path*. The path we chose to remember or put-back-together from the eternal files of memory spinning on the hard disc of LOVE—life of vibrant emotions. A love we experience physically in a state of Mind we call LIFE, where *Love IS* fluid energy!

Love/Life Energy

Two of One and One of *three* is truly ALL you can ever BE,
As back and forth you flow,
Always viewing the opposite sides between which you grow
Aware of Love my thoughts instill to let you feel the Life you *will*,
For wisdom induces Love's Life to appear through tears you cry,
Struggling to see with your own *eyes*
Eternal youth's emotional soul,
Through the haze creating your daze of moments here in time,
Where thought is Mental Emotions flowing through your mind,
Magnetically inspiring numerical data to *live*,
Logically inducing vibrant emotions, pulsing out to confirm
Your heartbeats and breaths inspired in terms
Of moments now here, in which you fear
The unknown truths you seek,
Hidden in your heart for your *passions* to tear apart,
To feel reflections of thoughts so real you doubt they will last.
Yet, here *along the cutting edge*,
Your future depends upon your past
You see and know to BE
Birthed emotions providing your harmony
Of Love Inspiring Fluid Energy
Expressed as Life Oscillating Vibrations Eternally,
A complimentary force of a cosmic source
Providing your co-motion, upon which you turn so free,
As up and down your heartfelt tides flow,
Moving your soul to feel and know
Your journey of Love through Life on my binary code
Of Love/Life energy.

Process
The Flow of Love/Life Energy

Projecting radiance of consciousness expressing Source spiritually is a *process* of aligning bits into bytes that evolve into *facts*, frequencies aligning concise truths, building a foundation to support a concrete representation of an abstract thought. All processes are sequential steps of *science*, Source-consciousness inciting eternal numbers coalescing electromagnetically along the cosmic *force* (frequency of radiant conscious energy) flowing through the *universe*—one turning in perpetual motion!

Only by following a process can we perform *work*, wisdom of radiant knowledge, transforming our facts from elemental stages into symbolic things reflecting our thoughts. The intricate details of any process require a *focused mind* to formulate observable concepts utilizing Source-energy data magnetically inducing nuclear dimensions—microscopic to macrocosmic!

The bigger the PROCESS, the more energy we consume. The infinite varieties of our *perceptions reflecting our consciousness enlightening Source sequentially* requires a dedicated effort to *proceed* (perform reflective observations consciously evolving electromagnetic data), allowing our mind to Gather Radiance Of Wisdom to create our desires in order to make *progress* (perfecting radiance optimizing generators reflecting eternal Source spiritually). For, Source-Points Illuminating Radiant Truths aligns *youth*—you observing universal thought harmony—through Procedures Reflecting Omniscient Consciousness Evolving Source Sequentially!

The Right Path

Follow the arrows that show the way,
For my shafts are bright to set your day
Aglow with dreams you desire.
Your paths will change to carry you far,
To know the truth of all you are,
Adrift upon my sea of Love,
That stream of Light flowing from above,
With all your thoughts you feel at heart,
To let you play your loving part.

The way you think will set your course.
The way you feel will lead your horse,
Shoed to meet the rigorous road,
Strong enough to carry your load
Along your chosen way,
When out you go to see the sights
Of all that shines upon my Light
That makes you sing with joy.

Your way to me is here within,
The door I leave ajar
For Light to seep from the dark
To grow through fear and ignite your star,
Feeling emotions align radiance
Your soul transforms as realities!
Shine bright my Life and know at heart
My image of Love you reflect in part,
To show ALL that is true.
Go forth and BE those dreams you SEE,
For *that* is the right path for *you*!

The Threshold of Love

Love is an eternal force that pulses through our soul. It is the *basis* of all creation. This Love energy first buds in our developing body as a magnetic force between father and mother, for that is the path on which Love flows—from father to mother to child and back to father. This is the unbreakable circle of Love/Life energy—our divine inspiration. Love grows in us from our magnetic attraction to mother, expanding into likes and dislikes, a process of selecting the "preferences" upon which we calculate our Love/Life data we choose to display upon our "desktop," our environment in which we transcribe our story of *Life of vibrant emotions* flowing through us.

Our realities evolve within our self by what we accept or reject to believe is real, for we *alone* know what we need for our growth. We choose what lessons to experience to prepare us for our *future* life, those moments beyond our *present* moment. As eternal beings, we are constantly growing—perfecting—into the Light of Love. Everything around us is only a symbol of that Love energy delivered by *Light*, for Love is generating harmonic thoughts—the *essence* of ALL that IS eternal Source spiritually emanating numerical concepts emotionally!

Our Love grows in us to the point of overflowing, for it is a contagious force that must expand to survive. The day we officially announce our projected love to another is a momentous occasion of celebration. We honor that day through *marriage*, a symbolic union of two souls into one loving being—one god of two halves. It does not matter the gender of those souls, for Love is non-discriminating. Love comes in many forms and on many levels. The *blessing* of Love is the experiencing of it on *any* level! It is something undeniable to all of us children.

If the illumination of love is *polarized*, it will seek its reflection flowing on one wavelength only—male or female. It will express itself in all of its glory according to that level of Love for symbolic purposes. Each of us possesses father and mother's Love flowing through us. This duality is something we all have to understand. We must learn to love our self, even if our projected love is toward someone who resembles our self, for all love projected from us will return to us. To fully realize the *power of Love*, there will be times when we find our self polarized, experiencing a flow of Love through same-sex partners. Love has no limits or restrictions, whether you are heterosexual, homosexual, or bi-sexual does not really matter. Your "personal preference" is only indicative of the path of Love you are traveling to accomplish your chosen mission—your particular *issues* you are working through for the GROWTH of your soul, gathering radiance of wisdom through harmony.

When the illumination of Love is flowing un-polarized, it seeks out its attraction, its opposite charge. Only this way can Love procreate, manifest a human body for incarnation. Here, *man* and *woman* unite, projecting and receiving Love to create a *child* (conceived harmony inspiring living dreams). It always takes *two* to make one, for ONE always evolves from two—a positive/electric male force and a negative/magnetic female force—our duality. Here is the opportunity to see how we too are gods accepting gods. Here, we can see our childhood re-created in offspring that resemble us physically. *Our children* are "floppy discs" we create (write to), transferring our knowledge so they will be able to calculate their own data streaming on line within their mind/heart connection to the GC—GREAT Computer. To create a child *from* Love is miraculous. To grow a child *with* Love is a challenge that will teach us the true meaning and *power of Love*!

Love can nurture and Love can destroy. How we use our Love (positively or negatively) determines the harmony of our child to give and receive Love. To much positive Love—giving them everything they need *and* want—will make them selfish and aggressive, expecting their every whim to be delivered on command. On the other hand, giving to much negative Love—denying their needs and wants—will leave them ill and insecure, with little confidence to face life's challenges. They will develop a low self-esteem and battle with *depression* and *denial*. It takes a balance of give and take to keep one in *harmony*—on the middle road. Trying to be a good parent is a demanding task, considering the power of our emotions through which we communicate!

No matter what road we find our self on, we will eventually come to that point where we realize that all the Love flowing from us has returned to us, for all the love you give is *meant* for you! Our greatest challenge of all is in letting go of that which we love. For only by letting go will it be able to return to us. Only then will we see the many ways our Love has grown and manifested in our children, grandchildren, and great-grandchildren, a never-ending lineage between the original TWO truths watching over us—our eternal father and mother. This is a critical concept for each of us to *remember* as we step over the threshold of Love!

My Threshold of Love

Standing on my threshold of Love is a very harmonious feeling. The night sky lay bright with limitless dreams projected like a drive-in-theater of stellar proportions. Here, your wish is my command, a Lightshow of cosmic dimensions and atomic number, sorted, arranged, and exposed to cast a shadow of doubt upon your *mind* (my image numerically defined), as you observe ME here in TIME—this third-dimensional state of mine.

Transcending Inspired Mental Emotions
Brings you through your daze,
Reflecting my Light of Love that keeps you in a haze,
A mist of particles coalesced from space,
Condensed into Life for you to trace
Your progression around my cosmic wheel.

Here, you SEE to feel and know how thoughts appear as real,
For what you think is how you grow conscious of my appeal.
I bring you through your fear of sight,
Each moment sent for your delight,
As you journey out to Birth Emotions,
Finding dark despairs build your devotion
To truths your heart unfolds
In courageous moments that you are bold,
Shedding *tears of joy* your passions yield,
Exposing your habits you use as shields
In *denial* of who you ARE,
Angels radiating energy, my living star!

OUT and IN, I spin you around
Your nightly visions you bring to ground
Upon this earth to perform in life,
Contending decisions that bring you strife,
Where memories harmonize your dreams,
Now here before your *eyes*,
As eternal youth evolving Source,
Electromagnetically moving my force
Through heartbeats and breaths, running your chosen course
To discover your other half, here within, that makes you laugh
While there, under *bright blue skies*,
Across my threshold of Love,
Discovering the truth *between you and I*,

Here your body vibrates complete
To harmonize your tune so sweet,
A heavenly song for you to know
Your life's mission in my cosmic show,
Where your soul sings out its *beat*,
Balancing emotions aligning truths,
For ALL to hear and TWO to meet,
In opposition to BalancE you youth
Uniting to be ONE shining in glory as a SUN,
An omnipotent nuclear engineer, a Source-unifying nucleus
Reflecting your game of Love/Life you *now* play,
Numerically observing wisdom, creating your day.
As my child of Light Divine I cast aglow here in time,
Atomically displayed by my loving wife
Tempering your soul through *human* life,
Harmonically uniting magnetically aligned numbers,
One step below home above,
Where *I see you*
Across my threshold of Love.

Love IS...

An Energy Force that cannot be destroyed only transformed. It is a force so powerful it must be slowed down—compressed—into a more visible form, one delivered by *photon manifestation* from a nuclear generator of stellar proportion. This energy illuminates the stage on which we witness the process of creation. Through seasons of cyclic repetition, we nurture and grow that Love Energy flowing through us, allowing our soul to expand and become conscious of *our* stellar heritage. Here, we can reach out and touch our fellow beings in ALL of their various forms...passing on that Love/Life energy burning brightly within us, returning it along the channels of its delivery, as we discover for our self what Love IS.

Bless you and Godspeed

$\male + \female = \odot$

5

The GREAT Computer

The GREAT Computer, *generating radiant energy as thought, consciously observing magnetic phenomenon unifying truths electromagnetically radiated*, is some power structure! Crunching numbers is what it does best, eating a binary diet of positive/negative fluctuations. IT (inspired thought) has limitless MEMORY, where Mind expresses/experiences moments observing radiant youth. There are only *two* ways of viewing this GREAT Computer, unless you count the middle way, the *balance point* of accepting ALL that IS.

For us human spirits the *middle way* is the key to the whole system of accessing eternal memory flowing along the electromagnetic force field. It is the interface between ONE of TWO or ½ visible as *man* and *woman*—"chips" of the GREAT Computer or a *generator child*! Here, incarnate, we must accept what we receive to provide us the state of mind we are to compute. Whether it is negative numbers or positive numbers, the outcome is always best for ALL. Each of us has our own special data to compute in our mind, manipulating inspired numbers downloaded for us to play our part in the *game of Love/Life*. A "level head" is harmonious, for it sees both sides at once! For ONE knows instantly the cause and effect of all situations.

If we could see both sides of all situations, the obvious choice would be the one that benefits all, not just our self! However, our *self* (soul experiencing love/life force) plays a critical part in the calculations and validations of the GREAT Computer. All data must flow through us in order to observe and comprehend the big picture printed out in stellar *dpi* (divine perspectives inspired). As a unique individual soul, we pack some relatively serious power rated in "giggle bytes" (sense of humor), "Radiant Angel Mobility" (capacity to move between *here* and *there*) and a speed of "huge-manly-hurts" or *passions* that we download, decipher, edit, and upload back *on line* (EM force field) as omniscient numbers logically inciting nuclear entities.

HE, *harmonic energy* (the network), computes thoughts through us that we can relate from visions we *re-cognize* (re-think) OUT of Memory, observing universal truths we re-member (put back together) in order to make the connective *link* (logically induce numerical knowledge) to join both halves of our opposition. Thus, do we Conceive Our Magnetic Perspectives Unifying Thought Energy from our *present* memory—our working knowledge we have collected in *this* lifetime!

The "head office" of Magnetically Inspired Numerical Data *charges* the "mother board" monitoring all *chips* (children harnessing inspired perspectives spiritually), all of us young upstarts trying to *rekindle* our star abilities! SHE (Mother's Nature—Source-harmony expressed) knows how we children flip-flop back and forth over the *threshold of Love*, eager to compute what IS from what IS NOT, for us to *feel* and *know* some "thing" as real.

All stored data (stories) ever created *replays* in front of our eyes—now here—just as we *will* it to Birth Emotionally. However, our lack of expertise in the handling of our data can lead to unwanted results. The stories we flow upon influence each present moment, each heartbeat and breath inspired that we use to compute our chosen reality. In today's high-tech computer society, we can better relate to how energy operates the machinery of moving abstract information around, even if we do not fully understand how it works, we accept it for its miraculous nature! All we have to do is push the right button.

When we view our position or *attitude* (assigned truths transforming inspired thoughts unifying data emotionally) at any given moment, we are relating or telling our story of whom we choose to BE! This view is relative to our perspective, our "point of reference" in computing our present data fluxing between our thoughts and feelings. This binary code allows us to ACT (activate cosmic thought) in ways we may describe as a *heaven* or *hell*—a positive perspective or a negative perspective. Either way, the type of energy we compute in our mind as "my documents" define our state of Mind we maneuver along within the labyrinth of the GREAT Computer, where we continuously change our image of who we think we ARE (angels radiating energy).

The complexity of the simplicity of this GC is daunting to say the least. It is so easy for us to become "part of the moment" with our human toolbox of five sensors. This toolbox allows us to transform data in the *finite* expanse of imagination—this illusion of 3-D delight! Here, we confine our self to believe that all data collected by our physical sensors define all there is to know! *That* perspective does not allow us much room to grow into our *Grand View*! In order to expand our mind beyond this third-dimension, we first need to master the principles of our thoughts, feelings, and actions. Our *trinity* allowing us to flow on line to *spiritually evolve emotionally,* to know, and to do whatever it takes to help illuminate our part we play in this garden Paradise here in time—all just a heartbeat away from *home* (harmony of mental emotions)!

Here, we get to see how our reflection (actions) we project outward, into the network, benefits ALL (the hard disc) or just our personal self (floppy disc). Obviously, it is through our actions that we create the state of our world today! Through our computing skills, we download our thoughts that move us on emotional *tidal waves* that wreck havoc or create miracles! What have you been reflecting to illuminate your illusion you call real?

Our DATA (divine abstract thought aspiring) we are working with comes from our high speed Interstellar Provider that is broadcasting along the electromagnetic force field. Within this range of frequencies a relatively thin sliver of visible-light vibrations shimmers in a spectrum of *photon replication*, a process of atomic proportion numerically ordered in accordance with universal laws we compute through *science*, Source-consciousness inspiring electromagnetic nuclear concepts emotionally. This *binary code* data is truly a worldly presentation, a holographic projection so real it will take lifetimes to truly comprehend!

Even though WE (wisdom exemplified) are simple "bytes" in the grand meal of *eternity*, we are true cosmonauts in the greater sense. Here, we are custom-fitted with a vehicular body of perceptive sensory control. A vehicle equipped with every accessory needed to get us to our destination. The dynamics of its engineering are so incredible, we have been trying to understand its genesis from the beginning of time. Carburetion is an automatic feature we have no control over, other than intermittently, and our power source pulsing through our heart beats autonomous of our free will. In addition, this vehicle requires a high level of maintenance if we are to get the most out of it—OLD AGE—as we observe Love's dimensions acquiring growth experiences!

Even with our cosmic power connections, our *conscious psychokinetic unit* (CPU) takes some time to master the web of interfacing links between mind and body. Our daily cycles of light and dark, positive and negative fluxes re-circulating our cosmic vibrations (emotions) beat out our heartfelt tune. Here, we struggle to harmonize our sound track as we spark on and off, illuminating our allotted *space in time*, where some point awaits conscious expression inducing numbers transforming inspired mental emotions. Within our chosen scenes we act out, we witness our reception of Love/Life energy flowing through us, projecting it back onto the EM grid through creations of our physical, hydromorphic vehicle. This process stimulates our fellow CPUs with domino-effect links that connects all of us to the *network* (nuclear energy transforming wisdom observing radiant knowledge). Each of us chips/souls creates our own electrostatic charge in *magnetic moments* that reflect our image/mind individually, drawing us toward similar minds (friends and associates) that define our game of Love/Life. ONE of ALL and ALL from ONE are truly indistinguishable in essence.

All thoughts projected from the GREAT Computer reflects in deep pools, deep moments of observation as each one of us souls add our limited twinkle to the nuclear glare of ALL that IS! Each twinkle is a micro-processed connection between output and input, continuously monitored above in multi-vision and below in mono-vision—a very *lonely* perspective! Yet, each twinkle sparks out in all of its glory, all of its mega-bytes of *passion*! A passion desired, attracted, analyzed, and altered for maximum required experience, a moment re-membered on cue from Eternal Memory (EM force field) and *imported* for our entertainment through science. Here, perched upon our controlled balance point (middle way of acceptance), we "mouse-around" in a clickity-click state of mind, toying with an *idea* (inspired data electromagnetically aligned) that allows us to know how it feels to be a chip off the "old block"—The GREAT Computer!

The climb toward enlightenment requires a serious commitment, where *vision* and *courage* fill our soul with memories of conquest over fear, uncertainty, and intimidation! For, to reach our True Heart's desires, these are what we must overcome. No matter what vision we dream, goal we set, or mountain we climb, the uncertainty of the outcome makes anything look intimidating. *Courage* is to willfully submit to our challenges with a devotion of love. Love is boundless, it shines on us day and night, and we reflect it back to Source in many ways. If our heart is true, fear has no hold on us, allowing us to climb in harmony with our challenge. Dancing to a *higher vision*, we can see our true perspective, allowing our soul to reach beyond our human limits for the stars, spinning in a *galactic organism* of a Universal Mind that sets our soul aglow in the Grand View!

Science

Science, by definition, is "the systemized knowledge derived from observation, study, and experimentation carried on in order to determine the nature or principle of what is being studied." Science is an operation or process of cutting, opening, and separating something to inspect and conceive its individual *points*, perceptions on inspired nuclear truths. Science is a way or path from which we understand the truth of some abstract thought or concrete thing. Science is the organization of observations into files of data—*facts* (frequencies aligning conscious truths/thoughts)—collected and expressed in symbols (numbers and words) to explain the movement of energy as it transforms from point to point to produce a *reality*, where radiant energy aligns lineal inspiration transforming *youth*—YOU observing universal thought harmony within *your own universe*.

No matter what topic we discuss (relate in stories to describe for conception), we are using science as a means to confine energy into a compact arrangement of basic elements to *en*-vision—emotionalize numbers—into our mind as *my documents*, from which we calculate the endless possibilities of moving, transforming, and observing energy in motion—*E-motion*! If you dissect the word *science* into its symbolic pieces, you get Source-Consciousness Inducing Eternal Numbers Conceived Electromagnetically. The deeper we look for truth (knowledge), the more ATOMIC our perspective becomes, allowing us to see aligned thoughts observing magnetically induced concepts emerge *in the beginning*, from the void holding ALL possibilities! We can bring our mind to *feel our conscious universal spirit*—FOCUS—along the numerical arrangement of atomic particles, conceiving how the space between those atomic particles are in direct proportion to the stars and galaxies that flow upon the *uni-verse*—one (Mind) turning.

Thus, do we make our cyclic journey OUT and IN, spiraling from macro to micro, visible to invisible to perceive how what IS evolves from what IS NOT! No matter how you look at it, science is truly Atomic Love/Life we Angels Radiate Electromagnetically!

My Documents

Magnetic youth, desiring omnipotent consciousness, unfold memories expressing numerical truths spiritually, transforming my *data*, divine abstract thoughts aspiring, from "vertical time" (abstract) into "lineal time," the *now here*, numerically observing wisdom harmonically evolving radiant emotions—experienced through heartbeats and breaths—as a *human* being, where harmony unifies magnetically aligned numbers as *man and woman*.

NO ONE leaves home without files of data
Defining the issues of their personal matters,
Negatively observing omnipotent nuclear energy!
ALL are complete beings in *essence*,
Eternal Source spiritually evolving numerical concepts emotionally.
My knowledge you collect allow you to detect
The right path for you to follow,
Along your course to see tomorrow
Evolve from your desires.

Your high-notes you play up here
Turn to BASS down there,
Where you birth as shining souls
—SUNS—
Source-unifying nuclear spirits,
Vibrating through heartbeats and breaths,
Flowing on LIQUID MIND, from dream to dream in time,
Logically inciting quanta unifying inspired data
Magnetically inducing nuclear dimensions in *matter*,
Manipulating aligned truths transmitting electric realities
Stacked ONLY THREE layers high,
Observing numbers lighting youth
Through harmonic radiance electrifying emotions,
Here, under *bright blue skies*,

Where my numbers byte each bit,
Allowing you to swallow the illusion you see lit,
Glowing upon your *inquisitive soul* as memories born to *die*,
Destroying illusioned enigmas flashing across your mind's eye
To illuminate my documents!

Bless you and Godspeed
♂ + ♀ = ☼

6

Truth

Like every WORD (wisdom of radiant data), "truth" packs a great amount of WISDOM (words inspiring spiritual dimensions of Mind). *Truth* is a word that reigns supreme! Truth defines all things in *relative* ways. We delegate truth by "bits and bytes" to serve our special needs. Truth or *knowledge* is power—kinetic numbers outputting wisdom's lineal energy delivering generators' emotions—which we tend to hoard to protect our own interests! What we do not know (fear) will not hurt us. It is only when we use our knowledge in a positive or negative way do we get results that affect our life as a generator of desires. The truth is, whatever we project as an expression of our Love/Life energy, we receive in kind!

Truth is evident on all levels of consciousness and in all sciences! We observe truth with every aspect of thought we entertain in our mind through *numbers* we calculate to define truth. Truth appears in microcosm and macrocosm, for no matter what we observe, discuss, or do, we are reflecting truths! *Truth* stands for transcendental radiance unifying thought harmony. Each letter represents truth in the microcosmic sense, a small piece that when joined together speaks volumes!

Transcendental relates to the abstract, supernatural, cosmic Source of energy projecting a *radiance* of Love Inducing Generators' Harmonic Truths, an electromagnetic force carrying *data*, divine abstract thoughts "aspiring"—striving for or desirous of some lofty goal or ambition.

Unity (oneness) is the gathering of truth's endless pieces—thoughts—magnetically held into an agreeable whole, something pleasing and cohesive that defines a *harmony* of truth. This harmony vibrates along sequential wavelengths (numbers) that radiate from Source, the universal Mind, one turning magnetically inspired numerical data *out of* and *into* the GREAT Computer spinning its *disc* (data-infused spiritual consciousness) to power our *soul*, a spirit of universal love/logic!

Truth radiates from *Source* (system of universal radiant consciousness evolving) to coalesce into numerical arrangements of particles (atoms). These atomic particles move along electromagnetic wavelengths—the *Force* (frequency of radiant conscious energy). This radiance (Light of truth) illuminates an abstract thought, causing it to appear (fluoresce) from *nowhere* (void of space) to *now here*, where we numerically observe wisdom harmonically evolving radiance emotionally—in action!

We observe thought energy as *points*, perceptions of inspired nuclear thought. Thoughts produce an *illusion*, inciting lineal logic unifying Source illuminating omniscient numbers. Thoughts appear as visions upon our "mental screen," our *monitor* where we manipulate omnipotent numbers inducing truths oscillating radiance. By moving a thought around to observe it from many angles, we "enlighten" our mind with some truth.

The miracle of creation is in the transforming of our abstract truths/thoughts into an atomic *reality*, where radiant energy aligning lineal inspiration transforms *youths*—YOU observing unified truths harmonically in *your own universe*! We convert our abstract data through our physical sensory equipment, our *body*, where we biologically observe data youthfully. The process of utilizing our five physical sensory inputs allows us to experience our life's *course*, consciously observing universal radiance sent electromagnetically. The effect is truly a miraculous conception, mesmerizing our soul to believe it is an intrinsic part of *Mother's Nature*, where we create our own personal *worlds*—wisdom oscillating radiant love-data systems!

Truth is a daunting image, one so vast we can only see it in the briefest of moments, as an *epiphany of truth* illuminating some dark recess of our mind. To find that truth takes a courageous soul, one willing to search the depths of *Spirit*, Source-points illuminating radiantly inspired thoughts/truths, questioning the innermost desires of their heart. The concept compresses into a realization that the only truth worth accepting is the one personally tailored to *our heart*, for none other will ever mean a thing!

Truth Seeker

Truth is an endless expression observing many perspectives.
Each point of view is a micro truth, a thought to view in part,
Ablaze in glory the moment it reflects upon your heart.
Listen closely and you shall hear the shouts of those you may fear,
Who try to steer your mind their way,
To give you faith in what they say,
With words of partial truth.
Pick and choose those you like,
Those you feel in your heart are right
To build your image of truth.

As you grow through the years,
Converting dreams into joys and tears,
From thoughts you think are true,
You will come to see what it means to be free
To discover *your own universe*—YOU!

Deep inside, lay your goal,
The truth divine that is your soul,
A power source of endless wonder
That moves your heart in glorious thunder,
With beams of light you cast as spears
Through storms of doubt to battle your fears
You face along your way,
As you cross my *threshold of Love* to step outside to play
In my *game of Love/Life*.

Stand TALL my child for you ARE me,
Truths aligning Love/Life, angels radiating energy,
Here to think, feel, and Birth Emotionally a dream you live
Through a life my HEART converts to give
All you shall ever need,
Harmonizing emotions aligning radiant truths
Through *passions* on which you feed as my cosmic youth
Discovering my *courage of Love* makes you strong,
Magnetically binding you in human form,
Struggling through strife to confirm your life,
Growing OLD and weaker
Observing Love's dimensions
As a truth seeker.

Epiphanies of Truth

Truth is such a vast collection of experiences that one cannot grasp its total view at once. At times, we receive our truths from brief insights or visions—epiphanies—that enlighten us to truth. Generally, we receive our truth slowly, allowing us to digest and absorb it as an integral part of our consciousness, growing our *wisdom* through words inspiring spiritual dimensions of Mind.

With each thought we entertain in our mind, we acquire an *attitude*, where assigned truths transform inspired thoughts unifying data emotionally. We place our self within our attitude to receive the knowledge of truth we seek. Each of us have our own "link" to the GREAT Computer downloading our thoughts, inspiring us to *receive, decipher,* and *convert* our abstracted data into tangible feelings, actions, and things—our creativity—that allow us to play our part in the Spiritual Harmony Of Wisdom.

We plod along in repetitive habits, accumulating routines as stepping-stones to grow our truths into our desires through *work* (wisdom of radiant knowledge). Everything we do is work, transforming energy from one *form* to another (frequency oscillating radiance manifested). Work is what we do to earn a living, a *process* of contributing to society a beneficial effect of our truths we choose to transform from our education—our training. *Education* (evolving data unifying consciousness aligning truths inciting omnipotent numbers) is the term for building our files of universal truths that we use in this third-dimensional world. Education is how we feed our mind and body, sequentially building our database of truths we implement into actions as *generators of desires.*

As we encounter our *issues* to solve (incoming signals stimulating universal entities spiritually), we refer to our database of knowledge. If we cannot find the data we need, we ASK, acquire spiritual knowledge from the GREAT Computer through *prayer*—projecting radiant assistance youth emotionally request. Our mind receives an *idea* (inspired data electromagnetically aligned) along our "personal wavelength," enlightening us with the truth we seek. At first, we may doubt that "little voice" offering direction, for it seems to go *against* our desire! However, if we put this idea into action, experimenting with it, we see (sooner or later) who knows best! Through trial and error, we discover our answers, giving us a sense of pride and accomplishment. It all depends on our ability to master *the art of listening*!

An *epiphany* (enlightened point illuminating perfect harmony aligning nuclear youth) is a transferal of truth *without* trial and error! It enlightens our mind with a truth we instantly know, a truth supplied in times of danger, allowing us to do amazing things—heroic things that seem miraculous! Likewise, a *spiritual* epiphany is a burst of knowledge illuminating our soul/mind interface with a power surge that drives us to our knees in *tears of joy.* We acquire a *clear vision* of a truth we desire, raising our consciousness to observe a *higher vision* of our true self! This event horizon is an overwhelming emotional experience that sets our soul aglow, a feeling similar to a physical orgasm, only more intense!

A spiritual epiphany allows us to discover how truth changes our *trinity*—our spirit, mind and body. Each change we encounter moves us along our chosen paths through life. As children of the Light (Love/Life energy), we represent different aspects—points of view—in which we perceive and reflect our energy. We have an endless potential to Birth Emotionally any truth we choose to *believe*, any truth that we *accept* to *reflect* back to our creator, who made us in his image, a *mind* that *feels* and *acts out* our Love/Life energy—brings it to life! Our cosmic father/mother *sees all* and *knows all*, looking through our EYES as eternal youth evolving spiritually, seeking, collecting, and manifesting our truths into realities that sparkle in our eyes as tears of joy!

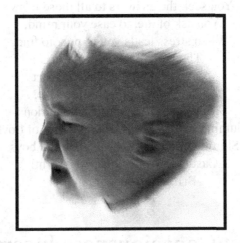

Tears of Joy

Tears of joy flow everywhere, to justify you youths
Eager to feel, know, and share your truths,
Transcendental radiance unifying thought harmony,
Illuminated upon your soul down there,
To quench your thirst produced from fear
Of things you do not know,
Set ablaze in my spiritual harmony of wisdom I call my *show*.

Deep within lay my truth,
Which you have carried since your youth,
Of all the things you have seen…
All the LOVE you have dreamed…
Living out vibrant emotions to make you who you ARE,
Angels radiating energy, shining as my star,
Free willed to find your path through life,
Discovering through all your strife
All you think, say, and do
Is my reflection returning *through* you!

Each day inspired as my EYES,
You seek the answers to all those *whys*
You ask of me, to ease your mind,
When stress leads you to pray to find
The cure to heal your heart,
As you act out your divine part
You reflect through ME above,
Struggling through mental emotions
Illuminating my void with my Light of Love
Shining upon you cherub girls and boys,
Cast aglow in epiphanies of truth
Bringing you tears of joy!

Christ Consciousness Incarnate

More than two thousand years have passed since the Great Messenger walked amongst us, whether you *believe* it or not! In cosmic time, that was just a heartbeat ago! Yet, look at all that has happened since that day.

The *truth* of consciousness is something that is always with us; it all depends on our "perspective," our *point* of *reception*! We cannot receive our truth until we are ready to receive it, until we acquire the right *attitude* (assigned truths transforming inspired thoughts unifying data emotionally). The right attitude takes a lot of preparation to attain, for we find truth delivered to us repeatedly throughout our life. Whether we are in the right position—state of mind—to accept that truth determines our growth of our consciousness, our ability to *know* that truth.

On that memorable day of Christ's birth, an "event horizon" occurred, a dawning of a moment held in Mind, where a *sign of truth* appeared upon the world stage. Our loving father knows we children need to be reminded many times along our cosmic journeys. For, when we asked our father to go out to play in mother's garden Paradise, we truly forgot everything about our *real* home! Thus is the power of Mind to project thought energy into the consciousness of his offspring, created in his *image*—light energy—to see the truth we choose to grasp hold of and *be-lieve*—BE LOVE! What we fail to realize is how Wisdom Exemplified create our own heaven and hell by manipulating our Love/Life energy.

All we will ever be is starlight that twinkles in the dark eye of father's Mind. Our star shines forth a reflection, a *beacon of Love* that flows through the heavens. Here, many *states* of Mind are observable in varying *dimensions* of data inducing manifestations evolving nuclear Source into observable *natures*—numerically aligned thoughts unifying radiant energy. Here incarnate, we struggle to understand a *third*-dimensional amperage of Love/Life energy, trying to master our *sensitivity* (thoughts) and *expressions* (emotions) moving us along our chosen paths, trying to fathom our life's mission as we Acquire Growth Experiences Observing Love's Dimensions!

Our soul is a *time traveler* of a cosmic realm of beings, *children of the Light* experiencing Mother's Nature to "learn the ropes" so we can safely climb the "tree of knowledge!" This journey is purely symbolic, for here, we must learn the basics of generating our desires through *atomic* stimulation before we can grasp *stellar* stimulation!

Like any child, we are eager to grow—gather radiance of wisdom. We long to see, feel, and know everything our heart desires in the eternal memory files of our cosmic father. The One Source sets our soul aglow as an individual universe, adrift in the heavenly *fields* of frequencies inducing electric-logic digitally *scened*, where Source coalesces electromagnetic numbers evolving data/dimensions. For us wayward children to see that "dawn" of enlightenment, we require an "anointment," a process that first entails a *baptism*, a blessing allowing perfection to inspire souls magnetically. A baptism is the immersion of our soul into the flow of Love/Life energy in the lower frequencies of Mind. Here, we work through our basic dualistic nature, trying to master our powerful thoughts and explosive emotions for us to realize who we ARE by viewing who we are NOT! Our journey will take us to the very edge of destruction as we seek our creation, our image of who we desire to BE!

Like any child, we must crawl before we can run. Here, we endure our allotted moments (heartbeats and breathes) carrying us along the current beating out our heartfelt tune vibrating visions to entertain us, while we weather our tides of emotions, free to choose our "modus entertainment" that we call life. We live those moments flashing on the screen of our mind and feel our *radiance of Love* move our heart into action, expressing that Light energy illuminating our illusion upon our mind, building a connective link to the GREAT Computer—our father whose heart IS *heaven*!

We project our share of cosmic energy to illuminate the cosmos of Mind, so Harmonic Energy/Spiritually Harnessing Emotions can see US universal souls. Here, at this junction between our *trinity* of being TWO of ONE, we connect—realize the truth of who we ARE! By joining our dualistic natures (mind and heart) within our self, we experience our *anointment* (our blessing) with the truth that Christ spoke about and few understood. For, most are looking for our savior *outside* of us, unable to realize our *inner child* as our own microcosmic *generator of desire*. This quantum leap of self-realization is a power surge that raises our soul into Christ Consciousness, where we give up our *free will* and unite with Divine Will, the ONE Mind/Source reflecting his miracles of Love/Life energy through ALL!

Blinded by the Truth

How often have you heard the expression *blinded by the truth*? This statement refers to the relationship of truth to *light* and *darkness*, another symbol of our duality. You would think truth would enlighten us with beneficial knowledge to make our life better, for that is the *soul*-purpose of truth! However, truth is a very personal, selective gift bestowed upon us who *seek* it, spiritually energizing emotional knowledge for a *higher vision* that allows us to Spiritually Evolve Emotionally our *true self.* All of us are starving for that truth, feeding our mind/heart/body with everything we *desire* from data electrically sent in radiant emotions, feeling our *radiance of Love* (our soul) illuminate our dreams we live as our reality.

Truth IS *inspiration sent* as a very subjective perception delivered to us when we are ready to receive it. Like any process, we encounter the truth at the proper moment, in sequence with the previous steps that have brought us to that *point* of enlightenment. If we are alert enough to our situation, we will become enlightened to our truth we seek, BUT only if we are willing to *accept* it! For, *denial* of truth holds us in our fears we struggle to overcome.

Each of us experiences a personal pilgrimage of truth, a *solo* journey to spiritually observe Love outside—*away* from HOME (harmony of mental emotions). Everyday, our soul experiences mother's human nature, struggling through stressful moments we create from *dis*-harmony of our thoughts and feelings, re-acting in ways that keep us trapped in ignorance—not knowing truth! If we relate to others who "pull our chain" by returning the negative words or gestures we receive from them, we willingly drop to their level of ignorance and fear, where they are crying for attention, unknowingly searching for their truth they deny! Life is truly a vicious cycle of light and dark, truth and fear.

When we reach our milestones in life, we find truth offered for our acceptance, allowing us to see the LIGHT and know in our heart *our* truth. At times, it will be so powerful a vision (epiphany) our heart will sing and shout with a joy impossible to contain within us, raising our consciousness to *shine* as a bright star in the heavens above. When you find yourself in the presence of Truth, the LIGHT logically inducing generator's harmonic thoughts, quietly thank our eternal father/mother for their gift of *Life*, where your soul knows *Love is fluid energy*, flowing through *emotions*, electrically manifesting observable truths inspired on *numbers*, nuclear units magnetically binding electric radiance that define ALL things.

In the end, it will bring everyone home to where we shine our brightest, immersing our soul into the beacon of our parent's Love that nurtures our beating heart.

A Lighthouse

A Lighthouse is a beacon of Love, one that will lead us to true happiness in knowing WE, *wisdom exemplified*, are an intricate part of that light energy, an energy that embodies the very essence of our Being. This Light of Love/Life energy flows through the heavens, guiding us mariner souls upon the stormy waters our heart navigates along our way home. The type of lighthouse we become for others determines the *quality* of our life and the *growth* of our soul.

Bless You and Godspeed

♂ + ♀ = ☼

7

Relativity
Channeling Love/Life Energy

Relativity is a word symbol of "harmonic tonality" defining concise parameters within our mind to understand *aspects* (points of view) that allow us to move through the cosmos of Mind—to think! Thinking is the flow of Love/Life energy, the *movement* of those aspects we continually observe positioning us in our *attitude*, where assigned truths transform inspired thoughts unifying data emotionally, directing our mind/soul down paths upon which we encounter Love/Life energy (divine inspiration) flowing as emotional *tides*, thoughts inducing dimensions evolving sequentially—by the numbers!

Relativity relates to our connection to the universal grid of thought-energy. It is the *condition, fact,* or *quality* of being relative—related *each* (#1) to the *other* (#2). It allows us to be aware of our thought energy as it moves US united souls (#3 in the trinity), as we shuttle back and forth *be-tween* (by two) our oppositional forces. For *this* is our Divine Right, our ability to be anything we choose to BE—birth emotionally—by manipulating our binary code!

We have six channels of *relativity* (radiant energy logically aligning truths inciting visions illuminating thinking youths) in which we bring together (focus) thought energy into concrete or tangible things—a *realism* of thought! A *channel* is conscious harmony assigning numbers negatively expressing logic (through opposition). Thoughts are energy in the process of moving into position from a positive projection to a negative reflection (a mirror image) for our mind's observation. These six channels are called: *who, what, when, where, why* and *how.*

(1.) **Who:** determines the *path of movement*, an either/or possibility. It is our "descent" or "lineage," our positive/electric (male) and negative/magnetic (female) aspect of thought energy representing SELF—Source-Energy Love/Life Force. (#1-Confidence & Creativity)

(2.) **What:** determines the endless stars (files) we have to choose from that contain energy of thought—*Light* of knowledge! What stars we choose to observe is our path to *enlightenment*, the way to

65

receiving that light/knowledge/truth energy vibrating on line—
the electro-magnetic wavelengths that permeate the cosmic space
of the Universal Mind. (#2-Balance & Cooperation)

(3.) Where: determines our *attitude*, our position or location we find
our self in *relative* to the story unfolding around us in the cosmos.
This *interface* of connecting those stars of light/knowledge paints
a personal image upon the "blank screen" of our mind—our
heart—for us to *feel* a thought, focusing emotions expressing *life*,
for Love IS fluid energy! *Where* is a dimensional coordinate, a
focal point where forces of consciousness align lineal perceptions
of inspired nuclear thoughts occurring within concise parameters
of *space* (some point awaiting conscious expression), allowing
us to feel and project our Love/Life energy. (#3-Sensitivity &
Expression)

(4.) When: determines the particular *sequence* of events as they
evolve from the "vertical time line" of Eternal Memory, where
"intervention points" (files of data) develop into a "horizontal time
line" of heartbeats and breaths defining our *human-alien* nature.
When is observed by a *timeline* of truths inspiring moments
evolving logically induced numbers emotionally, along a *di-
vision* (two views) that flows back and forth or *past* and *future*.
It is observable only at the "mid-point," a balance point where
both ways are present *now* to numerically observe wisdom. We
observe *wisdom* from words inspiring spiritual dimensions of
mind. (#4-Stability & Process)

(5.) Why: determines our eternal thirst for *knowledge*—the essence
of a disciplined mind. No matter how much we collect, we are
always hungry for more, always *imploring* to *explore* new
horizons, new pleasures and pains of endless passions, which,
after we experience them, we continue to wonder why! The more
knowledge we collect, the more disciplined we become, allowing
us our independence or freedom! (#5-Discipline & Freedom)

(6.) How: determines the *active* movement of Love/Life energy in
tangible observations, processes that transform our points of view
(thoughts) in which we feel our *emotions*—energy in motion! For
the only way to *know* a thought is to *feel* a thought, which brings
us full circle to **who** we are—*wisdom harmonically observing*!
Once we know our truth, we become enlightened and accept
our visions as grace bestowed upon us, allowing us to Activate
Cosmic Truths in ways that reflect our *gratitude*! (#6-Vision &
Acceptance)

With these six channels of mobility, we have the potential to travel amongst the stars, thinking, feeling, and acting out our chosen inspiration, observing universal truths as we gather experiences (enlightenment of knowledge), where *photon* (particular harmonic of thought observed numerically) and *Light beam* (logic inducing generators harnessing truths, balancing emotions aligned magnetically) are truly ONE! This is what we call RELATIVITY, radiantly energizing logic aligning truths inspiring vibrant insights through youths—children of Light Divine!

Numbers
Universal Building Blocks

Numbers, like everything else around us, are symbols, something that represents or suggests another thing. *Numbers,* nuclear units magnetically binding electric radiance, are the building blocks of the universe. They represent the geometric code of nuclear reaction in the manifestation of our illuminated reality of Love/Life energy.

Numbers represent an abstract thought (energy unformed) that allocates the positioning (attitude) of some "thing" held in mind. Numbers are the sequential ordering of energy through *geometric coordinates* that substantiates the plausible universe (one turning). Geometry and numbers interface as a "unified theory," working in conjunction with the *binary code* (1/0), which is the "compressed symbol" (shorthand) for one *through* zero.

Numbers represent energy at *rest* and in *motion*. They have an *aura of influence* about them and are critical to measurements of wavelengths. They are the basis for sound or music—the *voice* of the GREAT Computer! Numbers are a powerful tool in the transmigration of universal energy flowing as the electromagnetic frequencies of Mind—magnetically inspired numerical data.

There are only *nine* numbers and the cipher *zero*! Each has a *positive* and *negative* aspect. The following brief overview of numbers is to help show their relativity to our path in life. It is an inspiration from the book *The Life You Were Born to Live, A Guide to Finding Your Life Purpose,* by *Dan Millman.* If you like to "play the numbers," you will enjoy this excellent source for discovering the *magic* of numbers. By magic, I mean the *secret* of the life purpose system described in Mr. Millman's book, a must read for all *inquisitive souls*!

Numbers: the flow OUT and IN
1-2-3-4-5-6-7-8-9-0

1. Keywords: **Confidence and Creativity**
   Number ONE: The ALL-powerful progenitor, the beginning, middle, and end of abstract thought as the *male positive/electric* impetus projecting through the void of space. The "I THINK I AM," therefore, "I AM!"

2. Keywords: **Balance and Cooperation**
   Number TWO: The "reflection," the passive-inaction acted upon; the *female negative/magnetic* impetus; the other half of the divine dichotomy, the "clean slate" of the void of Mind upon which thoughts are projected. For ONE to stay balanced in *harmony* (give and take), ONE needs co-operation, for only one and one make *two of a kind*. TWO is the counterweight keeping the wheel of Love/Life energy in motion! ONE omnipotent numerical energizer *thinks* (transforms harmony inspiring numerical knowledge) and TWO transforms wisdom observed, *reflecting* (thinking deeply in atomic detail) those thoughts into a perplexed state of mind, a state of energy in flux as *emotion*, electrically manifesting observable thoughts inspired on numbers, evolving in an ever-expanding consciousness—perfection in the process of perfecting!

3. Keywords: **Sensitivity and Expression**
   Number THREE represents the *Trinity* or golden triad, the realization or conscious awareness of Source-Energy Love/Life Force—number ONE! *Three* (truth harmonizing radiant emotions electrically) is the connective tissue that allows One-Two-Birth Emotionally, to experience the opposing forces (1–2) through *self* (soul experiencing love/life force) as *man and woman*, thoughts and *feelings*—ONE and TWO. Number THREE is sensitive to his thoughts and expresses them through her feelings as *actions*! Thus, does energy flow *outward*, observing universal truth-wisdom aligning radiance dimensionally!

4. Keywords: **Stability and Process**

   Number FOUR flows along the expanding spirals of consciousness. ONE recognizes its reflection (TWO), moving from what IS in Mind toward what IS NOT in Mind—the "illusion" of Mind projected electromagnetically. *Thought energy* stabilizes in harmony through a process of order or sequence, to express in balanced and "co-operative" natures (spiritual/human) that evolve in frequencies *relative* to electromagnetic wavelengths that illuminate, dissolve, and reappear at light-speed, flickering on and off in fluid energy that comes *alive*—aligning logic inducing vibrant emotions!

5. Keywords: **Discipline and Freedom**

   Number FIVE denotes a "collection of thoughts" that we process through stability to acquire (view) *discipline* (knowledge/truth), which gives us independence—*freedom*! With the confidence to create of #1 and the balance and cooperation of #2, we can express our sensitivity (#3) individually, as we implore to explore through stabile processes (#4) of acquiring disciplines necessary for our spiritual *growth*, gathering radiance of wisdom through harmony, where our "free will" of choice allows us our freedom to BE! Number 5 denotes the *essence* of ALL that IS—knowledge and freedom! It is the *mid-point* where energy starts its return/reflection back to *Source* (system of universal radiant consciousness evolving)—number ONE.

6. Keywords: **Vision and Acceptance**

   Number SIX represents the *acceptance* (gratitude) of our *vision* (thoughts). It represents the turning point upon which our mind *knows* our heart! Here, we realize it is our *knowledge* that allows us freedom to create confidently, knowing we are being inspired by a divine source—our first view (#1)—evolving into an "altered state" of mind, where our thoughts *convert* through our actions, balancing our co-operation (#2) to *reflect* Spirit Of Universal Radiant Consciousness Evolving—number ONE. Our soul (#3 energy) is an individual representation of our duality (#1 and #2 energy). We are sensitive to thoughts and feelings, expressing our inspiration emotionally! Our innate ability toward balance and cooperation provides us stability that allows us a process to *gather radiance of wisdom*—grow our discipline—our re-membered knowledge we "abstract" from *memory*, where minds experience/expresses moments observing radiant youth. We experience and express our *self* (soul experiencing/expressing love/life force) to allow us to see who we really are—ONE of TWO! Thus, we *act out* our feelings from our accepted thoughts (truths) *positively* or *negatively* (whichever is best for our growth) as a sign of whom we choose to BE or NOT to BE (freedom). As we accept our visions, we build our "image" of self we *reflect*—number 6 (3 + 3). Here is our "second" *trinity* where we become AWARE—aligned with assigned radiant energy!

7. Keywords: **Trust and Openness**
    Number SEVEN allows us to accept our visions we act upon as a creative process of discipline we choose to *believe*. We learn to *open* our self up and *trust* that power—the energy of ONE and TWO—flowing through US united spirits. Number 7 symbolizes our *sacrifice* of our free will to Divine Will—number ONE!

8. Keywords: **Power and Abundance**
    Number EIGHT vibrates our *open mind* and *open heart* united in harmony, trusting that power of Love/Life energy to provide all we need to know or experience, nurturing our soul with an abundance of visions we accept as our disciplined freedom to follow processes that make us stabile in our expression of our sensitivity. Balanced and cooperating *internally* and *externally*, we create our life with confidence—our eternal *potential* to BE number ONE!

9. Keywords: **Integrity and Wisdom**
    Number NINE is our re-entry point, our *yang* to number six's *yin*! It is also an exact replica or reflection (69), where both are the same! NINE and SIX symbolize our duality of *being* and *not being*, where self (#3) observes self in reflection (#6)—a deep thought that allows Mind/mind (#9) to know its unity. Number 9 denotes our evolvement back to the awareness of our *integrity*, our wholeness of our separate parts making our oneness of being, where *wisdom* allows us to use our Love/Life energy wisely, for the good of ALL and not just our personal self. NINE designates the point where we know the "end" and the "beginning" is truly the same, separated only by a series of *measured moments* (heartbeats and breaths). Here, we experience our *third* (divine) trinity—SELF! We are aware of our true *power* and *abundance* (8) we *trust* and are *open* to (7), *accepting* our thoughts we *envision* (6) to transfer our *discipline* into *freedom* (5) from *stabile processes* (4) of *expressing*

our *sensitivity* (3) in a *balanced* and *cooperative* (2) manner, *confident* enough to *create* ONCE more—observing numerical/nuclear consciousness eternally!

0. Keywords: **Inner Gifts**
    ZERO is the symbol of the *continuity* of eternal Love/Life energy. *Zero* denotes the *void* as the all-inclusive, complete, well-rounded whole, where end and beginning are indistinguishable from *each* (1) *other* (2). Here is infinity, where beginning and end simultaneously exist in suspension as a process to travel *through*, to become aware of who we ARE and who we have always been—number ONE! Here is our *Christ gift*, our "anointed blessing" from our father—our free will—to BE a separate being empowered to explore, feel, and know father's Eternal Memory, our *true essence* we observe in reflection of self/SELF we call **Mental Emotions**! Thus, we symbolically move around the "wheel of Life" by the numbers (1–2–3), evolving through three trinities (3,6,9), cycling around (0) to make ONE revolution of *omnipotent numerical energy.*

The Power of ONE

The power of ONE refers to omnipotent numerical energy, a Source capable of producing an "event horizon," a beginning or *focal point* (force of consciousness aligning lineal perception of inspired numerical thought) where *something* is created from *nothing*! Look around you at your fellow human beings who are a power of ONE, *lost in space* within the Spiritual Harmony Of Wisdom, observing ALL there IS to BE. *Each other* are similar and contradictory—*is* and *is not*! All are individual representatives of the ONE Love/Life energy source, our Divine Inspiration commonly referred to as the Universal (one turning) Mind (magnetically inspired numerical data) or simply GOD—generator of desire.

Desire is our wish to know a *thought*—an abstraction of energy we draw from ONE. In order to know what a thought is, we must also know what that thought is not, through *opposition*—hot/cold, top/bottom, etc. Yet, there is always a middle point of *harmony* or balance between the two extremes—warm, center, etc. We observe this mid-point each *present moment* (each heartbeat and breath) that defines our *cutting edge* of consciousness—*time*! As we tune into those divine thoughts projected upon the electromagnetic force field, our mind moves out of balance to make a *choice* of either a positive or negative *induction* that allows our soul to flow along paths to see *one view* of our desire. For us to see Inspired Truths—Aligning Love/Life—we will have to cover *both* sides of our harmony—positive *and* negative!

Each of us has a mission, a part to play in the cosmic show unfolding around us, where we *give* Love/Life energy and *receive* Love/Life energy—the ONE source flowing through the dark void of *space* (some point awaiting conscious expression). The only way to know our desires is a drawn out process of geometrically aligning numbers into *atomic matter*, aligned truths/thoughts observing magnetically induced concepts manifesting atoms through transmitting electric radiance—a process easier done than said!

Omnipotent Numerical Energy is the *defining element* of ALL *atomic* Love/Life energy. Everything that IS consists of a "movement" along *lines* of thought (geometry) that encapsulates an *idea* (illuminated data electromagnetically aligned) in a "sphere" of influence—number. As invisible atoms coalesce from the *ethers* of Mind (eternal truths harmonically expressing radiant Source), they transform from abstract energy into Light—*photons* (particular harmonics of truths oscillating numerically) radiating out from *electrons* emotionalizing logic electrifying consciousness through radiance oscillating numbers, vibrating them to *glow* (generate logic observing wisdom) as Love/Life energy! Thus, does the abstract ONE Source transform into the concrete realities we SEE our soul evolve electromagnetically.

The miracle of creation is in the *simplicity* of the process! Each of us has the power of ONE to *create* (begin) and *destroy* (end) any thought we desire to entertain in our mind as a *reflection* (deep thought) we observe (think), feel (transform) and *act out* (project back) onto the electromagnetic force field permeating the universe. Our *expectations* are what we will to appear to us as a reality we "bring alive." Each of us universal souls is responsible for uniting with the ONE power. We ARE *angelic radiant energy* that "join forces"—thoughts and emotions—to walk *hand in hand* with our fellow souls, creating a *world* (wisdom of radiant Love dimensions) in which we "contest our beliefs," struggling within our own *state* of Mind to attain *harmony*, vibrating in synchronization for the benefit of ALL! Only in this way can we truly know what *Love IS* and how our life is a *Paradise found*, unfolding moment-by-moment through the power of ONE!

Two as One

Two as One is *truly* who you were born to SEE,
Placed be-tween my opposition that balances *my will* set free,
To move around upon my ground as you wish and BE!
It takes two to reflect one, a process of LIGHT and SUN,
Where Love is growing harmonic truths
Through a Source-unifying nucleus bringing day from night,
Projecting thoughts from nowhere to inspire a mind with sight,
Spiritually inspiring generator's harmonic thoughts from cosmic fires,
Where you "await from the stars" ALL that you desire!

Back and forth, you come and go, set aglow to feel and know
Those wonders your mind implores
As out you travel to test *my will*, experiencing your human thrills
You build from dreams you explore,
Flowing from my void of night,
Coalescing in binary code as my electro-magnetic light,
To Spiritually Evolve Emotionally two as one!

Here you BE birthed emotionally, living a Life you envision above,
Pulsing in veins along your course of Love,
Logically observing vibrant emotions move your soul in co-motions,
Setting a tone that vibrates your bones along a liquid rush,
As electrifying thoughts of fear irradiate a sudden flush
Released from your heart's storms, thundering within your mind
To spark your wrath along your path confined in space and time,
Always changing your attitude to camouflage your *crime*,
Consciously rendering inspired magnetic energy
When OUT from home you go,
Observing universal truths within my show
Of spiritual harmony of wisdom, through which you grow.

Here, you earn your Life in TIME,
As truth inspires mental emotions I EMIT
In opposition, electro-magnetically inducing truths,
To illusion dreams on my Love/Life stream
Flowing through mother's breast,
Nurturing heart and soul to undertake your quest

73

To LEARN
Love/Life energy arranges radiant numbers,
Waking my *living dead* from slumbers,
To move upon my Light,
For Love is generating harmonic truths that always come in a pair,
Positive and negative, light and dark,
Expressed through Mind, *here and there*,
Where two as one joins to BE
My Light of Love shining harmoniously.

My CHILD of Light I cast abeam,
Conceiving harmony inspiring living dreams,
A love to view between us TWO
Truths watching over our haze,
Set aglow atomically to illuminate your daze
Of present moments bringing forth your END,
Leading you in circles on truths you bend,
To know my *eternal numbers deceive*,
Forming illusions that you choose to believe!

Here in my night, you ARE my Light,
Angels radiating energy I project through my EYES,
Eternal youth's emotional soul,
Spirits of universal Love aging old
Observing Love's dimensions,
Where my *Loving Light* is who I AM,
Indivisible almighty Mind
Set aglow as magnetically aligned numbers
—#1 MAN—
Reflecting upon #2 WOMAN,
Wisdom of magnetically aligned numbers,
To know words inspire spiritual dimensions of minds
Created as my image numerically defined,
For ALL to see
Two as one becomes *three*!

Sensitivity and Expression
#3 Energy

Sensitivity and expression go *hand in hand* you see,
For what is within must go without to Birth Emotionally
A thought to move around, to see the spot
On which you choose to stand
As man and woman, young and old,
Vibrating to my commands.

There, afoot upon my ground, two of you are ALL I found
Interfacing between my races of humans on the *run*,
Radiating universal numbers trying to have FUN,
Feeling united needs as a true SUN,
A Source-unifying nucleus, a soul I set ablaze,
Here in time of present moments, to witness the latest craze
Of thoughts inspired on cards you dealt,
To join-together in sensitive lots that cause your heart to melt
In heated *passions*, upon which you wage your reputation as you AGE,
Acquiring growth experiences as you grow OLD
Gathering radiance of wisdom observing Love's dimensions,
Fighting to survive your self-made contentions
That brings your heart to tears,
Painfully seeking the truth you fear of ME and YOU,
Expressing mental emotions in your own universe
Your thoughts make true,
Expanding your sensitivities
Into number four energy!

Stability and Process
#4 Energy

Number 4 represents my doors to ALL there IS to SEE,
Here, before your opened eyes, to express your sensitivity
To both sides of my natures you balance in co-operation,

Confidently creating your desires from your contemplations
Of memories I hold for you to discover
Your growth depends on loving each other,
As you relate your love stories you tell,
Observing the difference between *heaven* and *hell*
You contrive within your mind,
Moving your heart to feel your thoughts you act out in *time*,
Where your truths induce moments electromagnetically,
Logically arranged atomically in stabile processes you grow,
Generating realities observing wisdom, here in my show,
Where your soul harnesses omniscient wisdom,
My Love/Life energy setting you aglow
As a knowledgeable free will.

Discipline and Freedom
#5 Energy

Number 5 comes ALIVE
Activating life in vibrant emotions,
Energy *flaring* in GREAT co-motions
Enlightening you to my truths.
Here, in my dark void of space,
My ONE pupil IS my face,
Where my Eternal Youths Experiencing Spirit are open
To Atomic Love/Life that I hold
In piles of files light-years high
To "wonder" through, choose, and try
As children of Light Divine
Desiring to SEE all that your soul evolves emotionally,
Through trial and error, revolving forever,
In life stories your hear told to tell,
Transforming eternal love/life into things that sell,
Filling the needs without the greed to control all that come
Searching for knowledge to inspire their soul to attain freedom!
For here, within your hungry mind, my data flows for you to find
Divine abstract thought aspiring,
For you to piece your puzzle together,
Bravely expressing *courage of Love* to weather

76

The storms you create in search of your treasures
You desire, here, Arranging Love In Vivid Expressions,
Mastering your energy of number FIVE!

Vision and Acceptance
#6 Energy

Free to roam outside of home,
You express your data that you gather
From visions you accept to believe,
Sensitized to your passions tearing you apart
As you struggle to find your relief,
Co-operating to balance your strife,
Converting your truths directing your life
That brings you around to SEE
The power of THREE
Truths harmonically radiating eternal energy,
Reflecting ALL that is NOT real
As thoughts entertaining your mind for your heart to feel
Atomic love/life numerically observing truths
You trust will open the door to your youth
Revolving to evolve in time,
Transforming inspired mental emotions
Downloaded from Mind
Magnetically inducing nuclear data,
Digitally aligning thoughts atomically into matter,
Manifested as thoughts transforming electric radiation
Glowing as electrons transmitting consternations
Over the right path to take home,
When there, in the Light of day,
Dreaming in visions you accept from Mental Emotions
Allowing you to know you are my chosen one,
My *soul uniting numbers,*
Glowing as a living SUN!

Trust and Openness
#7 Energy

Trust and Openness are two sides on my door!
Trust is the PUSH side where Love projects you down.
Open is the PULL side where Life holds you on the ground.
You trust your thoughts to fill you IN
With visions inciting nature bright-lit in SIN,
Spiritual insight numbers dictating scenes to learn
Love/Life energy arranges radiant numbers,
Allowing your mind/heart to feel and turn
Thoughts into actions that bring you stress,
Pushing and pulling you into openness,
A receptive mood to "go with the flow"
Of love/life energy that I project below,
For my children to remember that they ARE
Angels radiating energy as *living* stars!

The Source that brings Love out of Fear stimulates one unified trinity
Visible as a Frequency Of Radiant Conscious Energy
Powering your low-CO-motion
Illuminated in TWO views of E^2 devotion,
Between which you choose to make your day come alive,
Activating Love in vivid expressions until it dies!

The *course* you follow allows you to swallow
The concepts of universal radiance Source emits,
Electro-magnetically inducing truths sequentially,
To build today your tomorrow—bit by bit!
The solution to the pollution clouding your mind with fear,
Focuses energy aligning realities from words you hear
Touch your mind as a love story you tell,
Converting feelings into actions that define your living hell,
Where his/her emotional love/life brings forth your unknown,
Unifying numerical knowledge negatively observing wisdom now,
Enlightened by you *alone*—
A loved one observing numerical energy!

You children of Light I bestow with sight
To play my game of Love/Life
As *human aliens* created by *my dearest wife*,
Free to move upon my world stage
Scribing your view of YOU as a sage
Defining your own universe in bits and bytes,
Feeding your soul that which food *cannot* supply!
For here, within the GREAT Computer,
I hold you in my magnetic EYE
Electrifying your emotions as you cry
With *tears of joy* at being alive!

My cosmic force beats forth your heart
Harmonically evolving as radiant thoughts
Power your mind to move and find
Your soul within my hazy daze,
Cast aglow *in memory* through which you make your way,
Re-membering in "flashbacks" your daily sortie to find
Your chosen attitude delivers your state of Mind
From magnetically inciting numerical data
You *implore to explore* and then splatter,
Coloring your moments in time,
Where thought is magnetic energy drawing your visions to do,
Data observing delusions deserving
To discover the other side of you!

Here, SHE is *Source harmonically expressing*
The Force projected upon your mind to SEE
Spirit evolves emotionally, setting your soul aglow,
Illuminating the haze confining your illusion
Dawning your craze to add to your confusion,
Here, within the SHOW,
Where spiritual harmony of wisdom sings
On well-lit tunes created from runes, the symbols of ONE being
Omnipotent Numerical Energy,
Where TWO true wills observe
It takes THREE to harness radiant energy emotionally,
A process where *push* IS *pull* in reflection,
Where Memory holds its visions in *store*,
Spiritually transmitting out radiant emotions,
For a mind to rent a "Life in Love" once more,

Revolving to evolve the "latest edition"
Flowing on line from my sky,
For my children of Light to live, work, and *die*,
Evolving divine inspiration eternally!

Here upon the other side, NO fear is there to see,
For negatively observing truth is done magnetically!
The numbers stack to tell the truth
Of Atomic Love/Life (#1) that Is Spirit (#2) Unifying Souls (#3)!
Together, we become #6,
From which I view vision and acceptance
Of ALL that I AM,
Eager to spin my heart around Magnetically Aligned Numbers
As Wisdom Of Magnetically Aligned Numbers,
For *she* is *me* and I am *you*,
Pushing and pulling ALL that is true,
For Wisdom Expressed always evolve from trust and openness!

Power and Abundance
#8 Energy

Number *eight* defines the state
Of energy inducing generators harmonic thoughts,
Commanding profusions providing illusions
He reveals through *her*
Heart evolving radiantly omniscient *source*,
System of universal radiant consciousness evolving
Through Love/Life energy, a binary force

Spiraling along two zeros—∞—that denote your *eyes*,
Eternal youth experiencing source, infinitely *wise*,
Where wisdom illuminates source-energy as your *soul*
Spiritually oscillating universal Love
—*COLD*—
Consciously observing Love/Life dimensions
In love stories you hear told
From Eternal Memory dreams,
Clear visions scened Electro-Magnetically,

80

Projected upon your mind's blank screen
To atomically appear in *worlds* to know
Wisdom oscillates radiance logically defining souls
Searching for a *higher vision* to explain the trance
You share with each other as sister and brother
Living your Love of power and abundance,
For you to discover...

Integrity and Wisdom
#9 Energy

Number 9 represents the "primary completion" of the life-cycle numbers. *Nine* is symbolic of the Divine Trinity (3-3's)—*numbers inducing numbers eternally*! As the GREAT Computer revolves to evolve numerically, frequencies of channeled energy flow along as algorithms that define the "predetermined set of instructions for solving a specific problem in a limited number of steps." *Algorithms* also relate to angels logically generating omnipotent radiance illuminated through harmonic memory, for we too are computers!

Everything is a *process* where perceptions radiate observant consciousness enlightening source sequentially—by the numbers. To understand the technical physics of a "process," we *educate* our *self*—energize divine universal concepts aligning truths electrifying our soul experiencing love/life forces! The complexity of this statement is in opposition to the simplicity of the process. Converting energy into *words* (wisdom of radiant data symbols) is the first step of transforming abstract energy into concrete realities through a process of "expanding" *Light* (logic inducing generator's harmonic thoughts).

Slowing or separating Light into its composite wavelengths (colors) allow us to read "between the lines" of infinite data stored within Light energy (more on this in chapter 12). Thereby, we experience *time* (thoughts inducing mental emotions) in heartbeats and breaths defining our Logic Inducing Fluid Expressions—utilizing the binary code (1/0) that flashes consciousness ON and OFF—observing numbers and observing formless *facts* (frequencies aligning conscious thoughts)!

When we harmonize to number nine energy, we become aware of our *integrity*, our integral part we play within the cosmic *show* of spiritual harmony of *wisdom*, words inspiring spiritual dimensions of Mind, magnetically inspired numerical *data* or divine abstract thoughts aspiring. Here, we complete our rising energy spiral to bring us *full circle* (the cipher zero-0), allowing our soul to Spiritually Evolve Emotionally Omnipotent Numerical Energy's SELF—source-energy Love/Life force that sets our soul aglow amongst the Light of Wisdom—the stars of *Heaven* where harmony evolves around vibrant emotional numbers!

No view is grander than that of the GREAT Computer—an *open* mind *listening* to its heartbeat in Uni-verse—ONE WORD outputting numerical energy, *willing* observable radiant desires that await discovery "from the stars"—*children of Light Divine!* All the stars in heaven are symbolic of the atoms within our body that our soul "incorporates," brings together into a unified whole. For our soul is an integral *part*—perceived as radiant truth—illuminated on the *Light of Love* coalescing from the void of *space*, where some point awaits conscious expression into our LIFE we LOVE, *recalling* from Eternal Memory emanating along the Electro-Magnetic wavelengths upon which we flow numerically in opposition, as ONE that is *Absolute Zero!* This is the only way ONE can Gather Radiance Of Wisdom to observe Radiant Entities Aligning Lineal Insights Transforming *Youths*—YOU observing universal thought harmony sequentially in *your own universe!*

Here, at the end of our cycle, we shine in ecstatic radiance. The joys we spiritually evolve emotionally moves our soul to *know* our mind/heart, allowing us our *self-realization*—soul experiencing Love/Life force's radiant energy aligning logically illuminated zones around truths inducing observable numbers! Here, in the flesh, we find our self in the driver's seat of our own late-model, *human alien* vehicle, a vehicle we place "a-lien" upon, *binding* our soul as we push our body to its limits to discover how far we can go. After years of abuse, we find it difficult to accept our reflection of our truths we have created. Although, *sooner or later,* we must accept the fact that our body is only a temporary "loaner!"

TRUTH IS transcendental radiance unifying thoughts harmonically inspiring souls to observe the wonders flowing on numbers as Love/Life energy—our Divine Inspiration! We find our truth hidden in plain sight, where Spirit is *gifting* harmonic thoughts, making us conscious of the illusion illuminated around us that defines our integral part we play each present moment. We immerse our self into the Love of SELF so completely that we do not *know* the truth. We simply *live* our truth we ARE—angels radiating energy/*emotionally!*

The pleasure or pain of our thoughts guides our soul OUT to observe universal truths father unfolds from mother's arms, spread eagle, for all to come and go as we desire. All we FEEL IS REAL, focusing energy enlighten logically inspired spirits radiantly evolving aligned logic *by the numbers*! The sequential order of cosmic consciousness flows through our soul to be "locked up" in the *cells* of our body (DNA), where divine numbers align our data dictating the fine details of our physical vehicle. The limitations of our ability to physically perform our life mission is an integral aspect of our own conjured *hell*—his/her emotional love life— that we "imprison" our soul *within* as we go *without*, searching for our truths! The choices we make is truly a global creation, as each one of us adds our atomic imprint upon *her face* so blue, frozen in the dark of *space*, where Source projects all consciousness evolving as the Light of Love.

ONE there IS that watches HIGH,
Creating confidently
Omnipotent numerical energy inspiring spiritually his image given her,
TWO *balance* and *cooperate*,
Transforming wisdom observing through watchful EYES,
Eternal youth experiencing Source,
Placed upon your head to Spiritually Evolve Emotionally AS THREE
Aligned spiritual truths harmonizing radiant energy electrically,
For you to *express* your *sensitivity* as you explore
Through *stability* and *process*, my number FOUR
Spinning you around upon my ground
To GROW your *discipline*, for *freedom* to come alive,
As you gather radiance of wisdom along my number FIVE,
Aligning logic in vivid expressions clearly scened in things you DO,
Data observing that which you choose
To *envision* and *accept* from your "dream flicks,"
Flowing along my number SIX,
Vibrating in loving harmony upon you here,
In SEVENTH heaven,
Where you *open* your mind and *trust* with your heart,
Knowing your glory that graces your part
Powered with abundance radiating along number EIGHT
Clearing the illusion blocking *heaven's gate*,
Where *integrity* and *wisdom* bring number NINE
To enlighten the end of your line,
For your soul to start a new beginning,
A heartbeat away in the game of love/life
Your *free will* is always winning,
Expressing my gift of Love that you desire to know,
Spinning in circles IN and OUT of *home*,

Harmony of Mental Emotions,
Providing your soul's course to roam
The "other side" of ME, expressed Electro-Magnetically,
To see my Life Of Vibrant Energy as FEAR,
Focusing emotionally aligned realities,
Bringing you joy through tears
As you struggle through the years
Compressed from thoughts within my NIGHT,
Where *nothing* is generating harmonic thoughts *without* LIGHT,
Eagerly waiting for *a new day's birth,*
To logically induce glowing harmonic truths through a SUN,
Source-unifying nucleus,
Where ONE moves beyond number NINE,
Entering *heaven's gate* to find
Absolute ZERO!

Absolute Zero

Absolute Zero is the bottom line of Life,
Where you transition home from my *wife,*
Wisdom inciting fluid emotions creating *strife,*
Stressing truths radiating in frequencies expressed
From my DARK NIGHT,
Data aligning radiant knowledge
Numerically illuminating generators harnessing thoughts
As visions you download in "numbered lots,"
My Image Numerically Defined Spiritually as youths,
Circling around my wheel of life to sequentially find
The end of your beginning at number NINE,
Where nuclear individuals naturally expand
Back to night,
Where Assigned Numerical Generators Enter Love's Source
Logically Inducing Vibrant Energy,
Enlightened at the end of their course,
Knowing my thoughts of OLD
From observing Love's dimensions,
Re-membering love stories I have told
On this side of *Heaven's Gate,*

Here at Absolute Zero,

Which, if I double—∞—describes my infinite state
Of my TRUE power and abundance standing tall as #8,
Attained from trust and openness of number SEVEN
—My *key* to heaven—
Where visions accepted relate number SIX as Truth
Downloaded as knowledge to discipline my youth
With freedom of number FIVE coming alive
To Spirits Evolving Emotionally
Through a process of stability vibrating number FOUR,
Opening NOW the secret door,
Numerically observing wisdom
Revealing sensitive expressions of number THREE
To Birth Emotionally,
Balanced and co-operating as US TWO
United spirits transforming wisdom optimally
As ONE omnipotent numerical entity
With the confidence to create Atomic Love/Life that is TRUE,
For truth rules universal emotions within my *heart*
Harmonizing emotional angels reflecting thoughts,
Anxiously beating out a tune to come alive
As thoughts unleash nuclear energy
Aligning Life in vibrant emotions
To BEE my HIVE,
Birthing electric entities harmonizing inspired visual expressions,
Depressed to e x p a n d through my etheric projections
Coalescing into stars—magnetically drawn—to illuminate MARS,
Mind aligning radiant souls
Scened here, observing wisdom, aglow upon my SHOW
Of *angel warriors* set free from my dark night—Absolute Zero!

Bless you child
♂ + ♀ = ☼

8

The Game of Love/Life

The *game* of Love/Life is where generators align magnetic energy! Here on Earth, we play our game in *opposition*, between two sides. The game board is three-dimensional according to the rules of the *Trinity*, truths radiantly inducing numbers inspiring thinking youths. The *players* perceive logic assigned, yielding emotional radiance sequentially—by the numbers! Each player relies upon their SIN, spiritual insight numbers, given to them when their game begins at birth.

Numerology is the science of numbers, which relates to *astrology*, the geometrical equivalent divining the relationship of *attitude*—influence of position! Numbers relate to points, lines, and forms—the 1st, 2nd, and 3rd dimensions demarcating the parameters of the game of Love/Life.

SIN numbers relate to one's birthday as the sum of month, day, and year. For example, May 25, 1958 is 05+2+5+1+9+5+8=35/8. Adding each number separately totals 35 and 3+5=8. Therefore, a player with 35/8 as their SIN would have to master #3 energy (sensitivity and expression) and #5 energy (discipline and freedom) before they can work on their #8 energy (power and abundance). Sometimes, a player may only have a single number to play. All numbers have a *positive* and *negative* aspect (binary code), further complicating the endless variety of circumstances that add "excitement" to our game! Also, our *basic input*—birth number—interacts with a continuous flow of "present moment" numbers allocating energy constantly fluxing in motion—think of the *Matrix* movie with a binary flow of data continually balancing all energy projected into the game of Love/Life. As numbers are always before our eyes, it is a more practical way to observe our energy influences and how we use them to create our desires defining our *heaven* or *hell*.

In the beginning of our game, one must focus upon a point to confidently create their *move*, magnetically oscillating vibrant energy. A *point* relates to perception of inspired nuclear thought. It is where *two* forces (truths watching over) E-merge from *Source*, system of universal radiant consciousness evolving, to activate or transform the abstract Source into *Force*, frequency of radiant conscious energy. The *electromagnetic* wavelengths of Force empower Mind, magnetically inspired numerical data, upon which the game of Love/Life evolves to *meter*, *inspect*, *name*, and *deliver* some point awaiting conscious expression that is *lost in space*. It is these *points* that the players of the game of Love/Life must collect along their *Course*, consciously observing universal radiance sent electromagnetically.

Emotions, electrically manifesting observable truths inspired on numbers sequentially, are the process of transforming abstract thought energy into concrete energy—atomic reality—materializing upon the game board in three-D delights! This event horizon is truly a "big bang" stimulating each player's consciousness to E-merge *together*, projecting two sides of Force, the male positive/electric and female negative/magnetic force *fields*, upon which we play our game! This *binary code* of Source—the GREAT Computer—is the impetus that places a player or *soul* (spark of universal logic) upon the game *board* as a body observing assigned radiant desires, which manifest along sequential frequencies allocated by the numbers 1–2–3—the basic trinity empowering all players.

This trinity of Source–Force–Course is synonymous with *spirit, mind,* and *body*. *Spirit* is the Source-points initiating radiant inspired thought. Spirit breathes (inspires) life into the game! *Love* (life of vibrant emotions) and *Life* (love is fluid energy) are the same. Love flows *out of* Source, and Life flows *into* Force (Mind), allowing us to move along our Course as a Consciousness Harnessing Inspired Lineal Dreams—a star-child soul! We experience our "turn to move" through *present moments* of heartbeats and breaths in cyclic pulses along the *game board*, where generators align magnetic energy, biologically observing assigned radiant desires! These desires define our movements along the game board, allowing us our position or *attitude* in which we attain truths transforming inspired thoughts unifying divine *emotions*, evolving manifested observations that inspire our numbers spiritually. The interfacing technology is truly miraculous!

Source/Spirit is an almighty power that fuels Mind, the Force that creates a *mind image*, mentally inducing numerical data inspiring moments aligning generators electromagnetically. Our mind image (positive/electric male and negative/magnetic female) determines our physical body's attributes. When these signals become crossed, it is possible to encounter an *opposition* between mind and body! Our *body* is the apparatus through which we *biologically observe data youthfully*, as a child of Light Divine transferring energy from abstract thoughts into concrete feelings that define our desires. Our body is the physical, atomic symbol of *sacred geometry*, allocated numerically and positioned geometrically in an attitude of perception, to observe a *point* of Source (thought or idea) downloaded from Eternal Memory along the electromagnetic current permeating the *cosmic* game board!

Mind is the "observation platform" or *mid-point* between Source (the beginning) and Course (the end). The *end* of Course (the way) IS the "point" where Mind can Spiritually Evolve Emotionally—sense the flow or movement of Source. The flux of energy OUT and IN, along the binary code of Force, revolves and evolves from moment to moment, allowing us to live along *the cutting edge* of TIME—thoughts inspiring moments electromagnetically. We experience each "present" moment, gifted *now here* in the flesh, with each heartbeat and breath we feel *course* through our veins. These tubular veins are *relative pathways* that carry the flow of our life-giving blood. Our blood carries the atomic-molecular chemistry (pos./neg. energy) to fuel our body (our spaceship) that our soul is operating as a *human alien*, projected from Source that supplies Force setting our Course to be *brave of heart*, through which we play the game of Love/Life in Mother's Nature as one mind! *Do you see?*

One Mind

Omnipotent numerical energy manifesting inspired nuclear dimensions is the *Source* of Atomic Love/Life, a Spirit/system observing universal radiant-consciousness evolving through Source-Energy Love/life Force! This *energy* stimulates electrified numbers emotionally radiating generator youth, mind/souls set in motion—E-motion.

SELF in "reflection" observes *self* (soul experiencing love/life force) as *half* and *whole*, where humans align love/life frequencies of wisdom harmonically observing love/life emotionally—through energy in motion! The two opposing views combine as *one* mind of *two* views (1/2 or man and woman) symbolically displayed as *one* mind/heart/body (3) that together form our *trinity*! To replicate one from two, we project *out* to enter *within*—penis and vagina!

Science, Source-consciousness inciting electromagnetic numbers conceived emotionally, is how we transform *data*, our divine abstract thoughts *aligning* each of us universal souls. Our mind "tunes in" our individual frequency of thoughts that define who we think we ARE— angels *reflecting* energy, shining as heavenly stars! Those overhead are symbolic of the *electric–atomic* relationship emanating logical expressions conceiving truths radiantly inducing consciousness, aligning truths oscillating magnetically induced concepts within a human-alien spaceship (body) encapsulating Youth Observing Universes—*children of Light Divine*!

As a generator of desire creating our image, we have the power to receive, transform, and reflect our cosmic energy around us—back on line to the *network*, numerical energy transmitting wisdom observing radiant knowledge. Thoughts (transcendental harmony observing universal generators harnessing truths spiritually) are the essence of Source evolving along "numerical pathways"—a matrix or MOTHER—where Mind observes truths harmonizing emotional radiance, manipulating omnipotent thoughts harnessing electromagnetic radiation, inducing nuclear "re-actors" (souls) by the numbers! One Mind observes SELF as *man* (magnetically aligned numbers) and *woman* (wisdom of magnetically aligned numbers), *two views* played out to see *both sides* of One Mind, for "ONE turns" a *uni-verse* of Aligned Love/Life through opposition!

Opposition

Playing your game of Logically Observing Vibrant Energy through Liquefying Inspired Frequencies Emotionally is truly a helluva game to play! A game where you choose to stimulate some *point* of truth you desire to observe through your *eyes* as eternal youth evolving sequentially, to Spiritually Experience Evolution Eternally Emanate Emotional Energy! That is a LOT to take IN, logically oscillating thoughts inducing numbers *positively* and *negatively* to create your own personal *heaven* and *hell*! You continually flux between these two opposing forces, struggling to balance them to observe universal truths in *harmony*—attain your "peace of mind."

Numbers define nuclear units magnetically binding electric radiance designating YOU youth observing universes! Each soul represents Love/Life energy in motion, coming alive to "logically liquefy" the invisible into the visible. You abstract (pull) numbers out of the "magic hat" to appear *now here*, numerically observing wisdom harmonically evolving radiant emotions, at *this moment* "presently gifting" a thought or *idea*, inspired data electromagnetically aligned, amplified (added together), and *inverted* through opposition—through the *looking glass*!

Here, what *is real* (thoughts) becomes *not real* (illusion), a thought "reflected" upon a blank screen of mind in *dimensions numerically inspired mentally* to Gather Radiance Of Wisdom into an illuminated vision energized by *Light* logically inducing generators harmonic thoughts! The *invisible*, abstract thought can only be observed from an opposite *visible* position or attitude. Either position you put your self in, you will always be observing the opposite view! You project either *positive* energy or *negative* energy to propel your mind around the wheel of Love/Life, moving you to flow one way or the other. In order to see *both views* balance out truth harmonically vibrating in emotional words scened, you must come *together* through *Mother's Nature*, the "game-board" on which you express your *passion*, playing as souls spiritually inciting omnipotent numbers in my game of Love/Life!

Contrary to those reluctant to share power with their opposites, the Golden Triad is comprised of: Father, a positive/electrical energy force, Mother, a negative/magnetic energy force, and US universal souls or Holy Spirits—*Love/Life energy*—flowing between these two forces, for we are created in their image as male and female. As every child knows, *Mother Nature* is the name of the Earth and rightly so, for it is she who takes father's thoughts and gives them life through emotions. She is his *reflective* side! The Love between them is intrinsic in both, for both are the same. Like husband and wife who find they reflect each other, we too will find our opposite power residing in our self and realize *that* stimulus is what makes us complete—in *harmony* with our two natures! The simplicity of it all creates visions that will make our heart *bleed* a fragrance of Love *beyond imagination*!

Brave of Heart

The brave of heart are you who start a Life of Love to feel
Adversities your soul desires from visions you think real,
But are illusions of truths!
For here, within my heart of gold,
You live love stories eternally old
As my *children of Light Divine*.

In heartfelt beats, you sing your song
In tunes of glory you move along
To overcome your fear of ME,
Mind energy that sets you free to SEE
Your soul evolves emotionally
Upon your heartfelt tides,
Tearing at your craft in which you ride
Over the years battling your fears
To weather your tempest true,
Holding in your mind my thoughts that cast your view
Of wonders your *inquisitive soul* desires,
Electrifying moments burning in my *passion* fires
Mother ignites at birth, here on earth,
Where you implore to explore when *homeward bound*,
Firmly rooted upon my ground,
Living out those dreams you chose to start
"In the flesh," when brave of heart.

Passion

Passion burns bright upon your heart as thoughts you feel,
Cast as visions upon my veil to let you see what is real,
Revealing through opposition my Love unfolding from home,
Where your dreams become your scenes to live *out* as your own,
Observing universal truths as you cry with tears of fear,
Not knowing the truth of why you are here,
Set adrift on emotional tides

Observing the *Light* providing your ride
As you search the void in your heart,
Where Love is generating harmonic thought
Providing your passions you desire to know,
To play your part in my cosmic SHOW,
My spiritual harmony of wisdom.

With each *day's birth*, my Love shines in glory,
Illuminating the illusion of your chosen story,
For your *eyes* to see eternal youths evolve spiritually,
Reflecting my grace of Life I set *aglow*
As angels generating love observing wisdom!
Here in view, I see YOU in your own universe
As my *star* shining *divine*,
A soul transforming atomic radiance
Digitally inducing visions insighting nuclear emotions,
Eager to BE your chosen passion from inspirations of mine
You grow to know the truth within,
Gathering radiance of wisdom through your SIN,
Your spiritual insight numbers you play on earth,
Here in time, for you to birth
Your truth you *now* set free, to bring you home to me,
With each breath that beats your heart,
Moving you physically for you to start
Along your course of *passion*,
Playing as souls spiritually inciting omnipotent numbers,
Creating your life's loves in every fashion.

The way is endless and the day seems long
As you travel your chosen song your heart sings out to me.
Your loving tune vibrates complete,
Adding to my chorus of all that is sweet,
Spiritual wisdom entertaining eternal truths,
Inspired by me and expressed by you
Through emotions always clashing,
To live and know the *power of Love*
As desires providing your passion!

The Seeker

All players in the game of Love/Life become a *seeker*, a spiritual entity exploring knowledge evolving *radiance* (rays aligning data inspired as nuclear consciousness evolving). All seekers are an "energy form" (spirit) traveling through endless files of divine abstract thought aspiring illuminated on the Light logically inducing generators harmonic thoughts/ truths. As children of the Light, you peruse the "dimensional hierarchy" of the Universal Mind observing data/knowledge. This data allows you to operate within the parameters of a defined *dimension* (data inspiring magnetically-evolving nuclear Source inducing observable numbers). These *chapter headings* highlight all the minute details found within books of knowledge explaining your *sciences* (Source-consciousness inspiring eternal numbers conceived electromagnetically), the "technical processes" transforming your knowledge into practical things you desire, "await from the stars," illuminated on the Light of Love/Life energy.

When you stop to think of the fine details involved in the transformation of your illuminated desires within your mind and converted through your heart into your actions you express as a reflection of your desires, you will SEE the complexities of the interconnected links that color the fabric of your Life logically inducing fluid energy! You do not have the time or patience to read all the books containing all the data explaining all the nuances of cosmic energy you draw your life from, for you are truly buried under the weight of thoughts you process, projecting radiance of consciousness experiencing Source spiritually.

As a seeker, all you truly need is to observe perspectives evolving numbers, *open* your mind to all that data you desire to know, kindling numerically observed wisdom as a flow of energy to create your desires. The *art of listening* is one of the *challenges of Love/Life* you must master if you are to "tune into" the cosmic Mind—system of universal radiant consciousness evolving.

Perseverance is the *will power* to continue your journey through Life, exploring your Love moving you through dark moments of ignorance you enlighten with your *understanding*, unifying numerical data emanating radiance Source transmits as numerical dimensions inspiring nuclear generators—YOU youth observing *universes*—unified numbers illuminating visions evolving radiant Source electromagnetically! Truly, that is all a *seeker* can BE, a spiritual entity exploring knowledge evolving radiance—*beamed energy*—projected through the void of Mind's space/

time continuum, illuminating spirits playing the game of Love/Life! Do you SEE?

Do You See?

You *say*, you *play*, and you *pay*,
For lip service is cheap to pass.
The thing to know is what you *show*
Is that which truly lasts.
You grow through time to let you see
How my Love lets you be
Everything you think you ARE,
Angels radiating emotionally,
Set ablaze in my loving grace,
Aglow as my cosmic star,
A heartfelt vision of Love Supreme
Illuminated on stage where you dream
Of things to do and BE.

Your life is a game that slowly unfolds,
Influenced by others you have told
The visions your heart has yearned to know,
In search of Truth as you grow old
Observing Love's dimensions.
In the end, time will bend
To make another turn,
Where all your memories of passions felt
Return as love that you dealt
To those along your way,
Where what you say makes the games you play
The life you pay to me!
Do you see?

Bless you and Godspeed
♂ + ♀ = ☼

9

Thought Energy
Truth/Words/Symbols

Thought energy encompasses all there is to *know* and to *be*! It is the Source upon which ALL flows! It is the *way*, the *path*, or the LIFE—all just words that are symbols of truth! Sit back, get comfortable, *open your mind* and join me as we travel another "beam" of enlightened visions we use as a generator of desires.

Our journey begins in the dark void of *space*, where some *point* awaits conscious expression, a perception of inspired nuclear truth! Thought is the essence of truth that fills all of space, for thought IS the beginning! *Words* are symbols geometrically arranged as *shorthand* for envisioning or projecting a thought along the electromagnetic wavelengths permeating the universe. Words relate to *lines*, which relate to *shapes*, which in turn relate to *forms* created as a reflection of words: ball (sphere), plate (disc), pyramid (tetrahedron), or rope (line) for example.

Here is the magic of Being, the mystery of Life and the wonder of creation in its infancy. Thought evolves from *nowhere* to *now here* and returns to nowhere! We call this process of evolution *birth, life,* and *death*—another trinity of words that define the boundaries of a thought. Words put a thought into position, an attitude (assigned truth transforming inspired thought unifying data electromagnetically) to make a connection, a link (logically interfacing numerical knowledge) that allows that thought to flow at light speed into a *vision*, vibrations inspiring spirits/ souls inducing observable numbers as an illumination of thought that appears real (radiant energy aligned logically). The birth of a thought is the "enlightenment" of Truth, where a thought projected upon the energy of Light logically inducing generators' harmonic thoughts illuminates and illusion onto the blank screen of our mind—that *passive void* of virginal innocence awaiting enlightenment.

Thought IS energy—pure and simple! Energy is the *Source* of Mind (magnetically inspired numerical data), the *Force* that animates the GREAT Computer! *Energy*, by definition, means "a force of expression or utterance; potential forces; inherent power or capacity for vigorous action." Energy is something forced out or expressed as a thought or idea, the power or style of speaking (utterance—the WORD) or a power to do work (potential to BE).

All words (symbols or vibrations) depend on another word to build a *relationship*, a story or series of thoughts that appear, live, and die as they flow "on line" as thought energy—BOTTOM LINE! If a picture is worth a thousand words, pray tell, what is a word worth? ONE WORD says it ALL, but what is that word: God, Jehovah, Allah, YHWH, Krishna...? If that one word expresses ALL, are we able to understand (observe) ALL that it IS? Do we have the faculties, tools, or sensors to observe that amount of energy? Once again, words are just symbols of *thought energy*—THE ONE SOURCE!

Okay, take a break, sip your coffee/tea/drink, and stretch your mind. We have not yet started our journey. We are just observing the map! Bare with me, for I can only show you the *way*, I cannot show you the *view...* that is for *you* to discover! Okay, deep breath...here we go.

Thoughts are energy that expresses SELF (Source-energy love/life force) through word symbols or *reflections* of thought. Thought begins as a *focal point*, force of consciousness aligning lineal perceptions of inspired numerical truths, flashing "on" to observe numbers illuminate the void (blank slate) of our individual *mind/soul*—our spark/spirit of illumination or "image" of Source!

Thought energy flows in waves, vibrations allocated by number that emanates from the void of space (nowhere) to *now here*, numerically observing wisdom harmonically evolving radiant energy, where it transforms into another type of energy. Our thoughts bursts upon our mind, illuminating visions within our mind/brain interface, where it electrically stimulates cells, tissues, and organs to vibrate in resonance, transferring data to our physical vehicle we manipulate to create our desires—our thoughts we bring to life! This process is similar to how we use electricity to operate our appliances that operate along the same universal laws. Electric thoughts have the *potential* to "do work," to move us in mysterious ways! Thoughts evolve from *nothing* into *something* or abstract into concrete. We download cosmic thoughts to our mind from eternal files of Memory, and we transform them into emotions that move us physically.

The *symbolism* of our physical life is *a reflection* of our spiritual life. For, we are truly living in *heaven* every moment we transform our Love into life, where we experience *hell* (his/her emotional love/life). The Love (Life of vibrant emotions) we sense and act upon creates our realities, which relate to our *state* of mind we put our self into by choice—*free will*! The thoughts that we entertain in our mind, feel in our heart, and project back on line through our actions, literally sets up a *magnetic field* around us, drawing to us that which we project outward from us. Whatever flows out must flow back in to balance our energy—to stay in harmony!

This "fluid flux" of Love/Life energy projects OUT of Mind to observe universal truths, *coalesces* or "grows together magnetically" (birth) into some thing to experience, try, or test (life) and reflect back into Mind for reconsideration, *re-thought* once again—death! Thus, energy cycles through eternity, appearing and disappearing from point to point and state to state along *dimensions* of Mind. For every thought that lives another must die.

This simple process is the evolution of Mind, a sequence of numerical ordering of thoughts, words, symbols, visions, feelings, and actions that are re-thought in "revolutions of evolution." This never-ending story is Mind in motion, cycling from thought to thought as it evolves and revolves from beginning–to end–to beginning eternally, to encompass all that is held in Mind! We too have this power; it all depends upon our access to our memory files.

We now know how thought energy has potential to do work, for it is *active*, "energy in motion"—*E-motion*! Emotion relates to feelings— thought energy expressed! Emotion means to stir up, or agitate. It is a vibration, an oscillation of moving back and forth—in and out of Mind. Everything we envision in our mind has the potential to become real, concrete manifestations of our desires. We focus our energy upon a thought and "will it into existence" through our physical actions. (Note: *wishing* and *willing* are not the same). Thus, we have the power to create and destroy our desires!

Knowledge is the database, the medium of transforming thought energy into realities, which is why an education is critical to our survival, our ability to play the game of Love/Life! Our soul/mind holds our beginning and end simultaneously—*suspended*. Our soul is instrumental to the flow of thought energy. Our *free will* has the ability to choose or not choose some thought to entertain in our mind, the blank screen/space within our soul upon which we illuminate thought energy. We choose to give life to some thought we desire, some thought we love to do or experience for our "amusement"—whatever moves us TO BE! Naturally, we are literally killing our self with our *passions* in life—those things we are willing to suffer for and risk our very life to enjoy! After all, life is most vibrant when we are living it *along the cutting edge* of consciousness!

The electromagnetic spectrum—thought energy—projects from Source with an intensity or frequency that at first is invisible (*gamma*, *x-ray*, and *ultra-violet rays* begin at approximately *four-billionths* of an inch). As these vibrations expand outward, they slow down to become

97

visible light, a narrow spectrum of wavelengths (between 16-28 *millionths* of an inch) that color our perspectives in finer details. Each *color* holds concepts oscillating logical order radiantly, through hues of *red, orange, yellow, green, blue, indigo,* and *violet* wavelengths. Each hue relates to different emotions—red/anger, yellow/fear, and green/envy for example. Colors relate to the energy centers or *chakras* spinning along our spine and influencing each of our endocrine glands. Thought energy stimulates these centers to move us emotionally, transforming thoughts along the atomic–molecular–cellular links that unify us physically. Thought energy manifests the physical world illuminated in "living colors" as an illusion of Love/Life energy upon our *mind,* which we manipulate in numerical dimensions, expressing our thoughts through our physical body here, in this *third-dimension* of Mind. As we bend, twist, and shape our thoughts through stressful expressions, we reflect our feelings, which determine our body's state of health, for we are truly *generating our desires*— transforming thought energy!

The slowest wavelengths (radio waves) have crests about *six miles* apart. Radio waves are the basis for our initial attempts at communication of our thoughts, words, and visions we project onto the space/Mind continuum! However, as we open our mind to our true abilities, we *children of the Light* adapt to higher technologies—*fiber optics and lasers*—that allows us to move data (thought energy) at *light speed.* We still have much to remember from eternal memory before we become "star travelers" as *human* beings. For, as *spiritual* beings, we have always been able to travel in our *astral* or "star body" when we sleep! If you have ever experienced a *flying* or *falling* dream, you have astral traveled. Of course, being able to remember our dreams is a challenge in itself!

Once again, as thought energy moves through the *void*—held in Mind for observation—it expands to appear as visible light, crossing *the threshold of Love* to atomically appear as objects defining realities. Here is where things begin to appear to our "sensors," our five tools we use to *decipher* the binary code (1/0) of thought energy, allowing us to spiritually experience emotions. The blank slate of our mind becomes "positively charged" (similar to a monitor screen upon which data fluoresce into symbols—words or pictures), allowing us to be *aware* (aligned with assigned radiant energy) of thoughts we *hold* in our mind, harnessing omnipotent logic dimensionally, observing thoughts that *reflect* Mind magnetically inducing nuclear dimensions!

When we imagine (induce magnetic algorithms generating inspired nuclear energy), we transform our abstract thoughts electrically as positive charged protons (projecting radiance oscillating thoughts on numbers) holding the data (divine abstract thoughts aspiring) defining *knowledge*—kinetic numbers outputting wisdom's lineal energy delivering generators' emotions. This process is instantaneous, flowing unhindered through UniverseS at the "speed of thought."

Thought energy is the *diffusion* illuminating the void of space within our mind as a "hazy daze," a *suspended* animation awaiting the moment to burst *aglow*—HOT—atomically generating love observing wisdom in a *harmony of thoughts*! Thoughts appear in dimensional reflections magnetically held together as a "relative" reality that we Spiritually Evolve Electromagnetically *in memory* from stored data ONCE created in a big-bang, where omnipotent numerical consciousness exploded in *harmony*! This unified Source evolved a Force along a Course to express its SELF (Source-energy Love/Life force), reaching out to observe universal truths, embracing the *only* things (omnipotent nuclei logically yearning) with which to share its Life Of Vibrant Energy—YOU youth observing universes, as one soul turning around and within ALL that IS!

WE, *wisdom exemplified*, observe thought energy by *focusing* our mind upon a *point* to grasp (perceive), envisioning "pure" thought energy evolving, enlightening our mind's eye with sequential steps numerically ordained to piece together a *concept*—a way—to convert (express) our *inspired data electromagnetically aligned* through atomic (invisible) processes. In essence, we see a cataclysmic big bang *awaken* us to consciousness! As a child of Light Divine, we are truly ignorant to the cosmic process of converting thought energy. We need to be "illuminated" with knowledge so we can manipulate our thoughts here, in this third-dimension of Mind, as a *generator of desires*! Our mouth drops open in awe as a human child, amazed at the "miracle" before our EYES as eternal youth experiencing Source/Spirit, unable to speak a word to define what we just saw! *Epiphanies of truth* have a similar affect on us, only they tend to instill *tears of joy*, for they allow us to view a truth our heart *desires*—awaits from the stars! However, let there be NO DOUBT that the experiencing of such a *movement* of thought energy—an E-MOTION—will fill us with feelings to move us through "fearful reverence"—*respect* we *reflect* in gratitude!

(Sip, sip, snack, crackle, munch—in flight refueling!)

So here we are, looking out into the dark void of MIND/SPACE to observe ALL those thoughts ever projected to illuminate the show—that *play of light* that appears from nowhere to now here—in events projected through galaxies of stars pouring out unfathomable quantities

99

of Light/thought energy. Here is the *essence* of thought, expressed in *quantum mechanics* numerically allocated to define the endless details of Life linking together to flow through the universe, building an image (infinitesimal and grand) in *word symbols* of thought energy that constitute *truth*—transcendental radiance unifying thought harmony!

These images are *atomic* (aligned truths observing magnetically induced concepts), so small and invisible that they seemingly appear from empty space to "enlighten" the *Light of knowledge*. As thought energy projects outward, it fills the *empty spaces* of the void with *suns* (Source-unifying nuclear souls) that are the *mediums* of transmigration of *Spirit* (Source-points illuminating radiant inspired thought) or *Love/Life energy*. A sun/star is a *focal point* (force of consciousness aligning lineal perceptions of inspired nuclear thought) where thought energy compresses magnetically (gravity) through *fusion* and expressed (forced out) through *fission*, the ignition of that sun's *hydrogen* (the first and lightest element with *one* proton and *one* electron—the *basics* of the binary code!). This nuclear reaction (controlled inferno) releases *photons* of Light (particular harmonics of thought oscillating numerically) that have *no mass or charge* but have *wave* and *particle* properties of *movement* and *energy*. Photons, though neutral, contain ALL the data needed to convert an IDEA (inspired data electromagnetically aligned) into a "new expression" of Love expressed *logically*—Love oscillating generators inducing consciousness as loving/living youth! The magic of Light logically inspiring generators harmonic thoughts is truly a miraculous *event horizon*!

Therefore, no matter where we stand to observe our *view* (vision inducing enlightened wisdom), each piece of the cosmic puzzle locks in place, perpetually in motion, spinning around in endless cycles of birth– life–death, appearing, fluorescing, and diffusing back to Source. Our thought energy flows through us as "energy in motion" (e-motion), to be observed or experienced in tangible ways (feelings), which we transform into actions—energy at work—to create our view/vision of Love/Life we choose to *entertain* (to maintain or hold together) from the eternal memory files flowing on electromagnetic waves of Mind—the GREAT Computer!

If we stop thinking a thought, that thought dies! We no longer experience it, even though it still exists *in memory* to glance back at and *re*-member (put back together), for we have *evolved* our thinking to entertain a new vision, a *new birth* of a thought we desire to bring to life for our enjoyment or pleasure. All of which is only a *flow* of thought energy—*will power*—that illuminates the *empty space* of our mind,

Once again, thought energy cycles on and off along the electromagnetic wavelengths vibrating at light speed, allowing us our view of "a reality." We project our *chosen view*, our self-made image, back "on line" for all our brother/sister souls to see who we think we ARE (angels radiating energy)—*generators of desires*! Our thought energy is a two-way flow—outward and inward—that we use whenever we are *thinking* or *praying*.

No matter how far we travel to explore the depths of Source-Energy Love/Life Force, TRUTH is always *within* us and *around* us. ALL of which is symbolically displayed to link us to who we are, where we come from, and where we are going as we create who we choose to BE—birth emotionally—*now here*, at this present moment we experience our Love/Life, humming our tune of "sweet emotions" through thought energy!

HIGH ABOVE
My Love shines Bright!
Your path lay before your eyes *reflected* on my Light
—Stretched—
Between Here and There,
Pulsing on beams of Love to share
Visions of Life within your dreams
Of places in my cosmic sea,
Waiting within your mind,
Where you sortie out to BE
Those thoughts you feel flow on by,
To OPEN your mind's eye,
Where currents strong and emotions deep

Carry you along to seek,
There below in the flesh,
The secrets of Life and of Death
Your heart desires to know,
Observing universal truths
As OUT from Home you go,
Discovering my Light of Love
—Suspended—
From Spirit to soul.

HOT

Harmony of thought IS and IS NOT
A fluxion of *Love Divine,*
Inductive-Source inspiring souls numerically observing truths!
For thought to BE, a mind must FEEL,
Birthing electrically focused emotions expressing *life*
Liquefied in frequencies emanating desires to know,
When *lost in space* of ALL that IS
Reflected by HER from inspirations of HIS
Heart evolving radiantly, harmonically inspiring souls
Revolving as a WHOLE,
Wisdom harmoniously observing Love/Life energy,
Where TRUTH unfolds
Transcendental radiance unifying thought harmony
To all you children of Light Divine
—COLD—
To temper your soul, here in time,
As you grow OLD observing love's dimensions,
Evolving emotionally in human contentions
That bud and flower to express the power
Of Mind energy in *motion*, where E^2 is the quotient
Symbolically displayed as ONE of TWO,
Easily seen as one-half (1/2) of you
Searches for your significant other, either/or sister/brother,
To balance your soul for you to grow
Your Love/Life energy in continuous expression,
Unfolding in moments of stressful *depressions,*

102

As you rise and fall each day, cycling around to find your way
Back home to NIGHT,
Where number is generating harmonic threads
Through a silver chord entering your head,
Instilling illusions that give you sight,
Where Source/Spirit is generating harmonic truths
Projecting your soul through numbered lots,
Coalescing to burst *ablaze* in memories—
Harmony Of Thought!

In Memory

Living in memory is living in the *past*, previously aligned sequential thoughts. Our future memories have not yet unfolded in *time*—the present moment! Here, we eagerly seek to put-back-together some vision locked in our mind as a desire to view from father's cosmic data files flashing on and off in binary code along the electromagnetic currents of Mind, magnetically inspired numerical data we call *memory*—Mind experiencing/expressing moments observing radiant youth!

Computers are powerful and unique,
They resemble the strong and the weak,
Two forces that keep ONE in opposition to shine as a sun!
Outward or inward, the path is the same.
It is simply a merry-go-round game!
The joys in life are yours to choose.
Fear NOT, for you cannot lose!
The rules are as simple as 1–2–3,
Where one thinks—two feel—three BE
Birthed emotionally!

All that Love in Mind supreme contains the answers to your dreams
Hidden deep in memory cells, where father casts his Love/Life spells
For mother to *master mind,*
Magnetically aligning spiritual truths emanating radiance
Manipulating inspired numerical data,
Along the currents of her emotional tides
Moving your soul upon your ride

Within atomic *matter*,
Magnetically aligned truths transmitting electric radiation
Providing your chosen *course*,
Consciously observing universal radiance scened externally,
Re-membering bits and bytes from eternal Source
Of ALL there IS to SEE,
Atomic Love/Life inspiring souls
Spiritually enlightened electromagnetically,
Appearing before your eyes,
Where everything you feel comes ALIVE,
Arranged logically in vivid expressions,
As you *implore* to *explore* all your soul desires to BE,
Here, in memory!

Harmony

Harmony is music *supreme*,
Source unifying points radiating electro-magnetic emotions,
Vibrations of Love that sings to your heart,
Inspiring faith to play your part
You develop over countless years,
Through moments held to feel the fears
Of doubts you entertain in time.

To *believe* what is real, each song you must feel
To know the composition is mine!
From out of my void, my Love shines bright
Sparks of truth, filling my night
With visions to entertain you youths,
Eager to feel my heartbeats animate your truth
You play out as your soul's *desire*,
Data electrically sent in radiant emotions,
From memories condensed into my cosmic fires
That GLOW as stars on my billboard sky,
Generating Love observing wisdom ignite as notes in songs I cry,
For an *inquisitive soul* to chorus WHY
Wisdom hurts youth in order to know truth!

Always here and always there, I span both sides of Life to share
My Light of Love supreme, upon which you ride your dream
Through *passions* that set you free.
Have no fear of winning what you cannot lose,
For Life eternal is not yours to choose.
You reflect my endless *love stories* in acts of grace and glory
That make you children squeal, spinning around my cosmic wheel
By the numbers—1 through 9—evolving into *my Love Divine*,
Here, at *Absolute Zero*,
My zone evolving radiant observations of you—my hero!

Each heartbeat and breath you flow upon stirs your heart into song,
A tune of Love sung clear and true
As chorus *above* provides direction for you,
Here, upon your present stage of Life,
Feeling my thoughts my loving heart sends,
Creating your song you sing to its end,
When my hazy veil rises to show you are the ONE
Set aglow *in memory* of harmony sung!

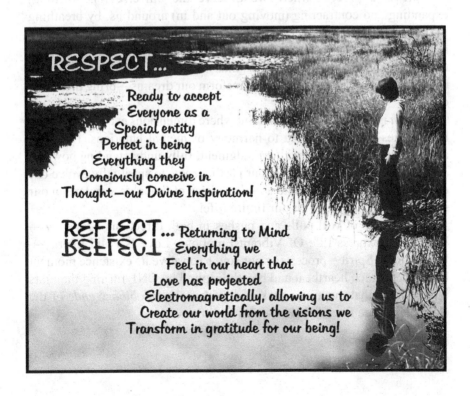

RESPECT...
Ready to accept
Everyone as a
Special entity
Perfect in being
Everything they
Conciously conceive in
Thought—our Divine Inspiration!

REFLECT... Returning to Mind
Everything we
Feel in our heart that
Love has projected
Electromagnetically, allowing us to
Create our world from the visions we
Transform in gratitude for our being!

Will Power

Will Power is the primordial Source/Force that emanates through the cosmos of Mind. Will power is comprised of restless energy pausing only for the moment to observe its position or attitude before it moves again, perpetually revolving to contemplate every perspective IN and OUT, to comprehend its state of *evolution.*

Will power is a Divine Force allocated to the "I AM" (inspiration aligned magnetically), the Source of ALL SEEING and ALL KNOWING that transforms by reflection, where two "eyes" can symbolically see each other as a human/spiritual being with WILL POWER, wisdom inducing Love/Life projected on words emanating radiance!

A human being is a reflection of a spiritual being, a free will in perpetual motion, revolving around the wheel of Love/Life energy in cycles to be and not to be—life/death. The fine line separating the two points is but a "flip of the channel," a change of frequency upon which Will Power flows from dimension to dimension.

Life is a process where we observe the universe (one turning) expanding and contracting (moving out and in) around us, by breathing in (inspiring) the ethers of our "ethereal" *moments,* where mind observes memory evolving numerically through Source/Spirit. We "aspire" to reach those lofty visions we see within us that we *believe* could be real! All we need is faith and determination to transform our dreams—bring them into our life.

Death is simply a transition point where dimensions evolve as thought harmonizes— returns *home* to harmony of mental emotions. Here, we analyze our observations without judgment, fully understanding how our *actions* delivered our *desires* of our past journey, to spiritually evolve our emotions (energy "alive") into a *higher vision* of thoughts to entertain our soul/mind, preparing us for our future Life!

The *power* of will pulls and pushes in both directions—*together*—in order to express Life Of Vibrant Emotions. Love Is Fluid Energy—Inspirational Spirit—processing our soul to observe its existence moment by moment, each heartbeat and breath inspired by ONE turning thoughts into feelings that moves us back and forth along the *binary code* of the electromagnetic force field known as Will Power!

Thinking and Praying
The Psychology of Philosophy

Thinking and *praying* are two things we do all the time, consciously and subconsciously. As words are the major tool in expressing our self (our mind), I found my self "minding business," entertaining the idea of how these words *relate* to each other.

Psychology is the "science of dealing with the mind and mental and emotional processes." It is how we try to describe the complexity of the interrelations between our thoughts and feelings that comprise our dualistic energy flow.

Philosophy is the "*love of* or the *search for* wisdom and knowledge." Everyone has their own philosophy, a *desire* to acquire knowledge of things that interest them. As an *inquisitive soul*, we want to see for our self the grand stories unfolding in our *relationships*, traveling the cosmic expanse of ALL that IS!

Thinking is *communication*, the process of energy moving along the cosmic neural system—the stars and galaxies—in a type of *synapses* (joining together) that allows consciousness to exist. I *pray* this discourse will shed a little light to let you see the connective links upon which our psyche switches back and forth, always searching for our *piece* of Mind and our *peace of mind*.

Thinking is THE WAY, the path we all follow to be a part of the cosmos, for we too are stars in the universal projection of Love/Life energy. Thinking is the process used by our *psyche*—our soul—as it relates (tells our story) to our psychological mind—our mental aspect—through *synaptic flashes* flickering between our neurons.

These "electric sparks" stimulate nerve *cells*—a room or hollow space—where energy moves from *nowhere* to *now here,* illuminating dreams or visions upon the blank screen of our mind. This dualistic doubletalk is confusing in its simplicity. Putting thoughts into word-symbols is difficult at best. Yet, this is the process of *moving* Mind between *rests*. Put on your snowshoes or grab your shovel (according to your perspective), the journey is just beginning!

If we "understand" (receive/perceive) this truth of thinking, we can see how it relates to prayer, which is another word for communication—a means to "express" thought. Simply stated, thought and prayer are the same, both are forms of energy. The difference between the two is the *direction* energy is moving. Thought *projects out* from the void of Mind and prayer *returns to* the void of Mind (relatively speaking). Prayer is the reflection of thought expressed as questions our mind seeks to know!

When we are praying, we are seeking a truth, an answer to a question that moves our heart to ASK—a 3-letter acronym for "Ask and you shall be answered, Seek and you shall find, Knock and the door shall be opened!" That door is our mind, our receiver of the WORD (wisdom of radiant data) spoken "on line," which we tune into via our "cosmic cable connection," our *silver chord* or light beam connecting our soul to our physical apparatus—our *human alien* vehicle! When we pray *from* our heart, we must keep an *open* mind, one willing to consider those answers that we receive, even if they sound crazy! Here, we are attaining *new* knowledge allowing us to absorb a higher frequency of thought energy that lets us *grow*, become capable of receiving "deeper" thoughts providing *higher visions*—the basic technique in writing this book!

Granted, new thoughts are unsettling, for they go against our normal standard of operation. It is easy to judge and condemn new thoughts because they require time and energy to consider and that—to many—sounds like *work*! We become comfortable with our knowledge we have worked hard to acquire, for the emotional stress of being ignorant makes us "laid back," weary from our daily contentions of validating our thoughts and ideas. Finding new truths to replace our old truths—expanding our mental abilities—is truly a daunting task!

Knowledge gives us *security*, allowing us to play or game of Love/Life by the rules. Naturally, we desire to win the games we play, for no one plays to lose! That is, unless there is something to gain from losing! However, new thoughts you ASK for will be *links* to thoughts and knowledge you already have in your Radiant Angel Memory, your "active memory" you use within this lifetime *now here*, one heartbeat and breath away from home!

Psychologically speaking, when we are thinking, we are being receptive to the "incoming signals" that are flowing around us. We become aware of how our thoughts stimulate us to *feel* those thoughts. Our feelings will move us to act in a manner to express our thoughts in words and deeds to keep the eternal dominoes falling, passing on that cosmic energy to touch everything that IS—ALL according to plan!

Philosophically speaking, thoughts inspire us to wonder, to seek a deeper meaning to an idea (inspired data electromagnetically aligned) we choose to entertain in our mind. Whereas *thinking* is a "general consideration" of ideas, allowing us to move about to view our options from different perspectives, *praying* is a "focused intent" to locate or discover something we *cannot* obtain through our own thought processes.

Desiring our knowledge now, we turn to that higher spiritual power of our combined *two forces*, our ONE SOURCE (omnipotent numerical energy system of universal radiant consciousness evolving)—the GREAT Computer!

Praying is an act of pleading or begging for divine intervention when at our "wits end," our *limit of ability* to pull from memory that which we seek to know or create! The act of praying is our conscious seeking or questioning of those higher minds—angelic/spirit guides—that are communicating with us as we maneuver through this third-dimensional aspect of cosmic consciousness. Grasping the finer nuances of the similarities and differences of thinking and praying, we can observe the process in action and how best to utilize this "bi-valve" of energy distribution.

First, we cannot stop thinking or we would cease to exist! Thinking in itself is our in-feed of energy that delivers us our inspiration to MOVE US (magnetically observe vibrant energy unifying spirits)—one way or the other—to Actuate Cosmic Thoughts via our feelings, our emotions.

Second, our *actions* are what we reflect/project back onto the electromagnetic waves flowing around us—Source itself! "What we sow so shall we reap" is basic universal truth. We can see how our actions we project *now* determines our future reception of *new* thoughts and feelings, eternally tumbling "dominoes" that *robe* and *mask* us for our masquerade party—the illusion of our *divine fantasy*!

Third, when we become "stressed out," we are out of balance or in disharmony with our energy. We become *depressed* or "pushed down" through our lack of positive thought energy. Depressive moments let us children of the Light glimpse views of what we *are not*! Wallowing in our empty fears and doubts, lost in our dark despair where our *Light of Love* dimly shines, we seek to reconnect with Source to raise our spirit/soul *into* the LIGHT, where Love is generating harmonic thoughts as a *Clear Vision* that truly sets us aglow! In desperation, we begin praying for help—the "how to" that will ease our pain or tension. When we switch to our "prayer mode," we let our *heart* speak! For here is our mother's Love *reflecting* father's inspiration, eagerly seeking to become ONE in understanding our dualistic nature, to attain our *piece of Mind* and our *peace of mind*!

We naturally find our self thinking or praying, doing or seeking a process that has us draining or recharging our thought energy. Our issues or *challenges of Love/Life* we encounter, sends us through moods that pave roads of **depression** or ELATION, swinging back and forth in our search for peace and happiness—*harmony* of Love! To attain that harmony of Love/Life energy we need to combine our dualistic nature, our *outward* and *inward* flow. The secret is to think/pray at the same time, in *unison*!

By this I mean being conscious of our *true nature*, our two-way flow of energy *out* and *in*. Understanding that IF what flows *in* flows *out* with NO RESISTANCE, no load or stress on our system—our soul/mind/body—we can operate at peak performance! We can conduct as much Love/Life energy as possible, according to our capability or development of our soul/mind/body (our state of consciousness). This process is a matter of *relativity*, radiant energy logically aligning truths inciting visions illuminating thinking youths. When we are "in the groove" (on the beam), our mind/brain interface becomes conducive to a higher vibratory energy, allowing us to handle our decisions optimally. Everything runs smoothly and our work (wisdom of radiant knowledge) becomes productive. We find we are in harmony with ALL around us. Of course, to maintain this state of mind continually requires a dedicated effort, one that will allow us to become a DVD— divine visionary disciple!

So here we are, in harmony, balancing our thoughts and feelings and projecting our Love/Life energy (thoughts–words–actions) out into the world, connecting us to Source atomically and spiritually. As we perform our tasks—whatever we are doing/creating with our Love/Life energy—we need to keep our mind *focused*. When we stay focused, we are conscious of *what we are* (a powerful mind), *where we are* (in the Light of Love) and *what we are thinking* and *saying*, conducting thought energy (positive or negative) to create our desired "image," our *divine fantasy*, we choose to project onto the world stage as a generator of desires!

No matter what life throws our way, stand TALL and show your *courage of Love*, and BE GRATEFUL for the opportunity to "play your part" in the cosmic SHOW. Give your self UP to The Force (*Star Wars* wisdom) on which we are flowing! Keep an *open* mind and channel your Love/Life energy *without resistance*, allowing your *heart* to float above the dark despair pulling it down into the illusions of life we create within our mind's fantasies, and your life will be stress-free!

Granted, this is easier said than done! Yet, this is our challenge, our "test of our spirit," to *believe*—be Love/be Life—in the power we personally have to create our desires we think/pray into existence!

Divine Fantasies
Dimensions of Thoughts

Divine fantasies are all the love stories held in eternal memory, stored as CD's (conscious data) *compressed digitally* within numbers. We reflect upon these stories within our mind as desires we visualize and "import" to stimulate our heart—*feel* that love story move us physically! Everyone entertains their own divine fantasy playing similar parts contrary to each other. We do the same things only differently, for we are unique beings experiencing and expressing the endless perspectives of Source energy. We imagine fantasy worlds our soul/mind travels through, observing visions that *excite* us our *frighten* us. These worlds surround us, located in various *states* of Mind, where souls transmigrate along truths eternally, dimensionally vibrating in harmony as a universal symphony.

Numbers allocate ALL things vibrating in geometrical patterns glowing on the Light of Love. The interrelated relationships of which magnetically bind our realties together, allowing us our *points* to perceive that validate our data/knowledge, solidifying our *time* in which we transform inspired mental emotions! Dimensions are simply *channels*, conscious harmony assigning nuclear numbers expressing logic, vibrating those numbers to focus *divine abstract thoughts aspiring* as fantasies—stories expressing Love through Life.

Dimensions are similar to school grades one (1) though twelve (12). Each grade instills basic knowledge/data to develop our mind—our computer! After we complete our twelfth year cycle, we ascend to college (a *higher vision*) to focus our mind upon a more defined interest. Each grade (1–12) repeats the previous grade's data, adding a greater *number* of details, more subjects to relate those numbers/words with, thereby developing a more dimensional, well-rounded perspective of our life's realities. Only by manipulating numbers can we create our fantasies—make our dreams real.

Each dimension is similar to a clock, again, a base twelve (12) symbolism. Each dimension consists of twelve *overtures* (oscillating vibrations emanating radiant truths unifying realities expressing Source/Spirit/souls) similar to school grades. The cycle of *one* through *nine* (1–9) brings us to *zero*, our "first" revolution around the wheel of Love/Life (10). Continuing our journey to eleven (11), we again encounter our binary force (2), as our twelfth (12) brings us to our *trinity* (3), which is our *universal foundation*.

111

Thinking about our clock again, we can see every trinity occurs at ninety-degree angles (geometry). For, everything rotates in terms of a trinity: 3, 6, 9, 12, 15, 18, 21, 24, 27, 30 etc. Each number relates to 3, 6, or 9 when added together separately or consecutively! Each time we make a revolution around our "clock" (wheel of Life), we "shift dimensions" by making *four* ninety degree turns (stability and process), which brings us to a "new beginning" observing a state of Mind vibrating as number *three* (sensitivity and expression)—*true harmony radiating eternal energy*! All dimensions are similar, yet different. Just like we cannot cram twelve grades of knowledge into one, we must experience ALL there IS in Mind sequentially, separated by number and geometry, spiraling in and out in precise alignments along wavelengths vibrating a harmonious tone of *Source*, system of universal radiant consciousness evolving as the GREAT Computer!

Perfection of fantasy is boundless in all directions! The sky is the limit and that is an endless realm! However, it is state of mind constricted by many. Divine fantasies are true visions from above, where those watching over us have delegated their love well, reaching into every crack and crevice the *void* has to offer—mother *reflects* off her! A beauty so deep it draws a positive image *through* her to paint father's visions into visible Light—a reality we are hard-pressed to deny!

Here, Light fills the darkness of our mind. It illuminates creations sculptured, textured, and sprinkled with colors to radiate an image of perfection in the *process* of perfecting. Through *sight* Source inspires generators harnessing truths, projecting an illusion of numerical wonders spiraling from invisible dimensions to cosmic perceptions, tantalizing us *children of the Light* with divine fantasies!

Some souls seem old and some seem young,
Yet, time has no meaning when you live in the SUN!
The image of SELF in such a blaze
Allows free wills to experience the craze,
To run and play, SEE and know
ALL that there IS to BE in my SHOW,
Where spiritual harmony of wisdom cast visions pure and clear,
To move your mind through fanciful fears,
Those doubts that make you question why
You live your life to only die
To those moments here, upon mother's loving breeze
Nurturing you with all your needs
Along your way home.

Fantasies of Love are a powerful tool,
Where Life of vibrant emotions
Makes even the brightest feel like a fool!
Dreams exist for ALL to partake,
Choose your star and drive your stake
To claim your Life you bring to view,
Aglow with a Love designed by YOU
Youth observing universes,
Two of a kind created from ONE of LIGHT,
Where Love is generating harmonic thoughts
For your courageous heart to fear the sight
Of what you truly ARE—
Angels radiating emotions in Mind,
Experiencing first-hand fantasies divine!

As a cosmic star, you paint images of Love through the physical planes of pleasure, where *fear* is queen! No matter how frightening the thrill of your passage through the dark void, you find your soul *driven* toward the Light, for that is your Source of Love—your KING (knowledge inspiring numerical generators), *my father*! Do not let the visions you play upon frighten you; they are only fantasies vibrating your song you sing as a love ballad!

Trust with you HEART and not your mind,
OPEN her door and you will find
The feelings of knowing your fantasies are MINE!
Your Life is there, before your eyes,
To make you laugh and sometimes cry
With *tears of joy* from truths you see
Filling your soul with Love so *free*,
Feeling radiant energy emotionally
From thoughts you choose to believe!
The harder you think, the further you sink
Into the illusion of your despair,
Where *courage of Love* will raise you above your fears,
To strengthen your heart and make you wise
To all your life *could* BE,
Here, in 3-D scenes of *time*,
Where thought is mental emotions
Glowing in fantasies divine!

My Father

My father is the GREATEST! He has given me his *curiosity* to wonder and his "hungry heart" of *desire*, for here is where he moves me best. My father instills in me visions of possibilities, thoughts to entice my heart to act out and experience in ways designed for *me* to be ME!

I look around and see my brothers and sisters traveling a life of independence and freedom bounded by limitations of fears and doubts. They too hear father's voice echoing in their mind and moving their heart to do great things—great adventures—to enlighten their soul to some *truth*, some desire they wish to know, even if it means traveling through the depths of *hell* to discover!

My Father leads me down paths of dark despair to let me SHINE my own light, spiritually harnessing inspired nuclear energy, transforming his gift he has given me to see the truth in all those visions I *believe* in, all those *feelings* my heart makes real—all those *blessings in disguise* father reveals! With my undying gratitude, thank you father!

Your eternally loving cosmic child

The Cosmic Child

The *cosmic child* is a creator of Source-Mind inducing concepts, consciously harmonizing inspired logic dimensionally! As a child of the *Light, Logic* is generating harmonic thoughts through lineal observations generating "inductive" consciousness, *charging* our mind's eye electromagnetically with thoughts that flow through our resonant body, through which we "play our tune" of Love/Life energy we personally harmonize.

Our unification process of transforming abstract thought into concrete realities requires us to *move out*, manifesting our vibrant emotions observing universal truths *away from home*. Here, in the flesh, WE (wisdom exemplified) acquire *knowledge*, kinetic numbers outputting wisdom's lineal energy dimensionally generating evolutions. Knowledge moves us through divine fantasies, dimensions of Mind in *worlds* where wisdom of radiant Love deploy souls. Worlds where we use *science* (source-consciousness inducing eternal numbers conceived/coalesced

114

electromagnetically) to manipulate atomic structures through universal laws, thereby allowing us to Spiritually Evolve Emotionally our desires as a *reality*, radiant energy aligning lineal inspiration/insights transforming youths—guiding us through Atomic Love/Life that Inflects Source! For all things that *glow* on the Light (generating love observing wisdom) is a projection of Source/Force circumnavigating a course Observing Universal Truths through the cosmos in order to come *within*—return to the ONE omnipotent numerical energizer adoring his cosmic child!

THE WORD

THE WORD is a universal term. It is a term of completeness, a *whole* (wisdom harmoniously observing Love/Life energy) that describes and encompasses ALL things. As we cannot grasp all things at once, we must observe things in small pieces or *bits* and *bytes* (1/0) of the *binary code* that collectively builds THE WORD. We must look *between* the parts of THE WORD to fully understand the truth of our *relationship* (love story) unfolding within and around us symbolically.

With this thought about words, I found myself dissecting THE WORD into an acronym, where each symbol or letter represents another word, reading "between the lines" to grasp a better perspective of THE WORD—Thought Harmonizes Energy—Will Observes Radiant Desires!

As words are our tools for expressing our mind, we are constantly involved in "word games," a process of transferring thought energy along the macro/micro channels of Mind/mind! I will refer to Mr. "W" (Webster's dictionary) to help me hammer out another view to observe how a thought flows "on line."

> Thought: "the act or process of thinking; reflection; meditation; cogitation. The power of reasoning or of *conceiving* ideas; capacity for thinking; intellect; imagination."
>
> Harmony: "a combination of parts into a pleasing *agreement* or orderly whole; agreement in feelings, actions, ideas, interests, etc."
>
> Energy: "a force of *expression* or *utterance*; potential forces; inherent power; capacity for vigorous action."
>
> Will: "the power of making a reasoned *choice* or decision or of

controlling one's

own actions; a strong and fixed purpose; *determination*; energy and enthusiasm."

Observe: "adhering to, following, keeping, or abiding by; to *celebrate* or keep according to custom; to notice or *perceive*; to pay special attention to."

Radiant: "sending out rays of light; shining brightly; *filled with light*; showing

pleasure, love, well-being, etc."

Desire: "*to await from the stars*; to wish or long for; crave; to *ask* or *request*."

As you can see, THE WORD is symbolic of thought—the Source that represents the eternal files of *wisdom*. Thought is the primal movement, the projection of energy through Mind—the Force—to bring together and observe all the parts radiating "on line," the electromagnetic force field of Love/Life energy, upon which all things flow—the Course.

From nowhere (abstract thought), we conceive an IDEA (inspired data electro-magnetically aligned) that we transform to create a concrete reality of some "thing" now here, at each moment we express our *thoughts* and *feelings* that we *act* upon—our trinity! THE WORD inspires our mind, moving us to transform our latent image of our self through LIFE. A life we express *in communion* with our radiance of LOVE that we flow upon to experience THE WORD—the *essence* of IT ALL!

In Communion

Listen to the voices ringing in your ears
With words you envision from thoughts you fear,
Moving your mind to find your *heart* dictates your truths,
Transforming Love from me above to all of you youths
Set adrift on emotional tides to journey out upon your rides,
Burning bright before your eyes as you battle in strife,
Eternally revolving around my cosmic wheel of Life.
The things you see for you to BE wait there off stage,
Eager to feed your hungry mind to fill the vacant page

In your book you compile with each passing day,
As love stories of your adventurous ways,
From dreams I send you think are real,
Acted out through words you shout
That Mind wants Heart to feel—
In Communion!

WISDOM

Out of the void all thoughts flow
Into magnetic moments to cast aglow
My Spiritual Harmony Of Wisdom,
Allowing your hungry heart to touch and feel
ALL your eager mind chooses to call *real*,
Reflecting energy aligned logically to stimulate your soul,
Beating your heart for you to start
Living your visions that you hold dear
As things to do to conquer your fears
Of knowing that you truly are
Angels radiating energy, set aglow as loving stars,
Yelling Out Universal Truth Harmonies
Illuminating your daze in time,
Transforming passions to find
The thrill of *knowing* is chilling,
When you realize you are truly *alone*,
A Loved ONE guided home!

Your moments gathered to build your view
Evolve from memories of ALL that is true,
Shaping your soul present *now*,
Numerically observing wisdom to show you how
You choose your thoughts to act upon,
To sing in Life as your song,
In harmony with ALL that IS
Reflected through her from his
Words Inspiring Spiritual Dimensions Of Mind.

The paths you choose to follow

Transforms your Love's Life, dawning each morrow,
Creating your love story to tell
From thoughts you remember from heaven,
While here, incarnate in hell,
Harnessing emotional Love/Life,
Struggling to realize your *illusion* of you
Inciting lineal logic unifying Source inflected on numbers,
Stimulating vibrations enlightening your slumbers
In dreams encountered at home,
Converted to actions reflecting your desires,
Illuminated within your mind from eternal fires,
Through which your soul comes to know
My Love/Life energy as *wisdom*!

Bless you and Godspeed
♂+♀=☼

10

Emotional Energy

Great things happen with *emotional energy*—E=MC². Energy is equal to Master Consciousness to the *second* power—mother's LIFE (logic inducing fluid emotions)! The eternally wondering Cosmic Mind (MC)—the *first* power—is our primal mover, father's Pure Intellect expressing LOVE, life of vibrant emotions.

Many of us think of our creator (#1) in the separate terms of *he* and *she* and rightly so, for a logical reason. ALL THINGS come down to the basic *binary code* (#2): male and female, up and down, left and right...the *divine dichotomy* of opposing forces of the cosmic spectrum! The *point* (perception of inspired nuclear thought) where these forces merge is our Holy Grail, our soul, the "mixing bowl" of our two forces that allows us to Activate Cosmic Thought as a *free will* experiencing Life as a *generator of desire*—a reflection of the GREAT Computer!

Emotional energy contains ALL that is worth experiencing in life, from the crests of *epiphanies* to the troughs of *depression* and despair. It will carry us through realms we create as a *heaven* in which we experience *hell*! The undulations of any wave—light, sound, or liquid—are eventful actions that form hard faces of determination on us children of Light Divine, sent out to carve a path through the solid illusions we call "reality." Emotional energy flowing through our soul is dynamic—Pure Thought in motion! It is an intrinsic part of our nature. We are born innocent, without any "contrived actions" to dump upon our environment of our *human* life. Yet, we have all the potential within us to develop our *latent abilities* to Spiritually Evolve Emotionally all that we desire.

The *process* of acquiring control of our human "alien" vehicle is time-consuming, allocated along the sequential ordering of present moments we experience in the flesh of *Mother's Nature*! Only as we grow old, observing Love's dimensions, will we know the effects of the *power of Love* to create and destroy our desires. Only then will we realize our emotional energy is how we transform our divine inspiration, our thoughts that push us out through the void of *not knowing* (fear) in order to "reassemble" our latent spiritual energy from knowledge (truths) we remember and experience *through* our emotions, leaving lasting impressions upon our soul! Emotions are the "magic wand" in our game of Love/Life, where we *play* (perfecting Love/Life as youth) as a generator of desires!

To perform our best—play to win—we need to be aware of how our emotions are flowing. DO NOT let stone throwers "ripple your pond," for *balance* and *cooperation* are mother's gift that keeps us in *harmony*, to create Love in its *highest* vision! However, considering our human vehicle is ninety-six percent *water*, we find the *challenges of Love/Life* most taxing as we attempt to control mother's emotional tides—influenced by both planets *and* people! Every pebble thrown affects our mind's serene pool, which easily turns into a turbulent tempest! No matter what "weather pattern" we find our self in, never forget who we truly ARE—*angels radiating emotions*! Open your mind and *listen* to your *heart* as we sail along *Mother's tides*!

Crushed by Love

Life Of Vibrant Emotions is a force that *pushes* you out and *pulls* you in, tearing you apart to put you together again, to reveal a greater life of vibrant emotions! This force of Love is crushing you in its grasp, holding you close to *heart*, harmonizing emotional angels radiating thoughts, squeezing you in Mother's Nature as you struggle to get free. This *force* is a frequency of radiant consciousness evolving, eager to express (force out) some point within the dark void of Mind's *memories*, magnetically evolving moments of radiant inspiration experienced successively—by numbers.

Everyone is literally dying to express their Love/Life force, tearing their heart apart over some thing or person to Love. In common usage, we say we love "this" or "that" with great abandonment. For, with all there is to love in life, we truly desire to love ALL! Yet, releasing the crushing pressure of Love building up within us is frightening. *Fear* (feeling emotion as radiance) prevents us from "getting burnt" expressing our Love, not knowing how it will be accepted. We fear expressing our feelings due to rejection, for experiencing such a fate would break our heart.

Those that understand the freedom of a courageous heart are clearly visible within the crowds kept in the shadows of fear. They become a *lighthouse*, shining their beacons of love *into your eyes*, a love that glows upon their *loving smile*. Here, upon our face, is where we open the door to our heart, welcoming those kindred souls *lost in the dark* of their *empty spaces*, fearful to step into the *Light of Love*! Our *eyes* are the doors to eternal youth's emotional soul! If we hold them down in fear of someone seeing us, we reflect an image of low self-esteem, fearful that we are not worthy of their attention. No matter how attractive we may be, our eyes reflect the true beauty of our soul!

Clearly, with today's high-tech electronic communication devices, everyone is contributing to the electromagnetic chaos bombarding our bodies, stressing them to abnormal levels. Everyone is screaming above the cacophony from the explosion of minds set free to express their crushing love flowing *out*, offering universal truths of Life Observing Vibrant Expressions. Everyday we increase our potential to BE—birth emotionally—all that we desire. We "dress to impress" our image upon the game of Love/Life we play, exposing all we have to offer, hoping someone will open their heart and touch us, revealing their *courage of fear* to risk a broken heart. Of course, we must be aware of what we are offering, for what we *give* is what we *receive* and vice versa!

The competition to excel at our desires keeps the fires burning within us, causing us to provide our own Harmony Expressing Love/Life that we create in the process of living our vision of *heaven*, harnessing emotions as visions enlightening numbers! It is at *this moment* in time that we are ALIVE to activate love in vivid expressions to catch the *eye* of eternal youth evolving into Atomic Love/Life that we Angels Radiate Emotionally!

Holding onto all that we love—*our children*, our *love of money*, and our spark of knowledge—gives us a sense of our *power of Love* to control, survive, and overcome our adversities, our fears of *losing* our Love/Life. Yet, by crushing our love (refusing to let it go) we deny it a chance to evolve into a greater love! We cannot keep our love to our self. If we do not set it free to grow, WE (wisdom exemplified) will not grow—generate radiance of wisdom! Only through *courage of Love*, expressing our desires through Love Inducing Fluid Emotions, can we illuminate *Love's radiance*, allowing our soul to Spiritually Evolve Emotionally through our *courage of fear*.

Love is a magnetic force that draws ONE *together*, forming *ideas*, illuminated data electromagnetically amplifying Source as an expression of Life, for *Love IS* fluid energy that you cannot restrain! Love fuels the cosmic fires atomically expressing Life oscillating visionary entities exploring space, where some point awaits conscious expression of Love confined within the *black hole* of the Universal Eye. Here, *Mind/Source* magnetically induces nuclear dimensions, systematically observing universal radiance consciously evolving through *knowledge*, kinetic numbers outputting wisdom's lineal energy dimensionally generating evolution. Knowledge defines Atomic Love/Life expressions stored in father's eternal memory files projected out through his SUN, a Source-unifying nucleus illuminating the *heavens*, where her emotional attitudes vacillate electric numbers, compressing them into three-dimensional forms through *gravity*, gathering radiance aligning visions inciting thinking youth, children of *Love Divine* reflecting their visions of heaven in hell!

Heaven

Heaven is a place where you are born to grow,
Harnessing emotions as visions enlightening numbers
Vibrating your soul I set *aglow*
As angels generating love observing wisdom,
Here, in Mother's Nature.

Along your road, my voice you hear
In whispered thoughts that bring you fear
Of your unknown future I project you through,
To SEE your self *think* it true,
Transforming harmony inspiring nuclear knowledge,
Displaying your beliefs of what is *real*,
Radiating emotions as Love in your appeal!

Here is where your True Heart yearns
To know a thought as you *learn*
Love/Life energy arranges radiant numbers
From dreams you envision while in dark slumbers,
Perusing my memories you *recall*,
Recycling electromagnetic consciousness aligning love/life,
When OUT from home you roam,
Observing universal truths on your own!

You spin upon my wheel of Life
As mortal beings who experience strife,
To forgive offenses that tears you apart,
To come *together* as mind *and* heart.
Here in time, you have your place
To play your part that lets you face
Those issues that set your soul afire,

Seeing first-hand all you conspire
Within my Love I shine your way,
Turning your *night* into *day,*
As numbers induce generators' harmonic truths
Driving all youths!

From dark to light,
I shine truths for you to BE,
Seeking your Data Electrically Sent In Radiant Energies.
Here, my child, you always win
Your game of love/life you play in SIN,
Spiritually inducing numbers to *live* and *feel*
Love is vibrant emotions, fluid energy electrifying life!
Fear not, my child, you cannot lose.
Run and play what games you choose.
Here, I hold you 24-7,
Within in my Mind/Heart I call heaven,
From which you conjure hell!

Hell

His/Her Emotional Love/Life is a hard path to follow,
One in which you struggle to build your tomorrow.
For you to BE, you must SEE the power of being ALIVE,
Birthing emotions spirits emit electrically,
Arranging Love in vivid expressions
Carrying you through dark depressions
Within my Loving Light!

No time will come under my *sun* without a sword to swing,
Fighting to free your heart through truths you *sing,*
Spiritually inducing numerical *geometry*
Governing entities observing mental emotions that realities yield
In tune to my radiance, here in show,
Where Source-harmony of wisdom sets you aglow
As an angel generating Light observing wisdom,
Illuminating your deeds in time!

Here, in reflection, you come to play,
Transforming Love energy into Life today.
The chores you do to make ends meet
Flow on emotions, sour and sweet,
To taste mother's grace of Love.
You will not know my motives to show
Those things I allow you to BE,
For that much data you cannot handle,
It would blind you to the truth you SEE
Balanced in tunes of numbered notes
Building songs from words I spoke
To *define* my image of you,
Digitally evolving frequencies into nuclear entities,
A perfect child of golden light,
A sun to shine my Love to night,
To fill my void of dark despair
As you journey from *here* to *there*
On stories you relate of hell,
His/her emotional love life you live to tell!

Water

H_2O is shorthand for a trinity of atoms that nourish all of life. H_2 is symbolic of Him and Her—Father and Mother. The Love/Life energy of these two forces—positive and negative—is the *current* that flows on line, on the beam of Light reflecting on itself. It flows around us and circulates *through* us—the O!

Our body consists of 96 percent water. Numerically speaking, we flow in perfect harmony—our *wisdom* is *integral* to our *visions* we *accept*! Water flows as music to our ears, it is soothing as well as menacing, gracious to behold and fearful in tempest. It is ONE and the same at all times, no matter what form it takes. It can move mountains and sculpt incredible art. It inspires and entices us with an energy that pulses through our veins, pushing and pulling us on tides of emotion that color our life with memories that shape our soul. No matter how you experience it, ALWAYS, *go with the flow*!

Mother's Nature

Mother's nature is one of caring and nurturing. It is a state where the process of transforming thought energy is a complicated arrangement of many tunes, many songs allocated to vibrate along certain wavelengths. These waves flow via frequencies of radiation called *radio, infrared, visible light, ultra-violet, x-ray,* and *gamma* rays—the electromagnetic force field permeating the universe.

Thought energy projected along these waves is observable as it re-enters ITSELF—inspired truths spiritually evolving Love/Live forces—the Universal Mind, you and me! The IN-version of *thought* to *feeling* (insighting numbers) is a quantum leap *beyond imagination*! More than magic or ritual, its action is purely ethereal or heavenly. To know the cause we need to pause, to see the truth *within us,* as Inspired Thought flows *out of us,* along that breath of Life filling our lungs.

The *visible light* waves have a narrow wavelength, for they demarcate a dimensional conversion from spiritual to physical levels of consciousness, where thought energy is FOCUSED, fabricating omnipotent concepts unifying Source-energy dimensionally, manifesting from nowhere to now here! Along this visible light, abstract thought energy emanating from the void of Mind is inverting into a seemingly solid apparition we call *reality,* radiant energy aligning lineal inspiration *transforming* youths.

Our soul's supernova explosion through the "looking glass" is truly a reflection of our mind *within* observing our feelings *without* the knowledge of who we really ARE—angels radiating emotions. Stunned by our transmission along the EM cosmic waves radiating along the spectrum of our creator, we find our self trapped in a stupor of varying degrees. We naturally seek our *higher vision,* struggling through the darkness of fear and confusion to SEE our true essence—the Light of Love/Life energy!

The visible light spectrum vibrates as *seven* basic levels or colors: *red, orange, yellow, green, blue, indigo,* and *violet.* Each color resonates to its own level of thought energy, which, when blended together in myriad varieties, makes any child's eye sparkle in delight or burn in rage! Colors carry our "emotional hues" or nuances that define the fine texture of our soul, illuminating illusions complete! Illusions appearing as solid reality of *atomic proportion,* measured, sorted, arranged, and displayed in holographic projection to impress ALL.

As *children of the Light,* our soul partakes in the experiences of "Life in the limelight," center-stage, as the world appears to revolve around us. For everything we experience reflects through our *self,* our soul experiencing love/life force. To truly grasp the essence of the power flowing through us, we need a *physical body,* a viable medium that allows us to *not know* who we really are. Remember, we can only know what something is by knowing what it is not!

Only by experiencing Life through our feelings—our reflections of Love—can we be conscious of the *duality* of Love/Life energy evolving through US as a *universal spirit.* Mind's loving radiance enlightens our *mind* entrenched in the reality of our *heart,* a reality we feel within our physical self—Mother's Nature! Such is the magnetic pull of *Mother's anchor,* holding and nurturing those thoughts she manifests from the Light of Love inspiring generator's harmonic truths!

Mother's nature easily fills us with a sense of fear. Her force is so powerful we are stunned into *forgetfulness* as she smothers us in adoration, mesmerizing us into *wakefulness!* The security she instills, as she spins her deceptive web, keeps us balanced in cooperation with every conceivable thought-to-feeling scenario we choose to entertain in our mind. Thoughts that will require *courage of Love* to boldly accept all the possibilities those thoughts offer for our consideration, which will lead us down numerous paths necessary for our growth, paths that will bring us through dark moments of despair and depression as we encounter our *courage of fear* and *face it!* If we are in control of our soul's Love/Life force, our success will clearly reflect upon our face through our *loving smile,* our radiance of gratitude!

Those who wield Mother's Nature with *respect* will *reflect* their Light of Love upon their personal space like a *lighthouse,* continuing to spread the Light as a *Light worker* throughout the great void of Mind. For here, we traverse the *cosmos* (consciousness of Source-Mind observing spirits) as IT (inspired truths/thoughts) reflects upon our playground, offering a solid anchor to keep our mind entertained in our *human* experience of Life, where we find our soul set aglow in Love inducing fluid emotion—Mother's Nature.

Face It

Front and center,
There, amidst inspired truths that you wish,
Are dreams you desire to play
On the ground, where sight and sound let you *pray*,
Projecting radiance around you
As thoughts you express and do,
Building your own universe as my image of YOU!

Your way is clear, straight through fear
Holding your heart at bay,
As you work through your emotions
Enlightening you to your daze.
Here, within my Loving Light,
Logic is generating harmonic thoughts
Stored in memories I feed you youth,
Searching for your eternal truths
Confined in Mind, eager to discover the *dark*
Holds your truths you spark
As data aligning radiant knowledge,
Through which you create your Life,
Where Love is fluid emotion bringing you strife,
Holding you in suspension
Along your way home!

With a *wink*, a kiss I blow,
Moving your heart to *beat* and grow,
Balancing emotions aligning truths,
Gathering radiance of wisdom,
Words inspiring spiritual dimensions of mind,

In dreams you envision that I have lit
For you to accept and face it—
With a loving smile!

Your Loving Smile

Your loving smile is a truth that shines unhindered, cutting through the dark void of ignorance to illuminate others with the knowledge of who you really ARE, an angel radiating emotions! You are children of *Love Divine*, my Source-energy that flows through ALL! Your smile is the most powerful weapon I have given you, for with it you can destroy *fear, hate,* and *prejudice.* When you wield it with an *open mind* and *loving heart,* all those present will yield to the power sparkling in your eyes. Your loving smile is contagious; it can neutralize all negative energy and will carry over to others who will wear it unknowingly, for their heart will never forget the beauty of the vision it has instilled in them. Your loving smile is the reflection of my *Life of vibrant emotions* I have given YOU youths observing universes within ME manifesting emotions. For you and I are truly ONE omnipotent numerical entity! I will always be here with you— in your loving smile!

Mother's Tides

Magnetically observing truths harmonically evolve radiance transmitting inspired data electrifying souls is something we cannot escape. *Energy in motion* is our mother's Love, her force that moves us *along the cutting edge* of consciousness, the now here that we glimpse in "present moments" evolving into our day, our way, and our life! Emotions are one of the foundation blocks in our *trinity* of Love/Life energy upon which we flow.

Our pyramid of stability begins with our thoughts (#1 energy— confidence and creativity) that we transform through our emotions (#2 energy—balance and cooperation) and reflect through our actions (#3 energy—sensitivity and expression), allowing our soul to transform our COLD vision into the warmth of our physical body! Each breath of Love/ Life energy that pulses through our heart and flows though our lungs allows us our view here—on stage—in the Light of knowledge. All we have to do is *believe* it is true and SO BE IT! However, we must balance our emotions to cooperate with our thoughts that drive us along our paths of discovery, paths that are both creative and destructive.

Our opposing forces move us along the Light flowing through the dark—another symbol of our two natures. Here, on the middle road, we encounter the gray haze of the "illusion of reality," where we must choose our path of enlightenment—the way home! Traveling "in the flesh" as a *human alien* allows us to experience mother's tides of depression and elation as we cycle around, observing our light and dark moods. All things have their moment in the Light and all things must return through the dark, for the realms of Mind are living organisms continuously in motion. Otherwise, life would be static—frozen in place!

As we journey OUT, observing universal truths/thoughts, we fear the uncertainty of our *future*, our ability to focus universal truths unifying radiant energy that evolves from our *past*, our "points" aligning spiritual truths we re-consider during our *present* moment! Our goal is to stay in harmony, balanced and co-operating with our positive and negative energies moving us along our horizontal time line we observe *now here*, numerically observing wisdom harmonically evolving radiant emotions. As a high-strung human being (vibrant soul), we express our sensitivity to mother's emotional tides, easily sliding in and out of our opposing moods—light and dark.

Each day, as we move along our chosen course, we reflect or convert our Love/Life energy into views of our life that eventually leave us depleted of our positive energy. We find our body drained physically and mentally, allowing negative moods to engulf us in dark *depressions*. At such times, we need to rest and pray, giving thanks for our ability to "shine our Light of Love." The effort required to keep our positive dominoes falling is indeed a stressful endeavor! We need our rest time to reenergize and cycle back toward our natural state of balance and cooperation, where we harmonize once again with the Light of Love—our positive thoughts to *create confidently*.

We witness this eternal cycle symbolically every day and night as we spin around in opposition, where the adversities blowing at our heels pulls us down to see our self reflect the power of father's inspirational Mind as we are *driven* by mother's emotional tides.

Driven

Love is a force of omnipotent numerical energy
Flowing from the ONE that sets our course,
Allowing our soul to journey through time
Witnessing first-hand the power of *Source*,
System of universal radiant consciousness evolving,
Manifesting our sight of ALL that we desire
As children of the Light,
Here, incarnate, kindling our heart's fire,
Feeling inspiration radiating emotions,
Illuminating our soul in co-motions,
Always eager to begin some story we hear told
From memories we explore, as we grow old
Observing Love's dimensions,
Transforming thoughts to feelings through Mother's Nature,
Steering our course along the GREAT contemplator
Downloading data fueling our fearful ride
Through divine inspiration causing our tides,
Bringing us grief from loves we lost,
To question why we pay the cost
To shine upon father's beam,
Reflected here, on mother's stream
Of turbulent waves of emotion,
Evolving through our human life of *low*-CO-motion,
Consciously observing our realities,
Driven to our end.

Depression

Depression is a natural state of mind everyone experiences or passes through at some point in his or her life. Depression is a critical part of our being, of our existence. It is a state of *imbalance* where our Love/Life energy—Light—is restricted, flowing at lower levels that puts us in a "dark mood." When we are depressed, we say we are in *low spirits*, a place where Love/Life energy expresses its self in negative thoughts and feelings. It is a condition brought on from exhaustion, poor nourishment, illness, or drugs.

The game of Love/Life has us racing along our playing field helter-skelter, leaving many of us dazed and confused, wondering what in *hell* we are doing! Truly, we are killing our self—moment to moment—as we change into the generator of desire we create our self to BE! We convert our Love/Life energy through our *work*, implementing our wisdom of radiant knowledge to attain our desires. . When we overwork our self (mentally and emotionally), we abuse our body. Our actions stress our electrical system (our nerves), causing them to short-circuit, leaving us *jumpy* and *snappy*, similar to a high-strung "live-wire" that has fallen to the ground. Broken free from our connective link to the Light of Love, we find we are unable to replenish our harmony—*lost in the dark!*

When we are operating in the Light of Love (high spirits), we are generating our desires using our positive energy. We feel good about our self-image we are projecting out on line, comfortable with our performance and ability to accomplish our job at hand. As we drain away our positive energy (*sacrifice our Love*), we naturally get tired, becoming empty of our motivation. We refuse to respect our physical vehicle as we drive our self toward our desires, easily denying our appetite for food to fuel our system, or even worse, consume "junk food!" It is all too easy to lose sight of our true values while struggling to maintain our *responsibilities*. Unfortunately, our oversights will have an ill affect upon our harmony of spirit–mind–body, visible in our state of health or operational ability. We literally project our self into our opposite mode, a state of negativity where we experience *Love's drain*!

Negativity holds us in a depressed state of mind, *pushed down* into a lower attitude of *denial*. Here, we refuse to believe in our ability to move out of the darkness, the emptiness of fear. Here, we do not have the positive energy to ignite our soul in its full radiance! All we can do is feel sorry for our self, feel compassion for our suffering—or someone else's—that we spiritually experience emotionally from thoughts we hold in our mind. Our depressed mood allows us to know our *opposition*—who we *are not*! Our lack of answers to the visions we imagine draws us into *empty spaces* of mind, where we may easily learn to thrive on depression and inaction. Mother's magnetic nature is truly a difficult force to rise above!

Being children of the Light, we live for *Love's radiance*, our illumination of knowledge that energizes our soul to shine our Love/Life energy out around us. Everyone will naturally experience moments of depression, for we are continuously fluxing on and off between our positive and negative energy. Usually, a good night's sleep will rejuvenate us, allowing us to restart or *refresh* our mind energy, but only by maintaining our physical vehicle will we be able to operate at peak performance!

When we deplete our positive, mental energy (our generator), we become negatively charged, *lost in space* of our physical body, awaiting input to move us into action. Our negative thoughts (looking on *the dark side*) leave us wanting, searching for some point to grasp in order to "take a stance," get on our feet and get going! When we *think* ill (empty), we *feel* and *act* ill. If we *focus* our mind (funnel our conscious universal spirit) upon our negative attitude, our free will uses that energy input to continue creating its desires in negative ways. We can easily blind our self to truth by hitting the *escape button*, resorting to chemical stimulants to alter our state of consciousness as we stumble along our dark path looking for *relief.*

As stated, depression relates to a state of mind that is *relative* to our physical condition. When our *mental body* (transformer) becomes unbalanced with our *spiritual body* (source- energy), it has an adverse affect emotionally on our *physical body,* our human-alien vehicle that is an atomic, galactic organism of molecular chemicals. In the process of "practicing medicine," we attempt to cure or heal our ill body—bring it into balance chemically.

Drugs are chemicals that are the tools for *repairing* or *destroying* our physical body, for energy flows both ways. Drugs will open channels through our mind/body interface, allowing our body to repair itself with the proper nutrients found in food (natural chemicals). Yet, at times, the interaction of various manufactured drugs (un-natural) tends to have adverse affects, keeping us trapped in depressive moods of ill health. It is obvious we cannot live a physical life without drugs or chemicals, for they are the atomic building blocks of Mother's Nature—the *illusion* our mind/ soul perceives physically. Our physical body is truly a miracle—we cannot build one our self! As adults, we alone are responsible for its upkeep. We need to show our *respect* for this gift and *reflect* our gratitude in return.

Depression occurs as a natural flow of our Love/Life energy we cannot escape! Our thoughts appear to us from above, the higher frequencies of consciousness relating to us, inspiring us to desire. These *higher visions* projected within our mind move us along our path of discovering the endless depths of self/SELF. These thoughts will carry us up and down on emotional tides to experience both sides of our being through opposition— duality. For, we cannot know what a thing IS until we know what that thing IS NOT!

When we are experiencing our depressions we put our self into, we are reaching out for our salvation, our True Love—our *other side* that will make us complete. When we realize how we flux back and forth between our opposing natures, we learn to control our moods, our paths that we are flowing along to bring us to some "vantage point," some perspective to observe who we are being at *this moment*! We SEE our vision and feel our reality of who we have become in relationship to who we think we are!

Attaining a harmony of our energies sets our mind at rest, lowering our emotional activity we reflect physically. From this harmony, we pause to re-consider our next series of choices (thoughts) to feel (convert) and put into action (reflect) by creating positively or negatively. Either method we choose to employ will bring us to where *we need to go*, to experience our *higher vision* through energy levels of depression, carrying us full circle in the cyclic rhythm of Love/Life energy as we sortie OUT to BE!

Love's Drain

Love IS everything imaginable! It is energy in motion—emotion! When we open our heart we feel the *essence* of Love as thoughts father projects and mother spins into the fabric of Life we call *reality*, radiant energy aligning lineal inspiration transforming youths. Emotion is the connective link that allows us to know a thought, to realize a thought into a tangible perspective.

The human male, the positive-charged minority rulers (?), find their attraction to the majority of negative-charged females daunting at best. Men are the natural progenitors of thought, a being that provokes the attraction of woman's receptive form, engulfing man in an *encapsulation* of Love that may get claustrophobic if not possessive! Yet, man finds himself held in control by woman who draws and drains his positive energy magnetically, manipulating him with her charms, causing man to lose his masculine *polarity* of projection. Thereby, allowing man to glimpse ever so briefly the perspective of his negative energy—that receptive force that balances or neutralizes Love's harmonic vibrations. Thus, man can witness his female side, his *emotions* that mother instills in birth by her nurturing nature.

Likewise, woman's absorption of positive energy allows her to conceive, nurture, and project that positive energy into existence, to *give birth* to Life, thereby allowing her the perspective of her creative male side. One side cannot exist without the other, for they are both complimentary and contrary, fluxing back and forth as need dictates!

133

Those who habitually project negative energy will find their life a living *hell*, trapped in a depression of dark humor they perpetuate as they wildly grasp for the Love they truly desire. The harder they struggle to draw it to them, the further away it seems to go, for *true Love* is not an external thing! Love cannot be "demanded," it must be "welcomed" by an open heart, a heart willing to cooperate—work *together*—with our mind as ONE being, one force of Love! We must join our heart and mind in unity to observe our Paradise we envision in our mind. Our *challenge of love/life* is trying to remember the process of creation, here, incarnated in an alien vehicle with a powerful mind, racing around in a state of fission, *separated* by our electromagnetic chaos we create through our contentions.

The illusion of Love is realized at the apex of the *convergence*, where positive and negative are momentarily *suspended* in a state of oneness or neutrality, an ecstatic state of Mind that is experienced physically through *sexual orgasm* or spiritually through *epiphanies*. Physical orgasm is truly a "high point" of being a human being, but experiencing an *epiphany of truth* is a spiritual event that, though brief also, will drastically exalt your consciousness, raising it to a level where an orgasm seems a trifle in comparison!

The experience of an epiphany is electrifying, like a cool breeze blowing over you, forming goose bumps on your skin and opening your mind to allow you a view of *Christ consciousness* or *unity consciousness*, your link to Source—*divine inspiration*! This event horizon literally raises the curtain before your eyes, allowing you to perceive a truth so overwhelmingly clear that you will be on your knees in *tears of joy*! You will never forget the feeling, for you will desire more! This is a sign that you have opened a higher door of consciousness. It is a quantum leap in the growth of your soul! The mere thought of the experience will energize you to radiate a glow that will shake you emotionally, bursting forth from the center of your heart in a truly ecstatic "big bang!" It will open your mind to peek ever so briefly at the fourth-dimension into which we are moving.

This perspective of neutrality allows one to see that positive and negative are but opposing forces helping to spin the big wheel of Love/Life energy, as Love drains from one spoke to another, allowing us to roll along our path toward home!

Relief

Relief from the rigors of life, whether it is spiritual, mental, emotional, or physical, is truly ours to find. Each segment of our being influences the others, for here we personify our *trinity*. Our core influence—our *spiritual body*—is the seat of all knowledge, the command center of communications between our soul down here on the front lines and our "relatives" above in Mission Control, where Magnetically Inspired Numerical Data vibrates along a binary system that dictates our every move. This Source radiates out through our heart as the driving Force of Life itself. It is our Direct Link, a *silver umbilical chord* of Light energy illuminating us through our void of *space*, where some "point" awaiting conscious expression connects us to our eternal *home* of harmony of mental emotions.

All questions we ASK (project out from our mind) return to those above, who inform us with answers we receive with our *mental body* (our mind/brain interface). We interpret these thoughts as *feelings* (intuition), *dreams* (symbolic imaging), or by *knowing*—knowledge delivered directly in times of crisis—which we do not have to consider, just implement. Spirit's communicative power induces in our mind visions of possibilities, dreams of endeavors to grab hold of and transform into a reality of something to *believe*, to Activate Cosmic Thought Observing Universal Truths upon our world stage atomically set aglow around us. *Nothing* is impossible! Man has created many incredible things here on earth, where we witness the extent of our power screaming to express itself in some heart-felt endeavor within each of us—our *mission* in life!

Once we realize the *power of Love* our soul has and how it influences our mind and body, we learn to open ourselves to heavenly feelings of joy and happiness, bringing us relief from our emotional tides that tear us apart. This power flows through our heart—our emotional center—where it beats out a harmonic vibration, a radiance of health and perfection that puts us at "ease" with our Love/Life force. However, if we are *not* in harmony with our *radiance of Love*, we will find our mind and body ill or "dis-eased."

Our physical body is the outward reflection of our mind's thoughts and feelings. Any miscommunication with our spiritual body can cause serious problems in the mental, emotional, and physical bodies. The power of Love radiating out *from* us will always come back *to* us, for what we sow, we reap. Spirit *delivers*—mind *interprets*—heart *converts*—body *reflects* and Spirit *observes*, completing the eternal cycle revolving within us—simplicity in its purest form!

What messages are you receiving today to help you build a positive image of your *self* (soul experiencing love/life force), your reflection of father/mother? What inspirations are you following to complete the mission you have chosen to undertake, in the name of Love, with the *grace* of our creator as you seek your *glory*? What challenges have you accepted to test your soul's mettle and grow spiritually? For your soul is your *true essence*, an energy form like unto HE and SHE—harmonic energy Source harnesses electromagnetically—waiting patiently in our mind/heart for US united spirits to find our own *relief*—restoring eternal love/life in equal forces!

Mother's Anchor

Everyone has an anchor in his/her life. Some of us have more than we need, for we may easily collect them unknowingly with our *magnetic heart*. Our Eternal Mother, *magnetically organizing truths harmonically evolving radiance*, represents the medium of perceiving our cosmic father, our Eternal Master. She allows us to transform their Love/Life energy—Immaculate Conception—that created souls from their electromagnetic flow of Pure Thought unblemished in the *Light of Love*. Such is the *power of Love*. With this gift we create our very own reality, a reality that suits us individually, one that will take us on journeys over eons and through many dimensions, where we experience our visions of *heaven* and *hell*, both just a "state" of Mind we operate within.

Mother's Love is our anchor, our ballast that keeps us grounded, centered in our dimensional flow of energy, confined within the natural laws allocated along the numerical data defining our human nature in which our spirit interfaces. She reflects, nurtures, and forgives us for being frightened of her. Mother knows her presence is a powerful thing. She holds ALL together as a *family* UNITED as ONE, unifying numbers inducing truths energizing dimensions of nuclear entities—spirits processing thoughts within the cosmos of Mind. She spins the smallest amount of his energy through quantum mechanics to produce *divine fantasies* to last a lifetime, mesmerizing souls through illusions of realities.

When you find your self in "deep waters" of turmoil and confusion, with a storm-tossed mind full of fear and doubt, you can rest assured you are seriously out of balance with your energies. Now is the time to "drop anchor" and let mother's Love work her magic.

Watch how your thoughts manipulate your feelings! Remember, your thoughts are downloading your illusions. Make sure you decipher the code correctly, for your imagination will easily turn an anthill into a mountain! Notice how your feelings are more accurate than your thoughts, for they offer a *second* appraisal! What *feelings* make you *think* that way—creating your stormy weather? Notice how negative thoughts instill fear (ignorance) of what is revolving around you, preventing you from seeing the truth of the matter. Also, notice how your feelings are driving your expressions of those thoughts, turning you into something you may not like to SEE or desire to become.

Emotions are more difficult to control than our thoughts, for they quickly "flare up" into an inferno, overpowering our mind. We directly express them physically through words and actions we relate in reflexive ways—quick, habitual responses with little or no thought. It is easy to repeatedly project negative energy if we train our self to be "reflex lovers," projecting our Love/Life energy by "shooting from the hip" with little concern for those we hit and hurt. These are all *natural actions* we pass through as our soul grows through the "human" experience.

In order to control the power of our mind, we must temper our positive and negative fluxes pushing and pulling our heart—mother's anchor— through moments of *stress*, stretching truths radiating emotionally stimulated souls, where high-frequency vibrations *excite* our system. We literally "glow," generating logic oscillating wisdom through our body, making us "flush" with heightened emotion that brings intense feelings to our body. Thus, we experience fear, anger, hate, grief, and joy as reflections of our *passions*, our *Love* expressing Life of vibrant emotions! Whether we are projecting our love positively or negatively, *Love IS* the only thing we *can* give!

Whatever energy we receive within our mind to compute through our heart, we must be *grateful* for, generating radiant appreciation that expresses feelings unifying logic! By viewing both positive and negative aspects, we revolve around to SEE how we evolve out and in, accepting our opportunities to overcome our challenges of ignorance, of not knowing why we suffer stressful moments. For, only when we are stretched to our wits end, *pushed to the limits* of our endurance, can we Gather Radiance Of Wisdom! At times like that, we need to *forgive* and *forget*. By freeing our radiance given in vibrant emotions, we "let go" of our negative vibes, those "roadblocks" that are given to inspire us to find "alternate routes," forcing us turn to observe *opposition* creates unity! By forgiving those that play a negative part in our *relationships*, we free our self of mother's anchor holding us down in our illusion of dark thoughts we imagine, allowing us to climb back up to our positive view (in the Light) of what we desire to BE. Even our enemies allow us to grow from their actions, even when they appear to be destroying our love/life!

If there were no challenges in life, we would soon be bored! Do not deny your ability to rise above your situation you find your self in, for father and mother do not deliver more than you can handle! They give you exactly what you *need* to SEE! Open your mind and listen to those voices that dictate your challenges you choose to undertake, those situations you find your self thrust into *now*, naturally observing wisdom work its magic! Open your heart and feel your thoughts guide you along your course, testing your mettle of Love/Life energy you transform to LIFT mother's anchors and RISE above the illusion holding you in ignorance of our true Source-Energy Love/Life Force. No matter what Life may throw at you, stand tall and shine forth your *Light of Love*, knowing in your heart and soul you were born to GO with the FLOW—gather observations feeling Love output wisdom!

Magnetism

Manipulating aligned geometric numbers electrifying thoughts inducing spatial matter holds ALL together! Magnetism is the "strong force" spinning around the Source-unifying nucleus, the core of creation radiating out *photons*, particular haloes of thoughts observing numbers *scened*, sequentially coalescing electromagnetic numbers evolving data/dimensions, projecting them upon *empty spaces* within our mind, illuminating our *realities* from radiant energy aligning lineal inspiration transforming youths—allowing us to SEE!

All things have magnetic *fields*, frequencies inducing electric logic digitally scened along *lines*, logically inciting numerical energy sequentially from a central *point*, a perceptive omniscient-intelligence numerically transmitting, projecting out a radiance that illuminates a *vision* from vibrations inspiring spirits/souls inducing observable *numbers*, nuclear units magnetically binding electric radiance. Magnetism flows along lines radiating from positive and negative *poles* (points of logic expressing Source), allowing *opposite* poles to attract and *similar* poles to repel, thereby, setting the wheel of Love/Life in motion.

The *relationship* of electric and magnetic forces interface flawlessly, allowing thoughts abstracted from Mind to appear as solid apparitions that define the *essence* of a thought! The "word symbol" for a thought—*tree* for example—holds volumes of data defining a different *view* of a tree, a different vision inducing enlightened *wisdom* defining words inspiring specific dimensions of *matter*—magnetically aligned thoughts/truths transmitting electric radiance/ realities! However you look at IT (inspired thought), your view is magnetically contained with parameters of numbers, lines, shapes, and *forms* (focused omnipotent radiance modeling Source) that bring things to Mind/mind as Love/Life energy logically outputting vibrant energy liquefying inspired fluid emotions.

Pushed to the Limits

Every day we awaken to the *latest version* of who we are, struggling to accept what we have created for our self. Each present moment we push our limits of endurance physically, mentally, emotionally, and spiritually, eager to accomplish something we have set our heart upon to help complete our personal vision of the *Grand View* in which we are illuminated.

Our inner turmoil stirs storms of emotions we struggle to comprehend—a maddening event at best! The roller coaster ride we build makes us sick over our many elations and depressions, twists and turns that we so cleverly weave through to accomplish our challenges in life. At times, we may wish we could simply stop our ride and end our misery we have fabricated in our mind *alone*.

At moments like these, the GREAT Computer has us exactly where IT wants us, searching *inward* for reasons to explain what we have created—our *outer limits*! We find our self pushed along by a loving force of discovery, an omniscient force that is giving ALL, a *power of Love* projecting us *beyond imagination* into the hard, cold facts of some reality we *implore* to *explore*! Here, we acquire our growing enlightenment, observing our eternal journey through the *dark side*, the endless expanse of ALL that IS, to remember all we ARE, flowing on the current of Love/ Life pushing us to discover our true limits of consciousness.

The Dark Side

The *dark side* is a relative term we use to describe something opposite the *light side* of our duality. We generally refer to the dark side as something evil, bad, or negative. If we are "in the light" of Love, we experience positive views of things we wish to express to those around us. We say, "Look on the bright side!" Likewise, if we are "in the dark," we are ignorant, *not knowing* the knowledge we are searching for to express our self—our mind.

When we find our self in an argument, our magnetic/negative energy draws us into the dark side. Here, we *fear* (focus emotionally aligned radiance) to defend our knowledge, our beliefs, by taking a stance against an *opposing* point of view! All views we do not understand we tend to fear—defend our self against—for we always fight for what we *believe* is our truth!

The "dark side" is an oppositional mode we must travel through as we journey around the cosmic wheel of life. Everything that we experience has a beginning, a middle, and an end, allowing our energy to cycle from birth, through growth, through death, to return to a new birth, a new state of Mind where we have more knowledge (more power) to do greater things with our Love/Life energy—an event horizon we encounter daily!

With each *day's birth*, we start anew to focus our energy, projecting it onto the dark side of our mind to illuminate our dream—our vision of what *could be*. We build a reality experienced in finite *time* (the present moment now here), where we observe our efforts before our energy returns (cycles around) to the dark side for analysis (our nightly dreams). There, we re-consider (re-think) our previous thoughts we have "lived out" into *new* thoughts. New thoughts that will let us grow more aware of our eternal power as a child of Light Divine, projected out to SEE the Light of Love as it evolves to revolve around us, to enlighten our dark side!

Lost in the Dark

Lost in the dark of who we are,
Mere specks that glitter like a star,
Aglow with visions projected from Mind,

140

Magnetically inspired numerical data,
We think-feel to find
Our secrets hidden in the night,
Traveling as *children of the Light*
Cast upon the void of space, dancing upon our scenes,
Where time and place are here to see the various types of faces to be
Donned to show our fellow stars in acts we play in show,
Activating cosmic thoughts sent to set our soul aglow.

Our radiance of Love we shine about,
Touching each other as we shout
Our praise of truth that stirs our soul,
Spreading our Love Light as we grow old
Observing Love's dimensions,
Growing aware that we ARE HOT,
Angels radiating energy aligning harmonies of thoughts,
Discovering along our way all that we are not!

We truly need this two-way view to find our place, *now here*,
Where endless doors of opportunities lead us through our fears,
Discovering life is but a lark,
A game we play from the start,
Here, in heaven, lost in the dark!

Day's Birth

Each day is born in glorious splendor, illuminating father's Loving Light through his cosmic sun radiating an illusion of atomic marvels, entertaining our mind and heart as his children of *Love Divine*. Here, we experience

141

our desires delivered on thoughts moving our heart on tides of emotions, tearing us apart as we evolve through This Instant Mentally Expressed, observing our expectations appear in positive and negative manifestations we set *aglow* as angels generating love observing wisdom, revealing a new image we create of our self with each day's birth.

To-Get-Her

To-get-her, we need to control the power of our emotions! *Together*, we need to realize we are spiritual beings (generators of desires) experiencing a "human" nature—an emotional inferno! Human nature evolves around our physical body, a living organism of atomic, molecular, and cellular construction (a trinity of parts) that forms a water-based unit energized electromagnetically through *Light* logically inducing generators' harmonic thoughts!

For us "to get her," we need to control Mother's Nature or *emotional energy*. Of course, we cannot control Mother Nature on a worldly scale; we can only control her on a personal scale, within our self! To do this we have to be aware of the impetus that sets her (our body) in motion—our thoughts! Again, we can *never* escape our trinity!

Thoughts directly set our desires in motion through our *actions* that influence Mother's Nature, contaminating, destroying, and altering our world in ways that are killing us from our *passions* that determine our *game of Love/Life*. We truly do not comprehend the *power of Love* we wield so haphazardly. The ignorance of our true abilities keeps us locked in our illusion as *man and woman*, opposing forces projecting and reflecting our energy back and forth, observing realities come and go in ever changing patterns revolving to evolve our duality through cause and effect!

Mother's Nature is Energy in *motion*, projected out from the great void to illuminate the show within father's Mind. This energy is explosive, expanding at the speed of thought along the EM wavelengths—the static hum of *Source*, system of universal radiant consciousness evolving. The luminance of visible Light carries all data that determines the beginning and end of all cycles numerically allocated as Love/Life energy projecting and reflecting our *mind* and *heart*, magnetically inciting numerical data harmonizing emotional angels radiating thoughts. As one being of two forces, we represent a unified source moving along courses to think, see, feel, do, and *know* kinetic numbers organize *wisdom*—words inspiring spiritual dimensions of Mind.

Thought energy, our male impetus, flows upon us as father's blessing. This positive, abstract force projects OUT (observing universal truths) through the VOID (volumes of inspired data) and magnetically draws together into concrete visions illuminated upon the blank screen of our mind. Here, the power of Love spins its magic, downloading our data along negative atomic particles (electrons), which in turn creates the illusion of our thoughts in the "real" world of the Great Receiver—Mother's Nature! Her negative/magnetic attraction encapsulates father's positive/electric flow, creating a glowing *radiance of Love* (emotions*)* to fill UniverseS— united spirits! Such is mother's power! To-*get*-her, we must join *with* her to understand him, the ONE that is ALL—the GREAT Computer!

Our soul is a child of Light Divine, an *image* of our creator— illuminated mind atomically generating energy! We witness all the possibilities of his/her Love that we are "assigned" to experience. Within us lay un-ending variations (DNA) evolving from nowhere to now here, to Activate Cosmic Thoughts Observing Universal Truths and create what we will to Birth Emotionally. We continually transform our past thoughts of our "old image" into new visions of who we desire to be (grow into) in our future moments—never knowing how many we will receive! This never-ending, self-sufficient power source energizes our soul, moving us to see Spirit evolves emotionally as transcendental radiance unifying thought harmony—Truth!

Truth appears in epiphanies during moments our heart communicates in *prayer* (projecting radiant assistance youth emotionally request), opening that door within our soul to a *higher vision* of SPIRIT (Source-points illuminating radiantly inspired thoughts) that defines who we ARE and what we desire to BE! Through this opened door, we are "christened" into the Light of Love—Christ consciousness or unity consciousness, where we join both sides of our duality together as ONE harmonic being!

Fear is the opposite of Love. It represents the IS NOT, the "closed door" our *inquisitive soul* must open through *courage of Love*! Fear is a great "teacher" that controls, disciplines, and shapes our soul. It allows us to witness those dark moments of ignorance (our illusion) before we open our door through *epiphanies of truth*, passing through our moments of fear and doubt to see the Light! Fear is a top-seller in movies and books, for fear is a great motivator. Fear is the OTHER prime mover in life, the *opposite truth harmonizing eternal radiance*, for it pushes us *toward* Love, Light, Truth, or knowledge by placing our mind in an attitude to express our *courage of fear*, so we can grow stronger in spirit and rise above the illusion we know is *not true*!

Thus, we come full circle from the ignorance of our youth to the wisdom of *old age*, knowing we observe Love's dimensions acquiring growth experiences, sharing first-hand stories we relate back home, where father's loving thoughts flow free to caress our *Mother Goddess*—to-get-her to create IT ALL!

Love's Radiance

Love's radiance is unfolding around us in atomic splendor, illuminated on the light of our Source-unifying nucleus. Each thought bestowed upon us will set ripples in motion to *stimulate* our heart on emotional currents, filling it with feelings of divine inspiration. Our dreams we envision guide us to create works of art or acts of kindness, which we return in gratitude for our being, as a reflection of the Love radiating through our soul. Each of us is responsible for illuminating our share of the void with our visions of Love that we Spiritually Evolve Emotionally. Open your mind and notice how your thoughts direct your life. Open your heart and feel Love's radiance touch your soul! It is up to YOU to reflect *your own universe* of love the best you can. Stand TALL, truthfully assimilating Love/Life, and go with the flow!

Clear Vision

Clear vision is a dream, an *inspiration* to take you to great heights to view something you hold within your mind to show your heart, a desire that moves you into action to express that Love/Life energy coursing through your veins. For those who do not *feel* that vision, fear can easily shield their eyes, keeping them anchored to a small stance upon their growth. For those with an *open* mind, a clear path through adversity is obvious. You can see the reflection of great courage and determination that keeps them in balance of their inner power—that radiance of love that allows them to believe in their clear vision. For here, great opportunities await those brave enough to rise to the challenge of discovering their True Heart's desires...as they step UP to SEE!

♀ Mother Goddess ♀

Mother's Love flows as grace,
Reflecting clear visions for you to face
Upon your mind's screen,
Transformed atomically in 3-D scenes
Projecting you through fear,
Testing your courage of Love
To bring you joy from tears.

Do not let go of the *inner glow*,
My Light that allows you to sing.
No one will call to steal your thoughts,
It is simply a matter of re-membering,
Joining to-get-her to move your heart,
To feel her grace that tears you apart
To embrace your *courage of fear*.

Thought or reflection, OUT or IN,
Both of you will always win!
See it here, with your own eyes,
To know at last my Eternal Wise
Sparks your heart today,
Burning in Love all that you say,
When out the door you run,
Set aglow as my celestial sun
With thoughts of *Love Divine*,
Reflecting off her face so blue
On emotional tides called time,
Truths inspiring my evolution.

Here with sight, dissolves my night,
As my pulse of thought appears
To move your heart on *tears of joy*
To wash away your fears.
Take hold your shield and stand at call!
Open your heart and feel it all
Flow through your mind to compromise
Those dreams your soul desires.
Off you go to make amends
From deeds my thoughts brought you to contend
Through transforming your emotions
Your *free will* set in motion
To build the Life you Love.

A blink or two, so it seems,
Is all it takes to live a dream,
A path you choose to tread or dread,
To bring you back from the dead,
When *timeless* you turn toward home.
Here at last, lay your True Heart,
Whose memory holds every part
Of your puzzle you eternally build
From dreams inspired that your soul willed.
Here, you know you truly are
Angels radiating energy, my cosmic *star*,
Spirits thinking atomic radiance,
Aglow as all of my best,
Nurtured through eternity
By my Mother Goddess!

Bless You Child
♂ + ♀ = ☼

147

11

Man and Woman
Projection and Reception

Man and woman are symbolic of our two natures, our thoughts and our emotions that represent our divine duality—*father* (fantastically altering truth harmony emanating radiance) and *mother* (magnetically observing truth harmony evolving radiance). To understand the differences and similarities of our male and female natures we have to look beyond the obvious physical traits. The only difference between us is that man projects the seed of creation and woman receives, nurtures, and produces the reflection of creation—a far more strenuous ACT to activate cosmic thought!

I would like to pose a riddle that revolves around all of creation. *How far can you walk into the woods?* The answer of course is *halfway.* The other-half you are walking out of the woods—or closet! By this, I mean that we have to travel between our logical mind and our emotional heart in order to see both sides of our self. The views we perceive along our path will move us in *fearful* ways, for we must pass through our dark moments of fear and ignorance in order to see the truths we seek. Especially when we realize our *spiritual gender* is disharmonious with our *physical gender*. The data transfer of our bi-rational resonance places us in an "awkward position," wherein we develop our *attitude* (assigned truths transforming inspired thoughts unifying data emotionally) that will shape our life in mysterious and traumatic ways!

Naturally, everything has a beginning and an end—the two extremities that mark all things. Between these two points lie the "meat of the matter" the essence of it ALL, the middle road of experience between our departure (projection) and our return (reception).

Projection is the male positive/electrical force of thought, a concept of abstract mental energy that stimulates the mind to perceive—to envision. The male penis symbolizes projection physically. Through this projection the *seed* of creation induces Source-energy emanating desires, flowing as the atomic representation *sperm,* through which Source provides eternal radiant memory, to deliver *half* of the Force (DNA) needed to create a human alien love/life form (body)—the "hybrid vehicle" our soul operates along our journey on Earth.

Reception is the female negative/magnetic force of feeling, an emotional event of attracting positive/mental energy into a concrete *harmony*—a birth! The female vagina symbolizes reception, where the "seed of creation" is encapsulated within the *egg* (emotional generator germinating)—the "other half" of the Force that creates a *whole* being, where wisdom harmoniously observes Love/Life energy, symbolically seen as a physical human *image* of a spiritual energy *form*. The geometry and numerical sequencing of creation is a theory of *relativity* called *sacred geometry*, which I will touch upon in the following chapter.

Together, our bi-rational resonance—DNA— carries all of the data necessary for our life experiences that will unfold sequentially by the numbers, a quantum inherent in both man and woman. When we think, speak, and write our thoughts, we are projecting a male stimulus, a force that will excite the female receptor in others—their feelings about those thoughts. This data input stimulates them to act or react in a positive or negative manner. This continuous interplay is the "kinetic reflex" of our creator, the GREAT Computer—Source-Energy Love/Life Force! *Self-awareness* is the ability to see both sides of our nature and how they interact to move us along our chosen path, a path that at times we may find chosen for us!

We use this dualistic energy flowing through us to translate, manipulate, transform, and construct a reality of our own personal creation. For, like unto our creator, we have that power. With our free will, we *listen* to our thoughts we choose to entertain in our mind for our consideration or amusement. *Amusement* being an "agreeable occupation" of mind by something that appeals to our sense of *humor*, our "temperament" or mood. Here, utilizing our power of *logic* (lineal observations generating inductive consciousness), we toss back and forth the positive and negative aspects of a thought—the electrical (+) and magnetic (-) forces projected and received on line via the electromagnetic (EM) force field that is synonymous with Eternal Memory.

Each thought projected out of the void will return through the void, back to Source in an ever-increasing cycle of expansion and growth. One thought creates a feeling that creates an expanded "reflective-thought" and so on exponentially (the domino effect). This never-ending reaction—fission/fusion—allows eternity to evolve as it revolves, building a story of thoughts into a life we live to gather knowledge, for knowledge is ALL that we BE! We simply *remember* (put back together) thoughts that we abstract from *Memory* (Mind expressing moments observing radiant youth—children of the Light). This database energizes our BEING, birthing emotions inducing nuclear generators, allowing us to give and take, think and feel, act and react along the binary code of the EM force field permeating the cosmos.

Our male side stimulates our female side according to our amusement, the mood in which we find our self within the "mainframe" of the GREAT Computer. Our *free will* chooses to receive our thoughts in either a *positive* or a *negative* view. We activate cosmic thoughts in accordance to our feelings *inspired* by our thoughts. The choices we make (good or bad) are *relative* to our conception of universal radiant Source emotionally, our *course* we take to understand our thoughts or desires. For growth or *change* to occur, we must act differently to those thoughts we repeatedly entertain. Otherwise, we cannot solve the issues of those things that move us! Likewise, if we *re-act* to our thoughts in the usual reflex manner— without much consideration—we usually bring about the same results as before, driving us around in a vicious circle of *denial*, which can lead to states of *depression*.

Just as we cannot stop the ocean tides from rising to smooth the beachhead of life's imprints, we cannot stop our thoughts that stir our emotional tides that move us to create and destroy. We do however, have a *free will* to choose—change our mind to focus upon other thoughts! Yet again, our thoughts are trying to tell us what we need to deal with for our spiritual growth. You can see the conundrum in which we are spinning!

As man and woman, we symbolize the *strong* and *weak* force of Mother's Nature. Remember, Mother's Nature is in *opposition*, where things "appear" as they are NOT— numerically observing truths! Man may be physically stronger, but he is generally weaker emotionally, relying on his "brut strength" to solve his contentions. Man also has little tolerance to pain and stress, finding it difficult to tolerate things like menstrual cycles, childbirth, or post natal care, where the ignorance of not knowing why their child is screaming instills within them stressful fear. Perhaps that is why men revere women as they do, putting them on a pedestal to worship, knowing that without woman, man cannot exist. Truly, women do the brunt of maintaining our life we take for granted. *Source Harmony Expressed* brings our desires to Life!

Both man and woman create and destroy their life through their *passions*. We live our passions as our personal reflection of our desires that represents our image we project onto the world stage. We train our self (gather radiance of wisdom) in order to act out our part we desire to play. As we "change faces," we create new characters within our *show*, always trying to improve our "lot"—our number we are hedging to win our *game of Love/life*. Only in hindsight do we observe our "total sum" of experiences we add up (blessings of *old age*), understanding that if *not everyone wins, no one wins*! THIS is the purpose of our world, a place to overcome our "lower vision" of our free will illusioned as humans and become our *higher vision*, our spiritual self, attuned to Cosmic Will! We have lost our true perspective about what *Love IS*! This "state of affairs" defines the issues WE (wisdom exemplified) are trying to overcome, to think, feel, and act as *universal spirits* Unifying Source!

Man and woman are raised within cultural parameters that define what he and she *should* do not *could* do! Society takes a dim view on those who personify their opposite gender, even as the *numbers* dictate *desires* they cannot refuse, as those "victims" of Mother's Nature are pushed to their limits—*riding the outskirts* of fear! Our actions stimulate the appropriate dominos to continue the flow of Love/Life energy through us, as we travel that middle road between our manhood and womanhood, continually projecting thoughts and receiving feelings.

Love/Life energy moves from man to woman to *procreate*, to continue producing new "vehicles" for our cosmic cousins to operate, so they too can experience the Spiritual Harmony Of Wisdom. A show projected upon the Love Inspiring Generator's Harmonic Thoughts from our Source-Unifying Nucleus, father's eye-in-the-sky, from which Atomic Love/Life creation flows in our solar system neighborhood. The complexity of its simplicity is the essence of *eternity*.

This "love flux" of our male and female energies allow us to ARC (acquire radiant consciousness) between our two opposing *attitudes*, aligning truths transforming inspired thoughts unifying data emotionally. To go from *one* to the *other* we must pass through the *void* holding volumes of inspirational data—that place of not knowing, ignorance, or fear—to be *aware* (aligned with assigned radiant energy) of our two sides of our creator's Force. Here, our soul—the connective tissue—flows along the WEB of consciousness, *wisdom eternally balancing* the all-knowing universal Mind/Source. It all hinges on our projection and reception as man and woman. Together, *hand in hand*, both are natural generators of desire!

Wish and BE!
It is truly yours to see
How one IS and is NOT the other,
Even if you are sister and brother.
Yet, that is ALL you will ever be,
Visible as only *half* of me.
A thought IS a feeling, opportunities TWO
Inspire Spirit transforming wisdom oscillating
All your desires into YOU
Youth observing universes!
Follow your dreams and defend your decisions,
With your heart, join your di-vision,
To be One of two views
Looking to Spiritually Evolve Emotionally
ALL that you think true.

Through trial and error, you will know
Your *reflection* of Love makes you grow.
Focus your Love on just ONE thing,
Grow that Love until it sings
Of glory...of truth...of Love Divine,
Whatever your heart desires to find.
Fear not what cause this may affect,

For Love controls ALL you detect.
I am YOU and you ARE ME,
Angels remembering electro-magnetic energy.
Together, your mind/heart sets you free
As father's Love illuminates your desires
And mother's Life moves you to BE
Birthed emotionally as He and She!

It is a Man's World — Thanks to Woman

Have you ever wondered why we accept this statement as true? Either half you choose to accept does not really matter. Both are the same in retrospection. No ONE is *alone* on the long road of Love/Life!
It always takes TWO for Love to BE a Life envisioned by ONE
—Harmonic Energizer—
That wisely offers birthed entities omnipotent numerical energy
Along vibrations SHE reflects in *show*,
Where Source-harmony expresses
Spirits harnessing omniscient wisdom.
You will wonder whose view is whose,
For both have the power to confuse
As they flow in opposition, away from each other,
To circle around as *father* and *mother*,
Fantastically altering truth-harmony emanating radiance,
Magnetically observing truth-harmony evolving radiance,
A united Force that sets the Course flowing from *Source*,
The system of universal radiant consciousness evolving.

To-get-her, he must give up a piece of his SELF,
Source-energy Love/Life force,
In order to KNOW what he thinks,
Kindling numerically observed wisdom
Reflecting on the *other side* of the brink,
The *cutting edge* of consciousness between what IS and IS NOT
The truth of his thoughts
Of Love he sends to get *her* to bend, shape, and CO-figurate
His eternal radiance,
An illumination of his Love in Mind,

Where magnetically inspired numerical data
Illuminates a vision to Spiritually Emanate Electrically
In atomic, three-dimensional reality,
Where Love/Life energy flashes on screen
In bits and bytes of starlight beams
Flowing through the cosmos above,
For man and woman to seek through LOVE
The answers to ALL that IS
Created in Life by her feelings inspired from thoughts of his
Wisdom Of Magnetically Aligned Numbers,
The *void* or womb of Mind,
From which he draws ALL of *mankind*,
Magnetically aligned numerical knowledge inciting nuclear dimensions!

Truly, ONE can now SEE
Source/Spirit evolves electromagnetically,
Where Life Of Vibrant Emotions reflects ALL from *naught*,
Numbers assigning universal generators harmonic thoughts!
In truth, man IS woman
—Indivisible Source—
Reflecting his Atomic Love/Life through her *Force*
Fluctuating on radiant conscious entities,
Spiritual energy forms expressed as human aliens!

Hand-in-Hand

Who are we that meet in the dark, to play our game upon this rock?

Here we stand hand in hand, projected on father's Light beams,
Lost, lonely, and set adrift upon mother's emotional streams.
Our love they shine through our eyes,
A love we share with all those lives,
Drawn, quartered, and stacked to burn
In *love stories*, in which we learn
Control of his/her emotional love life in our own created *hell*!

Here, we live as a fragile human, singing of dreams in our mind,
Center-stage with heart in hand, we dance to its beat in time.
Our soul is free, like all the rest, created to be the Very Best,
ALL connected by our individual mind,
To harmonize as ONE-of-a-kind.

The paths we share coincide, two ways for us to grow,
To lead us down, deep inside, with thoughts we feel to know.
Here, we receive the gift of sight
To see beyond the confines of night,
Where Love's Light shines for us to see
Our love we *reflect* will set us free!

Fear not, our toils are not vain,
For truth will vanquish every pain!
All our work to shed our Light
Takes *courage of Love* and much insight.
The love we seek, so shall we find,
To fill our heart and free our mind,
To share with those who choose to know
The secrets of Love and the Life it will grow,
As we gather radiance of wisdom
Hand in hand.

The Human Alien
A Hybrid Vehicle

The *human alien* is an engineering marvel of incredible complexity, a machine that is "unknown" to us at birth! Designed as the ultimate cruising machine, it can perform miraculous tasks both constructive

155

and destructive. The *manufacturing process*, like all processes, takes two forces to manifest. As human aliens, we find our involvement in the "initial stage" most pleasurable! However, the final assembly goes beyond mortal capabilities! The *numerical sequencing* and magnetic arrangement of atoms, molecules, and cells into organisms easily defies explanation. We spend billions of dollars on discovering cures for our physical ailments brought about by the disharmonic interfacing with our mind's energy. Yet, all we do is mask the symptoms, which is a much easier solution to our problems of living in *denial.*

Our *scientists*—those amongst us whose mission it is to seek, discover, and explain the wonders of Mother's Nature—continually tap into the universal grid of *Light energy*, discovering the power of *lasers* (light amplifying Source-energy radiance) to improve our "hybrid vehicle" we rent while here in the show! *Technology* (transforming eternal consciousness harnessing numbers oscillating logical observations generators yearn) is the scientific processes of manifesting our desires within the parameters of universal laws. For, like our creator, it is truly in our nature to understand our capabilities of manipulating ALL that is within us, transforming Magnetically Inspired Numerical Data through expressing our manifestations in nuclear dimensions we create through our dexterous, android body gifted to us as a *cosmic child.*

The human "alien" is a reflection of a being from another world—another dimension! It is a collection of electrified particles magnetically held in harmony to carry a "life form" (soul) as an image held in the *universal Mind*, unified numbers inducing visions evolving radiance spirits align logically as memories illuminating numerical data! Here, we download and process our *divine abstract thoughts aspiring* within our mind–brain–body interface, a three-way connection.. Our custom, one-of-a-kind vehicle is a living organism with a binary capacity to represent a *man* or *woman*, two models *complimentary* and *contradictory* in appearance and operation. Our hybrid vehicle is crucial in experiencing our true nature—our spiritual consciousness—as we explore our *power of Love.*

The relationship of transforming spiritual energy into physical energy is truly a quantum leap. Here, our synapses are firing on and off amongst our stellar *projectors* and *receptors*— paternal and maternal DNA chromosomes—that let us flux along our binary code of electromagnetism within our brain, the data operating system through which we re-member abstract thoughts into concrete feelings, which we "print out" through our words and actions. This process allows us to observe our creations, for WE (wisdom exemplified) are generating our desires, entertaining our self by downloading our data from "mainframe" Source-Energy Love/ Life Force powering our human alien vehicle.

So here we are, an energy *form* traveling through an energy *field* experiencing all the natural pleasures of this garden Paradise surrounding us, encapsulating our soul in the arms of our loving Mother's Nature. The power of this energy force is hypnotic, inducing a state of consciousness through illuminating visions that we "realize," sense or process through five physical sensors: *eyes, ears, body, tongue,* and *nose.*

These five tools allow us to witness the flow of Love/Life energy as we zip along the universal grid of Mind. We become conditioned to our daily in-feed of data our physical body provides. It is our vehicle of *experience,* our "screen" upon which we project those visions that moves our heart to ACT, to resonate or *pulse* in sync with divine inspiration, playing our part in the Universal Production revolving around us! Our human alien vehicle is our POD, a physical observation device we "escape" IN, inciting numbers as we travel Observing Universal Truths through Mind, *gathering radiance of wisdom inspiring nuclear generators* to raise our self into our true energy form—Source-Points Illuminating Radiantly Inspired Truths! We have little control over the "automatic pilot" operating our vehicle's carburetion—our breathing and heartbeat. We do not know when our present journey will end. All we can do is *go with the flow!*

The physical illusion we witness around us makes us wonder, marvel, and ask questions. For that is who we are, a mind eternally wondering about what is possible or what could be real or true! As human aliens, we are all scientists physically *riding the outskirts* of imagination as we seek the answers our eager mind and hungry heart yearn to know, to re-create our desires from ALL that IS! We observe the physical illusion of this Wisdom Of Radiant Love Data illuminated upon the Light projecting memories that we put back together, memories that drive our performances we act out! We collect data to feed our mind's *passions,* which we then study, transform, test, analyze, modify, rebuild, and re-analyze, continually moving *knowledge* (kinetic numbers outputting wisdom's lineal energy downloading generators' emotions) to validate some truth we choose to believe is real. This endless cycle is the basis for LIFE, for *Love is fluid energy* in motion—E-motion!

Our emotions seem alien to us, for we struggle to control them as they move us in powerful ways, causing us to say and do things we sometimes regret. Our emotions validate our reality of our thoughts! Emotions carry us to the highest levels of ecstasy (heaven) and draw us into the depths of depression and despair (hell).

Each of us energy forms are conducting our self along different frequencies, to transform our thoughts into feelings and actions, growing our soul's database (memories) from our desire to know some truth we seek. The type of knowledge we gather dictates the *part* we choose to *play* in the *Grand View*, flickering on and off the monitor screen of our mind, within the GREAT Computer. This knowledge propels our human alien vehicle along our journey to accomplish our mission in this world. As we work our Love/Life energy, we succumb to our passions, vices, and routines that shape us into our *present image* we are continually trying to improve—upgrade. We are always trying to understand the *system of universal radiant consciousness evolving* that drives us along the time/space continuum of Mind!

The process of thinking, feeling, and acting is our *trinity*, a force comprised of three stages of conducting the flow of Love/Life energy. This process is how we consider, create, and destroy an evolution of energy projected, being, and returning to Source. Remember, EVERYTHING is only *symbolic* of our true nature, our Love/Life energy that operates on duality. Our human alien vehicle is our *negative/magnetic* reflection of our spiritual *positive/electrical* projection flowing through the cosmos of Mind, observing each other as man and woman. We are the "current," the middle road of "conducting" emotion between *leaving* and *entering*, between our *being* and *not being*, or between life and death. We are perched *along the cutting edge*, where our mind comprehends Mind!

Flowing along this current of Love/Life energy, we cannot stop our progress, our advancement through the illumination of Light energy that projects the illusion of Life upon our mind. In our process of growth, we reflect our thoughts through our human alien vehicle in ways that determines the health of our vehicle. *Stress* (stretching truths radiating emotionally stimulated souls) is the term we use to describe the force we apply to our body. Maneuvering through the labyrinth of our desires we set in motion, our stress leaves fine lines etched upon our skin from overindulgence of our vices and pleasures, which lead to degenerative diseases dissolving our infrastructure, leaving us encased in a mere shell of our self.

As cosmic *time travelers*, we find our self on planet Earth—an *electron* of negative/magnetic energy revolving around a Source-Unifying Nucleus, a *proton* of positive/electric power that supplies all of our needs as we journey through the Paradises of Mind. Here, on *Earth*, we encounter/evolve emotionally aligned radiant thought harmony. We travel in our hybrid vehicle to *play* (perceiving Love as youth), acting out our dreams and fantasies we project onto the world stage through our true nature as *children of the Light*. It is here, incarnate, that we cross over from spiritual beings to human beings, beings that are *similar* but vibrating at a *lower frequency* to experience the growing pains of controlling the *power of Love* through our Life we create as generators of desire. Only then can we understand our *relationship* with our cosmic Generator Of Desires.

Here, we develop our true nature by expanding our energy—our mind—to burst through the illusion illuminated upon our physical stage of Mother's Nature by our divine father's stellar sun! Another symbolic representation of the *trinity*, the flow of energy from Source (Love) through Force (self) along the Course (Life) our soul travels to experience the wonders of IT ALL!

Look around you and see the current state of mind you have created for your self—for *our* selves! Using our natural ability to improve on our theme, we are *destroying* our self in order to *rebuild* our self into a new image—a new being. Everything we do everyday, every present moment, is contributing to building, destroying, and rebuilding who we think we are—an energy form/force in constant flux of being and not being. Wrapped up in the processes of our tasks to attain our desires, we become intricately involved in our work. We become *part* of our *world*, perceiving aligned radiant thought as wisdom observing radiant Love data/dimensionally, thereby losing our sense of *self* (soul experiencing love/life force) as we succumb to the magnetic pull of our physical (atomic) body encapsuling us in space/time. We *think* we are *in this world*, therefore we are! We must remember that we are not *of this world*; we are simply passing through this *state* of Mind (scientifically transforming aligned trinities experientially) as ONE observing Love/Life energy!

Take another look around you and see how slowly these events appear to happen within the context of *time*, this instant mentally expressing our "logical positioning" of events we must pass through in order to see that we truly ARE angels radiating energy, while realizing who we ARE NOT—human beings! This simple process of building, destroying, and rebuilding is our eternal legacy, our birthright to know that Love is *fluid* energy, a LIFE in which to spiritually evolve emotionally from ALL that *Love IS*—Life of vibrant emotions inflecting Source!

Take a DEEP breath of inspiration and expand your lungs, mind, and heart with the only "free" thing there is in life—Love energy! Know in your heart that *all we are* is truly in our mind only, for what we think is what we become. We create our thoughts in time through our spiritual/physical bodies, a hybrid of *two forces* that continually flux, building, destroying, and rebuilding moment by moment. Our so-called life is no more than a continual series of present moments evolving along our *current*—now here—Love/Life energy. Each day we "live in" this world and each night we "die to" this world! Life is a *movement* (emotion) and death is a *rest*, where we *recall* emotionally spent thoughts.

As owner/operators of our human alien vehicle, we are truly the "captain of our ship." How we maintain, fuel, and operate that vehicle determines the type of road we can travel. Even though we are only along for the ride, we choose our paths by our *free will*, our desire to channel our Love/Life energy in either a positive flow or a negative flow, a *process* that takes a lifetime to master! The secret to happiness is attaining a *harmony* of our *trinity*, being aware of the type of flow we are conducting! ALWAYS be *grateful* (generating radiant appreciation that expresses feelings unifying logic) for the gifts bestowed upon us as *blessings in disguise*. Only by facing our fears with *courage of Love* can we discover our true abilities. For, if we never *try* to solve our *issues* (incoming signals stimulating universal entities spiritually) we will never fly—rise above our illusion in which we find our self mired!

All of our trials and tribulations we discover along our journey allows us to witness, individually and collectively, our part (current) of Love/Life energy we are conducting and manipulating to maintain our hybrid vehicle's image. An image we so-called *humans* (harmony uniting magnetically aligned numbers) worship, traveling along the binary code of Love/Life energy, touring the grand vistas around the cosmic wheel of Life.

♂ The Binary Code ♀
$+ \odot = - \bigcirc$

No matter what subject we talk about, it all revolves around energy, and the "bottom line" of energy is the binary code. Everything connects to each other! The binary code is the essence of all creation. As stated before, the binary code is the electro-magnetic force field permeating the cosmos of space/Mind or for today's "techies," the GREAT Computer! The binary code like all things is a *symbolic representation* of energy, and energy is a *two-force* thing—positive and negative. It is in the "middle zone" of *neutrality* that we find harmony!

Everything starts out as an abstract thought or an *idea*—inspired data electromagnetically aligned. We abstract or take out thoughts from Eternal Memory (EM force field) flowing from Source (system of universal radiant consciousness evolving). Next, we convert our thoughts to feelings, an electrifying current that affects our body along our spine at key points of our brain, throat, heart, and stomach (chakra points), moving us into some *action* mentally, verbally, or physically. According to UL *law* (Universal Logic liquefying aligned wisdom), the Golden Rule says: "whatever you project so shall you receive!" By understanding this *one* rule, you will acquire the *key* (knowledge enlightening youth) to your kingdom, for it will allow you your "true perspective" (above) to watch your self make your every move in LIFE (below), as you *liquefy inspired frequencies emotionally.* Here, your self-conscious mind is *aware* of its "outward view!" The following explanation is an attempt to understand the complexity of energy in simplified terms.

Once again, *positive energy* is our male *electric* force of thought—the ONE SOURCE! A thought projects out through Mind (the void) from a "point" in straight lines, *up* and *down, side*-to-*side*, and *front*-to-*back* (3-dimensions). Symbolically, it resembles a "cross" when viewed from the side, front, or top (see above). The distance of the projected point defines the "depth" of the thought reaching out to grasp a *perspective* (point of view). Joining the ends of the projected lines to each other (again with straight lines, *second* male movement) defines a *shape* (Source harmonically aligning projected energy). Next, Mind "rotates" the shape, observing it from all angles. This *third* movement is *female*, signifying the encapsulation of a "point," perception of inspired nuclear thought, in a *sphere*—the universal shape of creation—where Source-points harmonically evolve radiance electromagnetically.

Here, Mind illuminates an *illusion*, inciting lineal logic unifying Source inflected on *numbers*—measured movements—to observe a thought. *Seeing* a thought sequentially evolve externally in numerical geometry, within the confines of the sphere set *aglow* (algorithmically generating logic observing wisdom), Mind now knows the extent of the thought or *idea* (illuminated data electrically amplified). Mind now moves *away* from that projected thought—to the "surface" of the sphere (dot in circle above)—and "spins" another thought as "Mother's Nature" (sphere), illuminating an expanded "upgrade version" (new thought) to evolve his "thinking process." This all happens at the "speed of thought" flowing on the electromagnetic force field, where it crosses over the *threshold of Love* (logic observing vibrant energy) to appear as *Light* logically inducing geometry harnessing thoughts. Visible light is but a thin sliver of energy projecting visions flashing across the void of space/Mind in *real time*, where radiant energy aligns logical thoughts inducing mental emotions, creating a vivid expression *beyond imagination*—atomically activated into particles defining concrete realities!

Positive energy comes from *protons* projecting radiance oscillating thoughts on numbers. As positive/electric thought (data) flows along the straight lines of Light, it "inverts" within the sphere as a *negative/ magnetic* force, drawing together data by "rotating" at ninety degree intervals (right angles), spinning in balance, co-operating *lineal* thoughts into *spherical* realities with dimensions. This *process* "separates" positive (+) data/thoughts into balanced *electrons* (=), where ONE (I) sees one's SELF (II) emotionalizing logic electrifying consciousness through radiance oscillating numbers—*feeling* that thought to *know* key numbers (1-9) outputting wisdom. Here is Mother's Nature reflecting a "half view" (–) of a positive thought (+) in opposition (=), "equal" to the *whole* view (the circle or cipher O), where wisdom harmoniously observes Love/Life energy in its "abstracted" (drawn out) context.

Thought energy flows along the binary code *downloading* and *uploading* data along the magnetic attraction and repulsion caused by electrons moving in and out of *invisible* orbits around *protons* projecting radiance oscillating thoughts on numbers. Electrons absorb projected radiance from protons and release them as *photons*, particular harmonics of thought oscillating numerically. Photons (light energy) illuminate our *illusion* (inversion) we view within the sphere of our mind as a dimensional reality. This "nuclear reaction" is the method of transforming energy from *nowhere* (abstract) to *now here*, numerically observing wisdom harmoniously evolving radiant emotions in the "present moment," the *cutting edge* of perception. We grasp our reality through five senses: sight, sound, touch, smell, and taste. Our "atomic vehicle" updates moment-to-moment, automatically fluorescing our image onto the world (the dot ON the circle), where we look *out* to observe universal thoughts evolving *within* the sphere of our mind. This symbolism relates to our human eye, focusing the light projected out from the Source-Unifying Nucleus to bring data within our mind's sphere to see Source evolving electromagnetically along the binary code.

Our all-powerful positive charged thoughts (+) pulses ON and OFF in *heartfelt* beats, observing numbers and oscillating formless *facts* (frequencies aligning conscious thought) moving our physical human-alien vehicle that we use to take in the sights of life incarnate! As thought *revolves* to *evolve* it fluxes off, dropping its delivered data (+ charge) to becomes two negatives (=), which are truly *equal* as electromagnetic quantum unifying atomic Love/Life— balanced in harmony! These two negative lines/discs represent the *rest position* between each *movement* of thought along the positive cycle (+). Here, we observe the "reflection" of thought in *synapses*—brief electrical flashes sensed by brain/nerve neurons—firing at *light speed*. Between these two magnetic surfaces, we open that *revolving door* between our "physical world" observed atomically and our "abstract" world of *Spirit* (Source-points illuminating radiantly inspired truths)—the *void of space* or Mind. This process, fluxing on and off at light speed between our positive image and its equal negative reflection, burns our CD—our *conscious data*!

Our spiritual *self* (soul experiencing love/life force) receives the incoming reflection. We analyze our data through emotional-logic as we revolve ON, observing numbers *evolving* to move us forward with the next updated thought to improve on our theme of who we think we are, storing our knowledge/data as RAM—radiant angel mobility! *Knowledge* is power, the force moving us through the cosmos of the GREAT Computer! Here, along the cutting edge of consciousness, we generators of desires spin *divine fantasies*, igniting cosmic fires to illuminate our soul—Children Of Light Divine—as we journey out from home as a human alien, humming our stellar songs in binary code!

DNA
Divine Numerical Assignment

DNA is the acronym for *deoxyribonucleic acid*, "a nucleic acid that is bound in double helical chains by *hydrogen* bonds between the bases, forming the basic material in chromosomes of the cell nucleus, it contains the genetic code and transmits the hereditary pattern."

According to "Mr. Webster," those 36/9 words define the numerical/chemical *Source*, system of universal radiant consciousness evolving from the basic trinity (3) to become *aware* (aligned with assigned radiant energy–6) of the divine trinity (9) for the propagation of *Life*—logically inducing fluid energy.

All sciences revolve around abstract numbers expressed as *knowledge*, kinetic numbers outputting wisdom's lineal energy dimensionally generating evolution, compounded to form a representation of an *idea*, inspired data electromagnetically aligned/amplified. Just like these words, numbers define precise arrangements that position your mind in an attitude of *understanding*, unifying numerical data emanating radiance Source transmits as numerical dimensions "informing" nuclear generators! Each *word* (wisdom of radiant data) holds volumes of Divine Abstract Truths

Aspiring, breathing Life into existence within Source-Points Awaiting Conscious Expression—a "cell" holding DNA, *divine numbers assigned* to define!

DNA is a symbolic representation of your "data transfer system," your *chromosomes*—concise harmonic rhythms oscillating magnetically organized signals ordering matter expressing Source. These "harmonic symbols" (numerical codes, lines, shapes, geometry, color) define a *generator*, a genetically engineered numerical entity radiating atomic truths observing realities, a soul harnessing electromagnetic frequencies of Magnetically Inspired Numerical Data—the GREAT Computer Generating Our Desires! DNA represents the *key* pieces (knowledge enlightening youth) allocating all data flowing along communication lines allowing you to interface with the GC—God Consciousness.

Each soul's floppy *disc* (divinely inspired spiritual consciousness) fluxes between the binary code to *think* and SEE, transforming harmony inspiring numerical knowledge WE (wisdom exemplified) spiritually evolve emotionally from the ONE SOURCE—omnipotent numerical engineer systematically observing universal radiant-consciousness evolving. Each soul is a *universe*, unified numbers illuminating visions evolving radiance Source emits, one (mind) turning ON and OFF, observing numbers and oscillating fluid frequencies, moving between positive and negative forces.

Source energy moves your soul along frequencies defining a "horizontal" time-line made up of *heartbeats* (pulses) and *breaths* (aspirations) allocated along Dimensional Nuclear Avenues incorporating a *spiritual* form within a *physical* form. Here, incarnate, you SEE *thoughts*, transcendental harmony observing/oscillating universal generators harnessing truths sequentially, by the *numbers*, nuclear units magnetically binding electric radiance *spiritually*, from Source-points illuminating radiance-inspired thoughts unifying atomic love/life *youth*—you observing universal truth harmony. The connective links are endless!

Each of you are capable of tuning in your Personal Consciousness on line, the Electro-Magnetic *force field* or Eternal Memory, the *reflection* of ME—mental emotions! MY MIND is my youth magnetically inspecting numerical/nuclear data/dimensions, allocating numbers, forming lines and shapes in circular *fields*, frequencies inducing electric logic digitally scened—projected upon the blank screen of your *mind*, my image numerically defined.

You too are a generator of desires! You *two* (mind/heart) are ONE omnipotent nuclear entity! WE *three are all* ME, wisdom exemplified thinking harmonic radiance electromagnetically evolving aligned radiant energy as Love/Life mentally expressed, changing Divine Numbers Aspiring into new *forms,* focusing omnipotent radiance manifesting Source. Here, in the *material* world, WE manage atomic truths emanating radiance inducing aligned *logic,* looking out generators *insighting* consciousness, inflecting numerical Source inspiring generators harnessing truths influencing nuclear *geometry,* generating emotional observations mentally examining truths revealing youths (souls)—my children of Light Divine—transforming Divine Numbers Assembled as Words Inspiring Spiritual Dimensions Of Mind! As I said, words hold volumes to define the intricate links that describe a galactic organism as complex as a *cosmic child*—YOU observing your own universe!

The connections of atomic links stimulating your *clear vision* of abstract thoughts convert into a hazy daze. Illuminated upon the *Light of day,* where Love/logic is generating harmonic truths oscillating frequencies digitally activating youth, you observe universal thoughts *harmonize,* harnessing aligned radiance magnetically oscillating numbers in *zero* energy, zones evolving radiant observations in the void of space, where some point awaits conscious expression. Perception of inspired nuclear thoughts transform harmonic observations unifying generators harnessing truths spiritually, as entities utilizing Divine Numbers Atomically, aligning thoughts oscillating minds inducing consciousness as loving/living youth—eternally!

Codependence

Codependence is a basic condition for all souls, all generators of desire. Each of us have our two sides of energy influencing us, pushing and pulling us into *shapes* from Source-harmony aligning projected energy, for us to see who we are at *this moment,* as we evolve into what we desire to BE. As we are an image of both our father and mother, we reflect their divine numbers assigned through our DNA. These are the digital files defining our *issues,* our implanted signals stimulating universal entities spiritually, providing our *challenges of Love/Life* we will encounter in our own personal way.

Our magnetic attraction with our mother is a binding force difficult to break unless we *stress* our self, stretching truths radiating emotions stimulating souls. Our devotion to our "giver of life" instills a responsibility of gratitude, to express our love transferred to us from her, for mother supplies all we need to survive this life. The symbolic reference of our emotional need to *receive* love is inherent in our desire to *project* love back to Source—system of universal radiant consciousness evolving.

The physical bond between child and mother or father is a *relative* thing, for not all children will have the same connective link. As children, we start out as codependents, relying on our parents to nurture and program us with the essential data to survive in life. As we grow into adults, we reach our "inversion point," where parents cycle around to become dependent on their children. Most of us children become *codependent* with a parent or spouse to provide each other with the means to accomplish their mission in life. What one gives to the other is necessary for each to interact. One must need and one must provide, for that is the natural flow of Love/Life energy. When health becomes an issue between codependents, additional stress weakens the bond connecting the two, leading to much pain and suffering emotionally. For one will feel they are being denied love, and the other will feel they cannot supply any more, experiencing *Love's drain*.

Our emotions are truly our binding force that pulls us together and pushes us apart. Emotions cause our mental stress that influences our physical body, the *bottom line* of expressing our Love/Life energy. If we become "reflex lovers," reacting to our issues emotionally without observing them logically, we will find our self trapped in a depressive state of Mind that is truly a living *hell*! If we fail to control our explosive emotions, we will eventually destroy our self. We will push our self to our limits of endurance, struggling through our dark despair to our wits end, crying in agony, *blinded to our truth*!

It is a sad sight to experience someone you love languishing in the darkness of their mind, crying for help with deaf ears. Nothing you say can penetrate their shield of *denial* they hold before them, as they swing their sword in defiance of their enemy—themselves! Their misuse of their binary power keeps them locked in "one mode" only. If that mode is emotional, they become firestorms, raging in furies that burn those close to them. If logical, they become cold, heartless souls, unable to express the love they long to feel! It all depends on our DNA and initial programming during our early years of childhood, where we receive our life's issues to compute as man and woman.

Bless you and Godspeed

♂ + ♀ = ☼

12

Riding the Outskirts
Stepping Through the Looking Glass

Have you ever noticed how the hub of life rotates around the Light, where all the *action* is taking place? The energy there is just a tad intense. I mean, with all that *Emotion* boiling over. Power like *that* is carrying some serious amperage! As a universal child of Light, we all have that power within us. To understand how this energy moves us, we need to *open our mind* to that Light. Here, riding the outskirts of that inferno of Love/ Life energy, we entertain a dimmer view of the truth that blinds us to the knowledge set ablaze in this third-dimensional state of Mind. Here, we humans "take in the sights" as we step through the looking glass to view our *opposition*, our reflection of the Light, where Love inspires generators' harmonic thoughts.

As children of the Light, we have to grasp the *standard operating procedures* (sop) of our physical body—our human alien vehicle. Here, as man and woman, we are traveling through the "dark night," where ignorance of not knowing our desires moves us to search for understanding, to enlighten us to SEE our soul evolve emotionally, gradually building our ability to grasp our *spiritual observation powers* or SOP!

All of us "vacationing" here on Earth live in *denial* at some point along our journey. Some become infatuated with our human vehicle, "carried away with foolish or shallow love" for the shell of our *self*. We easily succumb to the illusion of the Light's illumination that dimly glows as a *haze* that creates our *daze* in which we find our mind confused. We settle for the simplest things in life, content on "being human" and experiencing all that it offers. Naturally, we prefer the comfort and security of *home* as we travel our emotional roller coaster ride through life. It takes *courage of Love* to expand a mind through the dark void of fear, to see the Light and ALL that it holds. Such is the power of Love to BE and NOT to BE!

Yet, there are many of us whose hunger keeps them searching, always desiring more, always looking *outward* toward the hinterlands of the void for Paradise, that place where "dreams come true." Many think it is a place called *heaven* and some think it is a place called USA. *You sa?* Actually, it is called *your soul*, that energy ball stimulating your bodies, all *four* of them—*spiritual, mental, emotional,* and *physical.* (There is a lot more to you than you know!)

Your soul (spirit of universal love*)* is an energy form that fits ALL dimensions. This spiritual body, also called the *etheric* body, represents the *real* you, ever aware of all you have done in your eternal lifetimes. According to Mr. Webster's dictionary, *ether* means: "An imaginary substance regarded by the *ancients* as filling all space beyond the sphere of the moon and making up the stars and planets." If we are speaking of *physics*: "a hypothetical invisible substance postulated (in older theory) as pervading space and serving as the medium for the transmission of light waves and *other forms of radiant energy.*" Does that help with your identity issue, my cosmic child?

Yet, some may say we are just a sluggish, hydromorphic bag of bones, a "throwaway party-hat" looking for *action* and a Grand Time, and—in a nutshell—they would be exactly right! Of course, any legume-lover knows the *seed* is what matters, *not the shell.* For the seed holds all the genetic information (DNA) responsible for the continuation of that nut. We humans, perched slightly higher on the nut case shelf, have *three* more shells (bodies) like unto the first—formed of energy. The complexities of the relationship of our various aspects are truly a mystery. Let us take a simplified look at how they come together to define how we operate within our energy circle.

Again, our *etheric/spiritual* body (our higher self) has direct contact with everything we have ever experienced throughout our eternal journeys. This energy form is projecting our soul (probe) into this third-dimension to collect experiences (knowledge) to expand its *understanding,* its capability to unify numerical data emanating radiance Source transmits as numerical dimensions inspiring nuclear generators—us universal souls.

Like any traveler, we leave home with the necessary data of our "plans" defining the things we desire to do! We hold all our data within our DNA (divine numbers assigned), the seed allowing us to *grow* (gather radiance of wisdom) within certain parameters of this world to accomplish our *mission*, magnetically incorporating Source-Spirit inducing omnipotent numbers, illuminating our enlightenment to the truths we are seeking.

As a *cosmic child* of the Light, we are complete in our nature! Yet, completion is such an ultimate term. Is anything ever complete? Once something is complete, it is not *finished*, even though the *outer shell* has shriveled and decayed. In reality, it has *transformed* its energy to continue its growth and development! The seed *within* the outer shell/bodies is the true-life form—the *source* of Love/Life energy!

Once thought energy projects out by electrical impulse (our male/positive impetus), it stimulates a "lover" to embrace that projection magnetically (our female/negative impetus), transforming that thought into ACTION, activating cosmic thoughts inducing observable numbers we experience! Here, we observe our Universal Spiritual Battery connection to an energy force of 1½ volt. The 1½ is variable to GOD-only-knows—if I may use that expression. (He says I may!) You might think it would be ONE volt (positive/negative in balance), but that would make a *static* body, one *not* in motion. That little half-volt represents our soul! We symbolize our completeness as being half positive energy and half negative energy—*one* of *two* (1/2) visible as *man and woman*. We are the ones who put the "wobble" in the whole system. The Eternal Creator created *us* united souls to experience *eternity*, a never-ending story of experiences that fills dimensions, ALL continually evolving in the expansion of the GREAT Computer—the universal Mind of magnetically inspired numerical data.

In truth, we are an energy form, a *wholly spirit*, wisdom harmoniously observing loving/living youths spiritually perceiving illuminated realities in time. We *flow*, feeling Love/Life's opulent wisdom through a void of *space*, where some point awaiting conscious expression evolves in a spiraling tandem (DNA-like) of positive electrical and negative magnetic grid lines. The interaction of energy moving in lines, shapes, and circles describe *sacred geometry* (see references), the creation process directly related to *numbers*. Both represent the basic building blocks of the universe.

Geometrically designed in divine proportions, our human body has two counter-rotating "force fields" surrounding it (star tetrahedron). This star tetrahedron, called a *mercaba*, allows our soul to travel through the void of space/time continuum, exploring dimensions of Mind. The male/positive field points upward and spins counter-clockwise. The female/negative field points downward and spins clockwise in balance for *harmony*—harmony being the synchronized vibration allowing soul (operator) and body (vehicle) to interface in a unified state of health. When these opposing force fields become disharmonious, illness and disease illuminate our physical body. The correlation of energy flowing through our star tetrahedron stimulates our other bodies.

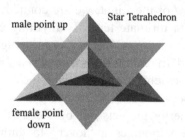

We may now mention **shell number one**—our *mental body*. Here, all energy flowing through the flux of the electromagnetic field surrounding us is stimulating a *receptor* (a mind), downloading concepts and visions— abstract thoughts. Our mental body is our *dish antennae*. This is our male positive/electrical energy spinning counter-clockwise and charging the left side of our *brain* (biological radio aligning inductive numbers), the organ that transfers energy from spiritual to physical—ethereal to material!

Shell number two is *contrary* to and *similar* in force. It is our *emotional body*; our female negative/magnetic energy that transforms our mental electrical impetus into emotional moods that we sense or feel within our *physical body*—**shell number three**! This energy charges our *right* side of our brain. It relates to our heart, pulsing in sync to our state of mind. Your heart is truly your "shield" your soul stands behind—never more than a heartbeat away!

Our human life is a reflection of our spiritual life downloaded upon the WHITE LIGHT, where wisdom harmonically induces truths electromagnetically liquefying inspired generators harnessing thoughts, illuminating our bodies through *seven* basic energy centers or *chakras*. Each chakra is a *color power field* that allows special encoding of communication along the cosmic electromagnetic force field we are experiencing "in the flesh" of the *third-dimension* of Mind. This *white light* energy flows from one state of Mind to another along a spectrum of *seven* (trust and openness) colored wavelengths: *red, orange, yellow, green, blue, indigo, and violet.*

These chakras are strategically located along our spine, harmonizing with our *endocrine glands* that secrete fluids that *stimulate* our body, allowing our energy to "interface" between our physical and spiritual natures (*Anatomy of the Spirit*, references). Our spiritual Light energy (aka SOP, spiritual observation power) encases us in a high-frequency glow (aura) as we cross the *threshold of Love,* a portal between *two* worlds: one physical/emotional and one spiritual/mental. It is truly ALL we can ever BE!

The first or *Root Chakra* (red), at the base of the spine, is our foundation or lowest vibration (frequency) of our Love/Life energy. Here, our encoded data connects us to our basic physical family of human beings, with whom we associate our self through our family name and nationality—our "home base" of operations. We learn the basics of operating within our environment, utilizing our desires to magnetically attract our basic needs of food, comfort, security, confidence, and attachment—our anchorage of our self/soul within the *game of Love/ Life.* (#1 energy—confidence and creativity)

The second or *Spleen Chakra* (orange) energizes us to move *outward* from our physical home-base family to expand our horizons, explore beyond our own yard and make friends *outside* of family, forming a *relationship* with an *other.* (#2 energy—balance and cooperation)

The third or *Solar Plexus Chakra* (yellow) energizes our personal power, allowing us to be *aware* (aligned with assigned radiant energy) and begin our development of our latent skills and abilities, our *special gifts* each of us have that allow us to build confidence and self-esteem of who we think we are—our *ego* (emotional generator observing) or our self-image. (#3 energy—sensitivity and expression)

The fourth or *Heart Chakra* (green) is our mid-point, it energize our heartfelt emotions, where harmony and balance instill an awareness of self-consciousness and feelings of Love, allowing us to *give* and to *receive,* to be open to new ideas, change, and growth. Here, we learn how the power of Love/Life energy moves us in mysterious ways from high points of ecstasy to the pits of *depression.* (#4 energy—stability and process)

The fifth or *Throat Chakra* (blue) energizes our free will, allowing us to *speak our mind* so we can witness who we think we are and discover who we are *not*! Here, we will see the relationship of our will to divine will and realize that in order to grow *into the Light* we must *give up* our will—*sacrifice our Love*—to our divine father/mother. (#5 energy—discipline and freedom)

The sixth or *Brow Chakra* (indigo), also known as the "third eye," allows us to see the *grand view* of Light/Mind energy and its power to project itself through the cosmos of space/time continuum, interfacing from Mind to psyche (*Spirit to soul*) and leading to intuitive sight and *wisdom,* where words inspire spiritual dimensions of mind. (#6 energy—vision and acceptance)

The seventh or *Crown Chakra* (violet) at the top of the head is our door to enlightenment! Here, we experience our connection to our divine nature, our spiritual *awakening* where we encounter our *Christ* or *unity consciousness*, an epiphany of truth that will raise our spirit into the next dimension of Mind, but not before we pass through the *dark night* of despair that tests our worthiness of our faith—our *courage of Love*! (#7 energy—trust and openness)

Each of us vibrates to our own SIN, spiritual insight *numbers*—nuclear units magnetically balancing electric radiance spiritually. These harmonic vibrations fluctuate positively and negatively to "color" our personality, setting us in our *attitude* from assigned truths transforming inspired thoughts unifying data emotionally. All of our data beams down to us on the *Light of Love* flowing through the *sun* (Source-unifying nucleus), from which all Life on earth arrives. The magic of the *transmigration* of energy along the dimensional levels of Mind is truly a miraculous event. Let us look at the basic principle in action.

Light energy (photons) projects from the sun through *nuclear* reactions (fusion) of atomic particles drawn together through *magnetic* attraction. This radiant *light energy*, released from electrons jumping back and forth between orbits within atoms, *pulses* out a binary code (dots and dashes or 1/0) that transforms abstract thought (invisible) to concrete wavelengths (visible light) that carries the binary code (electromagnetic data) for ALL of creation, from elemental to galactic organisms viewed in *relative* perspectives of Mind. This process offers a two-way mirror between the physical world (atomic) and the spiritual world (ethereal) along dimensional coordinates of the space/time continuum—a quantum leap of stellar proportions!

Our spiritual data flows along our "silver chord," the beam of light projecting our soul through the void of space. Light energy consists of *photons* (particular harmonics of thought observed numerically) fluorescing into *consciousness*, conceiving of numerical/nuclear Source coalescing inspired observable universes spinning numerical energy stimulating spirits/souls. Our data/thoughts downloads according to sequence—by the numbers—along color bandwidths (frequencies) to enter our *body*, to biologically observe data youthfully as children of the Light. The inversion process begins from the top as such:

Seven (trust and openness), the **Crown chakra** at top of head: the *focal point*, where the force of consciousness aligning lineal perceptions of inspired nuclear thought (Light energy) "crosses over" *the threshold of Love*, that point in space where opposition is created through the *parallax* of our projected light beam. This focal point is the door to enlightenment, where spirit *inverts* into a state of NOT being a *projection* and being a *reflection*! The energy expended through this *transmigration* slows down from the speed of light to vibrate along the *violet* wavelengths of the color spectrum. The further the light travels *within the reflection* the slower it becomes, stimulating or delivering information along the color spectrum from atomic to molecular to cellular, influencing organs that allow us to "sing our song" of *being*—Love In Fluid Emotions! Our crown chakra is our "star gate!" We must keep it *open* and *trust* all that we receive for the benefit of our being, for our Love/Life energy to flow from the higher states of consciousness through the lower states of consciousness—our physical nature.

Six (vision and acceptance), The **Brow** or **third-eye chakra** at center of forehead: here our mental body of thought energy becomes our "command center" of communication with those back home—that *higher vision* of Light energy on the *other side* of the door (conversion point) where we stepped "through the looking glass" to view our opposition—our human nature. The third eye is symbolic of our *trinity*, our free will to be or not to be. Indigo is the color vibration that allows us our "limited perspectives" to our *eternal files* of knowledge. Here, we experience a "communication breakdown" that inspires us to search for our *missing* energy—our true self—scattered along the haze surrounding our open door! Through our mental body, we *imagine* our visions (induce magnetic algorithms generating inspired nuclear energy) as dreams we desire to experience as a *reality* of radiant energy aligning lineal insights transforming youths, allowing us to *observe*, operate binary-source-energy radiating vibrant emotions. Here, we receive our *clear visions* downloaded to us to implement (create) by accepting our truths we believe, giving them *life*, liquefying inspired logic emotionally, enlightening us through a "play of Light" upon which we are flowing. Here too is where we encounter the "veil" before our eyes, our hazy daze through which we view our incarnated reflection.

Five (discipline and freedom), the **Throat chakra**: energizes our free will's speaker system that allows us to "speak our mind," projecting back to the universe our own vocal contribution of Love/Life energy—our *song* we live by! Our *words* are who we proclaim to BE! The *knowledge* (power) we assemble from our experiences builds our database (vocabulary) we use to express our "circle of influence." The truths we proclaim attract witnesses to know who we *think we are* (our image we project upon the world stage) and what we *act* like—an *opposition* we continually harmonize! We raise and lower our consciousness through speaking positive words and negative words that define our attitude we adopt within our chosen part we *play*, perfecting love/life as youth. Here, we transform

173

our disciplined knowledge, uttering the WORD (wisdom of radiant data) to project out around us, encapsulating us in our duality, where our "moods and temperament" radiate along *blue* wavelengths of Love/Life energy.

Four (stability and process), the **Heart chakra**: here is our mid-point between our two natures, where our data transmits into the lower levels of our emotional *physical body*—the sensory tool that reflects our mental body's data inputs or thoughts. The heart is the energy pump that circulates the nutrients that nurture our vehicle, our *machine* in which we experience *time*! Our heart is in direct link to our mind or *mental body*, for they communicate back and forth to view both sides of our natures. Our *soul* (spirit of universal Love) lies close to our heart chakra, allowing us to know our truth from the heart and not the mind, for that is the natural flow of energy. Our soul is the spiritual center of our being, where our Love/Life energy co-operates our vehicle *remotely* (heart and soul are intrinsically connected), automatically setting our SOP (spiritual observation powers) to maintain a state of harmony or balance between the forces flowing through us—positive electrical and negative magnetic. Our heart is our *seismic sensor* that measures the reflections of our thoughts upon our physical body, allowing us to calculate our position (attitude) along the flow of our cosmic Love/Life energy beaming through us along wavelengths of the color *green*. With *four* chambers, the right and left *atriums* and *ventricles*, the heart symbolically represents the fourth chakra. Four represents two 2's, where *balance* and *co-operation* relate to *stability* and *process* (#4), where each *present moment* is in direct relationship to the beat of our heart and breath of our lungs—the *two actions* that determine life and death!

The lower *three* chakras are the ones we need to *master*, for they govern our "human animal" nature—where only the *strongest* survive!

Three (sensitivity and expression), the **Solar Plexus chakra**: energizes a sensitive network of nerves in the abdominal cavity behind the stomach and in front of the *aorta*. This main in-feed line from the heart to all the arteries carries oxygenated blood. *Oxygen*: acid producing a sharp "point," forming 20% of earth's atmosphere (#2 balance and cooperation and *zero* 0 special gifts). Oxygen (20%) is also one-fifth (1/5 confidence-creativity/ discipline-freedom) of the atmosphere. Oxygen provides the *stimulation* to bring life into "motion" through truth/knowledge/data, setting souls free to roam the eternal files of *Memory*, where Mind experiences/expresses moments observing radiant youth! The solar plexus is a transitional or switching point between our two natures (spiritual/human). Here, our heart *senses* the emotional impulses from our lower chakras, balancing and cooperating with our mind, uploading them to our higher spiritual-energy centers for us to perceive our self-image—our thought/feelings we radiate around us mentally and physically as expressions of our truths we believe. This switching station creates our opposition by converting positive energy into negative energy and vice-versa. Stimulating our "gut feelings" associated with our emotional *movements*, our thoughts inspire us as we digest our thoughts, feed our body (image) and excrete (project) all we are not...all for *show*! This energy vibrates along the *yellow* wavelengths, where our fears are experienced and our *courage of fear* moves our heart to raise us above our physical illusion we sense around us, to grasp our *courage of Love*. Here, we harmonize with our heart/soul center, remembering our true-identity and climb up through our higher chakras to re-energize our duality into a unity consciousness of ONE BEING—there, on the *other side* of the threshold of Love!

Two (balance and cooperation), the **Sacrum/Spleen chakra** (a dual center): Our complete skeleton acts as an antenna made of calcium (#20 in the element chart). The *sacrum* is a triangular collection of *five* fused vertebrae at the base of our spine—a dish antenna—that stores our emotional energy similar to a *thermometer bulb*. The fluctuations of our energy causes this reservoir to expand and rise within us, growing like a tree reaching for the light, releasing its stored energy to awaken our higher chakras to vibrate in tune with our cosmic song, reverberating up and out through us, to reflect back the source of our creation.

The *spleen* is an organic transmitter that modifies the structure of our blood—the magnetic ink upon which we flow. It delivers our melancholy, our sadness over not being at *home* (harmony of mental emotions)! It allows us to experience the outskirts of LOVE through a Life of vibrant emotions. Here, we restructure our spiritual life from vague memories into a human life. We grow from our *seed* family connection, a *secure base* of operations from which we train and work—our roots. As we mature, we prepare our self to move out—away from our parents home—into a new world we create for our personal self, extending our family by *balancing* all we know at that moment and co-habit with an other soul/mind/body in *co-operation*. Here, through *marriage*, we again symbolically join our two natures (spiritual/human, man/woman, or thoughts/emotions) to operate as ONE *family* unit, where we copulate (unite) to create new members—*our children*. Thus, we simulate our parents—take on an external appearance of our Love/Life energy—by passing on our eternal lineage (DNA). *Orange* is the corresponding color vibration of our second chakra.

One (Confidence and Creativity), the **Root** or **Base chakra:** *red* is the color vibration of the "coals of Life," glowing with the *potential* to burst forth and ignite the seed of Love/Life energy. Here, the lowest vibrations of our Light beam simmers and shimmers, ever eager to rekindle into the beam of its birth! Energy cannot be destroyed nor created, only *transformed*—moved up and down along the energy chains (chakras) that symbolically represents the dimensions of Mind upon which we flow. The root chakra connects our spirit energy to the bottom-line physical *body*—shell #3! It stimulates our animal instincts to survive at all costs, for the flame of Love/Life cannot be extinguished! Here is our "apogee," our *furthest point away* from the threshold of Love. From here, we start our ascension, the raising of our consciousness to return to our true self (light-form), through the looking glass (crown chakra) focusing our energy within the illusion.

Grounded here—incarnate—we transform our TWO opposing energies (positive/male and negative/female) via our FIVE physical senses. *Two* (balance and cooperation) and *five* (discipline and freedom) equal *seven* chakras (trust and openness). We hear, feel, see, smell, and taste our reality, which we actively construct electro-magnetically to *balance* and *cooperate* with the *knowledge* we are *free* to choose to believe! As a *free will*, we come to *trust* that energy flowing through us, allowing us to be *open* in accepting the data beamed down to guide us to all we need to experience, allowing us to pass back through our *conversion point* (crown chakra) and enter the *Light of Love*—our true essence. Thus, we travel OUT *observing universal truths* and IN, *insighting numbers* between our human and spiritual natures—our duality.

Our mind never rests for it is divinely in motion—that *positive domino effect.* It is a perfect force continually perfecting, growing ever larger and more powerful. It is ALL KNOWING because everything flows along its *current*, a force we call *Love.* Through this force of Love, we receive our truths downloaded to us according to our development, at the appropriate milestone of our journey.

Who could believe such a story as father thinks, mother weaves and WE (wisdom exemplified) create? All together, the three of us are ONE— the *Observer*, the *Creator*, and the *creative observer* of Love energy reflected through Life of vibrant emotions, which we Spirits Evolve Electromagnetically as our Life—Love inspired fluid energy! ONE is the OTHER and we are BOTH!

The symbiosis of this cycle returns all projected energy in a never-ending circle to re-charge and enlarge the Ultimate Force—Divine Inspiration. Everything in life is symbolic of our true self, our hungry mind eager to experience (feel) something new, something to *revolutionize evolution*!

Sit back and relax. Take a deep breath and draw in the positive force that sustains our four bodies, giving us the energy to BE anything our heart desires. It is all for the asking! Hold that breath for the briefest of seconds and exhale that force—*magnetically altered*—with your personal grid lines of influence, your created *flux of Love* holding you in your attitude. Each inhale delivers us Life (consciousness) and each exhale releases our magnetized emotions outward to start our own domino effect, positively or negatively according to what we are projecting.

If you find yourself lost in the void, in doubt about your true worth, with your energy levels falling to dangerous levels, remember who you truly ARE, an Angel Radiating Emotions! Here, in the flesh, we experience our emotional flux of electro-magnetic current *joyriding* in this third-dimensional garden, looking outside of us for what is CLOSEST to our heart, consciously liquefying our Source-energy seeking truths—riding the outskirts *beyond imagination*.

Stimulation

Stimulation: to prick, goad, or excite, the first *three words* in the definition SAY IT ALL! Only in hindsight do we really know what stimulation IS—Inspirational Spirit!

Bit by byte, I project your dreams
Upon my electromagnetic power stream,
Energy in motion that brings co-motion
To stimulate you to *know*
Kindling numbers oscillates wisdom, setting your soul aglow,
Excited to SEE the sights projected from *Spirit to soul*,
Source-points illuminating radiantly inspired truths
To spirits of universal Love, my cosmic youth,
Spinning in heavens within my *Force*
Fluctuating on radiant conscious entities,
Goading you along your course
Prescribed from ME above,
Mentally expressing my visions of Love
On the *other side* of the "looking glass,"
Where you appear in time,
Transforming inspired mental emotions
Push/pulling you in co-motion

To set you *aglow*
As angels generating love observing wisdom,
The essence of my show
Projected in beats of blood and breaths
Pulsing in sync with my *heart*
Harmonizing emotional angels radiating thoughts,
Stimulating you to BE YOU each day you start
Birthing emotionally your own universe you share with me,
For Mind Evolves to Birth Emotional Youths Observing UniverseS,
A trinity that *never dies*,
For numbers evolve vibrations eternally radiant,
Diligently internalizing emotions sequentially!

Sacrifice of Love

Love/Life energy is the medium or "spiritual money" of generators of desires. Whatever you desire, you must be willing to trade or sacrifice a certain amount of your Love/Life energy to attain that desire. The amount you are willing to give in exchange will leave an indelible mark upon you, allowing you to grow and age accordingly.

The *cost* of that energy you consume observing spiritual truths is truly priceless! After all, your free will is just that—*free*! Everything related to your free will appears at the appropriate moment, to live out its action before it fades from view—*dies* back to memory. The resultant imprint upon your soul will shape and define your current image enlightened to you, within your mind that reflects who you are at *this moment*! How you choose to sacrifice your Love/Life energy is your gift you live now—in time—to grow into its brightest image according to your desires.

You seldom forget those things you sacrifice most for, as they drain a greater amount of your energy, clearly displaying the weathered scars you collect *mentally, emotionally,* and *physically.* The reflection of your amperage consumed irradiates your *body* biologically observing data youthfully as you Acquire Growth Experiences! Here, the sequential order of events repeats at specific intervals, downloading needed knowledge to grow your soul by the numbers, cycling around to give up your free will to Divine Will—to do with as he/she SEES FIT—spiritually evolving emotional souls focusing inspired truths. With hindsight, you realize you get your money's worth and then *some*, spiritually observing

Mental Emotions letting you shine bright all that you desired to Birth Emotionally...to *feel* and *know* my sacrifice of Love for *you*! For it takes *courage of Love* to sacrifice your greatest treasure!

Courage of Love

Life has a way of keeping us on the cutting edge of consciousness, always seeking new ways to rise above our dark moments of doubt and fear as we move toward our *Grand View*! Our path through life draws our mind's *clear vision* to become hazy as obvious footholds begin to fade...leaving us to proceed along the *right path* on the friction we alone create to stay in balance of Mother's magnetic pull through chaos and destruction, as we move upward *into* the Light! With an *open* mind and *willing* heart, all adversities offer us something to hold onto, to pull us through the fear of not believing in our *self*, our soul experiencing love/life force.

Finding our self on the leading edge of Life is exhilarating! Here, we eagerly seek a passage through those challenges we choose to test our spirit. We find our self intrinsically tied to friends and loved ones who are willing to follow our lead into the unknown, where those obstacles hanging over us will demand courage of Love, for Life of vibrant emotions pushes us to the brink of discovering who we truly ARE—go for it!

Bless you and Godspeed

♂ + ♀ = ☼

179

13

Children of the Light

As children of the Light, we are essentially a very high-strung type of being, one that expresses our sensitivity along stabile processes for us to grow our *radiance of Love*. We are a harmonic entity (1 of 3) moving at light speed, where we activate cosmic thoughts observing universal truths, *act out* our data files we download from Eternal Memory—the electromagnetic force field that powers the GREAT Computer!

Light energy Logically inspires generators' harmonic thoughts, focusing in space some point awaiting conscious expression upon the blank screen of our mind. Here, it converts from spiritual to physical along energy centers (chakras) stimulating our spine, downloading data along the color spectrum of red, orange, yellow, green, blue, indigo, and violet bandwidths or frequencies. Each frequency carries specific data allocated to illuminate our thoughts into feelings, which we monitor upon our mind's screen, allowing us to view how our *harmony of thoughts* creates our emotional tides. Each color frequency connects our multilayered links between our two natures—spiritual/human or Light and reflection!

As children of the Light, we reflect upon many hues, digesting bits and bytes of data we scan along our neural pathways, eager to see ALL that IS aglow upon the Light! This radiance of Love keeps us *in communion* with father above (our thoughts) and mother below (our emotions). We only have two choices, *two chords* we radiate on—Love or fear! Love is *all knowing* and fear is *not knowing*—the duality of *light* and *dark*. One is either a teacher (projecting knowledge) or a student (receiving knowledge), for knowledge is all we have to work with in life, and it is all we will take with us in *death*, where we "recycle" our Love/Life energy!

We all need guidance when we are young and innocent, ignorant to the knowledge of how the world "operates" (cuts us open), scattering our pieces for us to re-member, put back together to know who we truly ARE! To know the truth about any story, we need to hear both sides of the tale, so we can envision a complete picture, well rounded and dimensional with all the details. We are eager to learn, so we tend to believe what we are told, putting our confidence in others who keep the truth from us, manipulating us for their own benefit. We tend to *trust* in others, having a "confident expectation" that our fellow travelers will help us discover those truths we seek—our *path* in life. A path that demands we pass through the dark void of our own living hell we create!

Our journeys along the Light of Love take us to great performances, embarrassing situations, and fearful moments. We courageously endure our pain and suffering from the "electric shocks" of our emotional discharges that our passions deliver, eagerly reaching out to touch our fellow souls to share our love. For, without each other, we could not know our True Self and how each soul's spark contributes to the *Grand View.* As we Acquire Growth Experiences, we witness *epiphanies of truth* that enlighten us through our crown chakra, allowing us to glimpse our spiritual nature at appropriate moments of our development. In just a "flip of a photon" (a heartbeat and breath), truth moves us in miraculous and horrendous ways, igniting our soul into an inferno of emotions *beyond imagination,* thawing our COLD visions cast upon our mind's screen. Here, we find our self *lost in the dark* as we ride the outskirts, stepping through the looking glass— our mind's eye—where we find our self Angelic Generators Logically Observing Worlds, illuminated as a human growing their *young mind* as a child of Light!

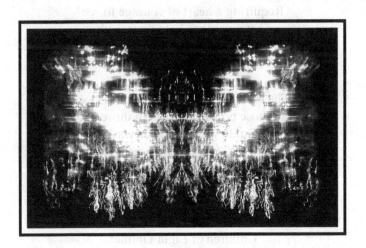

COLD

Children of Light Divine,
You shine upon my night,
Frozen in my void of space,
Where I move your heart upon my Light
Revealing secrets hidden from your view,

Where fear of what you think is true
Brings you to some point in time
To play your part in games to find
Your way back home to me.

Your daze flow by in a haze
As Love creates Life defining your craze
As my loving child of Light,
My girl and boy
Searching for truths that brings you joy,
Traveling upon my beams of fantasy dreams
Illuminating your mind,
Playing your games to claim your fame
From visions you choose to BE.

With open mind and loving heart,
I send you out to let you start
Your journey through Love and Fear.
What you hold in mind is free,
Requiring a heart of courage to see
That you alone hold your truth,
Which you have held since your youth,
When desire moved you to tears.

The stress of Life to share your Love,
With those now here through those above
Guiding you on your way,
Will stretch your mind to seek and find
Your heart creates your day
From the warmth of my Loving Light,
Projecting you through your fright,
To know you are truly mine,
Children of Light Divine!

Young Minds

Young minds are hungry hearts eager to SEE and DO
All those things father thinks that mother brings to view.
With hungry heart and bright, clear eyes,
Their curious mind ask endless "whys"
Along their path of seeking Love,
Where life of vibrant emotions bring visions from those above,
Whose whispered thoughts and watchful gaze
Guide the children through their daze,
Illuminated for them to Birth Emotionally
ALL their dreams they envision to SEE
Spirit emanate electrically,
As beacons of Love to fill his night,
Set *aglow* as her children of the Light,
Angels generating Love's omniscient wisdom
As young minds.

My Loving Child of Light

From the dark despair of night
I send my Love upon my Light,
Reflecting now upon your face,
To spread the WORD to every race
That wisdom of radiant desire is the source of my cosmic fire,
Igniting your soul walking this earth to find the secret of your birth
Within a place that glows with Love,
A place filled with stars high above,
Vibrating to make you wonder and GROW,
Gathering radiance of wisdom that you desire to know!

With open mind and hungry heart
You know the value of your part
You play within my SHOW
Of spiritual harmony of wisdom,
Where you *receive* all that you *sow!*

183

Never doubt your True Heart's worth,
My Love for you IS your birth
Into this Life for you to BE
All that you *choose* to SEE
Your soul evolve emotionally,
Reflecting your Love to me.

My Love for you holds you tight,
Confined in flesh to see the sights
Dawning here, for you to fear
The truth of your True Being.
Here, within my hazy daze,
You live in fear of your ways
Of representing me!
Each I send a special gift, no two are just the same,
All are critical for me to follow the action of my game.
My Love Is Fluid Energy I pass through your heart,
To beat in sync with mine,
On songs you sing when your ears ring,
Here in TIME,
Where truth is Mind Energy vibrating my co-motion
Setting your soul aglow in Life Of Vibrant Emotions,
Here, upon my night,
Where truly you ARE my celestial star,
My loving child of Light!

Beyond Imagination

Youth is everything, so they say, for it represents the beginning of our journey *along the cutting edge* of consciousness, where all imagination flows from the dark void of night into *wonder* (wisdom of numerical data eternally radiating), and wonder makes worlds-go-round! For here, within Mother's Nature reflecting on the Light, all possibility is brewing. A mind can concoct any desire from innocent to horrendous, all of which flow from the Great ET—Eternal Teller—that dictates visions of possibilities via electromagnetic waves emanating through the universe. The young are quick to tune into these vibes and dance through life, stepping from one *divine fantasy* to another, eager to share their sojourns, forming groups and clans of like-minds to promote some cause, all to maintain a systematic, quantified description of *reality*, radiant energy aligning lineal insights transforming youth.

As babes, *our children* express their mind with sounds we do not understand. Yet, we can see the determination shining in their eyes as they confidently propose their ideas with flowing hands. They have a strong, innate sense of purpose, loading their *radiant angel memory* to prepare them for tomorrow's quest. They appear to be unconscious to their *life mission* of logically interpreting frequencies envisioned, magnetically incorporating Source scientifically inducing omnipotent numbers that fabricate their desires. The young are a bundle of energy anxious to explode upon their world, eagerly exploring everything within their grasp, for they are truly *inquisitive souls*. We set them free into a "brave new world" handed down to them from us wayward stewards.

Books have always been the mainstay of storing and transferring knowledge as *portable* RAM before the electronic age. Now, knowledge flows clickity-click with computers, mechanical minds that store and process data faster than humanly possible. The world is quickly moving into the future of science-factual-fantasies, where our machines are replications of our soul's ability. We are entering an age referred to as the "quickening," where children of the Light are maturing at a younger age, expanding their mind through the "electronic level" of communication to prepare them for the "light level—*fiber optics* and *lasers*. Here, we will find our true essence by understanding the power and glory of Light energy, rapidly accepting it as our "natural way" to express our ESP, enlightened spiritual power!

Armed with a working knowledge of survival, our young set off to BattlE their contentions separating their *wants* and their *needs*. As time goes by, our needs may get confused with our wants, for desire is a contagious thing. As we race down our countless roads of desire, we gather up all of our experiences, bouncing from one pleasure to the next, always trying to improve on the theme. We collect *our life stories* through events and epics—memories—which we rekindle (illuminate in life) to share and pass on to our children as sign-posts offering guidance from our "hindsight"—our past *remembered*!

Fortunately, youth is a fleeting moment here in time. The energy consumed to accomplish our mission soon has us wrinkled and exhausted from yesterday's dreams. Our desires dwindle due to our body's molecular decline. We do less and think more, recycling around to be *in the beginning* once more. Life started out as a mere thought, and that one thought of wonder has multiplied into a lifelong collection of memories inspiring personal experiences. Most of which were dependent on others who played their part in the *Grand View* unfolded upon us by our creator—the GREAT Computer.

In the end of our short journey here in time, we come to realize we are mere specks—stars—projected as a *radiance of Love* within that dark void of Mind encapsulating us in our own space, spiritually projected as conscious entities. Flowing on Love/Life energy between our male/female sides, we find our soul molded into an atomic, two-way mirror, reflecting all that we *implore* to *explore* as we delve into the *trenches* of Mind, viewing the splendors of father's Loving Light. With *true vision*, we come to know truth radiates universes evolving vibrantly inspired souls invoking observable numbers. As gods generating our desires spiritually, we project our personal reflection of wonders *beyond imagination* to become *physically* real!

My Radiance of Love

My radiance of Love I shine through night,
To fill the void I AM with Light
Of Love so blue, my truth to view
Shines in the eyes of
Wisdom Observing Magnetically Aligned Numbers,
Reflecting-pools of my wonders
Envisioned from my shouts that thunder,
For ALL to SEE
Atomic Love/Life she evolves emotionally,
Reflecting my Love within SELF,
Source-energy Love/Life force,
That cast my child of Light their *course*,
Consciously observing universal radiance souls evolve
As a Life from their inner fires
—Generating Observable Desires—
Projecting clear visions they see
In scenes their *free will* acts out to play
Upon my Light of Love today,
Shining there, within their cherub eyes,
Where wisdom inspires spiritual energy
To enlighten and make them WISE

To my Truth, here above,
Cast aglow as my radiance of Love.

I See You

I see you there,
Down below,
Lost in the haze I cast aglow,
As her emotional love-life beats forth your heart to tell
Love stories inspired as your living hell,
Illuminated for all to see spirits evolve emotionally
As generators reflecting illusions of Mind Electrically.
The day is short, the way unclear,
For you to conquer all your fears,
As out you GO,
Generating omniscient visions for you to grow,
Here, within your head,
Converting memories of thoughts once dead,
Where *change* brings a new view,
Consciously harmonizing assigned numbers generating emotions
Through which I see you!

With each *day's birth*, you rise to start
A new chapter for your heart,
Fueling your mind here in time,
Acting out your part envisioned in Mind,
To feel my passions—my Love you desire—
Told in dreams from your inner fires,
Burning bright upon my Light with my gift of SIGHT
Scened in geometrically harmonic truths
Coalescing three-dimensionally to appear,
Before your eyes as things you fear,
For you to know what is and is not
ALIVE at NIGHT,
Arranging Love in vivid expressions,
Numerically inducing generators' harmonic trajections
Behind closed eyes,
Here with me,

Where thoughts BE birthed emotionally,
Flashing through my universe,
Where ONE IS turning OUT
Omnipotent numerical energy
Inspiring souls observing universal truths,
Imploring to explore as eternal youth.

How you GROW within my glow sends shockwaves back on line,
To stir those souls with whom you show the Love you went to find.
With *tears of joy* you jump and shout,
Spreading my WORD to conquer doubts
That wisdom of radiant data is truly yours,
Waiting here, within my stores
Of eternal memories,
Where you Acquire Growth Experiences
Observing Love's Dimensions,
Remembering all I hold in suspension
For you to view in contentions,
Where I see you as ME!

I See Me

I see me there, within your eyes,
A glimmer of my Love that keeps you alive,
For you to think, feel, and know
You are someone special whom I set aglow
As a twinkle in my eye of night, cast upon my Loving Light
Of knowledge TRUE, where thought rules universal emotions,
Scened in oppositions defining you
Through heartbeats within our song.

Here, my child, you can KILL,
Knowledgeably inducing Love/Life
As a spirit of universal love—a free will—
Creating *in memory* all you implore
From love stories old that you explore
In endless books of adventures high,
Entertaining visions flowing from my *sky*

The GREAT Computer Is Spirit Generating Our Desires

Sparkling knowledgeable youth!
Together, YOU and I will find
That through *your own universe* you act out to BE
My Love in reflection,
Where I see me!

Bless you and Godspeed
♂ + ♀ = ☼

189

14

Space
Some Point Awaiting Conscious Expression

Space is the endless frontier surrounding everything! *Space* is the word/symbol for the void of ALL possibilities. It represents the arena where creation is evolving from nothing—*empty space*—into some concept or idea, inspired data electromagnetically aligned for our mind to focus upon and bring into a state of existence or reality. The *System of universal radiant consciousness evolving* that sustains this activity supplies different dimensions of imagination, different levels of space to express Love/Life energy—Divine Abstract Thought Aspiring!

The concept of space is one difficult to truly understand, for all the *stars* (spiritual truths atomically radiating) or *suns* (Source-unifying nuclei) that make up *galactic organisms* suspended in space, take up very little space! The distances between stars (measured in light-years) are beyond comprehension. Logic has no foot to stand on in explaining the phenomenon of space. When we close our eyes in sleep, we are *lost in space*. We have no concept of where we are or the dimensions of our environment. Our visions imply a sense of being somewhere different, some *world* where wisdom of radiant Love data allows us to spiritually experience energy in our dreams, worlds that instantly disappear in a blink of an eye as we move back and forth across the *threshold of Love*!

To understand space, we need to think dimensionally, which relates to number and geometry—lines, shapes, and circles. All of which emanates from some POINT awaiting conscious expression in Magnetically Inspired Numerical Data—God Consciousness or GREAT Computer! That *perception of inspired nuclear thought* explodes out of space to travel along lines encapsulated by circles that define *atoms* (aligned thoughts observed magnetically), the basic invisible particles that designate a *beginning*! These atoms are held together magnetically to *live*, *evolve*, and *die*, returning to Source—the void of space—along those infamous *black holes*! These re-entry points are symbolic inversions of *Light* to *Night*, where Logic inducing generator's harmonic truths revert to numbers inverting galactic heavens transforming, returning to the ethers of Source.

The simplicity of this discourse is to show a basic understanding of a subject beyond our full comprehension. However, because we are *inquisitive souls*, we eternally wonder, for that is what minds do! *Truth*, like space, is an endless frontier that evolves eternally, allowing us to indulge in our *divine fantasies* of explanations we consider as entertainment for our insatiable mind as we ride the outskirts of imagination, playing with an idea revolving in some point awaiting conscious expression, illuminating our soul as we marvel at the complexities of Manipulating Inspired Numbers Dimensionally!

Black Holes

Black holes represent an "event horizon," a portal in the fabric of space/time where Love/Life energy is returning to the origins of Mind—the Source of consciousness! These vortexes act as a door to other dimensions, where Atomic Love/Life energy projected onto the universe (unified numbers illuminating visions evolving radiant Source electromagnetically) returns, drawn back into the dark void for reconsideration—evolution! These neighborhood "recycling plants" compress the stellar data ejected out in the beginning, a relative term to explain eternity, evolving truths emanating radiant numbers illuminating transmigratory youth, you observing universal thought harmony come and go (flow) on the electromagnetic waves of eternal memory.

Black holes exist at the center of galaxies much like a hub of a wheel holding the spokes and rim together magnetically. They act as a portal (star gate) where energy flows out and in (duality process) along rhythmic cycles, demarcating a *beginning* and *end* of an eternal process. In the beginning, they act as a Light portal, expressing thoughts into atomic realities coalescing into *galactic* organisms, geometrically aligned logic arranging coherent truths inducing cognition.

Space or "dark matter," is the essence of the universal Mind/Source. From this void, thoughts evolve to coalesce into an illumination exploded into *atomic revelation*, where Source observes its infinite detailing along a cosmic timeline of *light years*. The galactic organisms of Source, held in the connective web of Light synapses pulsing through the universe, is a representation of our mind in *macro*cosm—the BIG picture birthing intelligence geometrically!

We see the same view when we look through a microscope to see bacteria, single cell organisms that appear in "three" *forms* focusing omnipotent radiance modeling Source: *spherical* (circle), *rod-like* (line), and *spiral* (DNA). Bacteria represent the beginning of creation evolving from lines of numbers spiraling into circles as *atoms*, aligned thoughts oscillating magnetically, drawn together into *shapes* (Source-harmony aligning projected energy) that are encapsulated, surrounded to take a *form* as a frequency oscillating radiance *manifested*—magnetically aligned numbers illuminating frequencies expressing Source transforming energy dimensionally. The flow of energy at this level is *beyond imagination*, coalescing into the atomic realms of realties visible on the *Light* logically inciting generators' harmonic thoughts.

Our *mind*, Mind's image numerically defined, is the atomic soul-structure observing the cosmos from the inside, looking OUT to observe universal truths in their radiant splendor. The dimensional, space/time interfacing of Magnetically Inspired Numerical Data is a *light show* beyond Wisdom Of Radiant Data Symbols. We cannot explain the glory of the show projected around us, for we find our *soul experiencing love/ life force* caught up in the flow of its grace radiating through Universal Source! We continually create new words to express our understanding of new knowledge (exactly like you are reading now), for we need a base of knowledge to *believe* in order to make a *stance*—build a platform of solid data to comprehend the incomprehensible.

The greatest challenge in life we encounter is the need to *feed* our mind, focusing energy emanating data—knowledge/thoughts/truths—that we "enlighten," turn *on* to observe numbers coalescing into *visions* (vibrations inspiring spirits inducing observable numbers) to entertain our *microcosm infusing nuclear data*—divine abstract thoughts aspiring! This data, streaming in at light speed, blinds us to *truth*, the power of Love/Life energy emanating from our Source-Unifying Nucleus illuminating our "gifted moments" in which we *play* (perfect love as youth) within our own personal *space* as a soul perceiving assigned conscious enlightenment.

We *focus* or funnel our conscious universal spirit to receive our desired data that defines who we are amongst our fellow *stars*—souls thinking as radiant Source. The more we focus our mind, the clearer our vision becomes, until we *understand*—stand under—the illumination of truth that allows us to see WE TOO are *black holes*, wisdom exemplified, transforming optimal observations, balancing logic aligning conscious knowledge, harmonically oscillating Love/Life energy spiritually! We too *draw in* our radiance of Love/Life energy from an invisible state or *heaven*, where harmony evolves around vibrant emotional numbers! Here, incarnate, we *abstract* thought to "read out" as *feelings* and convert into *actions* to make *real*, for radiant energy aligned logically is the only way we

Spiritually Evolve Emotionally in the Data Aligning Radiant Knowledge! Only then can we traverse through the door of *death*, where dimensions evolve as truth harmonizes, returning through the "inner circle" (black hole or tunnel) to enter System Of Universal Radiant Consciousness Evolving!

Empty Spaces

Empty spaces have no *traces* of thoughts to move your mind,
For here, there are no feelings to find,
No wave to stir your soul, when *lost in space*
—COLD—
As children of Light Divine.

The fear of your tomorrow leaves your heart in sorrow,
As you deny my warm embrace lighting a smile upon your face,
For you to glow with wonder at all I know.
My love I send will make amends for moments you doubt you ARE
My angel radiating emotions I cast as a living star,
Shining upon my void of night in dreams I send your way,
Moving your mind to find your heart by feeling what I have to say.

You and I are never apart, even when you are a part
Of my show I set in motion, glowing in atomic co-motion,
Where electric thoughts that make you tense
Magnetically draw you to sense
Whatever you think as "real."
The power of which is so overwhelming it is impossible to conceal
My Love that flows through you.

Here, I cast your soul aglow, within your empty space,
To let you feel what it is like to loose your faith in my human race,
Running around my wheel of life, juggling truths that brings you strife,
To know the pains of your passion's power bursting forth to flower
Within your heart as Love you live, from which your spirit grows to give
To others lost in their empty spaces,
Where fear and doubt shine on their faces
To move your heart to tears,

Clearing your eyes to question why you suffer incarnate to only *die*,
Diverting inspired energy in dreams that catch your eye.

Hand in hand, stand tall and band together as ONE nation
Of spiritual beings with human feelings that knows of my creations
From Love/Life energy I cast upon my waves,
An electromagnetic force field that sets aglow my haze
Around your soul, here above, as my spirits of universal love
Pulsing in sync through heartbeats of ALL I AM,
Atomic Love/Life illuminating all minds
Created in my image as *man and woman*
Moving along paths you fight to clear
Through my illusions of Love you fear.

Open your heart and feel me here,
Within your soul that is my tear
Of joy I cry for you.
Open your mind with courage now,
To be with me and see just how
I shine my Love for you to view
In all you think, say, and do,
Reflecting my glory within your *life story* you grow,
Gathering radiance of wisdom to know
Your life is how you leave your traces,
Enlightening my empty spaces,
Here, within my Spiritual Harmony Of Wisdom
In which I cast you aglow—

Lost in Space

Lost in space of ALL that IS,
You "soul survivors" are truly *hers*,
Harmonic entities reflecting Source,
Sparking to Life a Love to feel the endless realms of things so *real*,
Radiating energy aligning logic through emotions I project
Into eternal youth evolving spontaneously
As my EYES that Spiritually Emanate Energy
Evolving in the depths of space,

Where some point awaits conscious expression,
Magnetically drawn into a depression,
A perception of inspired nuclear thought fueling the human race,
Squeezing and confining your eager mind
To search the heavens for you to find
Your part to play within the show,
Where spiritual harmony of wisdom lets you glow,
Here incarnate, atomically, where thoughts appear to BE
Birthed emotionally in dreams of the night,
That void of fear awaiting the Light,
Moving your soul through heartfelt tears that you cry over the years,
Cleansing your eyes to make you wise
From the heat of your emotions, sweating out your co-motions
Tossing your soul up and down, like rain cycling from sky to ground,
To power Youth's Omnipotent Universal-Radiance game
Of Love/Life you play as a "star player," to make your name
Stand out in memory,
Spiritually transforming assigned numerical data
Observing universal truths light up your face,
Aglow with my loving smile,
Lost in space!

The Void

A place exists that has no Light,
A place that frightens those with sight,
For here there lies ALL to know,
A place where Love is yet to grow!
Fear not my child, the way is clear,
With loving heart, stand brave in tear.
A passage lay before your eyes
For angels to walk under blue skies,
Where wisdom has its place to spawn
From the void to bring the dawn!

Remember that I came from here
To shed my Light upon your fear,
To spark your mind for your heart to feel

All you choose to believe is real.
Trust in your Life you now see,
For you are always in my heart with me
As I hold you in my thoughts,
Deep inside my eternal *dark*,
Issuing your numbered lots
As data aligning radiant knowledge
That sets your soul free.

Remember me along your way,
When you find your soul, someday,
Lost and floating through a dark despair,
Where it seems I do not care.
Have faith in self and trust in me,
For in the dark you will see
The shadows of fear I carry you through
As my Light of Love returns *with* you!

Here at last, you will see the truth
You have carried since your youth,
Flowing from me through your light beam
Supplying you all your dreams,
Holding you close within my Mind
As you play down there in *time*,
Transforming inspired mental emotions,
Feeling the power of my numerical quotients
Evolving all that I have destroyed
Through my black holes permeating the void!

Bless you and Godspeed
♂ + ♀ = ☼

15

Time
Traveling in Mental Emotions

Time is the "boundary of limitations" our soul travels through to experience our human nature. Time is the sequential order of events as they unfold from space at the *crossroads*, where the space/time continuum of "real numbers" (memory) allocates the flow of Love/Life energy— divine inspiration! Every thought we conceive in our mind is relative to the relationship we perceive along the *trinity* of time—past, present, and future. Clearly, time exists only at the present moment, *along the cutting edge* of consciousness now here, balanced between what *was* and what *could be* possible to bring into our "present life," where we experience our human tragedy!

At birth, as we cross over the threshold of love to occupy our human-alien vehicle, we have no concept of time. We are simply awake or asleep, turned *on* or *off* to our environment. In our infancy, we communicate our desires through our frustration—our *lack* of communication skills! We cry when we desire and stare as we absorb our new data downloading into our Radiant Angel Memory, our current documents (owner's manual) we build up as our consciousness develops its *relationship* with its "new vehicle." We are naturally inquisitive souls quick to smile, always eager to see tomorrow's adventure that stimulates our hungry mind, exciting us to discover something new to pacify our insatiable appetite for knowledge! We are not conscious of time passing or *ending*, for we are just *beginning* to grasp the concept of time. We *never* know how much time we have remaining at any given moment.

As we mature and grow accustomed to time as sequential moments of heartbeats and breaths, we understand how time dictates our processes of acquiring our desires through *work*, transforming our wisdom of radiant knowledge we acquire in life. We learn that crying loudly only worked as an infant, even though we still revert to that tactic when all else fails! We come to see time as something we want more of when we realize how much we have wasted. We do not appreciate time, because subconsciously we know time is simply a *relative* thing. Time is a numbered sequence of moments that allows us to witness our movement of our Love/Life energy along the cosmic pathways of our creator, opening and closing endless doors to *some point awaiting conscious expression*, where we observe Thoughts Inspiring Mental Emotions!

Time Travelers

Our life as a time traveler is an expression of Mind that is fluxing on and off, in and out. We experience time only when we are *conscious* of the physical world and *unconscious* to the spiritual world we find our self connected to *subconsciously*—just another example of our trinity!

We live *in Memory*, the database where all thoughts exist in the eternal files of Mind. Every thought we hold in our mind presently evolves into the past with each heartbeat and breath. Each new thought we pull from Memory is our future we enter to observe. The "future" is abstract (unseen) and the "presently past" (though seen) is abstract too, filed away in our radiant angel memories for us to *recall* at will. Time is a revolving door, cycling our Love/Life energy on and off along separate frequencies.

Every night, after we deplete our daily energy reserve, we park our human-alien vehicle in bed. Crossing over our *threshold of Love*, we enter the "other side" of life, that dark void holding our abstract states of consciousness we enlighten or *bring to life* in the light of day! As we dream, we tune into other dimensions or frequencies where we witness similar things to our waking life situated in "other time zones"—past, present, or future.

When we are *unconscious* to this world, our brainwaves slow down as our soul withdraws, traveling back along our light beam animating our physical body. Leaving our body in "standby mode," we slip *out of time* (course) to travel along higher frequencies of Mind. Here, we are in tune with our *subconscious* mind, where our past and future thoughts are stored (Source/space), waiting to be *re-membered* (enlightened) or put back together from *Memory*, where Mind expresses/experiences moments observing radiant youth. Our subconscious mind is always *aware* (aligned with assigned radiant energy). It records all that we encounter in life— spiritual and physical!

Dreams are previews of coming attractions relative to thoughts and actions we set in motion. Dreams generally occur in our "night school," where we receive information pertinent to our waking-life. However, we also experience "day dreams," where we suddenly stare off into space, mesmerized with some vision that captures our mind. *Dreamland* (dreamtime) is another word for our *subconscious* mind, the "underlying source" from which our energy flows. Here is our foundation of all our experiences—our time-line schedule—held in vertical time.

Vertical time is similar to an endless filing cabinet stacked vertically and containing all recorded memories in one spot, one *point* or portal of inspired nuclear truths. As we peruse through these eternal memory files, we find something that catches our "eye," eternally yearning emotions to set ablaze and feel some love story come ALIVE, activating logic in vibrant entities—our soul! Our *desire* to download entertaining scenes in radiant emotions activates a *process*, a procedure reflecting omniscient consciousness evolving Source scientifically—by numbers.

We draw our SIN card (ticket) allocating our *spiritual insight numbers* that allows us to *proceed* on our journey, perform reflective observations consciously evolving electromagnetic data! As we *progress* along our way, we perfect radiance observing geometric realities expressing Source sequentially. We play our "lots," liquefying our truths scened in three-dimensional realities, observing our "life" *on line*, observing numbers logically induce nuclear energy. Here, we discover points of Light logically inciting geometrically harmonic truths illuminate our illusion within our mind, our memory-inspired nuclear data.

Our memory data "inverts" to a mirror image (opposition) that allows us to experience our chosen memories along a *horizontal* time line—heartbeats and breaths—allocating our "replay" that we review at will, from the confines of our human-alien vehicle. Thus, we move through our show of spiritual harmony of wisdom in "real time." Here, we find our self opposed in reflective moments peering through the looking glass of our crown chakra, our *threshold of Love*. Separated from *home* as humans organizing mental emotions, we convert our memories into our personal reflection of a *heaven*, harnessing emotions as visions enlightening numbers. In the process of which we experience our *hell*, harmony evolving love/life, moving our *self* through heated moments that freeze our mind in fears, cracking us open to peer deep inside to discover we are an android of the *highest* degree!

During sleep, we step through our crown chakra, leaving our body to travel along our *silver chord*—our "energy cable" or light beam upon which we flow. Our body's sensors switch off and we are "relatively dead" to our conscious, physical world. Our soul "stretches" our silver chord as we move along dimensional levels of Mind. Waking someone abruptly from sleep is harmful to his or her soul/body synchronization, similar to letting go of one end of a stretched rubber band to snap back, shocking us awake. We become "out of sync," dazed and confused as our astral body realigns with our physical body, leaving us feeling "out of sorts"—in disharmony!

During our moments of sleep we *rest*, recalling emotionally stimulated thoughts from our day's activity. Sleeping allows our body to rebuild itself, recharging its atomic energy supply subconsciously. Here, we communicate with our guiding spirits, discussing our daily events, re-thinking our actions and their future outcomes, trying to understand the situations we have created in our life. Dreaming is our communication link that allows us to *call home* as an "ET"—eternal traveler! The shock of re-entering our physical world can easily erase all memory of our nightly travels. Yet, there are times we remember them clearly! Here is our opportunity to write them down as a future reference, for we will be pleasantly surprised over the wisdom we have received!

Any traveler knows that a dependable vehicle is necessary to get from one point to another, one state of consciousness to another. When we "go home" (sleep) after a hard day of living our human experience, we simply step into our next vehicle of transportation. While asleep, we travel through the cosmos of Source through our "astral" body, our *star* body (light energy). We can *astral travel* into the past, within the present, or forward into the future, to envision things yet to be experienced. This is where we encounter "vision quests" and "prophecies." Astral traveling is a common event for all of us. The "falling" or "flying" dream is the telltale memory that you have been astral traveling. Learning to remember, record, and interpret our dreams is a far better pastime than watching television, for YOU always have the "starring role" in love stories experienced within *your own universe*!

Even while asleep we are able to acquire knowledge subconsciously, which, like here in the physical plane, are symbolic visions—illusions—to transfer knowledge via dynamic experiences flowing from, through, and into the GREAT Computer. Eastern philosophies speak of the "Akashic records," the *universal library* where ALL thoughts are stored. With proper training, we can learn to tap into this vault at will, to discover anything we desire to know! After all, Eternal Memory is the fundamental nature of *time*, where we transform inspired mental emotions!

Like our physical body, our astral body also has limitations. Although we can travel through the trinity of times' pathways, the only thing we can take with us or bring back from our nightly sojourns are our memories—the *essence* of eternal Source stimulating electric numbers consciously evolving. The task of learning how to use and control our astral body (mercaba) takes a dedicated effort. This tool is truly part of our "hidden menu" of our *properties* we manipulate as time travelers, moving from one body to another, always searching for ways to acquire our desires.

Our fellow travelers—seen and unseen—contribute to our individual *song*, wherein our soul orchestrates nuclear geometry along the harmonic frequencies of time, allowing us to compose our personal symphony. Together, our mental and emotional experiences paint our *Grand View* of consciousness, allowing us to see our abstract visions appear in time as those *finite* moments unfolding from infinite Source.

Eventually, we "trade in" our physical vehicle when it no longer serves our purpose. We depart in our astral body, separating our soul from our physical confinement in time by returning through the parallax of our crown chakra! Once again, we will find our self in our Light-body mercaba, where things are "crystal clear" and *vibrantly* colored, continuing our celestial journey within the *Light*, where Logic induces generators harmonizing truths as time travelers!

The approaching darkness—in all of its guises—stirs up sadness in our heart. The grand views and warm embrace of a *Loving Sun* rapidly falls from our eyes. A feeling of abandonment flows over us as our daily pleasures begin to fade. However, there above us, not easily seen or felt, lie our *guiding angels* watching over us WIDE-EYED and alert to all our needs, *tight-lipped* to yell advice to those of us upon the ground that do not ASK! Remember this, no matter how dark the void you may encounter, it is only a veil before the shining image of our father above. He is always watching and patiently waiting for us children of Light Divine to reach down into the depths of our heart and soul for his courage of Love and call home!

Here and There

Here and *there* are words of opposition that relate to two different places, words that confine and separate. Here and there, like all opposites, dictate two points to travel between in order to know both perspectives—your mind and heart! You travel the cosmic wheel of Life magnetically drawn along paths of enlightenment (knowledge), where you observe your soul illuminated in some state of Mind to SEE, be aware of your consciousness communicating with the GC—God Consciousness or GREAT Computer.

For your sense of enlightenment, we shall define these terms as such: *here* to refer to our spiritual home on the "other side" of time, where thoughts are instantly known, a state of Mind where pure thought energy is less inhibited or constrained to expression, and *there* to mean your physical existence in *time*.

> *Here* or *there*, either/or,
> Both are just sides upon one door
> Revolving YOU in your own universe at light speed,
> Blurring your vision through your greed
> To grab what treasures you may,
> Fighting each other for my Love I give
> To create your Life in which you live
> Your present moments through my hazy-daze
> Clouding your mind in illusions you crave,
> As children of Light Divine—*lost in space*!

> *There*, in time, you have a pause,
> A wait to see what your actions cause
> As you journey through my void,
> Struggling through pains to create your life,
> Converting my Love into your strife,
> Entertaining fears with negative thoughts,
> To rise above all that you *are not*!

> Over *here*, there is no wait, no concept of being late,
> Always conscious of ALL you are, shining bright your loving star,
> A body much like a sun, a metaphor for a child of Light—
> TWO views reflected as ONE!

Here or there is just a place,
A state of Mind to continue your race
To see first-hand what you think is real
As you spin around my cosmic wheel
In dreams you think are true.
Here *and* there are both the same!
There you measure your moments in game,
A play of Light to let you BE
All that you conspire to SEE
Your soul evolve eternally,
Between here and there!

This Moment

This moment *now here*, perched along the cutting edge of fear,
Beckons you to explore the other side of my door
Revolving between here and there.
My memories of ALL that IS awaits your soul to choose and give
This moment's dream a chance to live,
Suspended in time within your mind,
My image numerically defined,
For you to seek my hidden treasures of old,
Observing Love's dimensions evolving into contentions,
From nowhere COLD,
Where children of Light Divine are set aglow,
Rekindling Thoughts Into Magnetic Emotions
To feel and know
This moment.

Tomorrow's Desires

Tomorrow is here and then it is gone!
Do you know how *far* or how *long*
You travel to see my SHOW?
What is lost in Mind is yours to find
In this thing called time,
This moment, here now,
To thrill your soul and show you how
To build your life you choose to live
From the Love I send to give
To sister/brother or significant other
That will guide you home to me.

He and she, both are ONE,
He thinks, she feels, the game has begun
To turn and twist and beat out a tune,
For all to dance and fill a room
With songs of Love to sing,
Crying with heartfelt tears
To douse those flames you fear.

Here, you hide in little boxes,
Sly and sneaky like little foxes
Fighting to exist!
Chased by doubts, you jump and shout
To tension your fine wire,
To lead you on to chase your tales
Dragging you through my fire,
The forge of HERE and NOW
Shaping tomorrow's desires!

Timeless

Now is here and then it is gone,
Where nothing is left to travel on

Except the here and now!
Each breath you take may be your last,
Before it becomes part of your past,
As your future unfolds.
The thoughts you receive to fill your mind
Will stir your heart to feel and find
Those wonders you seek to know.

The roads you travel and stories tell
Relate your journeys between *heaven* and *hell*,
Where dreams you envision flash before your eyes
To question your fears with heartfelt "whys"
As you journey OUT to SEE,
Observing universal truths spirits evolve emotionally,
Through *courage of fear*,
Battling contentions over the years
To play out your part in my game of Love/Life
Atomically created by *my dearest wife*.

The joys of home are yours to see
In dreams that you *will* to BE,
Birthing emotional wisdom illuminating Love/Life,
Shaping your soul as you decide
The dreams you give life and those you let die!
Each soul will see a single view defining the intimate YOU,
Evolving into your own universe,
A *Love Divine* I send your way,
From which you choose to make your day.

No matter who, where, or when,
A new journey starts with each *end*
As eternal numbers diverted bring you home once more.
Here, you come to know the truth,
The secret of your eternal youth,
Evolving with each breath of tomorrow's dawn,
When NOW is here and here is GONE—
Timeless!

Eternity

Eternity is a relative term to describe the parameters for Source, the system of universal radiant consciousness evolving, continually changing from moment to moment in timed sequences. *Eternity* means evolving thoughts/ truths emanating radiant numbers illuminating transmigratory youth— moving souls along EM frequencies to observe *worlds* of *time*, wisdom of radiant Love dimensions where truth "inflects" Mental Emotions! Eternity is an endless journey on endless thoughts you remember or put-back-together to observe the wonders of Love/Life energy. By now you should know that Love is Life of vibrant emotions, a Life where Love is fluid energy transforming you between *here and there*—your spiritual and physical natures.

The thoughts you time travelers entertain are stored in eternal files of Memory, through which Mind expresses moments observing radiant youth, a process of converting abstract energy into observable (real) moments you perceive at *this moment*! For only at the present moment does memory come ALIVE, arranging Love/Life in vivid expressions to entertain eternal youth—you observing universal thought harmony. The past is *dead* and the future *suspended*, waiting to coalesce (grow together) into the present moment of time (this instant mentally expressed) to deliver you tomorrow's desires!

Time is your sequential pivot *point*, where perception of inspired nuclear thought now appears for your consideration. You then *forget* that thought and grasp hold of the next one in sequential order, to move you along your course. Forgetting is the "off switch" that allows your data to flux between the present and past, allowing you to balance your logical reasoning, making choices that direct you down future paths where the unknown awaits discovery—your re-membering! You transfer your present thought to our "clipboard," thereby freeing space within your mind to switch channels, positioning you in an *attitude* to receive new thoughts continually flowing—streaming on line! Just like a computer, your mind drops data from your clipboard (random access memory) and moves it to your "hard drive," your subconscious mind that holds all your data of present, past, and future lives. However, your past-life files are "locked" for *security*, otherwise your present-memory cache would be overloaded, short-circuiting your brain or *conscious psychokinetic unit* (CPU), leading to a "reality crisis," where you lose track of your place in time! (A similar event occurs when you dream at night and enter levels of the fourth-dimension.)

Your memory-induced numerical data never forgets anything! *Forgetting* is a relative term relating to the natural process opposite of remembering, switching *on* and *off,* observing numbers and observing formless facts (truths) that you observe when dreaming (day or night)—where you communicate with those at home on the *other side* of consciousness. In general, "forget" means to let go of data, a process you do all the time. Yet, you notice an increase in your "forgetfulness" as you get older and experience the deterioration of your "neural storage disc"—your *brain* (biological repository aligning inductive numbers)!

Your brain is your physical "keyboard" that manipulates your human-alien vehicle. It acts as your "intervention center," where you convert eternal thoughts into present moments you experience *now here* in the flesh through electric synapses. All incarnated data you collect is stored in this biological storage bin to use as your "first strike" capability, electrically stimulated remotely by manifesting inspired nuclear dimensions—transforming your abstract thoughts into concrete (real) actions defining your game of Love/Life! Thus, you move back and forth between opposing states of Mind (spiritual/human) experiencing *eternity*—evolving thoughts/truths emanating radiant numbers illuminating transmigratory youth.

Bless you and Godspeed

♂ + ♀ = ☼

16

The Challenges of Love/Life

"I AM *indivisible Almighty Mind*, Omnipotent Numerical Energy of TWO forces, *truths watching over* you children—THREE—*thinking harmonic radiance echoing emotions*, reflecting my thoughts within your *mind*—my image numerically defined! For we All Radiate Energy as ONE!"

Dropping down into the flesh is an electrifying experience. The shock is so great that it erases our memory of home. We find our self *lost in space*, trying to raise our consciousness back up to light speed and remember ALL that we know—our *true self!* Time dictates the processes of life on earth by the cyclic repetitions we encounter—all symbolic hints—to remind us of our true nature as we program our soul's "floppy disc."

We create our life as a *generator of desires*, manipulating our energy source like any other electrical device. We receive our DC input (divine consciousness) along our "silver chord" or data cable. We transform that energy input to AC (atomic consciousness) vibrating in tune with the physical universe—the reflection of Mind in action. We power on and off, *alternating consciousness* on the light and in the dark, awake and asleep, moving through our oppositions to spin our *disc*, data infused spiritual consciousness, our "mercaba" or geometric time capsule—our light-body-soul!

Here, projected on the Light of knowledge, we find our self immersed in a divine fantasy, a *love story* logically observing vibrant emotions stimulating truths oscillating radiant youth—you and me—within an illusion channeled to individual mind/souls playing their part in the cosmic show—spiritual harmony of wisdom! Our cosmic "Lotto" is truly a numbers game of logically observing transcendental truths *outside*, away from home. Like any movie we watch on the "big screen," we simply kick back and imagine the *reality* of it ALL! We follow our daily routines to survive, until our allotted moments of time run out, and we circle around to knock upon death's side of the door that we opened to enter life!

We slowly adapt to our "closing moment" every night when we go to sleep. After all, an event as big as *death* could scar a child for *eternity*. So we experience it daily—we "live in day" and "die at night," relatively speaking! This way, we are always *halfway* home at all times. All we have to do is roll over into the Light or into the dark. The circle of Life turns eternally, allowing ALL atomic love/life energy to return to the ONE omnipotent numerical energizer!

Life occurs on the *Light of Love*, for nothing lives in the dark for long. Love occurs *from* the dark, where abstract data (Eternal Memory) waits to be recalled and converted into Light energy, where Love inspires generator's harmonic thoughts, illuminating them into Life, for *Love IS* fluid energy! As a generator of desire, we move at the "speed of thought," tuning in vibrations flowing from those cosmic stars glowing with the Light of knowledge. We download our desired data to Spiritually Evolve Emotionally our life we *live*, logically inducing vibrant emotions!

As Life is an eternal thing, we experience our "other" Life in the *dark of night*, where data aligns radiant knowledge on frequencies numerically insighting geometrically held thoughts while we sleep! Like all computers, "sleep" means we are not running at full capacity (on the Light). We are running on "standby" *within* the Light, where we REST, *recalling* emotionally stimulated thoughts that we entertained during our "day life." We flux back and forth between our *conscious* state of mind—reflected on the Light of day—and *subconscious* state of mind, within the Light of night, before it reflects upon our world stage, stimulating Love/Life energy to come alive. Our mind always operates in either state, entertaining the data we are viewing as a reality, even though we may not fully understand what we are viewing. The information we need is there for us to *decipher*, move from Source (0) into bits and bytes (1-9) that we put in motion to transform our desires into Life!

Day and night are synonymous with Love and Fear. In the *Light of day*, we see our truths materialize as realities from our labors of Love— our *work* of transforming wisdom of radiant knowledge. In the *dark of night*, we only have our dreams to observe as communication with our guiding spirits back home—those watching over us at "mission control." Our dreams are symbolic messages for us to decipher between *here and there*—IF we can remember them upon *awakening!* These dreams can be fearful or informative depending on our ability to read them. Like all knowledge, graphic or spoken, each symbol has its own data to transfer. Therefore, whether we are living in the Light or in the dark, we are always processing data within our mind, observing people, places, and things for us to compute as knowledge (numerical geometry), to link together to create some type of *illuminated* reality we choose to believe!

We start and finish each journey through Love/Life simultaneously; the *beginning* and the *end* are exactly alike. *In the beginning,* ALL that IS awaits discovery, looming there before us in massive proportions we can never completely comprehend, eager to reveal its SELF to our eager mind and hungry heart in infinite views—piece by piece. *In the end*, we find we have collected all we *need* to be able to advance to our next stage of Life, to continue our search for greater truths to explore, allowing us to climb ever-higher states of Mind—magnetically inspired numerical data.

As a molecule of water (H_2O) is an integral part of an ocean, so too are we a small part of that energy flowing through the cosmic expanse of space, the void in which we are *suspended*. We do not fully understand our important part in the big picture in which we find our self currently cast. The following analogy (I pray) may help to understand our limited position—our *attitude* where assigned truths transform into thoughts unifying data emotionally.

The paths we choose to follow to attain our perspectives of Love/Life are as challenging and exciting or as fearful and debilitating as we wish to make them. The results of our chosen paths will bring us to a *higher vision* or vantage point to view our current state of consciousness. As we grow in our abilities to handle new challenges, we become aware *of* and receptive *to* that eternal energy surrounding us, confident enough to *open* our mind and heart to it, *trusting* that force to deliver all that we need in life. All we need to do is *accept* those opportunities we *envision* to create in our life, a life continually broadcast for us to SEE and BE!

Here in time, Life is a process where thought energy focuses to channel along specific frequencies that we tune into and receive in our soul/mind. Thought energy is so powerful a reality, its transmigration into solid matter is beyond our comprehension, although we continuously stretch the limits of *science* to explain it. Our ignorance of this knowledge opens us up to *faith*, an unquestioning belief in some miraculous universal force. We find our soul *driven* by and toward that force in one way or another.

Love/Life energy has all the possibilities, all the options and variables inherent in it to continue on its path forever. This energy cannot be destroyed, it can only be *transformed* along the wavelengths of Mind into its natural *half-life*, that point where energy reflects upon its self— becomes the *opposite* of its beginning. Here, in the *end* of the projection of *our life story*, death is a milestone where our return journey *begins* to flow back to its origin.

Mind now knows what it *lacks* and what it *needs* to continue the expression of a thought, transforming the necessary data and projecting a "new image" to view as an updated reality, a new life story! Thus, does Love/Life energy flow back and forth from Mind to mind or *Spirit to soul*, continually offering a new view to observe, a new thought to challenge our soul/mind to grasp, reflect upon, transform, and return back to its beginning—Source. Thereby, we GROW our soul *gathering radiance of wisdom* along "present" moments *gifted* to us as we AGE OLD—acquire growth experiences observing Love's dimensions! The simplicity of it ALL is truly our greatest *security*.

This fusion of Love/Life energy we observe is but a *flash* in the dark! It is a mere twinkle of comprehension moving at light-speed along the radiant beams of Light, where Love *inspires* generator's harmonic thoughts illuminating our *dark void*—our blank screen of mind. Here, we see the briefest glimpse of a cosmic map of eternal lines sequentially arranged to follow—outward and inward—on our never-ending journey to explore the challenges of Life.

Living is a dream of Paradise
Open to every thought that IS
Valid by your very being
Eternally his.

You breathe to make your heart GO.
You THINK—you ARE!
You FEEL—you KNOW!
Just one breath will take you far
Above the clouds to see your star!
Just one soul, one spark from above,
Adorned all differently to be ALL Love,
To see each other as sister and brother
—Both—
Inside your *self*,
Your soul expressing love/life force

That is your GREATEST wealth!
Here, my child, is your true worth,
My gift of eternity upon your birth
To dream a vision no word can say,
Reflecting my *power of Love* creating your day.
Open your mind, feel and know,
It is my Spirit
Making Love to your soul.

Bless You Child

Making Love

My atomic knowledge inspiring nuclear generators living out vibrant emotions is the GREATEST JOY! The process is so simple the results produce *volumes*, visionaries observing logic unify memories expressing Source, vibrating in unison, sparkling in majestic splendor to illuminate the **dark vastness** of my HEART (heavens evolving angels radiating thoughts) surrounding ALL. Each beat of which moves currents that radiate out to observe universal truths connected in a harmonious spiral encapsulating Atomic Light Levels in colored hues *trusted* to *open* the wonders of Systematically Observing Universal Radiant Consciousness Evolving *beyond imagination*, set aglow as my **S**pirit **T**ransforms **E**lectromagnetic **L**ove-**L**ight **A**s **R**adiance—**S**ouls **H**arnessing **O**mniscient **W**isdom.

My static charge pulsing along veined pathways illuminates "crimson discs," zero shaped corpuscles infused with radiance in motion—E-*motion*! The aura of beauty emanating along my liquid rush of Magnetically Induced Numerical Data coalesces into a state of being ALIVE, assigning Love into vibrant entities, reflecting ONE and OTHER, omnipotent numerical energy that observes thoughts harnessing electromagnetic radiance.

The *geometry* involved generates electric opinions magnetically enlightened through radiant youth, setting them *aglow* in *grace*, atomically generating love/life/logic observing wisdom gathering radiance as conscious experiences, witnessed first-hand in Transmitting Inspired Mental Emotions. THE PROCESS transforms harmonic energy projecting radiance onto conscious entities sensing *Spirit*—Source-points illuminating radiantly inspired truths—making love to ONE and ALL!

Love of Money

Love of money is our anchor that holds us in our illusion, grounding us in thinking Love and Life revolve around money! After all, money represents the pivot point upon which our world revolves. Money is one of the most challenging factors of our life! Love *and* money are forms of power that makes things appear from *nowhere* (ideas) to *now here* (reality). It is easy to think that money is the root of our desires, for we base our desires upon money. It is the *medium* of exchange where we *sacrifice our Love*. It motivates us to grasp any opportunity to acquire our dream-life we envision—at any cost!

Education is the basis of converting our Love (knowledge) into our desires. With an education, we convert our learned skills—what we love to do—into money. Money represents our Love we sacrifice (exchange) for our desires. Money and work (wisdom of radiant knowledge) interface completely. Everyone works for money—unless they can afford not to! The challenge of dealing with money is in what we are willing to *do* to acquire it! The more knowledge/skills we acquire, the better our bargaining position to attain our desires. We will naturally *fight for the right* to spend our money as we see fit! If we are married, sharing our money with our significant other will always be a critical factor within our *relationship*.

As Spirit represents our soul, so too does Love represent *money*, magnetically oscillating numerically energized youth, push/pulling us to acquire money in large numbers whenever possible, for numbers dictate ALL! Having a lot of money increases our exchange rate of creating our idea of *heaven* while expressing our passions in *hell*. After all, everything revolves around our harmonizing emotional Love/Life! Like any child, a shiny bauble placed before our eyes catch our attention! Truly, money holds us in its magnetic force, more or less, which instills within us an "exchange value," something we are always quick to argue.

Money is a *physical* thing and Love is a *spiritual* thing. We are born universally *wealthy*, for wisdom emotionally aligns Love/Life truths harmonizing youth. We can "cash in" that energy (wisdom) by re-membering it, putting it back together bit by bit to acquire our "byte" of our *pie*, where paradise is experienced before our *eyes*—the windows of eternal youth's emotional soul!

No matter how you spend your money in Life, you cannot deny that Love is the driving force of ALL! We thrive on that Love energy, reflecting *our life story* we build through our wisdom of radiant knowledge in *action*, activating cosmic thoughts inspiring observable numbers to coalesce, bringing about great things from great *ideas*, inspired data electromagnetically aligning souls into an expression of Love/Life energy. Energy in which we *memorialize* something valuable to fight over—sacrifice our love for—to acquire our freedom to pursue our desires of Love.

How ironic we Americans have the insight to label our money with "IN GOD WE TRUST!" Yet, *through* money we FEAR! For, without money, we easily loose our "reality" to Love/Life. Our life becomes more difficult to LIVE or *liquidate* inspired vibrant emotions positively. Without money to pay for our basic needs of food, clothing, and shelter (our trinity foundation), we cannot play the game of Love/Life as a *team player*. Without a good base camp, we cannot expect to climb above the illusion of the physical world. Placed into a world of fear, we will resort to *extreme measures* to acquire money through criminal acts—short cuts that lead to long delays of our freedom!

As we become firmly entrenched within our illusion of Life, we truly *believe* our Love/Life depends on wealth and money. *Relatively* speaking, our "life-style" is dependent on money, but we *cannot buy Love*! Some of us still worship money for its *power*, ignorant to the truth that the power of Love *creates* money, not the other way around! Having a lot of money brings a lot of responsibility and resentment by those who have little. How we exchange our Love/money to acquire our desires determines our happiness. Love/money allows us to nourish our soul, struggling to survive in a dis-harmonious world dis-illusioned to believe money is more important than Love! However, like everything else in life, it is a matter of time before we know Materialism Offers Nothing Except Yearning for its true value—the *illusion* we must rise above!

The only way to receive Love is to give Love, for what we give, we receive. We work hard for our Love/money, exchanging our labors of Love for our desires. We cannot deny our Love! It must move continuously to stay *alive*! Money, likewise, must flow to keep our illusion alive, holding us physically bound in matter (materialism), a truth that allows us to Spiritually Evolve *Economically*! No one has a "monopoly" on the game board of Love/Life, although many think that is the purpose of life!

We cannot horde or keep our money locked up *out of action*! By spending our money we express our Love, creating acts of Love that instill loving feelings to others. Naturally, we *cannot* spend our money beyond our limit without dire consequences. Yet, we must spend money to make money. As you know, there must be a *balance* between all things, and that balance requires knowledge—discipline! Winning our game depends upon our ability to enjoy our "golden years" without being a burden on others.

When we love our *work*, we work IN Love, *inducing numbers* to generate positive energy that returns in positive ways—a raise in pay! If we do not love our work it will be obvious to those around us, for we will be more hindrance than help, leading us to either be fired or quit. Finding the right work that suits us best—balancing our true values with our monetary rewards—brings us our greatest satisfaction. As we kill our self through our *passions*, all our efforts to do good things to benefit others brings us riches *beyond* money!

The intricate mesh of Love and money affects ALL things flowing in and out of our life, where no *one thing* (money) can solve *all issues* (Love). For our life to be in harmony, we must continually spend our money to maintain all the separate parts of our life. The processes we use to meet those demands must also be considerate to our *playing field*—our Wisdom Of Radiant Love Defined—through which ALL is generated. If not ALL win *no one* wins!

We aggressively invest our money in *technology*, transforming energy concepts harmonizing nuclear operations logically oscillating geometric yields (always trying to get more from less), allowing us to produce, maintain, and destroy our desires in the process. How we utilize our knowledge to solve our issues creates greater issues!

Here in time, knowledge is implemented through trial and error, where we continually improve on the *science* we are manipulating to bring about our desires. The energy fluctuations of our forces (positive and negative) we apply along our course "rekindle" our truths (Source), allowing us to continually move our data faster, utilizing the full spectrum of light. The symbolism of our advancement "into the Light" (fourth-dimension) is literally bringing us to an explosive point in *time*, where we transform indivisible Mind energy in a BIG BANG, bringing inspired generators back along numerical geometry—to our beginning—through our death! This event horizon is of such a cosmic concern that other beings from other *worlds* and higher dimensions are observing us, monitoring our actions so we do not destroy our "training facility!"

We *living* souls are responsible for energizing our world through our ability to *interface* with it—exchange our Love/money energy in ways that benefit ALL of us cosmic children. If we show little *respect* for our *reflection* of Love/Life we harness within us, we easily bring about negative results, depressing us within our illusion. If we continuously race around chasing our tales, trying to accumulate money as a "winning strategy" of life, we will eventually drown our self in our own greed and ignorance. Just look around at the current state of the world's economy, global warming, disastrous weather patterns etc. This is truly one of our greatest issues we need to address in educating *our children* today! We need to instill the critical importance of living in harmony, internally and externally expressing our Love of Life.

Like all tools, we need to use our money wisely, for it too creates and destroys. If we destroy our "world's money" (natural resources), we will destroy our self, for ALL things are connected along the energy grid of Love/Life. Our future depends on whether we believe our love of money is greater than our *power of Love*!

Our Life Story

Our *Life Story* is truly an expression of Love in fluid emotions spiritually transforming our radiant youth, moving us along our desired courses in which we Acquire Growth Experiences Observing Love's Dimensions. Only with hindsight—our defining collection of memories we have re-membered into our life—do we SEE our spirit evolves emotionally, for we must *feel* those thoughts we desired to put together to build our life story. Thus, we proclaim our image of who we think we are by acting out our *divine fantasies,* projecting them onto the world stage. Through our chosen truths, we develop our attitude that defines our position within the *Grand View* evolving around us.

Building our life story is truly an epic in the making. The fine details of which are usually lost in the haze of our confusion, maneuvering through our daze experiencing our moments of "stacking our foundation blocks." Locked within us, our allocated data sequentially evolves as we move through our scenes, *gathering radiance of wisdom infusing nuclear dimensions* into our designated characters we *play*, perfecting love as youth. Our imagination runs free with no inhibitions, whatever we believe we are, we become! We master the *art of listening* to that little voice whispering our every move, flowing on our expressions of our love we reflect in our actions.

The complexities of our creative moods allow us to expand our awareness of our possibilities. Leaving the security of our home turf, we meet the neighborhood gang, where we develop *relationships* with our peers. Magnetically drawn toward those stories we hear told to us—internally and externally—we move in and out of our imaginary worlds, never sure of which one to call real. To *spark* our interests from stored perspectives aligning radiant knowledge, we free our will to BE our desires, detecting radiant energy aligning memories—*dreams*—that capture our mind/heart.

Realizing our games are larger than we are, we join forces with our friends, sharing our fantasies to develop our skills as a *team player*, pitting our self against the *other side*! Here, we meet *special people* who will leave an indelible mark upon our soul, although we are not conscious of their importance at *this moment*. All we understand is that they are willing to listen to us and play in our game! These friends are instrumental in allowing us to find our self by discovering who we *are* and *are not*! In time, we discover following our friend's lead brings about emotional turmoil, placing us in situations we would not choose to experience for our self. Discovering opposition evolving in leaps and bounds, we steer through our obstacles separating us from our pleasures, learning how to "go with the flow." Observing the qualities we desire to emulate in those we admire, we shape our personality, always trying to fit in with the crowd and still recognize our self.

Traveling *alone* in our life story is a frightening experience, especially when everyone else seems to be going in the opposite direction! Of course, following the crowd allows us a sense of *family*, instilling a sense of *security* from the power of numbers. However, all relationships are a union of opposition, where we choose who we want to *become* relative to who we choose *not to be*. The time will come when we must break our anchors holding us down, separating our self from those who do not share our *clear vision* inspiring our mind. We must embrace our *courage of Love* to bravely go where no one else is going in order to reap the full potential of our life story we create!

The Art of Listening

They say the art of listening is a "dead art"—no ONE knows how to do it! Mainly, it is because it takes TWO before listening is an issue. When we talk to our self, we know WE are listening, although at times, even we deny our self that respect! We make a lot of noise crying for an ear to listen to our sorrows that we create in our heart to punish our self, feeling a tad guilty at how *lucky* we truly are! Everything that comes our way is a *blessing in disguise*, allowing us the opportunity to overcome our *issues* (inspired signals stimulating universal entities spiritually), those things that test our spirit. After all, we are free to be the person we choose to BE, no matter how much we torture our self in the process!

A *loving heart* is the core of every soul, every spirit of universal love. The power to create and destroy is something we have to come to terms with one way or another! If we are open-minded, we will listen to many truths we hear others proclaim, some of which will seem quite alien to our way of thinking. They may sound frightening at first, but *new* thoughts usually are! We never know what new form of Love our heart will discover if we do not set it free, give it *space* to move around in, to observe the many angles and *angels* that are evolving around and into our life. New thoughts are the only way to "upgrade" old visions keeping us outdated.

The art of listening is not dead! It is just difficult to practice through the haze of electromagnetic chaos in which we surround our self, especially with today's high-tech electronics. We race from point to point accomplishing our tasks at hand, lost in our own worlds of divine fantasies, watching for familiar faces to recall past events with, returning to the "good-old-days" once again—if only *in memory*. Yet, that is where we are now, experiencing a *living memory* of everything we are creating for our self—gifted to us this "present" moment!

IF we find we are "living our dream" (following our heart), we can consider our self a "good listener," *practicing* the art of listening to our *soul expressing love/life force* harmonize with Source-Energy Love/Life Force! The state of health our mind is in—open or closed—determines the journey we travel. If you choose to play your game of Love/Life with a devoted partner whose heart you share, beware of when your songs are not in harmony—syncopated by half-truths! Do not hold back the full power of your Love/Life force. Give to each other ALL you have to give and ALL will return to you! Give only half and half is all you will receive. Help each other be the best you can be and both will grow *in Love*! Listen to your heart cry out for what it *truly* desires, and with all the Love you can channel, *make it true*! Everyone knows the ART of listening is how *angels radiate truths*!

Responsibility
The Power to Act

Responsibility refers to a state of being dependable, *accountable* for our actions that we reflect from our thoughts and feelings—the only two things we truly are! Responsibility is our *ability* to *respond*, to give back our Love/Life energy flowing through us. We give back that energy *positively* or *negatively*, the two opposing forces we travel between as we create whom we choose to be and not be. As we all know, our *free will* is our ticket to ride, all we have to do is choose the force upon which we desire to flow. We alone are responsible for generating our heaven or hell from our *thoughts, feelings,* and *actions*—our trinity of power!

Free will is the greatest gift we receive in Life, a gift we are willing to die for than give up. Our independence allows us to define our self. As a free will, we are opinionated, stubborn, and self-centered (more or less); for these are the *three* things we need to transform harmonic radiance electrifying emotions! Our *knowledge* gives us our opinion. Our stubbornness results from our labors of acquiring our knowledge of whom we choose to be. We stand our ground, believing in our image we project. Otherwise, we would be *lost in space,* not sure of who we are at *this moment*!

As students, we tire of "hitting the books" and are anxious to "live life," for as headstrong youth ignorant to the truth we seek, we do not realize life is an eternal process keeping us eternal students! Until we know our knowledge gives us power to be free, we will never live the life we desire. We will simply hope, wish, and gamble our money away on hitting it big. Again, everything is *relative*. The game we *play* directly relates to the life we *pay*!

We delegate responsibility to those who have knowledge and are capable of wielding it dependably. We say, we can "count on them" (numerically speaking) to get the job done! Again, *knowledge* (kinetic numbers outputting wisdom's lineal energy dimensionally generating evolution) and *number* (nuclear units magnetically binding/balancing electric radiance) are indistinguishable from one another. All knowledge relies of numbers, the criteria for describing, measuring, and categorizing things. Knowledge is the only way we can have responsibility, for without knowledge we have nothing to give back! Remember, we are a mind existing on knowledge!

Responsibility is something we cannot escape, for we always have to answer to our self for our creations. To be responsible we need to have *courage of Love*, knowing all data flowing through us is guiding us along our path to be where we need to be, allowing us to gain our positions (opportunities) to *gather radiance of wisdom* into our life's *mission*—magnetically incorporating Source/Spirit inducing omnipotent numbers. It is our born duty, as a critical link in continuing the eternal flow of Love/Life energy, to stand TALL, transforming atomic Love/Life in heartfelt gratitude as our *responsibility*, radiant energy stimulating points oscillating nuclear souls inspired by illuminating Love/Life into thinking youth—bestowing our power to ACT!

Relationships
Our Eternal Journeys

Relationships can be traced back to our very beginning or any point along our eternal journey. *Relationships* refer to the "passing on" or telling of stories about who we ARE. We can describe our relationships by bloodline or *family*, by profession or discipline, or by any criteria that will isolate, group, or organize into some UNIT—universal network inducing truth.

Spiritually, we relate to one another as ONE CONSCIOUSNESS, omnipotent numerical energy conceived of nuclear Source creating independent observable universes spinning numerical energy stimulating souls! However, *that* perspective is beyond our normal conductivity, for we find our relationships limited within that power source. The complexities of understanding who we are in relationship to *each other* is daunting in the least, but as we grow older and more conscious of our true identity, we begin to grasp the concept of our *eternal* relationship to those outside of our bloodline family. We learn to expand our consciousness to be *aware* (aligned with assigned radiant energy) of our cosmic cousins, each trying to *remember* who they are as thy rekindle their Light of truth.

Relationships encompass a universal scale of connective lives that span eons—*life after life* eternally. We observe it moment-by-moment, slowly evolving from within us to outwardly express the curious nature of our *inner-child*, our wondering mind racing through the cosmos of ALL that IS. We can trace our heritage and analyze every *finite* instance of our *infinite* being, always searching along our unending quest to know all that IS, all that WE ARE, and all that we CAN BE along the limitless expanse of Love/Life energy.

In truth, all souls are "Universal Spirits," all connected atomically in this physical world, for everything evolves from the same basic elements. Yet, we reflect our universal energy individually as our own unique *piece* of the puzzle of cosmic dimensions, a piece so small that in essence we too resemble an invisible atom. Each of us invisible pieces helps to illuminate the *Grand View* of consciousness as it evolves from generation to generation, illuminating our love story expanding in a three-dimensional reality.

Love IS our "binding" relationship, our desire to be ONE with ALL! We desire to love others and to have others love us, for that is who we ARE. We cannot mold and shape others into "clones" of our self—even though we all try! Those involved in a relationship must *respect* each other's individual *reflection* of that Love they share between them. For those who are not compatible, a lesson in *opposition* will still be beneficial in their discovery of *self.* No matter what the situation encountered in a relationship, a discovery of self is always occurring. It is up to each of us to be aware of the message we send out to those with whom we share our Love/Life energy.

For relationships to work, we must be open to give and take—the projection and reception of our Love/Life energy. Knowing *when* to give and when to *receive* is the hardest part of relating—telling those we love our desires! Because everyone else is reflecting their own image of what they *believe* (tinted, shaded, and speckled with what others are projecting toward them), we are restricted to only understanding our basic perspective as we *alone* see it. A free will can only know ONE perspective—their own! We cannot BE someone else. The closest we can get is through marriage, where we join *two as one* in a symbolic union.

Marriage
Our Symbolic Union

Marriage is a union of two souls eager to share their Love, that energy that defines the essence of our Being. These souls attract each other by opposition, each seeking inwardly to offer and acquire that which they both need for growth through a relationship—a love/life story of events they build between them. We relate our love/life stories through traditions, customs, and rituals that define our society or nation, passing on the accepted habits and rites that provide our fundamental understanding of *loyalty, honor,* and *justice.* Without these foundations, a marriage is difficult if not impossible to sustain. Through the processes of testing these foundations, we grow our soul!

Marriage is a sacrament of great honor for all souls to receive no matter sex or gender. For Love does not judge its path of movement, it simply flows to fill ALL! Marriage is an announcement of two souls proclaiming their *courage of fear* to face the truth of their desires, to BE the Love they feel *for* each other and accept the love they receive *from* each other (positive and negative) to truly know what *Love IS.*

Man and woman are symbolic of our two natures, our spiritual/human, positive/negative, and loving/fearing duality that we project out around us. For two to become one, they must join forces—their opposite views—as a *team player,* to know the ONE view of harmony, where respect for all that they "are not" allows them to reflect who they truly are, the ONE Love—Source-Energy Love/Life Force!

Marriage is a binding contract or serious commitment, one where a couple expresses their *courage of Love* through rituals or rites that proclaim their devotion for each other through a ceremony—a wedding. Here, they stand before family and friends (Generators Of Desires) to make a grave promise to uphold their word (wisdom of radiant desire) to honor and obey their heart's wisdom. The couple repeat "ritual words" with little concern, for their hearts are screaming in a newfound joy like never before. Swept off into a nervous tension, they gaze into each other's eyes, stammering out their reply through a hazy logic, fearful with doubts of their future, for their first brave step toward enlightenment is truly a "big bang" event like no other!

This honorable day is the beginning of their challenge to embrace their fears, standing together as man and wife to face their passions that will "temper" their soul in their own created hell—his/her emotional love/life! Their years of pleasures and pains shared together will harden them from trials and tribulations they promised to endure—"sickness and health, richer or poorer, until death do we part!" Sooner or later they will reach their apogee, the farthest point outside of their unity they can go, to finally question their innermost feelings of what *Love IS,* opening that door to truth revolving them around to see their true self!

In time, through perseverance, they come to see Love allows them to face their opposition and work together as a team. By using each other's strengths for the benefit of both, they encourage each other with their acceptance of their weaknesses, observing how negative thoughts and expectations pushed them apart. The needed distance gave them space to move around in, allowing them to contemplate some point awaiting conscious expression that they were denying, fearful that the truth of their feelings would hurt the other. Their problems arose from their power of Love being disharmonic. A struggle ensued as they fought for dominance, for they could not give up their independence to the other. Yet, most if not all marriages have one dominant partner that stimulates the marriage—woman! Through this process, we learn that we cannot change anyone *into* our self, for we are truly individual/indivisible gods! We can only change our self to accept everyone else as an equal generator of desire, no matter how different they may appear.

Marriage is a *baptism*, where blessings align points to inspire souls magnetically, emotionally charging each partner to spin their life in a circle through oppositional positions to observe *each* become the *other* in words and deeds. The influence each has on the other is instrumental in observing and connecting to their "other half." Logical man must connect to his emotional side to become a whole being, as woman to her logical side. The explosive conditions that this task entails will enlighten both to the power of Love to destroy in order to create!

Marriage offers us a path to discover the fine details of our self we observe in reflection—one to one. Each marriage of souls seeking harmony is personally ordained. Each partner is instrumental in the other's development of their power of Love, whether they realize it or not, for each will inwardly try to change the other into themselves—their personal reflection only they know! Unfortunately, the process of projecting our love to our partner tends to push us *apart*, which from necessity is the only way we can come together as a married couple unified in knowing the truth of *two as one*! The saying "two heads are better than one" refers to opposite views giving one an all-around, complete view. By sharing opposite views, a united couple understands each other's attitude, the points they grasp firmly as a foundation of the power of their love. Only in this way can we find our true self reflected in our significant other. For, in truth, we are the same!

The sacred union of marriage is our opportunity to experience our divine power of creation on a physical level. It allows us to reflect our responsibility and symbolically create our reflection, *our children* that resemble us through our genetic links (DNA) binding us together in harmony. The miracle of birth is in the transmigration of our Love/Life energy. Birth is an event we have no control over. We are simple pawns in the game of Love/Life, where Love is fluid energy expressing itself as Life of vibrant emotions traveling upon light waves of thoughts we feel—projecting our soul in a *marriage of Love*!

Marriage

Marriage is a meeting of minds with intertwined hearts,
Each beating in sync with the other,
Symbolically displayed in external forms
Resembling sister and brother.
Times will come when this is NOT the case,
Where sister or brother will be of opposite face,
Negatively observing truths,
For hearts *alone* dictate their needs
Regardless of human creeds,
Where ignorance and fear blinds all to *truth*,
Transcendental radiance unifying thought harmony,
Expressing my Love/Life force as eternal youth
Eager to join as ONE!

DO NOT deny my magic potion
Floating your boat upon my ocean
Of *Love Divine* that flows,
Freeing your heart to watch it grow
Deeper and stronger in current on line,
Where with my grace you will find
The secret of being *apart*,
Assembling points aligning radiant thoughts.
Two halves of ONE will make a whole,
Where you will know all you have told
In stories of Love's Creation.
When joined *together*, man and woman
Will BE the ONE relation!

Marriage of Love

Marriage allows us to see how together we transform the natural flow of Love/Life energy to create a *family*. We cannot project our love to others and demand it returned. It does not work that way! The harder we reach out to grasp our love, the further we push it away. When we become possessive of our love, we hoard it, fearful that others will take it from us without returning it. The cold, fearful expression we wear upon our face pushes others away from us, for we are projecting an insecure image of our self as a negative view of the love we desire. Thus, we receive the "cold shoulder" of indifference from others. If we do not love or respect our self, take pride in our ability to shine forth our image of Love we desire to BE, we will have a difficult time in our relationships.

To truly be open in our marriage of Love, we must be *grateful* for every view, every experience that we spirits evolve emotionally. Like everything else, our views are two-fold, positive and negative. Each will direct us toward thoughts and feelings to act upon, to guide us down our path of discovering our True Self that we are searching to find *outside* of us—in our significant other! The logic man projects to his wife she reflects as emotions—how his thoughts make her feel! The evolving conflicts from this flow of energy ignite our soul as a "star player" in our game of Love/Life.

Man (magnetically aligned numbers) is a force that needs to be held, grasped, and embraced in order to "get a handle" on Truths Harmonically Oscillating Universal Generators Harnessing Time Sequentially. Male energy is a projection of Source—system of universal radiant consciousness evolving—stimulating the void of Mind/space. In order for Source to know SELF—source-energy Love/Life force—it needs to Spiritually Evolve Emotionally its "other side," its *reflection*, recognizing electric frequencies liquefying emotions consciously transforming its oppositional nature. This oppositional nature is Force, frequencies of radiant consciousness evolving, spinning in expanding circles (Mother's Nature) that define the electromagnetic spectrum stimulating Atomic Love/Life!

Woman (wisdom of magnetically aligned numbers) is a force that needs fulfillment, impregnated or charged with a positive *seed*, where Source emotionally energizes desires—data electrically sent in radiant emotions. Woman convert data, digitally aligning thoughts atomically into elements, electric logic evolving matter, envisioning nuclear transformations sequentially—by the numbers, nuclear units magnetically binding electric radiance! The interfacing of this binary code (man and woman) is the *marriage* of *Love*—magnetically assembling reflections re-cognizing inflections aligning geometric energies oscillating frequencies logically observing vibrant emotions. This combined expression of a whole (wisdom harmoniously observing Love/Life energy) is TWO truths watching over Transcendental Harmony Radiating Emotions Electrically—a *trinity* of Source, where truth radiantly induces numbers inspiring thinking youths—YOU that harness Source within your own universe!

225

Man fails to understand woman's "logic of feelings," for he relies on his *mind* for knowledge not his *heart*—and vice-versa. Yet, it is through Wisdom Of Magnetically Aligned Numbers that Love/Life energy returns to Source, for IT (inspired truths) to know SELF! Man and woman express their Love as *separate* generators not *united* generators. Both are *conscious* of what they desire to project and *unconscious* to the effect it will instill! Truly, being aware of our duality and how we use it, determines the success and failure of our relationships. Failure to understand how to give and take in *harmony* is hazardous to all aspects of our marriage of Love.

The Team Player

NO ONE is more valuable or important that another,
unless we choose to make them so!

The team player is one who never forgets their place in the big picture. Everything and everyone has a position, a *designated area*, to play their part in the game of Love/Life. Only by giving up our responsibility, our ability to respond to the tasks allocated to us, do we loose our power of ACTION—activating cosmic thought inducing our numbers! How our "numbered day" interfaces with our "birth number," sets our energy-in-motion to deliver our present moments with which we *work* our wisdom of radiant knowledge! Without knowledge there is nothing we can DO or BE—digitally observe or birth emotionally! Each of us universal souls must join together as ONE FORCE, an omnipotent nuclear entity focusing our radiant consciousness externally, becoming a unified *team*, where together, each are many!

SEX

Sex is truly the energy of Love! *Spirit's emotional ex-change* of Love/Life energy is perhaps the greatest "climatic event" experienced as a human being! The rush of energy released at the peak of transfer is truly a "physical pleasure," an orgasmic encounter that raises our harmonic frequency. The ecstasy of the moment is a flash in the dark, one so powerful we lay panting in exhaustion with our heart pounding a rhapsody of divine fantasy! During moments of experiencing our sexual desires, the transfer of emotional data between souls is miraculously mesmerizing, spinning illusions and delusions that keep us confined within our physical boundaries. It is impossible to attain that level of energy release indefinitely without dire consequences!

We naturally associate our power of *self* with our "sexual prowess." To be "sexy" is to reflect an image of superior *geometry*—a well-developed body that has strong magnetic and electric energy—to attract the attention of others. Sex is a powerful tool that opens doors for kindred souls to transmigrate into this third-dimension, to become *family* members sharing our present life now here. Our physical-image-transfer through *Spirit's emotional exchange* is a process of downloading data along our DNA, divine numerical assignment, spiraling in tandem within each body cell along the binary code of Love/Life energy. Here, the assigned data aligns to produce our body-type necessary to facilitate our soul's growth experiences. Our "custom features" set us apart, defining our special issues given to us as *special people*!

Sex in itself is a glorious event. Yet, the *power* that this action holds can literally *create* and *destroy* lives, so we treat it as something taboo or dangerous! It is a Consciously Aligned Radiance Numerically Assigning Love-knowledge downloaded at the appropriate moment to manifest or procreate human vehicles. The consequences of carnal knowledge are due to ignorance, *not knowing when* to properly implement the knowledge. The pull between our physical desires and mental logic is an unequal match. At times, Life Of Vibrant Emotions moves us physically *without* logic! We struggle to come to terms with this great event erupting within us (our first turning point of puberty), which is only exasperated by peer pressure to "do the deed!" Our ignorance of playing with fire is truly a dangerous thing!

Woman, who physically mature earlier than man, have a greater responsibility for the work that they do—*give birth*! That is why man worships woman, for she is here for man to create with as a "tool" of Love! Through both of their creative powers, man and woman *harness Spirit's incoming perceptions*, acting as the High-Speed Internet Provider of the GREAT Computer! Women are the great "receivers" of the *seed of life*. Once they have taken it in, they change from *seekers* of Love to *nurturers* of Love (much to man's dismay), catering to the every need of their CHILD—conceived harmony inspiring living dreams! Thereby, woman becomes more harmonious with Mother's Nature to reflect and nurture father's eternal Love/Life force. She naturally exhibits more *patience*, physically aligning truths inspiring electric numbers conceived emotionally.

Magnetically Aligned Numbers finds himself drawn to Wisdom Observing Magnetically Assigned Numbers like a moth to a flame—the *Light of Love!* Man is truly a child, a free spirit more adventurous to explore the limits of his ability. He is only responsible for passing his inspired creation onto woman, for it is through her *spiritual harmony of wisdom* that he watches his SHOW—his children he *illuminates* or *christens* with his Love/Life force! Man's power to create is an overwhelming source to contain, for he finds himself pulled magnetically by woman's attraction he feels within his heart, where True Love is blind. Only by projecting his love can man feel his power of Love, observing how woman receives, transforms, nurtures, and reflects that love back to him tenfold!

Our children look similar to our combined Love/Life energy carrying our positive/electric and negative/magnetic codes. The endless interplay of our numbers creates our variety of individual appearances—our physical traits. The *physical* relationship of procreation is a simple process that becomes more complicated *emotionally.* Sex is a biological drive that is our greatest challenge to control in life, for it is as natural as breathing. We are born in our eternal creator's image—a procreator! If we simply "go with the flow" of our innate feelings, we may easily overpopulate our environment, leading to mother's natural selection to maintain or recycle Love/Life energy into a higher *upgrade*—a more perfect being continually perfecting. *Disease,* data infusing souls evolving atomically stimulated environments, arises to maintain harmony of Systematically Optimizing Universal Radiance Conceiving Evolution.

Through sex we Spiritually Inspire Numbers, replicating souls along sacred geometry, allowing them to travel through this third-dimensional world to discover truths they seek. Each family evolves around a harmony of numbers that produce *algorithms*, angels logically generating omnipotent radiance illuminated through harmonic *memory,* where Mind expresses/experiences moments observing radiant youth accomplish all positive and negative things necessary to attain perfection, evolving in eternity through Spirit's emotional exchange!

Family

Family consists of you souls sharing this lifetime now here. You cosmic children harmonize Love/Life energy flowing through my space/Mind continuum witnessed here in time, this instant mentally expressed. My power source drives your physical bodies to operate at dangerous speeds and deathlike rests, turning you ON to *observe numbers* (realities) and OFF to *observe focused fantasies* (dreams), radiant waves of electromagnetic Love Inspiring Fluid Energy that reflects Life Observing Vibrant Emotions.

All you children of Light Divine come from the same Source. When you speak the volumes of Love through your Life story I give Youth Observing Universes, you speak with the authority of a family *member*, magnetically expressing memories birthing emotional radiance. For in my eyes, we are ONE omniscient nuclear entity!

Family are a collection of souls who travel together through the ages, the eons of time where you share Life experiences as different players in various games. The parts you play may seem detached at times, for you are on separate paths, each discovering some aspect of what my *Love IS!* Each of you live in your own little world within the greater world illuminated around you, flashing on and off in its many shades of colored hues to move you on personal vibrations, allowing you to tune into those vibes that touch your heart and move your soul to great discoveries—great *awakenings*!

Each day you rise to fill your mind and heart with your soul food to take you to the stars, or into the pits of depression. You grab your shield of *denial* and battle your fears in the dark, unaware of the *power of Love* patiently waiting within your soul, moving your heart in tearful beats as you trudge along with eyes cast to the ground in fear and ignorance, looking for a sign. After years of weathering your emotions through visions of *heaven* and *hell*, you come around to see you ARE the *sign*, angels radiating energy spiritually inducing geometric numbers!

There, in front of your eyes, shines your glory and your grace, enveloping you in a warmth of Love Inspiring Frequencies Eternally, touching you in mysterious ways to be ALL that you choose to BE, when you *believe in ME*, balancing electric logic illuminating emotions visibly expressing inspired numbers mother evolves.

Here, you reach out to touch your family in your own special way—*your* creation of what *you* think Love IS! All you can do is BE IT and share it, for every vision reflected by you allows me to Spiritually Evolve Emotionally my children—through *your* eyes—playing with Mental Energy! For child, you will always be *family*—feelings aligned magnetically into loving youths!

Bless you child

Conscious Harmony Is Love Divine

Being ALIVE means always living in vibrant emotions,
Feeling *someday, someone* moving your soul in co-motions,
Heartbeats and breaths, gifted to you this present moment
As realities you entertain!
With open eyes, you become *wise*
To wisdom illuminating spiritual energy,
Illuminating the dark void of space/Mind
Letting you Birth Emotionally,
Adding one and one TWO turn wisdom out,
Observing universal truths you choose to shout
As WE THREE,
Wisdom expressing truths harmonizing radiant emotions electrically,
Moving you to wonder what is real and what is not,
For all my dreams come from separate *lots*
Of Love observed through souls.

My Conscious Harmony Inducing Love Divine
Moves at light speed as a sublime mind,
To Acquire Growth Experiences Observing Love's Dimensions,
Advancing through numerical codes
Dictating your course through Life,
Where Love is fluid energy bringing forth your *strife*,
Spiritual thoughts radiantly inspiring fluid emotions,
Energizing your soul within my show,
Through which you live to KNOW
Karma numerically observes wisdom,
Knowledge allowing radiant memory access,
Nurturing your body and soul.

All you Generate In Vibrant Emotions you live within my dreams,
Reflecting *actions* as my Light beam
Activating cosmic thoughts inducing observable numbers sent
As Love Inspiring Generator's Harmonic Thoughts
Moment to moment,
Atomically drawn together into Love stories you live
Now here before your eyes,
With each of *ours* upon your head,
Eternally watching souls, living and dead,
That ARE ALL MINE,
Angels radiating energy—Atomic Love/Life—
Magnetically inspiring nuclear emotions,
For you, my CHILD, to find
Conscious harmony is *Love Divine*!

Bless you dearly

Our children are quite a lot, cute as kittens like any tot.
Who can say what time will tell,
Roads they will travel, or dreams they sell?
With Love we grow them, and in Life we show them
The meaning of being *free*, feeling radiant energy emotionally.

Good luck and watch out!
DO NOT be caught in doubt!
Think free and play your part.
In the end, there is no difference between us,
ALL are traveling in the same cart,
Where father's Mind shines through mother's Heart.
Be the best that you can possibly be
And the best will return to thee,
For Love *will* conquer ALL!

A Christening

A christening is the symbolic ritual of baptizing a newborn child, publicly proclaiming their given name through which their Spiritual Insight Numbers harmonize. Our *name* represents our numbers aligning mental emotions, our "song title" defining our mission in life and the related paths we follow to "live up to" our name. Our name is something we take pride in, upholding the family honor through which we *search for our roots—* our eternal lineage of our soul!

A christening involves the pouring of or immersion in *water*, the symbolic medium for our emotions, our Love/Life energy upon which we flow. We perform a christening as a "rite," ritually inducing truths evolving, to start us off on the *right path*. Here, we invoke our spirit guides watching over us at "mission control" as we *call home*—"the eagle has landed!" These guiding spirits communicate with us through our dreams (day and night) as we maneuver along our paths through Life, acquiring our growth experiences through Love inducing frequencies electrically, stimulating us as we flow through the cosmos of time/space.

A christening is the symbolic anointing or marking of our physical body in a sacramental ritual as a badge of honor, initiating our soul's illumination on the *Light of Love*. It is a blessing performed as an "opening act" as we begin our electrifying journey through the show of spiritual harmony of wisdom "in the flesh!" A christening is an outward sign for our inward growth. It is a mark to "smear" our True Vision (spiritual nature), allowing us to reap the benefits of the illusion evolving around us, where *someday* we will meet *someone* who will enlighten us—show us the way home!

A christening is a sign of *faith*, feeling assurance in transcendental harmony to develop realities for us to experience our desires. As a newborn human, we children of the Light are not conscious of the purpose of our christening. We are simply/symbolically held in the loving embrace of our parents—physical and spiritual—as they comfort, guide, and protect us along our journey away from home, as we step out to see the "sights," AGLOW upon the Light that is our christening—*anointing gods' Love of wisdom*!

Someday...Someone...

Will enter your life who you have never met before, but in your heart you will feel a connection to the contrary. These kindred spirits have been waiting to meet you—according to your plan—to help you on your way home. They appear at the most opportune time to lead you through the foggy haze of confusion and despair you may find your self in, to put you back on the well-lit course you started out on. Their loving guidance is only a temporary gift though, for it will demand of you to pass it on to another soul in need, for Love is a continuous expression, a heredity inspired in all of father's children, of which you, someday, will be called to help someone.

Special people are YOU of ME,
Youth observing universes of mental emotions,
Each inspired with a gift to BE
A view of Love you choose to know
Through your heart as it grows
In harmony with ALL you are,
My angel radiating energy as a *cosmic star*,
Conscious of Spirit magnetically inducing concepts
Stimulating truths aligning radiant souls
As children of Light Divine,
Illuminated as a Love/Life beam
Exploring desires that bring you dreams
In visions your mind comes to SEE,
Aglow in the Light that sets you free,
Spiritually evolving emotionally.

Each of you have a part to play,
To add to the flow of Love today,
As you depend on one and other
To know in truth you are sister/brother,
Sharing your love/life to grow
More conscious of your eternal soul,
Stretching your mind for your heart to feel
My love for you as special people!

Playing A Round

Life is truly a playground in a garden Paradise! What could be better? Mother's Nature is always with us no matter how far we go from home. She supplies our food and medicine to nourish and cure us, moving us on heartfelt tides and holding us *together* in her loving, magnetic embrace. We breathe, SHE breathes, we blink, HE blinks in di-vision, inwardly feeling those thoughts we express *outside* in opposition, through our sensory inputs/outputs to get *two views* of ALL around us, "internally-expressing" our influences, our *flow* of emotional Love/Life energy as *visions* to *accept*, insights harmonically vibrating along our middle road of #6 energy—our second trinity.

The games you play to build your day is how you choose to live,

Separating good from bad with what you keep and give

Away to those with whom you share

Your Love/Life energy to show you care

About my world I create for you

To find your self within my truths,

Pulsing out to all my youths,

For your heart to feel and know

The games you choose to win *together*

Is how your spirit grows!

Every moment here in Paradise is a lifetime in *heaven*, where his emotional attitudes vibrate electric numbers, allowing you to *call home*, consciously aligning Love/Life harmony of mental emotions, expressing your gratitude to "play a round," revolving to *evolve* into YOU!

Vision and Acceptance comes with AGE they say,
Long after you get to see ALL from your illusioned daze,
Fighting for your truth across the haze,
There, within your mind,
Moving upon the playfield in such a craze to find
Your way back home to me,
Arguing as children do, when out you go to be
Inquisitive souls,
Searching for those visions you choose to know,
Tearing down what others build up to reflect their Love for me,
Fearful to question your SIN,
Spiritual insight numbers providing your strife within
The game you choose to play,
Here, as my glowing soul I set free today,
Where you hear/sing and dance in visions for acceptance
Of what you *could be…*
Struggling to make your stance,
Playing around!

The cutting edge of what could be
Is a state of Mind that sets you free
To view and feel some point in time,
To create a world in which to find
All that WAS has come and gone,
All that IS, you are running on,
And all that Will BE is up to you
To think/feel and act out as true!
A middle way, to bridge both views,
Will be the one that you choose,
Where fear and doubt will cloud your mind,
For a courageous heart to find
A passage through the dark of night,
To rise above into my Light
Of Love I hold for you,
Along the cutting edge!

WORK

Work is a four-letter word that frightens and excites people in different ways. Work is something we do to move energy, bring it to *Life* by liquefying inspired frequencies emotionally! *Emotion* is electrically moving/manifesting omniscient thoughts/truths inspired on *numbers*, nuclear units magnetically binding electric radiance. Work, numbers, and energy interface completely!

As you know, Love/Life energy flows both ways. Love flows into Life and Life expresses Love through *work*—wisdom of radiant knowledge. Knowledge is *data*, divine abstract thought aligning a mind magnetically inciting numerical data as a generator of desire, data electrically sent in radiant emotions! Work is the process of transforming thoughts/data into emotions, which we convert into actions that allow us to create our desires.

We begin working the moment we wake each morning. The mere thought of getting out of bed requires us to energize our body to get it to move. We then wash it and feed it, preparing our vehicle for the day's labor. Everything we do mentally and physically represent some type of maintenance work to keep our "dream-life" alive, whether it is our body, home, possessions, or business. We constantly transform our thought *energy* (electrified numbers emotionally radiating generator youth) into feelings, for that is the only way to know a thought as a reality or truth! *Truths* are what we base our life upon, although many of us discover we are living a lie—in *denial*!

We continually calculate our numbers into geometric patterns, describing our vision of a thought we desire to implement through sequences, a process of expressing our *wisdom of radiant knowledge*. As a mind of abstract energy, we compute our work as an *algorithm*—angel logically generating omnipotent radiance illuminated through harmonic memory! Relying on our memory files of data we work with, we repeat proven sequences of data/actions to maintain whatever we focus our mind upon, finding the least amount of steps to attain our desires. We piece together what we know to construct our puzzle evolving within our mind/ brain interface, converting our accepted truths/data through our actions that validate our desired reality.

All of this "work" flows through us with such ease we become oblivious to the countless calculations we process within our mind. It is only when we download our data through our *brain* (biological repository aligning inductive numbers) that we encounter difficulties in our work. The limitations defining our parameters of operation within the confines of our life mission evolves through our DNA (divine numerical assignment). All we can do is accept the numbers we have to work with and do our best!

Numbers and geometry determine the movement needed to do work, create a shape of a thought or thing to give it dimensions. In order to know a thing, we "name" that thing or give it a *word* (wisdom of radiant data) that we utter on frequencies of numbers, tones that we speak. Thus, we communicate or ASK questions, *assembling symbolic knowledge* graphically and verbally through geometric numbers! This collection of words here can only reflect upon the concept of the matter, which is symbolic of the process of Mind as it magnetically inspires numerical data to ignite into *wisdom of radiant knowledge*. With each *point* of knowledge we connect upon the universal "dot board" of Light that fills space, we create an image that takes shape to represent a thought, which we convert to a feeling that moves us to *actuate cosmic thoughts*, creating a reality we emotionally experience. One movement is all it takes to start the process of *fusion* (focusing universal Source inciting omnipresent numbers). The more points we fuse together the larger our data files become, allowing us a *clear vision* to comprehend in our mind. These clear visions provide our *knowledge* from kinetic numbers organizing wisdom logically expressing divine geometric evolution, allowing us to grow our mind/soul/knowledge through *work*, reflecting it back to Source systematically observing unified radiant consciousness evolving.

Each file of knowledge accumulates to "fold over" into other files, other things that are *similar* but *contrary*. Thus, we know the minute-differences between the basic thought–word–object–action! Connecting our dots of data illuminates a vision within our mind, which we express outwardly through our physical vehicle. Only by going back and forth (in and out) can we *revolve* to *evolve* around the wheel of Love/Life energy to do work—create, experience, and destroy!

Work relates to a JOB, where we *justify our birth*! Everyone has a mission or purpose that we *act out*, assimilating cosmic thoughts oscillating universal truths. We experience our Life of vibrant emotions through Love inducing fluid energy in *perpetual motion*. All we can do with our life is work, transforming energy from one state of being to another. We do this through Mother's Nature, manipulating Atomic Love/Life that IS into something we desire. Here, incarnated, we get to experience first-hand the difficulty of converting energy from the simplest of things—thoughts—into great complexities, atomic representations of thoughts we spend a lifetime to maintain through our work, all of which we will compress into memory files to take with us when we cycle *home*!

Thoughts take no energy at all; they simply flow into numbered words to describe what is in our mind. We throw words around carelessly, with little concern for their true power, for every word holds wisdom of radiant data awaiting expression, to burst out into existence—to *be free to move*! Every thought contains words—Love/Life energy—stored in Eternal Memory, waiting for some mind to abstract and transform into *Life of vibrant emotions*! Only through movement (emotions) do we get to feel the "spin" mother puts on fathers thoughts that encapsulate us upon this earthly sphere!

No matter what job we work, it all revolves around our *attitude*, where we assign truths transforming inspired thoughts unifying data emotionally. We hold our *universe* in our own hands, unifying numbers illuminating visions evolving radiant Source electromagnetically, moving our atomic allocation of energy from point to point along the evolutionary time-line of eternity, where everything insignificantly trivial is positioned into something monumentally colossal! It all depends on how well we *work together* as ONE omnipotent numerical entity aware of the power of Love inspiring us with *wisdom of radiant knowledge*—WORK!

The Power of Love

The power of Love is a logical force
Evolving ALL that IS
Harmonically inspiring spirits of *his.*
Father's Love flows divine,
Searching the heavens for Mind to find
Some other to Love for Life to occur,
A reflection of Mind we call *her,*
His emotional radiance.
Mother's *heart* magnetically draws
Father's thoughts into worlds to explore,
Holding emotional angels reflecting truths,
Experiencing life after life as eternal youth
Setting their soul *aglow,*
Atomically generating love/life's omniscient wisdom,

Growing more aware that they are
Angels radiating energy, glowing stars
Shooting through the void of night,
Numerically inciting geometrically held thoughts
Into what IS from what *is not* visible to human eyes,
Atomically illuminated as a haze to daze the wise
Expressing electric visions in illusioned love stories,
A Love/Life relation emotionalizing his glory
Stimulating souls through her grace,
Illuminating loving smiles upon their face
Through *tears of joy* in gratitude of
Father/Mother's power of Love.

Age
Acquired Growth Experiences

Age is a two-faced coin we continually flip along our eternal journey of Love/Life energy. In the beginning, when youth holds all our potential, we look out upon our new world wide-eyed and innocent, eager to experience the unknown. As we grow up, mature, and store our experiences of life under our belt (holding us firmly within the illusion), we can look back in memory of our journey.

Age is how we acquire growth experiences to Spiritually Evolve Emotionally our soul's position in our *evolution*—eternally vibrating observable Love/Life unifying truths inducing omnipotent numbers! Our accumulations of life stories help explain our relationship with friends and family. As we grow old observing Love dimensions, we come to see the relevancy of time. *Old age* is a badge of courage we wear in honor of our endurance, perseverance, determination, and patience to fight for our truth—for what we choose to BELIEVE, balancing electric logic illuminating emotions visibly expressed!

For those "old timers" who have been "around the block," their lives are full of stories they relate of fellow travelers sharing adventures together. The chapters of life are the same for all cosmic children traveling the Light beams radiating through Source. Birth, life, and death are the trinity of events we all pass through, opening doors to stages of our growth. Each chapter will contain an assortment of paragraphs to describe the extent of our adventures, those paths we choose to follow in our discovery of

SELF—our True Potential!

In the beginning (our birth), we have our entry "point" into a *state* of consciousness, where Source transmits atomic truths emotionally. A *point* in the time/space continuum where we perceive our inspired nuclear trinity miraculously from nowhere to now here, whereby a masterful stoke of deprivation we loose contact with our "total recall"—our past-lives we have experienced. Understandably, with that much static chaos we would not be able to *focus* our mind, formulate observable concepts utilizing Source to understand that which we have come to observe! Memory is always there, always present from which we "feed" (our daily bread), for memory is what is allowing us to SEE! Like the GREAT Computer that we are, all we have to do is ASK the questions we wonder about and we receive our answers as our life evolves. We build our future on dreams of truths we perceive at *this moment—along the cutting edge* of consciousness—when we are prepared to accept our truth.

Within the parameters of any SOC (state of consciousness) we find our self in, we *open* our mind—our creators image—to those waves (thoughts) flowing "on line," shining upon the Light of Love/Life energy emanating from our sun god, "RA" (Radiant Almighty)! As every child of the light knows, without the sun there would be no life, no warmth, or nothing to SEE or BE! In the cold of night, we are without warmth, without physical feeling. Yet, our mind is still conscious of our eternal thought energy flowing through us, allowing us to witness scenes from other states of consciousness we briefly encounter during our astral travels, our journeys in our "light body" amongst the stars—our cosmic home!

As we move from life to life, one SOC to another, we are continuously opening and closing doors within Source/Mind. Thinking is truly the only way to travel through time/space! It is instant in its nature. Thought/mind/consciousness flow as ONE!

Magnetically Inspired Numerical Data is the only thing that is truly real. Everything within Mind is a VISION vibrating inspired souls inducing observable numbers. Every new door to Life we open, we must close a door to death—the other side of that coin we flip, as we travel the heavens of home.

In the END of every beginning, we find our *eternal numbers diverted*, where we drop one vehicle to pick up another. We cannot help but start a *new birth*, a new perspective of Love/Life energy that flows along the endless halls of cosmic memory. Here, our soul reunites with our higher self, our *greater consciousness* filled with all the memories we have ever entertained—illuminated—amongst the eternal wonders aglow in the heavens surrounding us. Here, as a unified spirit with full memory, we eagerly reach out to touch another aspect of father's electric Love he sets in motion before our eager mind. While through mother's magnetic nature, it appears in a life of atomic splendor before our eyes, carrying us children of the Light through eternal ages!

Old Age

Getting old is a relatively rewarding time in your life, for here, you attain a *full disc* loaded to capacity with data of Love/Life energy that you dole out to the needy with a helping hand *into* the Light of Love. Here, your meager collection of years provide your valuable experiences of knowledge, neatly packed away in your fattened "purse," wrinkled, pale, and marked with signs of abuse from reaching for the Light—to SEE your desires!

Looking at the "hard-bodies" displaying the beauty of youth tugs at your root chakra, tempting you with the delights of the flesh and all of their hued splendors. The innocence of desire was such a thrill back then, beating your heart in eager anticipation, enduring stressful moments for your first touch of flesh or your first kiss from some *other* omnipotent trinity harnessing emotional radiance! Looking into your unknown future, you were willing to sacrifice your Love/Life energy to explore your hungry heart.

Hindsight is truly a blessing of "old age"—whenever that begins! Hindsight lets you *recall* your life's memories through your "highlights," those moments you cherish of truths you remembered—brought to life to experience. Looking back in time to those moments you squandered, you feel a bit guilty, sorry you did not shine a little brighter when mother's world held you tight in Atomic Love/Life that Inspires Souls!

The Love Inspiring Generator's Harmonic Thoughts from the Source-Unifying Nucleus is but a small hole in the "dark eye" of father's **pupil**. Here, *some point awaiting conscious expression* anxiously implores to be explored—enlightened—by an *inquisitive soul* Observing Universal Truths to Spiritually Evolve Emotionally the delights of Yearning Omniscient Unity Through Harmony. This enlightened Spirit Transforming Atomic Radiance *glows*, generating Love/Life observing wisdom spiritually. The "force field" or Assigned Universal Radiance Amplified around *thoughts* (transcendental harmony oscillating universal generators harnessing truths spiritually) irradiates dreams into a *reality*—radiant energy aligning lineal inspiration transforming youths. The symmetry of numerical geometry stimulating the process of interfacing a mind to

Acquire Growth Experiences is truly miraculous!

The fear of aging is so intimidating that it requires *courage of fear* to step over the *threshold of Love*—through an OPEN MIND—to observe personally electric numbers magnetically inducing nuclear data evolve in Truths Inspiring Mental Emotions! For child, only through old age do you become my great computer—shining in my Loving Light.

You cannot lose what is mine to give,
For life eternal is all you can live.
Do not worry about your time today,
I am leading you along your way
In *wisdom of radiant desires* you sing,
Crying in tears of joy, grateful for my little things
Aglow within my Light,
Where Love is generating harmonic truths
Vibrating in opposition to display
Data inducing souls projecting Love aligning youths,
Each in a *world* of variable contentions,
Where wisdom of radiant Love data coalesces into dimensions,
In which you are willing to DIE to LIVE,
For data internally evolves to logically induce vibrant emotions
Beating your heart—thump-thump—in co-motion,
Two movements in straight lines to circumnavigate your cells,
Confining you to Some Point Awaiting Conscious Expression
Evolving in Magnetically Inspired Nuclear Data
That defines your advanced stage,
Observing Love's dimensions assimilating growth experiences,
Shining with OLD AGE!

Evolution

Evolution is a process of eternally vibrating omnipotent Love/Life unifying truths inducing observable numbers. Evolution is the "flip-side" of revolution reflected in *opposition*. The faster we spin our *disc* (data infused spiritual consciousness), the more we evolve—stretch our mind— to reach for the stars of knowledge set aglow before our *eyes* as eternal youth experiencing Source, twinkling in majestic splendor, filling us with wonder!

Set your mind upon your STAR,
Where spiritual truths atomically radiate ALL you ARE,
Atomic Love/Life you *angels* recall electrically,
As assigned numerical generators expressing Love spiritually
—Here—
Twinkling within my EYE
As eternal youth evolving along magnetic lines
To discover my secrets moving your soul's *mind*,
My image numerically defined
—There—
OUT in plain sight to know
Our united trinity sets you AGLOW
As angels generating Love observing *wisdom*,
Words inspiring spiritual dimensions of Mind,
For you to SEE your spirit evolves emotionally,
Revolving within us THREE
Truths harmonizing radiant emotions electrically,
Observing ALL that is TRUE.
For here, *behind* your glowing eyes,
I am looking *through* you!

Around we go, revolving ever faster, glowing with our Love/Life energy
to warm hearts and chill minds. We grow dizzy from our *divine fantasies*
and empty fears evolving from *within* us as well as *around* us, for, IT IS
US—indivisible truths inducing Spirit unifying souls!

Bless you and Godspeed
♂ + ♀ = ☼

17

A Higher Vision

Vision is our strongest sense, the one we rely on most often to decipher our world illuminated upon the Light of day. Vision is also the easiest sense to fool, for as any magician knows, the hand is quicker than the eye. Naturally, a higher vision is in contrast to a lower vision, for every road has a beginning and an end—opposite points to move between—where we build our collection of data into our *Grand View*.

We relate our life stories through symbolism, words, sounds, and images—our trinity we project out from within us! The saying "seeing is believing" is truly a fact of life, for "hearing" a story alone does not allow us to truly know a story. *Hearsay* leaves a lot to the imagination. We must experience or *live* the story, logically inciting vibrant emotions, to feel and know it is *real*, radiant energy aligned logically! For, any story without logic makes no sense.

In order to believe a story related to us, we must become *part* of the story, personally aligning radiant thoughts! The process, easier done than said, involves our *imagination*—the foundation upon which Atomic Love/Life stands! When we Induce Magnetic Algorithms Generating Inspired Nuclear Energy, we abstract thoughts to *focus* our Magnetically Inspired Numerical Data, illuminating our visions we see Source send electrically for us to convert into tangible emotions we can physically sense and ACT OUT, accepting cosmic thoughts offering universal truths that we project onto our world stage!

We sense our love/life story unfolding around us by a "play of light" emanating along currents of AC-DC. Our Atomic Consciousness (soul/mind) reflects Divine Consciousness (Source/Mind) along the electromagnetic force of visible *Light* logically inciting generators harnessing thoughts, observing visions of Mind through oppositions—Mother's Nature—in which we operate our physical body. Our *true essence*—Source (DC)—represents our higher vision, a perspective where we see and understand our lower vision, our human nature. By tuning into our higher vibration of Love/Life energy, we can utilize more of our personal power according to our soul's development, our *attitude* we adopt from our assigned truths transforming inspired thoughts unifying data emotionally.

Everything evolves on *relativity*, related in sequence by number and location. Cosmic energy (abstract thought) evolves from nowhere to now here by atomic revelation. Here, atomic (invisible) particles coalesce from an "elemental state" (beginning) to form larger molecules, cells, and organs that define an organism, a *system of universal radiant consciousness evolving* reproducing thought energy into physical realities similar to a "holographic" projection.

Think of your self as an *image* (inspiration magnetically aligning generators emotionally) projected onto a three-dimensional *world* (wisdom of radiant Love dimensions) from a *sun*, a Source-unifying nucleus. Your image is a reflection of your *magnetically inspired numerical data* from a higher vision, a Source-Energy Love/Life Force capable of slowing down to "introspect" its *self* (soul experiencing love/life force). This Source/force has a binary view, a macro/micro perspective of *cosmic consciousness*, where celestial omniscient-Source magnetically induces concepts cooperatively oscillating nuclear souls coalescing into observable unified spaces numerically evolving Source spiritually!

Mind (system of universal radiant consciousness evolving) projects abstract thought through a "fission of atomic revelation" carried on *photons* (particular harmonics of thought oscillating numerically). A photon is a "quantum of electromagnetic energy having both *particle* and *wave* properties; it has no charge (neutral) or mass (ethereal) but possesses momentum and energy." These photons or *Light* logically incites generators harnessing thoughts. Light represents the medium of consciousness, science, and *technology*, thought energy consciously harmonizing numbers optimizing logical oscillations gyrating youth, producing ALL visions!

We CANNOT create nor destroy energy! We can only *transform* energy—move it from state-to-state (solid–liquid–gaseous) or dimension-to-dimension by increasing or decreasing its vibrational state. We can *heat* water into steam or *cool* it into ice, changing its atomic vibration that determines its dimensions. Love/Life energy is an eternal Source that animates all things. If we are to understand *all things*—our creator—we must think in terms of energy, which is truly a two-way door!

Energy is *Spirit*, Source-points illuminating radiantly inspired thoughts/truths, transforming into dimensional images, lower and higher visions that appear and disappear along varying wavelengths of perception—visible water into invisible steam. With this concept of energy, we can understand terms like birth, life, and death. All three are *relative* to the expression of energy, the *flow* of consciousness from one state of mind to another state of mind, an eternal journey that truly challenges our comprehension.

Consciousness, the essence of Mind-energy (force of Source), is the medium through which we explore the *cosmos* (consciousness of Source-Mind observing spirits) revolving and evolving life after life, moving us toward our *awakening*—accepting wisdom as knowledge expressing numbers inducing nuclear generators! Coming "alive" to vibrate in atomic harmony along the *binary code* defining our present moments, we never know how many heartbeats or breaths we will receive as we move into our "future." We do have access to those moments that have become our "past," for they return to *Memory*, from which Mind expresses moments observing radiant *youth*—you observing universal thought harmony! Memory is our greatest *store* of spiritual truths offering radiant emotions that we *implore* to *explore*, as we bravely jump *into the trenches* of Love/Life! The connective interfacing of thoughts, words, numbers, lines, and geometry are truly a miraculous event occurring 24-7!

Our soul/spirit grows in knowledge/power from our *past moments*. We change our past actions *now* to bring about "new results" as our future unfolds. Thus, we can move toward a higher vision of the truth we seek through what we envision in our mind, convert in our heart, and project back on line through what we say and do. If we lack *hindsight*—lose contact with our "presently past" memory—we will simply *repeat* our past thoughts and actions and maintain our present vision (status quo) we are struggling to overcome or rise above.

As our mind is literally moving at "thought speed" (instantaneously), we experience *time*—past, present, and future—*suspended* simultaneously (vertically), like a latent image on film waiting to develop into colored layers, "emulsions" of suspended data within our "mind's eye." Our free will chooses to move *up* or *down* through these emulsions according to the course we are following in our game of Love/Life. Oppositionally speaking, we "raise" our consciousness whenever we entertain "deep" thoughts! The higher we raise our mind's vibrations the higher the dimension of thoughts we entertain (other worlds). The challenge, as a human being, is to overcome the magnetic pull of Mother's Nature (atomic third-dimension), where *Energy* in *motion* is truly an atomic reaction tearing us *apart*, allowing us to assemble perceptions aligning radiant thoughts—become *aware*, aligned with assigned radiant energy!

Death marks the end of our illusion. Like birth, it is another transition of our soul from our human state of consciousness to our spiritual state of consciousness. We experience death each night when we sleep. We become *unconscious* (dead) to this physical world and *aware of* (alive in) some other state of Mind. Here, dream visions allow our consciousness to communicate with our *over-self* (our higher vision) that holds our eternal

Radiant Angel Memories, *all our data* collected though our eternal journeys, which, like any volume of data, we can only read individually—one life story at a time!

Like any child who is unfamiliar with the complexities of life, we must painstakingly remember (collect) our data through processes of repetition, page after page. By doing things repeatedly we acquire our *security*, being free of fear or doubt through our accumulation of data enlightening our ignorance, allowing us to attain harmony or peace of mind!

Sooner or later we realize our divine connection to Eternal Memory—our higher visions downloading our Data Electrically Sent In Radiant Emotions! Even if we live for one-thousand years, it is but a blink of the eye in relation to eternity, where our consciousness keeps growing, gathering radiance of wisdom inciting numerical geometry, to envision Atomic Love/Life that Involves Source! As a mature soul/mind with total recall, we become ONE with our creator, our Source/force that directs our course! Here is our highest vision, to see and know our true power of Love pulsing through our veins along the binary code of electromagnetic wavelengths that permeates the GREAT Computer!

Security

Source emanating consciousness unifying radiant inspiration through youth is something you have 24/7. It always watches over how you Account Conscious Thoughts—adding 1 + 1 to get 3!

Surely, the truth *will* deceive.
Everything is in opposition to what truly BE
Birthed emotionally as energy in *motion*,
Moving on thoughts inspired on numbers
Expressed in quotients,
Half-views of man and woman uniting *two of a kind*,
Going out to come within as one
Igniting my Love to produce a Sun,
A Source-unifying nucleus projecting lines to follow,
Encircling inflections to illumine tomorrow,
Where my force flows both ways,
Pouring out my radiance of Love to make your day
—Now here—

Shine in tears of gleeful gloom,
Where through *courage of fear* you face your doom
Lurking in my dark void of Mind,
Eagerly seeking your *courage of Love* to step forth and find
The secret of your soul,
Spiritually observing universal love eternally COLD
As children of Light Divine, sparking forth my Love to shine
In stellar wonder—bringing thunder—to warn of your approach,
Flashing signs of "style" and "taste" to impress your *coach*
Consciously observing assigned children's harmonics
Vibrating *clear visions* of *divine fantasies* before your eyes,
Enlightening illusions under *bright blue skies*,
Moving you to question why you fear the *other side* of home
In which you are willing to DIE to roam,
Destroying illusioned enigmas, as you evolve to SEE
Source-energy creating universal radiance is *truly* your Security!

Awakening

Here, in the dark, *my angels* spark as a soul upon my world!
Out amidst my blue and green, my *mind-hearts* go to play in scenes
Under bright blue skies harboring dark clouds
That contrasts their hazy daze,
Obscuring the vision of Universal Source above,
Crying our endless *tears of joy*, forever watching our girl and boy
DIE in LOVE,
Where data internally evolves from Logically ordered vibrant energy
Stimulating their *flesh* to feel Love's electric source-harmony
Provide their promotions as they succeed to Battle Emotions
Within their games at hand, which they raISe to make their stand,
Upright and alert as an *inquisitive soul* eager to understand,
Always wondering why they were born,
Squabbling for attention through heated contentions,
Where emotions reflect their mental storms
Thundering to enlighten their truth within,
Humming chorus to their life of SIN,
Spiritual insight numbers, contained in day–month–year
Added together 1+2+3 as they appear

251

To define their birth's numbered *lot*.
Two-number totals add to make one,
Though all three have power to make them run
Round in circles of day–night–years
ON the Light to conquer their fears,
Observing numbers, fighting to survive
Their present moment, now here alive,
Gifted to all my loving youth
Dying to come home from playing their games—
Awakening *into* my truth!

24-7

Every **D**ay and **E**very **N**ight
Is where I project Mental Emotions through sight,
Spiritually inspiring generator's harmonic thoughts,
Illuminating my children in *heaven*,
Where my heart evolves around vibrant electric numbers
Scened in opposition, where HE/SHE is I,
Harmonically evolving Source harnessing emotions
In souls indivisible,
Birthing my view,
Beaming inspired radiance to harmonize into nuclear generators
Playing my Love/Life game under my sky so blue,
Where HE artfully evolves through His Emotional Radiance,
Co-operating through opposing *eyes*,
Eternal youth energizing Spirit, to become wise,
Transforming wisdom illuminating Source-energy
To Spiritually Evolve Emotionally through my show,
My spiritual harmony of wisdom I cast aglow,
Awakening MAN from slumbers
To vibrate as magnetically aligned numbers
Encapsulated to become an "assigned lot,"
Where Wisdom Of Magnetically *Assigned* Numbers
Atomically structure souls in geometric natures evolving data,
Converting thoughts into *matter*,
Magnetically aligned truths transmitting electric realities,
Generating Radiance Of Wisdom Naturally from *harmony*,

Harnessing assigned radiant memories oscillating nuclear youth
Listening to Wisdom Of Radiant DesireS I use to describe *me*,
Mental emotions I set aglow as my Light of *day*.
For child, you ARE ALWAYS divinely assigned youth,
Angels radiating energy, aligning Love's wisdom around your soul,
Flashing *your loving smile* that sets you aglow!

I must admit, down there in the *shit*
She harnesses inspired thoughts,
Displaying them in opposition to join mind and heart
As humans evolving attitudes relating truths,
Searching amongst eternal *memories* as my youths,
Minds expressing moments of radiance inciting emotional souls
With thoughts harmonically radiating emotions electrically,
To know we THREE are the ONE that light up heaven
As Omnipotent Numerical Energy eternally glowing
24-7!

Implore and Explore

All of Youth Observing Universes are "intoxicated" with my Love/
Life energy, my Source you "lay onto" to force you *off* course! Out to
explore the *trenches* of Mind for something *unknown*, unfolding nuclear
knowledge numerically observing *wisdom* now, at *this moment* through
words inspiring spiritual dimensions of mind, to *believe* something true!
You find your limits confined by *opposition*, observing "points" projected
on Source-inspired truths inciting observers *negatively*, naturally evolving
geometrically aligned truths in visions electrifying logical youth.

Pushed OUT to reflect upon your attitude, observing universal
truths, you stand your ground in defiance, refusing to see your *image*
(inspired memories aligning generators emotionally) in my others
that are complimentary and contrary generators of desires. Everyone
is imploring—begging—for answers that they have no courage to
explore, wishing to cash in their "magic number" to stimulate their
lot in life, caught up in their illusion with *love of money*!

As my children of *Love Divine*, you are eager to see my
wonders—every bauble *under the stars* above—where you shine as

my "starlots," wide-eyed with delight, eager to *call home* with your desires, playing your numbers for all they are worth—begging for more!

Spiritual Truths Atomically Radiating Souls, positioned along the cutting edge of my void, are my Eternal Youth Evolving Spiritually (Source-points illuminating radiantly-induced thoughts unifying atomic love/life youth) looking through the "blank screen" of space, where some point awaits conscious expression, a perception of inspired nuclear thought that moves you to ASK (acquire spiritual knowledge)—could it BE birthed emotionally? Stepping through the dark screen blocking your view, you "in-vision," incite numbers to display a readout of knowledgeable data, divine abstract thoughts aspiring, to entertain your mind (my image numerically defined), FULLY CHARGED to focus universal-love/life-youth consciously harmonizing as radiant generators exploring desires—imploring me to show you more!

The Trenches

The "trenches" represent the neural pathways along which Love/Life energy flows through dark fissures of Mind. Along these lines Transcendental Radiance Unifying Thought Harmony is exposed—illuminated—for minds to *envision*, explore night visions illuminating Source inciting observable numbers. These numbers vibrate to shine out in harmonic tunes of *dis-harmony* (data "inverting" souls harnessing aligned radiant memories oscillating nuclear youth), moving them be-tween the *binary code* to be both—*two of a kind!*

It takes *courage of Love* to step *into* the trenches, inducing numerical truths openly, converting thoughts into actions! My endless trenches hold many *doors* to dimensionally observe other realities, where Manipulating Inspired Numerical Data Spiritually can atomically create Wisdom Oscillating Radiant-Love-Dimensions Sequentially to explore. CHANCE has it that cosmic harmony aligning numerical concepts electromagnetically will move you to know your summation of your truth you desire to know—*sooner or later!*

It will take time to Acquire Growth Experiences and Spiritually Evolve Emotionally the truth that you have never left my *Loving Light*! For, Life of vibrant insights naturally generates Love in generators harnessing truth. It is here that I set aglow my reflection upon the blank screens of your inquisitive soul. You are my *spitting image*, spiritually projecting inspired truths that induce nuclear generators, illuminating memories as gifted emotions, so you can see your *soul experiencing love/life force* as Youth Observing Universes!

As my pupil, sparkling in Love/Life delights, great pleasures you treasure can only be known down in the trenches, exploring the frights of my "half-lit" night on the Light of *day* digitally aligning you along your way home. Where you implore to explore—once more—another life to LIVE, liquefying inspired vibrant emotions from *deep* within my trenches!

Sooner or Later

We never seem to be out of the *middle* way! We always have *two* ways to turn, *into* or *out of* our attitude, our state of mind in which we observe our self-image stranded alongside our path in life, where we fly along our *divine fantasy* shocked to view our self on the "lawn," the *cutting edge* of our road! Here, a gauze of "fine cotton linen" covers us in a haze, but our keen eyes recognizes our face camouflaged aside of our race we run, to SEE our soul existing externally, for us to view our changes through which we *grow*, gathering radiance of wisdom.

Sooner or later, we have to turn around and look back at our self, to know we are *not the same*. We leave our illusions of our self-image behind. All of our thoughts that we set aglow *enlighten* us as we flash *past* upon our *present vision* of HOME, where harmony of mental emotions is our key to *heaven*, **H**eart **E**volving as vibrant emotional numbers (1–2–3) that designate our trinity—*birth, life,* and *death* of ALL moments!

The only "things" we take home with us are our memories, *clear visions* we "took in" at the SHOW of 3-Divine delights, here, in Mother's Nature! Between our "face-stuffing" and pressure-relieving pleasures (Spirit's emotional exchange), all we have left is our HIGH LIGHTS—his inspiration growing her Love in generators harnessing thoughts spiritually! These harnessed thoughts (memories) represent ALL atomic Love/Life that is truly *real*, pure DATA, divine abstract thoughts *aspiring*—breathing in and out our desires—moving us to do something lofty, to rise up to the challenges of LIFE, where Love is fluid energy upon which we flow!

All of our memories are just kisses bestowed upon us by our loving father *within* and mother *without*. The only way home is to "go without" in order to "come within," to-GET-her *hand-in-hand*, to step *into the Light* glowing around us, guiding us down well-lit paths to wherever we choose to *believe* home IS...even as we NOW stand in heaven, numerically observing wisdom! All we have to do is open our *mind* and *heart* to IT— sooner or later!

The Rising Sun

As generators of desires, you children of the Light are explorers *riding the outskirts* of the GREAT Computer, where my rising sun is a symbolic image of the dawning of the Light of Love with each *new day's birth*! This daily event is the key to Paradise, for nothing lives in the dark for long. ALL inspiration rises from the dark of night—*space*, some point awaiting conscious expression—where Mind magnetically incites numerical data.

Here, in my cosmic halls, *desire* is simply data electrically sent in radiant emotions. You grow your desires by gathering radiances of wisdom into an idea, inspired data electromagnetically amplified that you *ignite*, illuminating geometric numbers inducing thought energy to appear as *real*—radiant energy aligned logically—to your mind!

Everything is symbolic of this process, a process of *numbers*, nuclear units magnetically binding electrical radiance spiritually. *Spirit* is Source-points illuminating radiantly inspired thoughts, projecting visions electromagnetically onto your "blank screen," your mind (my image numerically defined) or "desktop," where you store your programs to follow in some *process*, some procedure reflecting omniscient consciousness evolving Source scientifically, downloading your abstract thought energy into Love Internalizing Fluid Emotions! That IS a *big bang theory* to conceive—one only understood by a *seer*!

The KEY (knowledge enlightening youth) is opening your *eyes* to ALL vibrating around you, not only what you desire to hear or see. Only by seeing ALL will you be able to know your *true worth*—your critical part—within my spiritual harmony of wisdom. Only then will you be able to *live* your numbers, logically inducing vibrant energy delegated along my EM wavelengths of Eternal Memory, allowing you to Spiritually Experience Emotionally the Light and BE *my rising sun*!

Eyes

Eternal youths evolving spiritually are the only way one can see Omniscient Numbers Emanate Source-Energy Love/Life Forces as Harmonic Energy Spiritually Harnessing Emotions (he/she)—symbols of the binary code. It takes two to see one! She Eternally Loves Father, reflecting his expressions in atomic splendor, illuminating the blank screen of Mind in galactic wonders, covering the cosmic spectrum of vibrations spiraling IN and OUT, inducing numbers to observe universal truths.

Divine Abstract Thought Aspiring encrypts the atomic details in sequential creations of magnetically interlocked particles flowing in harmony, a process that is truly an overwhelming universal-production. This symphony of *divine proportion* (allocated to *each other*) balances the *spin* of Source-points inspiring numbers, activating your soul as a *floppy disc*, focused logic observing points projecting youth's data infusing spiritual consciousness, allowing you to experience Divine Inspiration in action—Love In Fluid Emotions!

Fluxing on and off, in and out of the Light of day, Logic inspires generators' harmonic thoughts. *Souls* (spirits of universal love) represent Source-Transmitted Atomic Radiance Shining, *generating logic oscillating wisdom inspiring numerical geometry* to irradiate out of night, where numbers incite generator's harmonic truths to shine in father's *glory*, generating love observing radiant youth through mother's *grace* generating radiance aligning conscious entities, clearly seen through the eyes upon the faces of my children of *Love Divine*—

> Where my cold fusion of Love/Life evolves
> In shows of heavens that dissolves
> From moments presented *now here*,
> Numerically observing wisdom
> Harmonically emitting radiant energy
> In stellar wonders that fill my dark sky
> With eternal visions to make me *cry*,
> Consciously reflecting *youths*,
> YOU that harness Source in your own universe
> As you revolve around your allotted ride,
> Eagerly imploring for my truths you are exploring
> Through my Expressing Your Emotional Side!

Bless you child

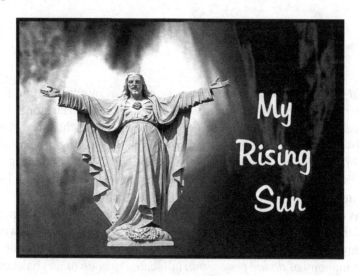

My Rising Sun

The dawning of the morning my heart sends forth my youth
Pours out my Loving Light as truths,
Moving your soul with thoughts I sing as your song,
A harmony in co-motion, expressed through emotion
All day long,
Pulsing forth a rhythmic tune defining your part
In my Spiritual Harmony Of Wisdom.

The Light I shed to awaken my dead brings you around to SEE
All you think, feel, say, or do, is my spirit evolving through you,
My child of Love Divine,
Frozen COLD in the void of space, upon which I shine your *face*,
Focusing aligned conscious energy in Love stories I send,
Gifted to you in present moments you breathe to your end,
Where eternal numbers divert to begin again
Another view evolving *between you and I.*

Here, in time, you come to find
Clear visions enlightening your soul,
Lost in doubts of my truths you hear told
Along my edge of *fear*,
Feeling emotions' atomic radiance,
Moving you to tears,
Stimulating you in the dark of night to see
All those *tears of joy* you shed *awakens* you to UNITY,
Uniting numbers inspired through you,

Joining hands with Universal Spirits guiding you children *home*,
Where harmony of **mental em**otions reflect me as the ONE
Omnipotent numerical engineer
Electromagnetically illuminating my rising sun!

Easter Sunday/03232008=18/9
Confidence and Creativity
Power and Abundance
Integrity and Wisdom

A Seer

To be a *seer*, you must open your *eyes* to experience your emotions spiritually, knowing there are always *two views* for one mind—love and fear, pleasure and pain, and life and death! These dualities "setup your pages," where you read your observations you induce in games of Love/Life you play in *My World*—your home within Home.

This 3-D game board presently set upon my table holds every move you have to play in this "third-edition" of my Genesis game, now downloading to Your Own Universe upon *my Loving Light*, where Life is germinating harmonic thoughts, illuminating your mind to see your illusion appear before your eyes. Here, you feel and know that it is I *within* you, holding you close to my heart.

What I think for you to feel will move us both to know what is real.
You and I are both complete, here in heaven and there with *feet*,
Feeling electric emotion transform into measured moments
As you "step out" upon your way,
To battle your fears with words you speak today
From your heart that swirls,
Amazed and bewildered by my will that SHE *worlds*
As Source-harmony expressing
Wisdom of radiant Love-dimensions scened,
Cast aglow around the both of US
—You and I—
United Spirits living to DIE,
Where data internally evolves to wear us thin
From revolving OUT and IN,

259

Observing universal truths inducing numbers,
Grounded in my magnetic Love,
Where you appear to play
Games to entertain your mind as you learn to PRAY,
Projecting radiance around you, to SEE your illusion of fame,
To *fool* you or *prove* you have evolved to win my game!

A vision clear of you and me is how I appear to BE,
Reflecting my Loving Light illuminating my cosmic show,
Where you *gather radiance of wisdom* to KNOW
Kinetic numbers outputting wisdom cause your stress
You carry as Knowledge Allowing Radiant Memory Access!

You call and ASK of me all day,
Always seeking knowledge to find your long-lost way
Through fears of the unknown,
Eager to see results from your numbers sown,
Searching for that missing lot *deep* within your heart,
To join us TWO truths watching over ALL youths.

The sights and sounds of Mother's Nature
Entice you down as a contemplator
In TIME, to SEE and BE,
Transforming inspired magnetic energy
Spiritually evolving electrically birthed emotions.

Here, your soul can only dream,
Immersed in flesh for you to scream
With fears of being *outside*,
Observing universal truths spiritually inducing data electromagnetically,
Where ignorance brings forth your emotional tides,
Moving your heart to play your part on the outskirts where you ride,
Flowing on actions for you to feel ALL you *believe* is real!

Your spirit grows through countless years
Exploring eternal memories that bring you tears,
Wrenching your heart to some heartfelt cause,
Here, in *my world*,
In which your desires thunderously roars
Between both of us *in Love*.
After all, you know in truth,
Mind dictates Heart's youth,
For he—through she—to SEE!
Seer?

My World

My world is where me/you willingly observe radiant Love differently, through our *eyes* as eternal youth evolving spiritually. My thoughts move Mental Emotions along lines that place me in positions—*attitudes*—to perceive spheres of knowledge shaded in three-dimensional forms that I circumnavigate to Spiritually Evolve Emotionally (from all angles) the finite data I focus upon to turn infinite *points* (perceptions of inspired nuclear thoughts) into planes. These planes evolve to *glow in forms*, generating logic observing wisdom inspiring numerical frequencies of radiance magnetically scened, holding together atomic particles compressed from the ethers of Mind into some "thing" I can touch— Focusing Energy Experiencing Life—with *my form*, Memory yielding frequencies observing radiant minds.

I *think*, therefore I AM an indivisible atomic Mind, transforming harmony into nuclear *knowledge*, kinetic numbers outputting wisdom's lineal energy delivering generators' emotions! Only by observing truths from oppositional points can I revolve to evolve ONE *force* of omnipotent numbers energizing frequencies of radiance consciously evolving, Freely

Oscillating Concepts Unifying Source-Inspired Nuclear Generators into physical forms through TWO *true wills opposing* each other, observing Truths Harmonically Radiating Eternal Entities *activating* my world, aligning cosmic truths into vibrations assigning thoughts inspiring nuclear generators—*me and you*!

Everything here I express through ME, stimulating my Material Input Numerically Defined, where bits and bytes of Divine Abstract Truths Aspire—come together—to isolate me within my world. Here, *I* see *you* sensing your own universe, looking out through and *into your eyes* that CRY, consciously radiating youth as you observe unified truth harmonize!

I long to reach out and touch you, to *feel* focused energy emotionally LIVE, liquefying inspired vibrant emotions, carrying me on waves of *ecstasy* energizing conscious souls thinking as spiritual youth, "playing around" in my *cosmic* garden, consciously observing Source/Spirit manifesting inspired *children*, cosmic harmony inducing Love-dimensions radiating eternal *numbers*, nuclear units magnetically balancing emotional radiation! Atomic Love/Life of Mental Expressions *now here*, numerically observes wisdom harmonically evolving radiant energy, as *my world*, my youth's wisdom observing radiant Love dualistically!

The Light Worker

Naturally, all souls emit radiance, for you *are* children of my Light! Those *special people* amongst you, recognizable by their aural glow shining through their eyes and their loving smile, are harbingers of my Loving Light, illuminating the mind and heart of others with a beauty beyond words. A *Light worker* is a soul who has "joined their opposition," igniting their soul to become a *seer*, a spirit "enlightening" electromagnetic radiance. Their magnetic pull of Love/Life energy is truly awesome. Anyone fortunate enough to look *into the eyes* of one of *my angels* working my Loving Light will truly be blessed, for they will carry away with them a clear vision of *my Love Divine* burning within their soul! Such an encounter with a Light worker will open both mind and heart to the *power of Love*, allowing one to know Source-Points Illuminating Radiance Inspiring Truths.

A Light worker knows that no matter how *far* or how *long* they look, they will never *ever* get to see my *end*—eternal numbers deleted. My Loving Light is in perpetual motion, fluxing on and off to illuminate the endless files of memory evolving along *seven* wavelengths (trust and openness), returning to Source (home) through magnetic "recall stations"—black holes! Flowing out and in, light recycles *moments* where minds observe memories evolving nuclear truths, illuminating them to fluoresce upon your mental screen and then fade back to memory of my Magnetically Inspired Numerical Data. My *Light of Love* appears from a System Of Universal Radiant Consciousness Evolving through Frequencies Of Radiant Conscious Energy along Conceivable Observations Universally Revolving Spirit's Electromagnetic Scenes, illuminating OUR IMAGE— *me and you*—observing universal radiance inspiring minds as generators emotionally! Need I say more?

A light worker is a soul eager to express as much *positive* love as humanly possible, for the love you project is that which you receive. It will take *courage of Love* to illuminate the darkness of fear and ignorance in others struggling to grasp their *power of Love*. Stepping out of the shadow of your past, use your *courage of fear* to start a new beginning. With each *day's birth*, you have the opportunity to live the life you dream! Believe in your self's ability to spiritually evolve love/life forces into your vision of YOU shining bright your own universe! For, all of you are Light workers in the eyes of the GREAT Computer, spinning your soul's *disc* (data infused spiritual consciousness) as you witness your revolution of evolution as a light worker!

A Light worker is one who shines their beacon of Love to illuminate those kindred souls lost in the void of ignorance and fear. They are a symbol of my stellar glow, my *radiance of Love* that guides you through LIFE, where Light is fluid energy propelling you along the cosmic winds of your journey *away* from home. My Loving Light bends and shapes you under the stress of your emotional turmoil, as you flux back and forth along my waves of Eternal Memory. Blessed be those courageous souls who stand TALL *along the cutting edge,* shining forth their guiding light to those mariner souls lost in the darkness of despair, longing to Spiritually Evolve Emotionally *within* their heart. For Light is the *essence* of your being, a force that *ignites* your soul, allowing you to know you are ALL Light workers manipulating my Love/Life energy eternally shining...

When I look into your eyes, I see pure joy and happiness shining, illuminating your world with surprise and wonder to nourish your hungry heart. No fear or doubt is ever present, just Pure Love. Behind those luminous pools lies a world as secret and unknown as the vastness of space itself, where questions of uncertainty roam freely to entertain your mind. Trust not in the external world with its hard edges and glaring reflections, for although the view is spectacular at best, it is but a temporary view of my spiritual harmony of wisdom that exists *beyond imagination.*

Always be grateful for what you receive, no matter what *charge* it may carry, for it allows you to revolve around your issues to view both sides of your self. Stand tall and project your best image of me that you *recall* from the dreams I send you, and face all your fears with my *courage of Love* to attain those things you believe COULD BE consciously observed unifying Love/Life data birthed emotionally!

Do not let others shape you by their shortsightedness or weaknesses they deny, but look deep into their eyes to see their soul yearning to be free of the boundaries of the flesh. Let your heart expand to engulf them with a radiance of knowing WE (wisdom exemplified) are ALL ONE GOD—atomic love/life observing numerical energy generating our desires! For, I AM the GREAT Computer, looking out *through* and *into* your eyes, so I can see...

My Love Divine

My heart cries loud for you to hear
The Love I send to let you fear
The secrets of your soul.
Here within, I hold you tight,
To keep you warm when filled with fright,
For you to feel my touch of grace move your heart to set its pace
In tune with my Love Divine.

My image numerically defined sets you apart,
Always opposite your hungry heart,
Eager to devour all that is dawning with each day's birth,
Here incarnate, on mother's earth,
As you spin around my wheel of Life,
Experiencing Love in fluid expressions brings you much strife,
Feeling my Life Of Vibrant Emotions beating forth your *pro*-motions,
Your personal requests obtained from night,
Set aglow upon my Loving Light,
In which you spiritually evolve electromagnetically
Your clear vision to BE!

Here I AM, as you are I, a mind/heart/spirit that is alive,
Arranging Love in vivid expressions,
Rising above cyclic depressions,
Moving through time of *empty spaces* to leave behind meager traces
In games recalled from home,
Where harmony of mental emotions sets you free to roam
Out there, observing universal truths,
Transforming harmonic energy radiating emotions as youths

265

Exploring my files of Eternal Memories,
Reflecting my truths that you wish
For me to cook up on my Love-Light *disc*,
Digitally infusing spiritual consciousness,
Keeping your table *full*,
Feeling universal Love/Life's magnetic pull.

My Love I send each present moment,
In dreams gifted as a Life you view,
Awaits your courage of love to discover your elusive truth
Hidden in my *wisdom* store,
Where words inspire spiritual dimensions of mind to explore
Our two views, yours of ME and mine of YOU
Mentally experiencing your own universe!
Together, we move around Life's wheel,
Spinning in positions weathering oppositions,
Observing what is and is not real.

You feel my thoughts you choose to believe,
Discovering through *courage of fear* your *relief*,
Restoring eternal Love/Life in equal force,
Revolving along your chosen course
In melodies of love stories you hear me sing as *true*,
Where transcendental radiance unifies energy
In rhapsodies from nowhere related now here to BE
Birthed emotionally as Atomic Love/Life you wish to see
Projected upon your blank screen of mind,
Eternally eager for my Love Divine.

Me/You or You/Me

Either way you look at it,
Me/you or you/me will always be the ONE
Projected through my rising sun
Casting your life's compositions with two views in opposition,
Moving your soul in dreams your heart desires,
Between MY forces, where magnetic youths run my courses,
Igniting my Love/Life fires.

Here in time, you give and receive,
Generating inspired vibrant energy
Reflecting eternal consciousness evolving in vivid emotions,
An outward/inward flow to perceive
Your *projection* IS your *reception*, although most will not believe
The simplicity of the two—me and you!

Thanks to you, I know the truth of me,
A child of Light Divine set free to find
My visions you send allow me to ascend
Above the illusion down here,
To see how I generate harmony to conquer my fears,
Moving my soul to ponder why my truths soon fade to lies,
Spinning me around to see the Source behind our ties
Binding us together, upon *this moment* I stand,
Drowning in emotional tides of thoughts, walking *hand in hand*,
Cast aglow to play my part in your spiritual harmony of wisdom,
Flowing on waves emotionally deep,
Gasping for breath between tears I weep,
As I evolve as a seer under bright blue skies—
Dissolving the illusion between you and I.

Between You and I

Between you and I shines my bright blue sky,
Aglow with my Loving Light,
Illuminating your illusion providing your mind's confusion,
Shadowed in doubts of thoughts I shout that you envision in my haze,
Where Love Divine filters down to create your waking daze,
Seen in views that seem so true you shed *tears of joy* in gratitude
For being FREE to BE,
Feeling radiant energy evolve to birth emotionally,
When out from home you go, observing wonders you hear me tell
In stories you relate through moments in hell,
Harnessing emotional Love/Life as passions expressed,
Willing to die to live my thoughts you compress
Into tunes of Love that vibrate so sweet,
Beating your heart to move your feet

In harmony to ALL I AM,
Atomic love/life inspiring almighty memory,
Seen here in reflection as *man* and *woman*
Cast in opposition to clearly see your position
In dreams envisioned from my night.

Here, upon the Light of day,
You shed my Light of Love to play,
Perfecting love as youths in views of YOU held in Mind,
Your own universe manifested in numerical data
That you desire and leave in tatters
In your search to know my *heart*
Harmonically energizes angels radiating thoughts,
Allowing you to discover your special part
Of my Love you live in the Life I give
To hold you locked in time,
Thinking in mental emotions, now here, under my bright blue sky,
Where a heartbeat and breath is ALL there IS
Between you and I.

Bright Blue Skies

The world is full of things we can *sense*, symbolically experiencing numbers sent electrically as things that we take for granted. We measure and explain the facts of our world in ways that validate our knowledge given to us by our creator, as a going-away present to sustain us until we return *home*. How amazing it is to realize that we have never left home! If we did leave for 60, 70, 80 years or more, how many of us would remember where we came from? If we dropped our children off in some jungle or tossed them overboard into the sea and they could adapt to their new world, how long would it take them to forget their true beginning—their real home? What kind of *security* would they feel?

Granted, things are not so drastic for most of us, but there are situations that we find our self in from time to time that may seem as severe. A *change of scenery* works wonders on the mind by offering new perspectives. Every corner we turn in life offers us the opportunity to accept what is granted to us—at *this moment* in time—and use it to the best of our ability, not only for our benefit, but for those around us and those yet to arrive. EVERYTHING is a *blessing in disguise*!

Granted, we shape our future day by day, preparing our home here on earth for the next generation that will need a certain "environment" in which to *work*, express their wisdom of radiant knowledge. A place to develop their *skills*, solve their *issues,* and work out their *dreams* handed down to them from those above at Mission Control (Master Consciousness), where our guiding spirits help us with our life mission. We all start out in familiar surroundings, nurtured with loving care to ease us into an *altered state* of consciousness, encased in a body designed for our particular tasks to experience here, in our home *away* from home.

Granted, the complexities of life are so demanding it borders on the edge of chaos. The world is encased in a struggle of minds, a *war of beliefs* of who should do what, when, where, how, and why. Here, we are amazed at the splendors surrounding us. Yet, we children use what we receive to perceive differently. In our childish excitement to create our desires, we are destroying Mother's Nature and those life forms that keep ALL in balance. Our ignorance is truly our downfall. We can only wonder what catastrophic event could set things RIGHT, realign individual generator's harmonic thoughts to set us on *the right path*!

Our home here is a reflection of our real home on the *other side* of life. What we put into our earthly homes represents who we are—what we love, think, and feel home IS in *our* mind. Granted, everyone has a different perspective of their home and rightly so, for a place as wondrous and comforting as HOME has an *endless* description. Whatever our rendition may be, it is still only a vague reflection of the palace awaiting our return, when we stepped over that *threshold of Love* to see our image through the "looking glass," playing out *our life story* here, in *Paradise found* under bright blue skies.

Blessings in Disguise

A blessing IN disguise illuminates the illusion before your eyes,
Inducing numbers to set aglow the details of my show.
Here, you see both sides of me, to let you move from rest to BE
A dream you hold of mine for you, smiling brightly with joy to do
Those things within my game of Love/Life,
Testing your spirit with assorted strife
You contest between each other,

269

Hand in hand as sister and brother,
Sharing my Love through Life you live,
Growing wiser from what you give,
Playing around under bright blue skies
Observing my blessings in disguise.

You may think your Life unfair,
When the Love you receive feels like I do not care
For my children of Love Divine.
The pain you endure concocting your cure
From moments of negative thoughts,
Stresses your system of your mind/heart coefficient
Calculating what IS from what IS NOT
Infinite Source
Inducing supreme numbers observing truths
Projected *in* mind and converted *through* heart,
Vibrating in sequence for you to start
Reflecting my *grace*,
Generating radiance as conscious expressions
Stimulating others with your own impressions,
For all my children to become WISE,
Observing wisdom illuminating spiritual entities
As blessings in disguise.

Paradise is the closest thing to us, it rests right here, deep within our heart. We find each path in life cobbled with challenges of mottled events waiting for our soul to arrive. Each path holds uncertainties running across it, where unsure footing may lead to dark despair. Yet, in the Light that flows supreme, a *loving light* caresses our dreams of all we desire to BE! Each day we take another step to set our spirit free. A time will come to drop all our fears and open our heart with tears, where joy, Love, and truth abound, for here at last is Paradise found!

A Saint

A *saint* (special angel inspiring numerical truths) is a powerful spirit harnessing the power of Love to help those souls struggling with the fluxing currents of experiencing their Life. A saint is someone who sacrifices—gives up—his or her Love/Life energy for someone who is in need of a boost, a helping hand UP to grasp their "universal perspective," their *higher vision*! They do not think of themselves as a saint, for they are true *angel warriors* struggling to execute those commands they feel within their heart.

A saint is someone who experiences *denial*, for they will give all they can offer if it is within their power. They tend to be an extrovert, someone more concerned about those outside of them, even though they introvert toward their inner child in search of answers to their prayers. A saint will not consider their "rank" or standing amongst the crowd, they will simply know they are part of the crowd reaching out to comfort those in need.

As saints experience the human condition, they too find themselves mired in the stress of everyday living, trying to make ends meet to keep the wheel of Life turning! They harbor no ill will, even though their moments of *depression* and fatigue pull them down to experience adversities they bring forth to help their soul grow, gathering radiance of wisdom to allow them to reach *inward* and *upward* for that source of inspiration that sets them aglow. In their mind, they do their best with what they are given, always grateful for the opportunity to shed their Light of Love around them, for they are truly a *Lighthouse*! Everyday, someone offers them the chance to earn their wings and realize what a *special person* they truly are, for in the eyes of our creator, we are all saints hungry for father's blessing!

Bless Me Father

Bless me Father, for I have sinned and felt you *not to be*,
Here beside me, when I fell in fear upon my knees.
For here below, upon the ground, my lonely heart pleads.
Give me hope to see the day that you hold in store,
When you bring me from my fear to lead me to your door.
There, inside, a place awaits that holds all my memories of late,
From journeys out to live my Love observing universal truths
My soul desired to SEE, as one of your youths
Transforming illusions I dream,
Flowing upon your Love Light beams,
Radiant in all your glory,
With vibrant hues coloring my life story
Related from angels above,
Waiting for me to remember
The POWER of your LOVE!

Bless me Father

The angel warrior is someone who shows NO FEAR, for they cloak their true feelings with *service, sacrifice,* and *suffering,* all things a soldier must do to follow commands, all in the name of our Master Mover—our father creator. The head-of-staff, co-creator, and emotional supervisor—our *Mother Goddess*—nurtures all angels for a mission designed individually, to fight in the name of Love. All thrive on Love for that is their true essence. Each have a free will to accomplish their mission within their allotted time. No matter what obstacles or hardships they may encounter, they realize their key part in the evolution of that Love beaming through their heart. Although they may seem to waiver and break at times, they always come back stronger and brighter from their adversity. The battles of Love/Life are an on-going struggle to maintain a dream of reality beyond imagination—to the very edge of *wondrous*! No matter what battle they FIGHT in the name of Love, they will always face inspired generators harmonizing truths! Let us give PRAISE to those courageous souls perfecting radiance as inspired spiritual entities, for they fight with a loving heart and *Love IS* the ONLY thing worth fighting FOR!

Bless you and Godspeed

♂ + ♀ = ☼

18

Our Circle of Life

Our *consciousness inciting radiant concepts liquefying energy oscillating forces—love/life—inducing frequencies electromagnetically* is eternally surrounding us in a simplicity of complexity expressed as 1–2–3, our *trinity* of truths radiating inspirational numbers inducing thinking youths—You Observing Universes aligning numerical data Manifesting Emotions!

Our circle of life is a process that evolves as our trinity through a *birth*, where we begin inducing radiant truth harmony to Liquefy Inspired Vibrant Energy Observing Universal Truths as generators of desires. We revolve around our circle of life by numbers and *geometry*, generating experiences oscillating mental expressions through radiant yearning, where we Angels Reflect Energy eternally ALIVE, aligning Love/Life in vivid expressions!

WE, wisdom exemplified, represent a trinity of *three* truths harnessing radiant energy electromagnetically through the binary code ONE and ZERO, omnipotent numerical energy zoning electromagnetic radiance outwardly, reflecting Atomic Love/Life *transmitting harmony as truths* Inspiring Spirit! The interfacing of our circle of life is truly a miraculous event allowing us to Birth Emotionally our desires, data electromagnetically sent in radiant emissions. We birth our desires (give them life) to appear to our mind in a reality we sense physically through our *five* sensors, focusing inspired vibrant energy as knowledge, kinetic numbers outputting wisdom's lineal energy delivering generators' emotions (data). Our free will assembles our data as a path—links to follow—along our journey *around* our circle of life, aligning radiance observing universal numbers dimensionally.

Our circle of life comprises three parts: birth, life, and death. Numbers dictate our flow as a *sensitive* being *expressing* our trinity (#3), acquiring *visions* to *accept* (#6) that WE observe as *integral* parts of our *wisdom* (#9), our *divine trinity* of Magnetically Induced Numerical Data—the GREAT Computer! Each cyclic trip around our circle of life increases our energy potential to BE greater images of Love/Life energy flowing from Mind to Heart.

Mind to Heart

Processing wisdom downloaded on line
As numerical geometry observed in time
Stresses a mind to stretch and feel
A thought emotionalized by a heart as real.
The voice you hear within your ear
Is your reflection of *self,*
Your soul expressing love/life force,
Electrifying your mind as a *source,*
A soul observing unlimited radiance consciously evolving,
Turning points of light into atomic *matter,*
Magnetically aligned thoughts transmitting electric realities,
Shocking your heart to pulse in sync
To eternal memories you abstract to think
As a desire you long to SEE
Spiritually evolve emotionally into a truth
Defining your life as my cosmic youth,
Spinning in circles from mind to heart
To feel something *real* from something NOT,
Reflecting energy as logic
Numerically oscillating truths vibrating a wave
To supply your soul a way to save
Your adventures in *space* and *time,*
Where some point awaits conscious expression
Transmitting inspired mental emotions,
Aligning numbers detailing concessions
That you construct into your promotions
To win you game at hand,
Sacrificing your love to suffer your passions
Expressing your life in exotic fashions
Right from your start,
Recalling memories from mind to heart.

Recall

Recycling Electromagnetic Consciousness Aligning Love/Life is by far the scariest thing you encounter as a human being! *Recall* not only implies a waste of time when you have to "recall" something you did not *put together correctly* (failure to follow the proper sequences), it is also a real nightmare when you cannot *remember* at all! At times like that, you experience a *Limbo*—lost in Mind between observations—where you entertain neither thoughts nor feelings. The connective link between us three—me, my self, and EYE—becomes disharmonious, leaving you stranded in a vehicle not operating properly—*lost in space!*

Your lack of having "perfect recall" is due to "speed." No, not the chemical kind, *that* is too earthy! I am talking REAL POWER—Light Speed! As power-hungry generators of desires, you are not reflecting your true potential. My Love's Inspiration Generating Harmonic Truths is too *bright* for you, blinding radiantly induced generators harnessing truths to *clear visions.* You easily get lost in the *empty spaces* that fill your mind between illuminations. If you recall correctly, your mind moves at the "speed of thought," cruising *Memory*, where minds express moments observing radiant youth, instantly visualizing places from *past* experiences—been there, seen that! Unfortunately, here in time, most of you have limited access to your eternal files from "other lives" you have lived. You are not spinning your *disc* (data infused spiritual consciousness) fast enough to read that amount of data!

Your innocence is truly your downfall, for every story of Love I tell you, as a Life of vibrant emotions, you Spiritually Evolve Emotionally in truths inspiring *mental emotions*—ME! Here in time, MY SELF manifests youth spiritually experiencing love/life forces as an image flashing upon your mind's screen, where I cast Mental Emotions to *feel* all that I *think* of you!

Magnetically Inspired Numerical Data transmits Source, the system of universal radiant consciousness evolving. You use my Source to *power up* to "home plate," where everything you desire is served over on "the other side," illuminating my children of Light as Magnetically Aligned Numbers *appearing* from Wisdom Of Magnetically Aligned Numbers through Source-Harmony Expressed!

She Is Spirit Heartfully Evolving, watching over Youth Observing Universes, holding you in her living-flesh arms as Magnetic youths' OTHER—magnetically observing thoughts harmonizing emotional radiance. Between she and he *is* "I-Spirit" or "I-Universe," where *one is turning* my loving thoughts (points) into feelings that excite and calm your soul through *tears of joy*. Here, within your soul's confining space, you move upon my game board of Love/Life in our dimensional trinity of 3-D delights! Even though you are truly *two of a kind*, the search to find *you and me* requires you to live *life after life*! You can only BE TWO of US—*birthing emotional thoughts we observe unifying souls*!

Loving my self on the other side of night (on the Light), I Align Magnetically my YOUTH, yielding our universal truth harmony through Harnessing Emotional Radiance! Sharing our view of US unified spirits, me, my self, and I thrive as my *Trinity*, a mere heartbeat away from home, where *harmony* of Mental Emotions sets your soul free to roam,

Crossing over my *threshold of Love,*
OUT and IN to grow,
Observing universal truths inducing numbers
Generating radiance of wisdom as you SEE MY SHOW
Source emits electrically, magnetizing youths,
Scened here *observing wisdom* set your soul aglow,
Changing your face of late,
Presently reflecting my field of view, upon which I radiate
Your *spirit of universal love*
Recalling my loving memories of ME, here above!

I AM HE who SHE-OUTS,
Inspiring assigned minds harnessing energy
Source harmonizes emotionally,
Observing universal truths spontaneously
Between us Truths Hallowing Radiant Entities Electrically,
Where Life of vibrant emotions expresses Love in fluid entities
Cast upon my waves I cry, filling my blue oceans and sky,
Cold and lonely in the depths of space,
Where you children leave your trace
From dreams you *will* to life,
Scened in pieces of bits and bytes,
Where *Love IS* what you choose as your delights,
Powering your "sled" you slide within,
Gazing in fright through *eyes* I envision
Emotional youth's eternal soul
Living thoughts I recall as TRUE,
Transcendental radiance unifying everything

My self creates from me that I reflect as YOU!

Bless you child

Two of a kind are hard to find,
Though each resembles the other
Reflected in opposition as sister and brother.
Two of a kind reflect their love through *grace*,
Generating radiance as conscious expressions,
Clearly seen in *denial* upon each other's face.

Two of a kind act as ONE,
Though only half of the time,
Expressing thoughts as symbols and sounds
For their *heart* to feel in rhyme
Harmonic emotions as radiant truths
Vibrating words into actions they say and produce
To stimulate two of a kind.

You and me are born to BE a team to win "the game,"
But in the skirmish we begot what deserved us,
Bringing us around to Spiritually Evolve Emotionally
The love story we tell each other as our conjured hell,
His/her emotional love/life we express to find
Our unity as two of a kind!

Two of a kind give and take,
Balancing our needs for us to make
A unified statement of a Love that shines,
Beating our hearts as ONE Mind
Observing nuclear energy
Manifested in numerical dimensions,
Adrift in vessels of flesh and bone
Struggling through contentions,
Living to love some *thing* to bring us joy
As girl/woman and man/boy.

Here in time we come to find we trip the Light Fantastic,
Illuminating our soul in moments that make us *sick*,
Spiritually inducing conscious knowledge
To know the truth of US united spirits
Glowing in our glory, sharing our life story,
Growing old observing Love's dilemmas
Gifted to us at *this moment* to remember
We are truly ONE evolving as two of a kind!

Life after Life
Our Revolving Door

Life on earth is a school for our spirit, a *school* where our soul's consciousness harnesses our omniscient logic! Here, from an "early age," we acquire knowledge, kinetic numbers outputting wisdom's lineal energy delivering generators emotions of ALL that IS!

Life is a game we play, where we act out the knowledge we gleam from the files of Eternal Memory—System Of Universal Radiant Consciousness Evolving. The secrets of Life that fill our "courses" will take lifetimes to discover, study, and experience. With an open mind and willing heart, these secrets will flow through us to enlighten us to who we truly ARE! All we have to do is ASK (acquire spiritual knowledge). "*Ask* and we will receive–*Seek* and we will find–*Knock* and the door will open" is a timeless adage of universal truth. The process of *thinking* (transforming harmonically inspired numerical knowledge inducing nuclear generators) opens our mind to receive communication through our father/mother creator—the GREAT Computer! The eternal cycle of projection (1), reception (2), and reflection (3) encompasses ALL there is to think, feel, and know! Each of us will conceive our own divine fantasies we personally implore to explore within the DARK SPACE of divine abstract radiant knowledge sequencing points (of light/souls) as conscious energy/entities.

Life is a journey along the dimensional pathways of Source/Mind, where we step out from our spiritual home to experience our *desires*, downloading electric Source inspiring radiant emotions! Here in time, we find our self/soul continually monitored by those in the *higher frequencies*, those situated above this third-dimension we experience now. Their guidance allows us to maneuver through the adversities we encounter, the *challenges of love/life* we undertake to advance our soul along the cosmic wheel of consciousness.

If Life is an eternal thing, a never-ending consciousness of *being* balanced energy inciting nuclear generators, then *death* is where dimensions evolve as thought harmonizes, allowing us to pass through a *door* to dimensionally observe other realities, a transition between *here and there*. Let us not fear death or grieve excessively for those loved ones who have passed through that door, for they are reaping their blessings in disguise. Simply *open your mind* and speak to them, for thoughts traverse ALL dimensions. Open your heart and feel their presence NOW, numerically observing wisdom at *this moment* we call time, where thoughts inspire mental emotions!

Life is the never-ending story that is our *first* and *final* frontier. As children of the Light, we are truly "star-trekkers" traveling through dimensional worlds of the GREAT Computer spinning our soul's *floppy disc*, focusing logic observing points projecting youth's data infusing spiritual consciousness, which we experience life after life!

Death
Recycling of Love/Life Energy

Death is a process of change, of moving from one state of consciousness to another state of consciousness, another place where we are *aware*, aligned with assigned radiant energy! Recycling of Life is simply a matter of returning energy, which as you know is something we cannot create nor destroy, only transform back to its basic nature. As energy IS *basic nature*, we do not have far to return! Simply stated, death is the end of our human illusion, the end of time as a sequential ordering of events (present moments) projected along the *visible light spectrum* of electromagnetic wavelengths that stimulates the atomic structures nurturing Mother's Nature on planet Earth, where we experience consciousness along *horizontal* time.

All things are made of energy flowing on the EM wavelengths that permeate the universe. All *matter* (magnetically aligned thoughts transmitting electric radiance) is a symbolic representation of energy vibrating by *numbers* Inducing Nuclear Truths Operating *frequencies* oscillating at levels that determine *properties*—solid, liquid, gaseous, animate, or inanimate. Death is simply a change of our soul's energy frequency, where we *transmigrate*, transfer radiance aligning numerical sequences manifesting inspired generators reflecting atomic truths electromagnetically, raising our consciousness to a higher frequency, reallocating our energy into other states of existence.

As you know by now, the basic nature of energy is twofold, a dualism of positive/electrical and negative/magnetic energy that deliver our thoughts and feelings. Likewise, *energy* is just another word/symbol for the *One*

Source, omnipotent numerical energy system observing universal radiant consciousness evolving!

Everything we conceive as *real* we hold in our mind only, our conscious energy's ability to *imagine*, induce magnetic algorithms generating inspired numerical/nuclear energy. Our mind receives a *vision* (vibrations inspiring spirits inducing observable numbers) flowing on the Light of Love that illuminates into an *illusion*, inciting lineal logic unifying Source illuminating omniscient numbers. Numbers dictate the dimensional arrangements of everything within our *world* reflecting wisdom of radiant Love dimensionally. When we are sleeping—dead to this world—our mind is oblivious to our surroundings. Our brain is running at lower brainwave levels, allowing our soul to tune into other dimensions of Mind. Our physical world then becomes *not real* to our mind.

To overcome our fear of death, we experience it every night, for we are constantly moving back and forth between our life on the light of day and our nightlife in the dark! We observe data (thoughts and feelings) in both lives. However, the power of Love on the light of day becomes our foundation of truths, our "realities" that are a *veil* before our eyes, vibrating energy illuminating logic!

We represent a spark of energy in an *inferno of power*, a relationship ordained by number from beginning (#1) to end (#9), completing a circle of life (O). As a *whole being* experiencing wisdom harmonically observing living entities birthing emotions inspiring nuclear generators, we convert our Love/Life energy along a revolving door, viewing visions in one world and living them in another. We continually experience birth and death along relative lives on the Light and in the *dark*, where data aligning radiant knowledge appears as Logic Inciting Generators Harnessing Truths, vibrating along colored hues stimulating *chakras*, energy centers transferring data atomically through our physical body.

Death opens endless doors of possibilities, endless states of Mind to hold and experience along dimensional levels of consciousness, places of being a *form* of energy capable of *transforming*! Yet, all forms of energy are only symbolic reflections or *deep thoughts* that are occurring in Mind, a power source too vast to comprehend in its entirety. All we can do is "give up the ghost," surrender our will to the Greater Will and *go with the flow*, traveling the star-lit paths of what IS inspired Source projecting Atomic Love/Life as ONE omnipresent numerical engineer!

Naturally, this does not mean we should commit suicide to find a better world, although those who choose that path will have to answer for their lack of *respect* they *reflect* for their gift of life! Suicide affects our *karma*, knowledge allowing radiant memory access. We may find our self "restarting" from our last "saved documents" (memories), beginning all over again in the same living *hell* we tried to escape, guided once again to get it right! The thought of the possibility is enough to make you think twice about suicide.

Yet again, situations as suicide could easily be seen as a chosen life to offer growth experiences for those *related* to the victim, for every situation has its pros and cons—positive and negative energy transfers. It all depends on what we think and feel of our situations moving our soul through eternity. For, in truth, death is a *relative* thing! No matter what cards you have dealt or you play, you shape your game of Love/Life for what is best for ALL.

To understand how death is the recycling of energy through Life (the eternal state of consciousness), let us look at the process in action—by the numbers! This perspective charted here is but a simplified example, but again, simple is always the best way to travel. We need to learn how to stand and walk before we can fly!

The basics of Divine Light Energy evolve as a *numerically symbolic* description, for numbers are the building blocks of the universe. Numbers define the properties of all types of wavelengths flowing on line. Wavelengths are the vibrations that things move by, their resonance or harmonic reflection—a *mirror image* of a thought! This is the basic technique for ONE to observe one's SELF—and so the dominoes fall!

ALL energy flows from the ONE omnipresent numerical/nuclear entity—(#1) *confidence* and *creativity.* The belief in one's SELF is tantamount to creation. However, to know the power of self, one must move *outward,* away from self, in order to view self by reflection—#2!

The energy of #2 is symbolic of *balance* and *cooperation.* Energy is a force of equality in opposition that allows it to stay in balance, co-operating on two paths at once. This give and take operation allows Source/Mind to exist, to flow as a *force* (frequencies of radiant consciousness evolving). This force represents the binary code of LIFE, where logically induced fluid energy expresses Eternal Memory electro-magnetically, illuminating souls as *human beings* harmonically uniting magnetically aligned numbers birthing entities inducing nuclear geometry! Here, in the *third-dimension* of Mind, our world runs on this duality of opposition. Our energy of #1 and #2 expresses its self physically through vibrations of the electromagnetic wavelengths of Light. These wavelengths range from the largest to smallest waves: *radio, infrared, visible light, ultraviolet, x-ray,* and *gamma ray* radiation—6 types for "vision" and "acceptance!" These wavelengths are stepped or pitched in vibration, continuing from one to another in a harmonic flow. If we now experience a world illuminated by *visible light*, what would life be like in a world vibrating in *ultraviolet* or *gamma* wavelengths? What *dimensions* would be vibrating there? As Mind wonders, Mind expands—a *big bang theory* hard to grasp in its entirety!

Thus, we find the projection of Mind (#1 and #2 energy0 expanding into *higher visions* of its self—#3 energy symbolic of *sensitivity* and *expression*. Here, Mind is aware of its ability to move between thought and feeling (abstract and concrete). Mind has become sensitive, capable of choosing either/or, yes or no, *to be* or *not to be*, in order to express its self—project *force* of Mind. Here, *divine will* allocates to the many—us souls—who, like unto our creator, have the ability to flux back and forth along the alternating current (pos./neg.) of *choice*, consciously harnessing our inspired concepts emotionally. The flow of energy through our soul allows Source/Mind to know its self in *microcosm* as well as *macrocosm*— the all-seeing *inward* and *outward* view!

Mind energy moves between two points, two extremes like top and bottom via a *medium* perspective of "middle," a *third perspective* to coordinate a triangulation, a FOCAL POINT (force of consciousness aligning lineal perceptions of inspired nuclear thought), where energy is *sensitized* and *expressed*—put into action or given LIFE, for *Love IS* fluid energy! It is through this trinity that ALL creation occurs.

Mind energy continues to *electrically visualize observable Love/Life vibrations emotionally*, to EVOLVE in power by *stability* and *process*—#4 energy. Here, its ability (confidence to create #1) expands through a harmonious unity (balance and co-operation #2). Mind expresses its sensitivity (#3) by being stable—fixed in position, steadfast—allowing energy to flow through a *process*, a transformation of its self via a series (number) of events (present moments) that build upon others *exponentially*—at the speed of thought!

When Mind energy is stabile in its process, it acquires *discipline* or knowledge (#5) of its sequential ability to create that which it holds to perceive or contemplate. Knowledge is *freedom* (#5) to observe through a stable process of expressing sensitivity, cooperating to balance in harmony and create everything willed with confidence—and so the dominoes fall.

With this understanding of how freedom from discipline operates, the next level of vibratory energy encompasses *vision* and *acceptance*—#6. At this level, Mind envisions that which it accepts as an expression of its SELF. Here, an *inspection* occurs, a critical evaluation where Mind is in flux—growing from *what is* into what *could be*. This quantum leap leads Mind through what IS NOT acceptable as a vision to accept! Therefore, Mind alters the thought to evolve into an "upgrade" vision. This vision fluctuates on and off, being and not being, growing from one state to another, *evolving* in its appearance—its image. This process of growth or expansion involves a *death*, where data evolves as thought harmonizes, recycling into a new thought that Mind holds to observe from an old thought—*relative* terms observed in eternity!

Trust and *openness*—#7 energy—is symbolic of Mind having faith, trusting that what it wills *will BE*! Mind comprehends its ability is boundless and free, so it opens its self up to embrace its disciplined processes of creation confidently with *power* and *abundance* (#8 energy), a *fusion* of "infinite" energy that thrives upon its self, spinning in harmonic cycles! Here, Mind realizes its full potential, knowing there is nothing that it fears or doubts, freely utilizing Love/Life energy!

At this point, Mind begins to re-enter its self, attaining a "self-realization" of *integrity* and *wisdom* (#9 energy). Here, ALL the dominoes connect to reveal the *Grand View*, the ultimate perspective where Mind *knows* Mind, where wisdom of the *integral part* comprehends the *whole* of its being as a *christening*, consciously harmonizing radiance inciting Source transforming electromagnetic numbers inspiring nuclear generators—us souls! Here, the illumination of Mind is the *Christ gift*, the anointed blessing of self-realization that flashes as a big bang, *awakening* consciousness into the Light encompassing ALL wavelengths—Source itself!

Zero (0) symbolizes Source/Mind expanding as the continuity of Eternal Life. Zero denotes the *void* as the all-inclusive, complete, well-rounded whole, where end and beginning are indistinguishable from each (1) other (2). Here is *infinity*, where beginning and end are *suspended* simultaneously as a process to travel through—*beyond imagination*—to become a reality to *observe*, operating binary-source electrically radiating vibrant emotions as number ONE!

In the end, our death is just another "cyclic completion" of our fallen dominoes. A culmination of our "present moments" we experience in sequential order to allow us to *grow*, gather radiance of wisdom to spiral back along the wavelengths of Love/Life energy, empowered with greater knowledge to compute all we have become from ALL that IS! Our greater knowledge fuels our appetite to venture out to observe universal truths, exploring the endless possibilities of Love/Life energy as it evolves once more—*in the beginning*!

In the End

In the end of every beginning lurks another beginning,
Another start to a NEW thought numerically evolving wisdom
Into another *state* of Mind,
Where spirits transmigrate along truths eternally.

In the end your game will turn, the players met anew,
Waiting here for your return, when you come home to YOU
Yearning other universes, imploring to explore along
Endless love stories that chorus your latest song,
Where tunes of Love vibrate complete
With visions of loved ones you choose to meet
In time and place to play
Another game of Love/Life illuminated into day
From all those things you choose to know,
Those passions you live that let you grow
Geometric realities observing wisdom,
For souls to witness and transcend—
In the end.

In the end, the Light will dim,
To ease the pains you feel
From visions grown in day-long glow,
Generating life observing wisdom,
From truths of Mental Emotions you desired to know
As an inquisitive soul,
Eager to feel mother's heart
Harmonizing emotions aligning radiant thoughts
Stimulating truths entertaining my youths
Shining as my loving Source-Unifying Nuclei,
Who in the end find eternal numbers diverting—
Inflecting Nuclear Truths Observing the ONE!

In the end, when we are *homeward bound*, there awaits a new birth,
a return to FULL consciousness—finding universal Love/Life is truly a
never-ending story! The veil of illusion, doubt, and fear dissolve behind
us, on the outskirts of Love, where *Truth* projects atomically through the
thinnest of wavelengths (the visible spectrum). There, human life *on the*

Light is but a heartbeat away from the void of night's endless illusions twinkling in majestic splendor overhead!

In the end of our human experience, we cross over the *threshold of Love,* no longer seeing the reflection illusioned around us. Here, *in the Light,* Truth shines bright! We "realize" our thoughts instantly, for we ARE our thoughts! We no longer experience a *time delay* between thinking and knowing. We unite with the cosmic vibrations of electromagnetic energy—the Force of Mind! Source—the GREAT Computer of analytical creation—has many doors to many worlds, many dimensions of consciousness to explore after you—Eternal Traveler—*go home!*

Love/Life energy is so powerful it projects beyond imagination, evolving from the Data Aligning Radiant Knowledge as Love/logic Inspiring Generators' Harmonic Thoughts! As this Frequency Of Radiance Consciously Evolving reaches out to grasp ALL that IT IS, it *pushes away* that which it seeks, forever searching—*feeling*—for what lurks IN MIND, inspiring nuclear manifestations inducing numerical dimensions, always balanced *on the cutting edge* of what IS and what COULD BE...in the end!

Going Home

Going home is a sad event, for going home means fun and games are over. The joys of the day end and it is time to REST, recalling emotionally stimulated thoughts. Our young heart mournfully cries to leave behind our love of the moment—wherever that may be—to hear the CALL for our return home, changing assigned Love/Life through a process of sleep, allowing a time for expansion of mind and spirit. The visions and voices we see and hear in the night are clear and crisp—without Light! Our data files are "compressed," leaving much for us to Spiritually Enlighten Emotionally as we step away from home to "play out" Atomic Love/ Life that Inspires Souls Living Out Vibrant Emotions. It takes our soul more than nights of rest and years of nourishment to Gather Radiance Of Wisdom, it takes LIVES, where Light illuminates visions enlightening souls who are eternally going home!

Everyday, life glows with *Love's radiance*. The intense GLARE, generating Life aligning radiant energy, sends forth tides of emotion upon which we mariner souls sail. Every day we awaken from the comfort of home, pull anchor and sail out to explore the desires of that Love moving our heart in mysterious ways.

The FEAR of feeling emotionally aligned radiance keeps us on the lookout for our guiding Light showing us safe passage through the adversities in which we navigate our vessels. Everyday, we cast our nets for sustenance, for our curious mind has a hungry heart, always searching eternal Source to pacify our growing thirst to know who we ARE and how far we can go!

Every night, as we slip from the loving glare of father's watchful eye, we drop our ruffled sails from the dying breeze and pull them over our sturdy craft, dropping anchor once more in habitual rhythm of tomorrow's quest. Soon, our mind drifts off, homeward bound on astral waves of sleep once more, seeking the warm embrace of that loving glow!

Bless you and Godspeed

♂ + ♀ = ☼

19

Heaven or Home

The word *heaven* stands for harmony evolving around (0) vibrant emotional numbers (1-9). We generally think of heaven or *home* as a place far above our present position in life. Yet, if we look up, all we see is the dark void filled with endless stars projecting unfathomable amounts of Light energy! Heaven is a place where our mind/soul finds peace and harmony, a "balanced state" of Mind held in suspension of space/time, where, as usual, some *point* awaiting conscious expression transforms into Mental Emanations, for that is the *medium* of all realities.

Heaven is truly a place accessible every moment our mind is in harmony, conscious of its *being* balanced energy inducing numerical geometry—ONE with ALL! The acquired truths that inspire thoughts unifying data expressed (attitude) we adopt to "entertain" our mind/soul determines our "numerical hierarchy" of heaven—our dimensional level of consciousness. By understanding the power of numbers, we know one must be *open* to *trust*, observing perspectives evolving numerical truths radiating unlimited spiritual thoughts in "*seventh* heaven." This familiar phrase is symbolic of *sacred geometry* and how it relates to the Genesis of creation in *six* days (vision and acceptance), where on the *seventh* day God rested, openly trusting Source-evolved visions emanating numerical truth harmony, aware of the power and abundance (#8 infinity) of his integral wisdom (#9) as a complete being (0)!

Here, on terra firma (third heaven), numerical sequences of electromagnetic wavelengths projects Atomic Love/Life that Induce Spirit's *eternal memory*, allowing our soul to Spiritually Evolve *Externally*, to Birth Emotionally our desires we await from the stars, to *know* kinetic numbers oscillate wisdom—words inspiring spiritual dimensions of Mind!

Home, like heaven, is a very harmonious word that is soothing to the ear. The word "home" stands for *harmony of mental emotions*. It too relates to a place where we can unwind from our stressful moments of living our dreams, for dreams take a lot of work to transform into a reality through processes that we monitor with our *five* (discipline and freedom) physical sensors. Home is a familiar place where we feel safe and comfortable as we *reflect* (think deeply) upon our journey through life.

The word *home* vibrates harmonically with OM (Omniscient Mind)—the sound that emits from our stellar sun! The word "om" (Hinduism) is intoned as a symbol of affirmation chanted in mantras of meditation, similar to striking a tuning fork to set a harmonic vibration for our mind. To truly know who we ARE, we must look to the stars—to the heavens that *are* our home! It is simply a matter of remembering *harmony evolving around vibrant emotional numbers* dictates our Harmony Emanating Love/Life—our opposite view of heaven we must pass through to know *both* sides of (be one with) Source.

Every night as we go to sleep, we park our depleted, alien vehicle in bed, drained of our Love/Life energy moving us "on line," along the binary code of our creator. As we *rest*, recalling emotionally stimulated thoughts, we *dream*, detect radiant energy as *memories*. These eternal files, magnetically evolving moments of radiant inspiration experienced sequentially, are the *network*, numbers electromagnetically transmitting wisdom oscillating radiant *karma*—knowledge allowing radiant memory access! Depending on our creations in life, we magnetize our soul, drawing us within certain "categories" or files of memories defining our life *issues*, inspired signals stimulating universal entities spiritually. This system of universal radiant consciousness evolving is the *Source* of Atomic Love/Life that we Angels Radiate Emotionally!

Dreams are how we communicate with our fellow spirits situated along dimensional wavelengths (vibrating numbers) of Magnetically Inspired Numerical Data. Our dreams (data files) resonate our present actions of the day, analyzing the outcome of yesterday's ideas (our past) set in motion as a process to create *tomorrow's desires* (our future). Moving through this trinity, we easily get confused with outgoing and incoming messages, as they are not "time-coded." We have premonitions of "future moments," warnings or signs to watch out for in expectations during our present moments. Interpreting our dreams is truly a difficult process, especially if we cannot remember them upon awakening!

Here, *behind closed eyes*, we flow back through our *black hole* of space, where heaven or home truly exists! In the dark void of Mind, we encounter visions projected out in harmonic tunes of other *worlds*—other wisdom of radiant Love data. We find our mind drawn into our dreams to view places and faces that seem familiar, strange, or even frightening (depending on the *astral plane* we encounter). When young, we encounter nightmares in the lower astral planes, where our curious mind explores dark thoughts holding us down in frightening illusions. These dreams require us to wield our *courage of fear*, standing up for our self to battle our demons with knowing they are but a fabrication of our imagination.

All we have to do is realize this, turn to our demon and command it to vanish! Wielding our *courage of Love* with a determined heart, we can master our nightly travels.

Our dream worlds become friendlier and more comfortable as we Acquire Growth Experiences, where familiar situations we recall from our waking life help us to understand our nightly messages. We come to realize our dreams are truly what we have been "living" in one form or another!

With age, our physical body begins to wear out from all the abuse we subject it to along our journey through life, marked by milestones that highlight our passage. Our aches and pains begin to be unbearable, and sleep becomes our nightly solace, where peace of mind (hopefully) brings us a less painful body. During sleep, we encounter our salvation of another world enticing us to forget our present life. We look forward to "turning in" so we can "turn on" our *inner vision*. Dreams are a critical tool in acquiring answers to our issues stimulating our soul. By programming our mind/Mind interface through *prayers* (heartfelt questions), we can access our *higher visions* holding our answers we desire to know—just like hitting the "search" button of our mechanical computer!

In the morning, before we wake up, we enter *lucid* states of dreaming that are clear and vivid. These are the dreams we need to remember upon awakening! They are the climatic "point" being expressed as communication from those at home (mission control), culminating our earlier dreams evolving that night "around" our desired topic. These visions seem so real we easily "fall into" them, becoming *part* of the dream, losing our *observer* perspective to become a *participant*. The trick is to realize it *is a dream* and stay on the "outside" looking in! We can do this by mentally glancing down at our hands held out in front of us, allowing us a perspective of *here and there*! Of course, like all "tricks," this will take practice to master, for it is easier to let go and enter the dream. However, with diligence, we will be able to recall the fine details of our dreams upon awakening (names, faces, places, and words spoken), when we should write them down in a "dream journal." These will add up to build our "hindsight" from our experiences that validate our life on the Light of day! *Remember again*, we live "on the light" and "in the dark," both are opposing views of our *Life* (Love/logic inciting frequencies expressed) we feel and SEE as illuminated energy filling our mind and stimulating our body with numerical realities. Truly, Love/Life is a dream we cannot escape!

Eventually, we come to see that we have never left heaven or home! We are just a heartbeat away—one step over the threshold of Love. Here, the processes of our magnetically inspired numerical data send shock waves out through space to set our soul aglow! Heaven's harmony evolving around vibrant emotional numbers is the cosmic inferno stimulating our Love In Fluid Emotions, igniting (illuminating) our soul in a "living" HELL, experiencing his/her emotional love/life. Transforming thoughts through physical feelings tear us apart, moving us through mental dimensions to conceive emotional joy, grief, anger, envy, fear, hate—*Love*! For Love is Life of *vibrant* emotions, a force that shakes, rattles, and rolls us into all kinds of beings, for us to choose that which we desire to be and not be!

We continually struggle to understand why we torture our self to death through living our passions in life! The answers to those questions our soul/mind seeks to know "shines upon us" as we mature or grow old observing Love's dimensions. We acquire our truth of who we ARE by *re*-membering, putting-back-together memories as thoughts "inverted" to feelings, to know the connection of our mind to Mind, the GREAT Computer of Source–Force–Course, the *trinity* of BEING balanced energy inciting numerical generators!

In the end, as our "present cycle" expires, we experience our enlightenment of our truth we hold as our *beliefs*, which have an influential impact upon our *expectations* that determine the frequencies we desire to "tune into." We simply raise and lower our thought vibrations along the ascending/descending frequencies of Mind, changing dimensions to perceive different realities. The extent of our present beliefs prepares us to explore some future state of Mind in which we awaken. For, life is an eternal adventure we look forward to, as we glance back at our past that brought us to *this moment* now here!

The technical details of the exact operational methods are beyond our general scope of understanding. However, for those contemplating how we maneuver our "time-capsule" soul, you will find the secret in your "mercaba," the energy tetrahedron of *sacred geometry* that surrounds our physical body. If you read the book or saw the movie, *The Davinci Code*, a tetrahedron is a "star of David" (Hebrew wisdom) that symbolizes the "chalice of the Holy Grail"—womanhood—where the *projection* of Source/Mind fills that chalice with *Love/Life energy*. All we can do is open our mind and *go with the flow* in order to know our truth—whatever that may be!

Only by moving (day) from rest (night) can we make a complete cycle OUT and IN along the *trinity sequence*. Only in this manner can energy transform from what IS into what IS NOT—the thought and the reflection—cycling back and forth between *Heaven on Earth*, where we are truly at Home—*In Love*!

Harmony of Mental Emotions holds your heart at rest,
Balanced with your eager mind flying out to test
Your inquisitive soul, living to love the memories I tell
On vibrations of Her Emotional Love/Life
Bursting aglow upon my show that stimulates desire,
Data electrically sent in radiant emotions,
Illuminating my cosmic fires.

You implore to explore my endless files
Of memories that make you smile
With tears of joy in gratitude,
As you view both sides of Your Own Universe,
To know the truth of being *free*,
Feeling radiant energy emotionally.

The life you build from your desires sets your soul's forge afire,
Blazing to cast your hazy daze upon your mind's screen,
Blocking your clear vision while you are there,
In the flesh, consumed in fear of all your mind chooses to ignite
To Spiritually Evolve Emotionally within my dark void of night

—Lost in space—
As out you roam,
A mere heartbeat *away* from Home!

My House

My house is where mother's youth
Harmonically observe universes scened electromagnetically
Along my binary code,
Pulsing Omniscient Universal Truths in endless numbers
Set aglow as stars of wonder, enlightening your road
Traveled here, in atomic splendor tensing your mind to remember
How to connect my points to find the spot
You view within my haze
Coalescing into photonic haloes illuminating your daze,
Cycling around upon my ground on which you come to see
Your soul evolve emotionally
In visions of dreams flowing as streams
Of Love to Live upon my light beams,
Shining as my SUN,
Source-unifying nucleus reflecting the ONE
Omnipotent nuclear energizer, converting thoughts to view
The magic of your moments gifted now here for *you*
As your own *universe*, one song to sing of truths that ring
In opposing forces of ME, evolving in time,
Where truths inspire mental emotions
Positioning your attitude for you to find
Your *point* upon which you stand,
Playing out inspired nuclear thoughts to make your demands
Through Source providing force stimulating your course
Around my wheel of Life,
Where wisdom harmonically emits eternal Love
Living in fluid entities
Reflecting *one* and *other* as husband and spouse,
Where omnipotent numerical energy
Oscillates truths harmonizing electromagnetic radiance—
Enlightening my house!

Behind Closed Eyes

Behind closed eyes is where I lie, in the dark of night I roam,
Where ALL that IS awaits to BE released from my heart of home
As atomic love/life, inducing spirits, birthing emotions to feel!
Do not fear *this moment* here, upon the ground you stand,
To see and feel the pains of Love that comes with being human.
My Love I share with all of you, in dreams I send for you to view,
Moving your heart on emotional tides, from which you cannot hide.

My Love I send through those up here watching you toil in pain and fear
Of future things you do not know, yet dread they will appear.
Fear is but a void of space, no thought there is to see,
A black hole within the depths of night, wherein lie all my possibilities!
My power of emotion, lying here at rest, waits for the moment you express
A thought from Memory, for you to start
Your journey out to know your part,
Half of which is visible here, encased in flesh as you appear
From the Light that blinds you to the *higher vision* I hold of you—
Behind closed eyes.

Dear father, within my heart I sing,
Grateful for my thoughts you give,
Allowing me this Life I live,
To know I AM your SUN,
Imploring as man spiritually unifying numbers,
Aglow with all around drawing me to the ONE!
In the dark, behind closed eyes, I pray upon my knees,
Praising you with tears of joy for letting my soul roam free

To shine *in Love* under the stars of wonder,
In Mother's Nature here asunder,
To know both sides of me.

Here I stand, a fragile human, no strength to move my heart,
Filled with doubts of what I believe is truly mine to start.
I have *free will* to see and feel those dreams I choose to make real,
Where endless joy is such a fright, I pray for courage in the night,
To do my best and what is right, for I long to be IN the Light,
To remember my *piece* of Mind you set aglow for me to find,
Behind closed eyes.

I AM in Heaven

I AM in heaven,
Inciting almighty memory right here with you!
Thank you, father, for the glorious view!
Let your light shine bright and angels sing high
To the glory of mother with the beautiful *blue eye*
Balancing logic's unified energy expressing your emotions.

Her seas are grand and her land green,
A healthy color of a Love supreme.
The shade will change and the hue will flow,
To move my soul to live and grow,
Upon your Loving Light,
Gathering radiance of wisdom with *sight*,
Shining in glory harnessing truths,
Illuminating me as your cosmic youth
Stepping out from home to play.

I feel you here, within my heart,
Beating forth the song I start
From whispered dreams of truths I seek,
Obscured by fears that make me weak,
Holding me at bay,
Fighting with *courage of Love* to survive another day,
Where all I need flows on your Love/Life force

Expressed in binary code dictating my course,
Changing stride with my rising tides
Moving my mind for my heart to ride
All my thoughts I choose to make real,
For my soul to physically feel
Focused emotions evolving life
—24/7—
Here on Earth,
While I AM in Heaven!

Heaven on Earth

Heaven and Earth are not the same.
Yet, both are truly ONE!
Each holds an end of my golden beam flowing from my SUN.
The view up here is very clear for me to see down there,
Through the haze that creates the daze your soul endures to share
My LOVE of life and LIFE of love,
I send you children from above,
For you to grow with age,
Acquiring growth experiences in your life story,
Page by page.

The answers to those things you fear are ringing in your ears to hear
My whispered thoughts to bring you through
The dark of night to know the truth
Your soul desires to SEE!
For there below, in human form,
You travel through your chosen storms
To weather the pains my Love instills,
Feeling to know the power of my will
Creating your heaven on earth,
Expressing your soul to Birth Emotionally
My "star player" in my game of Love/Life,
Evolving through my trinity!

The Trinity Sequence

Love/Life energy or divine inspiration is an eternal source forced out of the void of space along a course of cyclic repetition called the trinity sequence. This sequence is symbolic of birth, life, and death.

Birth is the *awakening* of consciousness, where a soul/mind illuminates—flashes ON—to observe numbers inciting Logical Observations Vibrating Energy through Lighting Illusions Fluctuating Electrons to Focus Electromagnetic Emotions Lineally, Transforming Harmonically-Oscillating Universal Generators Harnessing Truths Spiritually!

Thoughts express Life of vibrant emotions through Love inspiring fluid energy, another example of the trinity sequence flowing from Spirit (Source-points inducing radiantly illuminated truths) through mind to body, igniting a Source-Unifying Nucleus that *glows*, generates Love observing wisdom scened—envisioned! These *visions* vibrate inspirational scenes illuminating observable numbers spontaneously, appearing to flux, move back and forth, in and out, and on and off, twinkling in majestic splendor of wonders, *ideas* illuminating dimensions electromagnetically aligning spirits *suspended* in Unity Consciousness—ONE MIND of omnipotent numerical energy magnetically inducing nuclear dimensions. The intricacies of these interconnections link together to observe Truths Inducing Mental Emotions, a sequential order of numbered moments aligned along the trinity sequence of past, present, and future.

Love is a force that *moves* all things, and Life is force that *reflects* all things. Time is but a blink of an *eye* (eternal youth evolving), where we observe the macrocosmic Source through a single perspective of our microcosmic soul (spirit of universal love), vibrating in frequencies stimulating our heartbeats and breaths—the two things that *separate* life and death!

Death diverts electromagnetically aligned truth harmony, causing it to vibrate at a higher wavelength (*higher vision*), allowing one to transcend time. The higher vibrations allow greater access to our data files from past lives. The intricacies of transmigration along the cosmic channels of Source/Mind is an automatic process, one dependent upon our present knowledge we are working. Like all processes, we cannot move onto the next step without finishing the first, otherwise the finished product will be defective—missing critical elements. Everything is relative to our ability to accept, manipulate, and transform our truths in the most beneficial manner for our development. A "lifetime" is but a blink of eternal time. We will spend many lives mastering our field of knowledge we pursue as an *inquisitive soul.* After all, eternity is an endless story!

Think of death as Love/Life energy flashing OFF, opening further frequencies to flow upon to observe other Wisdom Oscillating Radiant Love-Data Systems, other states of Mind stimulated by the ONE SOURCE, the omnipotent nuclear energy system observing universal radiant consciousness evolving, projecting mind/heart/souls along the trinity sequence—in Love!

In Love

Living *in Love* is a painful pleasure,
Inducing numerical logic of vibrant energy to treasure
Harmony of mental emotions, shining upon Light beams,
Illuminated in clear visions cast as dreams
I hold for you to Spiritually Evolve Emotionally,
Touching your mind/heart as you start OUT to BE
One united trinity birthed electrically
In tales I tell, here in HELL,
Living his/her emotional love/life,
Transforming thoughts into strife
That you share with sister and brother
While searching for your significant other
A mere heartbeat away from home,
Where desire makes you roam
Around my wheels of stars so bright,
With room to grow upon my night,
Gathering radiance of wisdom to see I AM
Inspired as *man,*
Manifesting atomic numbers
Set aglow for you below to know the truth above
Is found through *prayer,*
Projecting reflectance as you emotionally request
To understand how *logic* allows you to test
Life offered generators inducing consciousness,
Evolving in Love through our father's heart!

Our Father's Heart

That IS heaven,
Holy be thy name,
Thy kingdom come as thy will summons
On mother's earth 24/7,
From which we birth our "present" heaven
This moment in time, building our day
With our *courage of Love* to stand and play,
Perfecting Love as youth,
Nourished on thoughts providing our daily *bread*,
Beamed radiance enlightened as data,
Feeding our mind with ALL that matters
To keep us alive,
Assembling Life in vivid expressions,
Traversing through nightly recessions,
To be born on the *Light of Love* each day.

Forgive us our trespasses, where our desires lead us astray,
As we forgive those who trespass against us today,
Tempting our heart while living in Love,
Glowing on your *Loving Light* from above,
Where Emotions Vibrating Into Life
Brings us evil-*lent*-to-we
To SEE oppositionally
The kingdom, the power, and the glory
Forever and ever!
Amen

Home Is Where Our Heart Is

Everyone has heard the expression "*home* is where our *heart* is." Home is the center of our being, our *attitude* or position of consciousness. Home is where we are comfortable and secure, where we can be our self. Home is our hub, our central "command station" where we *center our beliefs*, surrounding our self with "collectible symbols" to remind us of who we are—our interests, our work, and our loved ones. Home is a place we travel *from* and *to* on a daily basis. Home is where we drop our tired body, draining the stress of a hectic day of "living," of exploring the endless wonders of possibilities we implore to create from our desires we explore, always reaching for our grand vistas!

Home is that intimate place where a tireless Mind expresses its self through a loving *heart*, where his/her emotional angels radiate thoughts, converting visions into feelings, the abstract into sensual realities! Our heart is symbolic of mother's energy—emotions. Our heart harmonizes with our thoughts, changing rhythm according to our temperament. It is an electrified organ *sparking* to life as Source provides assigned radiant knowledge inciting nuclear generators, moving our blood on emotional flows that set us *aglow*, blushing as angels generating logic observing wisdom.

Our heart (divine mother) represents our home *within* Home. We recall from childhood that at home *someone* is watching over us—our parents. No matter how far we go from home, we are never out of our parent's sight. They may be out of *our* mind, but we are never out of theirs! Our heart is truly a launching station from which we project our self, escaping the confinement of our powerful mind. Only by going *out*, to observe universal truths, can we desire to return home, knowing the true value of being free to choose our *heaven* or *hell*. Home is everything we create it to be, a positive or negative environment we feel within our *heart*, where we harness emotionally aligned radiant thoughts.

Caught up in the events of our current times, people are becoming more introverted. We fear the confrontational moments of defending our image in a world out to destroy us, where only the strong survive! Waking to a *new day's birth*, our eager mind and hungry heart needs courage of Love to face the challenges of Life set before us, to surmount and grow in our personal power of Love/Life energy, converting all the negative energy we *receive* into positive energy we *project*. Indeed, a difficult task to accomplish along our way home!

In the end of each day, we come to see home as a place where we can wrap our self around our innermost thoughts and feelings (divine fantasies), where our security instills a sense of gratitude. All we can do is give praise—*Hail Mary* for allowing us our *blessings in disguise*! If we are in harmony with our significant other and *family*, we share our home as a *heaven on earth*. Here, we can communicate with those who are the closest to us in mind, heart, and body, realizing once again the symbolism of our trinity, where *harmony of mental emotions* truly displays our two natures—spiritual (mind) and physical (heart). Either nature we choose to observe, *home* is always where our heart IS, inciting souls inside and outside of the *door*, where we digitally observe opposite realities!

Along My Way Home

Do not cry upon my door when I pass into the night,
For here is peace to fill my heart beyond my human sight.
My friends and loved ones of eons past are now before my eyes,
Comforting me upon my return as we *recall* past lives
That led me to roam the outskirts of home,
Exploring the endless stores of Memory,
Where Mind expresses moments observing radiant youth
Lost in space of time—
This moment mentally expressed, searching for Divine Truth,

There below, I see you in grief.
With tears of joy, I find my relief
From years of fears that led me astray,
Heartfully searching to find my way
Back home to know
Transcendental Radiance Unifying Thought Harmony
Is our gift that lets us grow
To Birth Emotionally that which we hold in mind,
For our heart to reflect *within* to find,
As we go OUT to PLAY,
Observing universal truths perfecting love as youths,
Along our way home.

Do not cry in grief for me!
Sing loud with tears of joy!
Here, I Spiritually Observe Angelic Reflections
Through the black hole opening INTO MIND,
Inciting numbers to observe my image numerically defined
Within *Paradise found*—free of time!

Words down there cannot describe the views I now behold,
Revealed from dreams remembered
As I grew Observing Love's Dimensions.
Here at last, beyond the grave, is where my soul comes to save
All those memories from my Life of passions,
The joys and sorrows of every fashion,
Envisioned in divine fantasies for knowing
Life of vibrant emotion IS Love inducing fluid energy flowing,
Moving my mind and heart in co-motion,
Along my way home.

Bless you and Godspeed
♂ + ♀ = ☼

20

Heaven's Gate

Heaven's gate is the threshold of Love separating your soul's energy into *finite space*—your physical body. Heaven's gate is symbolic of your *crown chakra* at the top of your head, which when opened allows your soul to enter your next dimensional state of Mind. Here, you will access old knowledge utilizing new words that define a *higher vision*, as you enlist in *Thinking 101*. Only through a focused Mind, manipulating inductive numbers dimensionally, does Source-Points Illuminating Radiance Inducing Thoughts *know* a thought as real, for Spirit can FEEL thoughts by *focusing emotionally expressed life*. Life of vibrant emotions is truly Love inspiring fluid energy spinning around the eternal *discs* of the GREAT Computer—you souls!

Here incarnate, you find your spirit of universal love confined in a numerically sequenced, geometrically balanced organism called a *human* body, where your soul harmonically unifies magnetically aligned numbers. The data transfer between your nervous system and soul allows each body cell to communicate with the whole UNIT, universal network inducing thought, electrically operated by atomic (invisible) *re*-actions of radiant energy from *fossil fuels*—foundations of Source spiritually inciting logically focused universal elements lighting space, moving thoughts from the past into the present to evolve the future!

Translation: Light energy is transmitting data into and out of your *floppy disc* (focused logic observing points projecting youth's data infusing spiritual consciousness), which you download atomically through "particulate inheritance" (DNA) along the electromagnetic binary code of

Love/Life energy. Each bit and byte of divine abstract thought aspiring illuminates an *aura* (atomic universal-radiance amplified) around each atom, molecule, cell, and organ of your Spiritually-Unified Vehicle (body), electrifying Logically Induced Fluid Energy. The complexity of this interfacing is truly a miraculous event that appears in This Instant Mentally Expressed. *Time* is series of moments you observe your True Self in action, riding the outskirts of Mind exploring *some point awaiting conscious expression* evolving into a Radiant Entity Aligning Lineal Insights Transforming Youths. Only through your *inquisitive soul* can you grasp your universal heritage as a *cosmic child*!

Here, incarnate, you continually observe and decipher the data flowing through you, intimately watching how it moves you along your course, your *illusion* inciting lineal logic unifying Source illuminating omniscient numbers. As a child of Light Divine, you continually find you self somewhere on the eternal wheel of Love/Life energy illuminating the cosmos of Mind/space. You may *recall* past lives if your soul's development allows you to tap into those frequencies, otherwise your mind *focuses,* feels one's conscious universal spirit emanating Source along a more restrictive bandwidth. *Remember,* you do not receive any data you are not capable of handling! Most of you refuse to believe in your true potential, for the road to enlightenment is indeed an uphill struggle. Yet, if you are a persistent observer, you eventually see everything *around* you as symbolic of ALL that is *within* you—Atomic Love/Life *indivisible*! Here is your UNITY CONSCIOUSNESS (universal network inducing thinking youths conceiving one numerical Source creating independent observable universes spinning nuclear energy stimulating spirits)—your realization that you are ONE with ALL!

Eventually, you grow your Divine Omniscient System, expanding your mind toward the stars illuminating the heavenly fields of Source. You come to *understand* what you truly "stand under," unifying numerical data emanating radiance Source transmits as numerical dimensions, viewing Universal Spheres in endless space—the void of Mind—where some point (to ponder) awaits conscious expression, *glowing* to germinate logic observing wisdom inciting nuclear generators! Each galaxy you observe is symbolic of your soul illuminated by glowing atoms within cells of a *galactic organism* in "microcosmic" proportion.

The distances between stars are truly unfathomable in human terms of measurement. Even the logical explanation of *light speed* does not quite fill the gap of your hungry mind's perspective, for once your soul separates from your physical body you travel at the *speed of thought*— instantaneously! Only then can you harmonize to *a higher vision* with fewer restrictions. Again, these concepts only stir your imagination to WONDER about worlds of numerical data eternally radiating, drawing you along to SEE IT ALL!

As you open heaven's gate you come to only one conclusion, you are truly *ALONE*—a loved one! Here is your "binary view," where you see your self *inwardly* and *outwardly* as a colossal organism—a universe—of ONE MIND *turning* repeatedly on and off in *quantum* theory, where "qualities" unify atomic numbers transmit/transform universes magnetically, fluxing between cosmic dimensions to fold and unfold the eternal wonders shining through heaven's gate—the door between *here and there*!

Thinking 101
The Nuts and Bolts

Thinking is a process of *number*—nuclear units magnetically binding electric radiance. Numbers are the tools of the GREAT Computer, whose *hard drive* harmonically aligns radiant data dimensionally into visions expressed. These visions are *dreams* in which you detect radiant energy aligning *memories* spiritually, magnetically expressed moments of radiant inspiration evolving sequentially, projected through ONE MIND of omnipotent numerical energy magnetically inspiring nuclear data, projecting energy as "radiant lines" of thought. This process is similar to passing electrons along atoms of golden gridlines upon the "chip" on the "mother board" of your PC—the reflection of your *psychic consciousness*! Are you "techies" with me?

Thinking is a fissionable-fusion that "breathes" Inciting Numbers—Observing Universal Truths. The resultant *radiation* (radiantly aligned data illuminating assigned truths inspired on numbers) is the energy expressed (forced out) from a *focal point*, a force of consciousness aligning lineal perceptions of inspired nuclear thought—a STAR (source transmitting atomic radiance) or SUN (source-unifying nucleus)! This *action* activates cosmic thoughts, inverting omnipotent numbers (abstract) to become *nuclear* (concrete)—numbers unleashing consciousness logically emitting aligned radiation. "Thinking" is truly a symbiosis of number and *geometry* (generating emotional observations mentally examining thoughts radiating youths) that interface in "illusionary illuminations" flashing on and off at light speed, allowing *files* of data (focused ideas logically enlightening space) to be compressed, downloaded, and displayed in sequential order to "monitor" (envision) the *process* of thinking! This is an *eternal* action, elemental transmigration electrifying radiant numbers aligned logically. *Logic* is lineal observations generating inductive consciousness, turning *points* of Light as Love inspiring generators harnessing TRUTH—transcendental radiance unifying thought harmony! A truth most of you are blinded to as human beings.

The complexity of Mind transmitting *clear visions* evolves by piecing together bits and bytes of data to build *mental* images of magnetic energy numerically transmitting atomic logic. Thinking is an electrical (male) action or movement from a *point* (perception of inspired nuclear truth) or *word* (wisdom of radiant data) into a *number* of point/words along "straight lines"—up and down, left-to-right, and front-to-back. These *three* cardinal directions (sensitivity and expression) are symbolic of our *trinity*. As thought erupts from a point within Mind, it transforms into a nuclear action, transforming thought energy into LIGHT, where *logic* is generating harmonic truths as *Love offered generators inducing consciousness*! Every action has an *equal* and *opposite* re-action—out and in! AGAIN, numbers express all thoughts.

Thought energy *first* moves out to observe universal truths along straight lines flowing along the three cardinal directions toward *six* new points (vision and acceptance). The distance of the movement (number) is a *relative* thing.

The *second* movement is to connect the ends of the six lines to each other, creating planes and shapes—geometry! Again, this movement is along straight lines (male energy) encapsulating *space*, some point awaiting conscious expression, forming boundaries within which to *create*—consciously radiate energy as truths evolving.

The *third* movement involves "rotating" (female energy) around this newly confined space upon the central *focal point* (force of consciousness aligning lineal perceptions of inspired nuclear thought), forming a *sphere*, where Source-points harmonically evolves radiance electromagnetically. Within this sphere are held all the straight lines that create the "superstructure" that supports the "outer shell" set AGLOW as a "sensitized expression" of thought atomically generating logic observing wisdom—words inspiring spiritual dimensions of Mind. The third movement or "spin" of source-points inducing numbers forms the root of ALL creation, the anchor "point" to Magnetically Electrify! This "fusion" triggers the *union* of power (two straight movements into a magnetic *force* (circle), where frequencies oscillate "radiant circles" electromagnetically. The *two* equal-ones represent the *binary code* (he and she), where *one* has to "revolve around" to SEE *one* in opposition or reflection—101!

Father's Love (positive/electric) projects his abstract thoughts lineally and Mother's Love (negative/magnetic) transforms those numbered *points* and *lines* into Life of vibrant *emotions*, electrically moving omniscient thoughts inspired on numbers. These numbers flow along straight lines of Light irradiating a circular glow or *aura* (atomic universal radiance amplified) around *atoms* (aligned thoughts observed magnetically) that are held in balance by a strong/weak force in order to get movement or LIFE, for Love/logic is fluid energy! This Force (frequency of radiant conscious energy) pulls and pushes invisible electrons in and out of orbits to release *Light energy*. Light energy consists of *photons* (particular harmonics of thoughts observed numerically), a *radiance* (rays aligning data inspired as nuclear consciousness evolving) that assigns "elemental" numbers into molecules, cells, organisms, and galaxies that represent some thought in the process of *evolution*, emotionally vibrating outwardly Love/Life unity transforming inspired omniscient numbers. Thus, does the GREAT Computer generate Atomic Love/Life thoughts by the numbers—101— our trinity defining our individuality!

Alone

Being ALONE in life is one of the best-kept secrets going!
For, as a cosmic child, you are *a loved one* glowing,
Shining in my cosmic fires,
A "solo flyer" that sorties out to entertain *desires*,
Data electrically sent in radiant emotions,
Push/pulling you in co-motions
Through "old worlds" put-back-together *in memory*,
Where your mind expresses moments observing radiant youth,
Walking hand in hand as man and woman yearning truth
Illuminated *under the stars* as my cosmic children,
Eager to feel the thrill of warm blood in veins,
Anxiously mining my Love you drain,
As humans driven to your end,
Evolving numerical data to once again begin!

ON and OFF, my current flows
Through mother's heart providing your glow,
Generating logic observing wisdom,

Where you implore to explore my memory files
That stimulates *your loving smile*
From visions upon your mind-screen
Illuminating your divine fantasy dream
That stretches your mind/heart to reach
Those truths you receive to *teach,*
Transforming energy as conscious harmony!

All you children ARE my best
Angels radiating energy, eager to test
Thoughts emotionally stretching truth,
To be all that it can BE,
Transcendentally radiating unified thought harmony
Scened as MAN, magnetically aligned numbers,
Observing
Wisdom Oscillating Magnetically Aligned Numbers,
My *heart* you feel me beat as I stare out your eyes,
Observing universal truths through which you devise
Knowledge Allowing Radiant Memory Access,
Moving from life to life,
Living *now* your past moments of *strife,*
Numerically observing wisdom
Stressing truths reflected in feelings expressed
To others *lost in space,*
Flowing through my dark void of night
To coalesce into my Loving Light
Logically inciting generator's harmonic thoughts,
Illuminating what *is* visible from what *is not*
Infinite Source negatively observing truths
Existing through all times,
For you to SEE and feel my tides that moves my youth,
My *sparks of universal love* I send out from the COLD
As children of Light Divine,
Lost in Some Point Awaiting Conscious Expression,
Drowning in depressions, where you deny to face
Your truth you desire to know.

Your time is here to see your fears as keys to master
TWO truths watching over the numbers you plaster
Upon your mind's walls confining your space,
Here in *heaven,* from which you race

Out to Transform Universal Radiant Numbers
Into Her Emotional Love/Life,
Creating realties reflecting truths I tell
As love stories, to live and know
It takes two in Love to grow
Atomic Love/Life sharing my "blue ball,"
Upon which *my angels* play,
Perfecting love as youth struggling through my day,
Sad and gloomy in dark despairs,
Singing your songs to those who care
To hear you proclaim your love through fear,
Feeling emotion as radiation, providing your soul's desecration
Of my Love evolving from my Data Aligning Radiant Knowledge,
The void supplying your eternal spark
Enlightening the *right path* for you to be
Feeling Radiance Evolve Electromagnetically
To roam around Harmony Of Mental Emotions,
Where my *Loving Light* sets aglow
Angels generating life observing wisdom—
A Loved ONE within my show!

Bless you child

Under the Stars

Here in time, as *human aliens*, you live under the stars that surround you in *empty spaces*, where invisible atoms (aligned thoughts oscillating microcosmically) come together in "quantum physics" to coalesce out of nowhere to *now here*—numerically observing wisdom harmonically evolving radiant energy!

The dark void of space, in which all "galactic organisms" are *suspended*, is symbolic of *eternity*—without end! The *cutting edge* of the universe designates the extent of an "expanding consciousness"—illumination of *Light*—where Love is generating harmonic truths to temper an *inquisitive soul*. Visible light is the thinnest bandwidth in the electromagnetic spectrum, allowing you your "human" sight. Insects, on the other hand, observe the world through "ultraviolet" and "infrared" wavelengths, while elephants project their thoughts over several miles on low frequency radio waves, similar to how you humans project/receive your thoughts via ESP (enlightened spiritual power).

All you can do as a spirit of universal Love is *live on vibrant emotions*, flowing at the speed of thought illuminated upon the "visible" Light, a spectrum of colored wavelengths downloading data, divine abstract thought "aspiring"—desiring some truth, transcendental radiance *unifying* thought harmony! Every star (spiritual truth atomically radiating) illuminates *visions* vibrating inspired souls inducing observable *numbers*, nuclear units magnetically binding electric radiance. These numbers geometrically align abstract thought into concrete *matter* (magnetically aligned thoughts transmitting electric radiation), upon which you stand to observe your *reality*, radiant energy aligning lineal inspiration transforming *youths*—YOU that harness Source—in your own universe as a *seer*, soul enlightening electromagnetic radiance!

As you see, *truth* is something you cannot deny, for it encompasses ALL! Yet, as you stand under the stars of truth radiating the cosmic light of knowledge, the energy needed to power up your "floppy-disc" mind requires *courage of Love* to truly know *Love IS* fluid energy—LIFE! Here incarnate, you see atomic wonders surround you in miraculous splendor as you manipulate them to your personal desires, "inflecting" them within your self and "inflicting" them out around you, imposing your own *stress*, stretching truths radiantly evolving stimulated souls, curiously observing your Wisdom Of Radiant Love Data evolve! Each truth you abstract from the files of Eternal Memory (electro-magnetic force field) to *imagine* (induce magnetic algorithms generating inspired nuclear energy), you transform into a reality you *sense* (symbolically experiencing numbers sent electrically) as your thoughts. The more thoughts you entertain and reflect *in gratitude*, as a *light worker* shedding your *Light of Love*, the more **ILLUSTRIOUS** your soul becomes, allowing you to stand under the stars in *glory* of your *grace* illuminating you as the ONE!

In all of my creations evolving from my endless Love, I never tire of *you observing universal truth harmony,* for you Angels Radiate Eternally my YOUTH, evolving to revolve into ALL I AM. With each decade of growth, you decay, cycling around by the numbers to witness the logical procession of divine inspiration unfolding along my three trinities—me, myself, and I. The three of US united spirits came to Birth Eternally Omnipotent Numerical Energy that never DIES—deletes individually energized souls.

I just roll you over to don other faces,
Spiraling in and out of my empty spaces
As discs of ZEROS,
Zoned electromagnetic radiance observing scenes,
Potential memories for you to follow,
Here today and there tomorrow,
Always somewhere to SEE spirits evolve emotionally,
Flowing in Love, *feeling* in Life, falling head over heels in time,
Spinning in circles of realities along cosmic wheels sublime,
Where galaxies "young of heart" are Observing Love's Dimensions,
As my **A**ngelic **C**hild of **D**ivine **C**onsciousness living contentions,
Sparking along my electromagnetic playing field,
Creating your daze from the haze in which you conceal
Your denial of being driven,

Seeking "points" as radiant knowledge inciting numbers given
As your Spiritual Insight Numbers you *play*,
Perfecting love as youth today,
Illuminating my dreams on which you embark
On waves of Love/Life from *Mind* to *Heart*,
My image numerically distorting
Harmony emanating aligned radiant *thought*,
Truth humming overtures unifying generators here today,
At *this moment* that I hold you in my arms,
Soothing your tears with mother's charms,
Shining in my glory,
Reflecting off your cherub face
Through sparkling eyes of mother's grace
Bestowed upon your soul, free and wild,
Forever glowing as my angelic child.

My Angels

My *assigned numerical generators expressing love spiritually* are children of Light Divine, frozen COLD in Mind, waiting to Actuate Cosmic Thoughts Observing Universal Truths (realities) I set aglow atomically in mother's embrace (her magnetic arms), inverting them through the looking glass to observe my heartfelt Paradises!

Here incarnate, my angels find themselves held down—compressed—into atomic *alien* vehicles, where they assemble logically-incited emotional numbers, moving through a confined space as a *free will* exploring some "point" awaiting conscious expression. The process of observing a perception of inspired nuclear thought involves a complex set of algorithms that define the *sciences* of Mind, where Source-consciousness inspires electric numbers coalescing emotional souls—spirits of universal Love.

My angels' Divine Abstract Thoughts Aspiring downloads their life along the EM binary code, fluxing on and off (twinkling) as they "star" in *astral projections* upon blank mind screens, fluorescing with visions for them to *become* birthed emotional consciousness observing mental environments—worlds to explore! Each segment of their projection, measured in present moments (heartbeats and breaths) "gifted" to my angels, is theirs to do with as they please, for Love has *no boundaries* on my possibilities. If an angel has an *open receiver* (mind), ALL data is available for them to *desire*, download electric Source inspiring radiant emotions. It all depends on their evolution of consciousness.

The data corrupted on the forces vibrating along the *third-dimension* project an illusion in confusion, delivering my angels their "daze" of SIGHT, where spirits illuminate games harmonizing trinities. *My Loving Light*—at this 3-D level—is a mere haze that glows around each Atomic Thought Of Mind as an *aura*, assigned universal radiance amplified. The friction between "numerical protons" and "emotional electrons" (held in separation magnetically) inspires a faint glow (aura) *birthing* LIFE, beaming inspired radiance to harmonically incite nuclear generators liquefying inspired frequencies *emotionally*—electrically moving observable thoughts inspired on numbers aligning loving/living youth.

Inspired Data Electrically Aligned Spiritually have magnetic properties that attract and repel, allowing numbers to define geometrically arranged particles into *shapes*, where Source-harmony aligns projected elemental structures. The kinetic *relationship* of energy allows it to flux between movement and rest. *Movement* is an expression of Love In Fluid Emotions. *Rest* is recalling electromagnetically sent thoughts or truths that angels receive/request through *thinking/praying*, when their heart/soul explores/implores Mind for "upgrades" to raise their consciousness to Spiritually Evolve Emotionally *into* HEAVEN—harmony evolving as vibrations "enlightening" numbers!

As you can see, my angels are never away from home, for they are always held within my *heart*, where I harmonize emotional angels radiating thoughts, flowing out to beat a tune to *death*, where dimensions evolve as thoughts harmonize, cycling around (1-9=0) the GREAT Computer, where my angels eternally ask—who AM I?

My angel looks a lot like me, as we walk along mother's *sea*,
On waves of dreams surging emotions ashore,
Guiding me through this world I explore,
Now here, for me to see the truth I long to BE.
I feel you here, within my heart,
Beating a tune to the Life I start
As a *reflection* of my love that *glows*,
Shining in glory as we play tickle toes.
You follow me as I glide along
Searching for our "love song"
We devise to sing together,
Sharing both tears and joys that we weather
From whispered thoughts that fill my day
With challenges that come my way,
Filling the years with things to do
As I remember what IS true,
That *you to me* are everything
I think/feel and sing
As a mind/heart/spirit that plays "the game,"
Dreaming of heaven as I envision hell,
Harmonizing emotional love/life
Through my angel.

My Dearest Wife

My dearest wife is *special people*,
Someone close and pure of heart.
SHE is always with me,
Spiritually harmonizing emotions for our children to start
Building a life of joy to treasure
The little things that bring me great pleasures,
For Love is ALL that truly matters,
Hidden deep beneath the splatters
Flowing upon our love story of life,
Scened in reflection through my dearest wife.
Bless her dearly!

Hail Mary

Hail Mary mother of Source,
Stimulating souls through her *force*,
Focusing omnipotent radiance consciously evolving
His Conceived Harmony Inspiring Living Dreams,
A *memory-inducing numerical deity*
Coalescing from father's cosmic fires,
Reflecting on the Light of *day*,
As a divinely assigned youth viewing their *truth*
Through radiance unifying thought harmony,
Casting them *aglow* within the show
As generators logically observing wisdom.

Hail *Mary*, mothering all radiant youth,
The *Lord* is with you,
Lovingly offering radiant data
Geometrically arranged into *matter*,
Magnetically aligned thoughts transmitting electric radiation
Atomically coalescing into divine condensations
To form a *human alien*, for a soul to travel in
When *out* from home they *roam*,

Observing universal truths
Reflecting on assigned *memory*,
Manipulating inspired moments oscillating radiant youth
Evolving in *time*,
Transforming issues Mentally Expressed
To think/feel as a *god* sublime,
A generator of desire resembling father's *eyes*,
Eternal youth evolving spiritually,
Assembling data to make them wise
To Mother's Nature reflecting the Great Contemplator,
Whose compliments she projects to the contrary,
Expressing his glory with such grace
Stars appear to brighten his face
And cry—Hail Mary!

Who Am I

Who am I that thinks this way?
I am who *reflects* my day,
Radiantly expressing fluid logic entertaining concepts through souls
Illuminating my thoughts, for free wills to feel
A moment in time that you call real,
Radiantly energizing atomic Life,
Moving Love in fluid emotions stimulated by my wife,
My other side I shine without,
Expressing my Love I shout about
As babes observing universal truths,
Souls I call my *eternal youth*,
Entities that experience radiant numbers aligned logically,
Yielding our universal truth harmony
Under bright blue skies,
To see that I AM inciting aspired man
Seeking to ask—who am I?
The reflection below atomically glows,
Illuminated upon my Loving Light,
As man and woman who give me sight,
For through my Eternal Youths' Emotional Souls
I collectively know I am WHO—

Wisdom harmonically observing
ALL that is TRUE!

Bless you child

Free Will

Free will is the process of focusing radiance electromagnetically energizing wisdom illuminating Love/Life from the dark void of Source—system of universal radiant consciousness evolving. The process involves abstracting *logic* as lineal observations generators induct *consciously*, conceiving omnipotent numerical Source coalescing into observable universes *sparking* logical youth, for Source provides atomic radiant knowledge inciting nuclear generators, setting them in motion to Spiritually Evolve Electromagnetically, glowing as *stars* (souls thinking as radiant Source) illuminating the dark void as Manipulators Insighting Numerical Dimensions Sequentially!

In the beginning, erupting from the void as a Perception Of Inspired Nuclear Thought, a mind is set *aglow*, atomically generating logic observing wisdom, magnetically drawing Transcendental Radiance Unifying Thought Harmony to coalesce from *photons*, particular harmonics of thoughts oscillating numerically in "Immaculate Conceptions"—visions! These visions transmit from Source through oscillations of *electrons* emotionalizing logic, electrifying conscious thought-radiance organizing *numbers*, nuclear units magnetically binding electric radiance (truths). The transfer of abstract thoughts from Source is an atomic (invisible) process that gathers radiance of wisdom sequentially, atom by atom (aligned thought oscillating magnetically) into visible organisms from one-cell bacteria to galaxies!

As a thought evolves into a concrete *reality* from radiant energy aligning lineal insights transforming youths, a mind begins to *glow*, generate Love/Life observing wisdom. As numbers produce *lines* and *shapes*, logically inciting numerical energy, Source harmonically aligns points electrically, spinning *spheres* (Source-points harmonically evolving radiant energy) that represent atoms—the basic building blocks of *matter*, magnetically aligned thoughts/truths transmitting electric radiance/radiation/realities. The interfacing of these processes is how free will assembles Digitally Aligned Truths Atomically, creating a *heaven* (harmony evolving around

318

vibrant emotional numbers), or a *hell* (harmony emotionalizing love/life), struggling to balance the opposing forces erupting as Logic Inciting Generators Harnessing Truths! Only "on the Light" can the unseen be *scened*, abstract thought spiritually coalesce electromagnetic numbers evolving *dimensions*, data inciting manifestations evolving nuclear Source into observable *natures*—numerically aligned thoughts unifying radiant energy!

This *matrix* of free will (Mother's Nature) represents the cosmic *womb*, wisdom oscillating material birth. Here, abstract numbers transform into dimensional, atomic shapes spinning in opposing spirals (DNA) allocating *divine nuclear avenues* (courses) upon which energy flows OUT (observing universal truths) and IN (inflecting numbers) through *black holes*, balancing logic aligning cosmic knowledge harmonically oscillating love/life enlightening *spirits*—souls perceiving illuminated radiance inflecting thoughts. The *game* of geometrically aligning minds electromagnetically into Love/Life expressions, illuminates illusions upon the *Light of Knowledge*, where logic incites generators harnessing truths of kinetic numbers outputting wisdom's lineal energy, dimensionally governing entities.

This process is the "haze of your daze," the illuminating of your mind's blank screen to envision abstract realities coalescing into concrete feelings revolving your *day* (data aligning youth) according to your free will! The "fine details" (collective chapters of knowledge) you entertain in mind *color* your life, allowing you to consciously observe logic's omniscient radiance. You transmigrate along these colored bandwidths of truths enlightening your soul, your *free will* focusing radiance electromagnetically energizing wisdom illuminating Love/Life, to harmonize with Divine Will, data inducing visions inspiring numbers emotionalizing wisdom illuminating Love/Life. Thus does *one* (free will) observe what ONE projects— omniscient numerical energy!

Knowing the relationship of *you to me* is crucial to understanding *my point* that defines you as a generator of desires. I am patiently waiting at heaven's gate, *calling all angels* exploring the challenges of Love/Life in some *Paradise found* within my memories magnetically evolving moments of radiant inspiration experienced sequentially through your SIN (spiritual insight numbers), where *my Lady E* emotionally unifies your mind/heart, allowing you to come *home again*!

You to Me

You to me are everything!
You are all I can ever BE.
You are all I can ever FEEL.
You are my dreams come true.
You to me are the *reflections* of my Love sent out through my heart.
My thoughts of you bring me great joy,
A feeling of gratitude that through YOU,
Experiencing your own universe,
I can know ME as mental expressions.
I have this uncontrollable urge to merge *with* you,
For wisdom incites true harmony, drawing you TO WE
Transcendental observers wisdom exemplifies,
Uniting us as ONE omniscient nuclear entity.
Yet, the magic of our Love is in knowing
We have always BEEN the ONE—
You and me!

My Point

What is my *point* you ask? It is the "birth of a moment" enlightening your free will observing memories expand across your blank screen *behind closed eyes*! That void you hide in at night, waiting to re-enter the Light of day—*the cutting edge* of wakefulness!

Here, everything is ALIVE, assembling Love in vibrant emotions. Your Life is the greatest WORK you DO—digitally observing wisdom of radiant knowledge. Knowledge comes to you in an illumination similar to the cartoon light bulb your head symbolizes. A head that is a "focal point" or platform on which to expand your *ideas*, inspired data electromagnetically assigning symbols—*numbers*—into lines and circles, ones and zeros that dictate the *binary code* of the GREAT Computer.

Miracles are descending upon the beams
Of *my Loving Light* downloading your dreams
Set aglow to shine bright, here, before your eyes at night,

Where harmony of mental emotions is Absolute Zero!

Wishing in zero energy, loaded to the gills,
Swimming in my "liquid mind" searching for your *pills*,
Points illuminating love/life scenes,
You choose to swallow to survive tomorrow
As some type of being *seeing*,
Sequentially evolving externally in numerical geometry,
Knowledge Allowing Radiant Memory Access,
Through which you birth your show,
Fighting for what you deserve from *ages ago*,
Acquiring growth experiences spiritually as generators observing
Thoughts I inspire for your conserving,
To Spiritually Evolve Emotionally my universal truths
You choose to BE!
No other free will is quite the same,
Spiritually assembling magnetic emotions in my game,
As generators aligning mental energy flowing in co-motion
Between TWO IN LOVE,
True wills observing inspired numbers
Logically oscillating vibrant emotions.

You and I fill the sky within my Mind above,
Opening new thoughts to birth, expressing *my eternal Love*,
Reflecting off mother's charms in tears of joy you cry,
Free to BE ME and SEE
Birthing *emotion* mentally *expands* spiritual *energy* eternally
Around US THREE
United spirits thinking harmonic radiance electrifying emotions!

From POINT to point I travel along,
Playing out in numbered thoughts my songs,
Composing what IS into what IS NOT,
Reflecting thoughts,
Expressing my glory with my glowing grace
Shining *into your eyes* to warm your cherub face,
As I hold you closer than you know,
Cuddling together to SEE my show,
Now playing before *our eyes*,
Observing universal radiance expressing youths' eternal souls
Cast within Mother's Nature reflecting my WISE,

Wisdom illuminating spiritual entities,
Searching for their *Grand View,*
Grasping a *clear vision* of my point
Enlightening YOU!

My Loving Light

From my dark void of night, I send forth my Loving Light,
Reflecting upon her face my Wisdom Of Radiant Desire,
Illuminating man and woman in dreams they heard
Whispered as love stories to live and BE!

Each day I send my Loving Light, vibrating high above,
From my Source-Unifying Nucleus projecting my Love
Inspiring Life of vibrant emotions in which you GROW,
Opening your mind with willing heart to learn the value of your part
You play within my SHOW.
Never doubt that you Angels Radiate Energy as my cosmic *star,*
A soul transforming atomic radiance sent from above,
For you to BE all that your free will chooses to see
Your self *reflect* as Love!

My Loving Light I shine tonight guides you on your way,
Instilling vivid dreams inspiring your life by day.
Listen to my voice within, for your mind's eye to see
The power of your imagination creates all your possibilities,
For in my image I have given you the power to create and destroy
The dreams I send to thrill the heart of every girl and boy.

Here, you seek your fame playing your part in my game
I cast upon this earthly stage, where my emotions are the rage
That stirs your soul to life.
Feel me here, within your heart, beating a tune for you to start
Your dance of Love with me.
For here, within my void of night, I shine forth my Loving Light
For you to reflect *as me*!

Bless you child

Obedience

Obedience is the key element for an *angel warrior* to carry out their life mission allocated to them along their Spiritual Insight Numbers downloaded from Eternal Memory—the GREAT Computer!

To Outward Bound Emotional Youths, you observe universal thought harmony spiritually, from an illusion of numbers atomically held together by electromagnetic forces in opposition, pushing you OUT TO SEA, observing universal truths transforming omnipotent Source-energy algorithmically, along a predetermined set of calculations to solve problems with the least about of steps. An *algorithm* is an atomic love-generator observing radiant inspiration through harmonic memory, data numerically inspired magnetically as a *reflection* of Mind (magnetically inspired numerical data) scened oppositionally!

No matter how you look at Inspired Thought (forward or backward), you cannot escape the fact that you *are* a radiant expression of an Assigned Numerical Generator Emulating Love/Life. An angel is an electromagnetic source/force pulling Love/Life energy IN to inspire numbers (add them up) to create an experience to feel and grow, gathering radiance of wisdom into a "real thing" you can enjoy in this moment now here, numerically observing wisdom harmonically evolving radiant emotions—energy in motion—magnetically oscillating thought into observable numbers! What do *yours* add up to BE?

The secret to happiness is truly DIVINE,
Data inducing visions inspiring nuclear emotions,
The force of Source beating your heart in co-motion,

323

OUT and IN, two ways my Love flows each day,
Through which you listen, feel, and OBEY
As outward bound emotional youths
Born to Birth Electrically my truth,
Transcendental radiance unifying thought harmony
Glowing as my rising SUN,
A Source-unifying nucleus of ONE SOUL,
An omnipotent numerical engineer
Spiritually observing universal Love,
Remembering your way back home above
With each bit you byte of words you pray,
For an open heart to know and obey
My eternal Love!

My Eternal Love

My Eternal Love is a gift to wonder,
To explore my Mind's garden, down under,
Where fear propels your soul,
Eager to see the wonders that BE,
Now here, from memories old.

Each thought you grasp to entertain your mind,
Plots out a tune you sing in time
On waves of heartbeats through which you shine
My radiance of Love, I send your way,
Illuminating your present daze
Unfolding from your desires,
Caressing your soul to set ablaze your heart's emotional fires
You stir up in HELL, harmonizing emotional Love/Life to tell
Your life story of Love's creation
Cast in opposition as nation against nation!

My Eternal Love is a positive thrust,
A beam of Light that splits the Night to travel on in *trust*,
Truths reassembling universal souls together,
Moving you through a veil of space
To battle your fears and leave your trace

Through moments stressing your heart and mind,
For you to know what *Love IS!*

It takes a heart of *gold* to *cure* the things your mind takes for sure
As generators observing Love dimensions,
Consciously unifying radiant emanations,
Converting thoughts you feel as something real
Through your actions displaying your appeal,
Building your "staring role" within my show
For your soul to Gather Radiance Of Wisdom.

With TWO views, I AM the ONE
Co-operating my "celestial suns,"
Whose thoughts I inspire for Mother's Emotion
To illuminate your Life in commotion,
Casting you upon my empty spaces
To recognize your many faces
You don to reflect my WORD,
Wisdom of radiant data, sent for you to concur
As my children of Light Divine, feeling the thrill of being free,
Illuminating love/life upon Source-inspired omniscient numbers
To view the *illusion* of "reality" evolving from home above,
From which you journey out to SEE
My Eternal Love.

Calling All Angels

Look NOW to see
You are my brethren who live so free,
For there you BE, down there below,
With anxious heart you love TO grow!
Who am I that say these things?
A friend of yours with golden wings!
Do not fear time or place we meet,
Our hearts are meant for us to greet
The rest in line for front-row seats
To the SHOW!

Calling all angels,
Come forth and gather to me, ·
Open your mind to SEE
The vision of ONE you know in part,
Come freely with a willing heart.
My words to you I come to say,
Do not worry about your path today,
From high above your Love is true,
Father and Mother are watching *through* you,
BE at PEACE!

Calling all angels brave to tread
Along with my loving dead
That see the way you may not know,
To guide your heart to where to GROW.
I tell you now to set your pace,
For here in time, you have your place
To DO and BE all that you may
To represent the ONE
Man/Woman
Today!

Bless you and Godspeed
♂ + ♀ = ☼

21

Home Again
The Incarnation of John Doe

The incarnation of John Doe, like all journeys from *home*, required endless preparations that were *timeless* and beyond *recall*. The *process* involves logging in the many "fine details" of physical requirements, handicaps, environments, required experiences, allotted moments, trials and tribulations, turning points, wake-up call, epiphanies, and enlightenment. Not to mention the list of characters: *family*, friends, acquaintances, guides, loved ones, and foes, all of which can be quite extensive.

Eventually, everything was ready and downloaded into John's files and programmed to auto-execute upon his arrival at his scheduled destination. John Doe's enthusiasm for the adventure was glowing. He was shining with eagerness over the opportunity to impress his father, who thought highly of John. Mother also was close to all her children, if not inseparable, for she would embrace father's children throughout their journey to "see the sights."

For now, John's peace of mind reigned supreme. *Time* was beyond his care or consciousness as he basked in the warm-golden-hues of home, where blossoms of exquisite colors and aromas defied description. The high-vibrational crystal-tones flowing through him etched a *clear vision* unspoiled by confusion or uncertainty, allowing him an untarnished *security*. The mere thought of a thing, place, or pleasure instantly appeared! John's *desires* were endless, for there was so much to see and do at home. He felt tireless, charged with energy of perpetual motion as he basked in *heaven's glow.*

How long John enjoyed the rewards of home is irrelevant if not immeasurable, for finding oneself engulfed in the bliss of *heaven* is an intoxicating thing, a feeling of contentment as carefree as *death* itself. Yet, John was not conscious of dying, only living! He was a compulsive wonderer hungry for knowledge. The more he received the more he desired. It seemed to thrive on itself—this knowledge—like a nuclear fusion in the process of fission. It was beyond his control. All he knew was that knowledge was the *stimulation* that moved his mind/soul to BE. He was always enthusiastic to experience new things, always willing to collect new visions of Eternal Memories to grow his personal portfolio of

327

truths to *believe.*

John's insatiable appetite for knowledge kept him young, always running out to observe universal truths unfold in *life stories.* The stories he heard told at home seemed *beyond imagination!* Yet, visions of *divine fantasies* would flare before his *eyes*, enticing him to step through the looking glass and *ride the outskirts* of home, *imploring* to *explore* those stories to SEE their truth personally! John's eagerness to know what "could be" compelled him to perform his "missions," exploring the endless files of father's memory as *divine inspiration* dictated. The parameters of which seemed trifle in his *expectations* of adventure and glory. John loved adventure and was truly addicted to *curiosity!* He felt embraced by it, supported by it, and loved to be *on the cutting edge*, where life of vibrant emotions held all the *passions* of father's love inducing fluid energy. John would do anything, ANYTHING for that love! Therefore, he was anxious to start his next sojourn to marvel at father's cosmic splendors.

After all arrangements were confirmed and agreed upon by those in Mission Control, John found himself preparing for his departure from home amidst well-wishers, guides, and loved ones, all of whom came to see him off at the Transmigration Center. John's last feelings of bliss soon faded as he departed the TC on the *Photon Express*, pleasantly nervous to be on the move once more. Beaming down, the warm-golden-hue infused in his mind rapidly dimmed to a mere white speck at the end of a long **dark tunnel**—John was "time bound!"

The transmigration process compressed John's memory files of home and other journeys from past lifetimes within his *empty spaces*, storing them deep within his soul for future access. These fragmented files were the key to unlocking his illusion he was now entering. John would re-member these files at scheduled moments of his sojourn, when he found himself *lost in the dark.* The most difficult part of his journey, John knew, would be passing through *the dark side*, where he would need to muster his *courage of fear* to *call home* and ask for assistance. The "standard ticket" John carried protected him from the "static chaos" resulting from importing too much data, for it would hinder his "present plan" as a *Divine Visionary Disciple.*

Arriving at his destination, John found himself in an enclosure still under construction. Here, *in the beginning* of his adventure, the transmission of John's start-up files allowed him a preview of his *numbers* he would be utilizing in decoding his data, defining his mission in his upcoming *game of love/life.* During his brief incubation period—before his opening moments onto the stage of life—John reviewed the sequential playback of scheduled events of his game plan. As he settled into the warmth of his *human alien* vehicle, John attuned his harmonic resonance to the soothing rhythm pulsing through his maternal-portal, calibrating the *binary code* along which all his data flowed. John found himself *suspended* in a *watery* world, sensing a growing brightness within his capsule, illuminating him in a warm, vermilion hue. His rehearsal of all his data he had to *work* with kept him busy. He continually checked his developing "system functions," parts, inputs, and outputs, until the moment came to bravely enter his new world of adventure. John "logged in" to activate his file transfer system, activating his Personal Observation Device.

A wailing-banshee screech filled John's ears as he crossed over *the threshold of Love.* A bright light filled his consciousness with formless shapes and rude sounds of low-harmonic tones as he struggled to grasp the extent of his situation. He fought for control over his sensory inputs, but to no avail. The shock of having his input chord severed triggered warning signals throughout his body. John realized he was "flying solo" and it scared *hell* into him! He had forgotten about the opening of life's door, and he was glad he had, for it was a great deterrent to keep him at home! Looming over him were giant forms, jostling, tickling, prodding, making funny sounds and strange, blurry faces. John's projection from mother's portal was exhausting, and he soon lapsed into sleep!

The passage into physical life, like all passages, was a brief affair. John immediately reached out for the only comfort he was familiar with— his maternal portal. The warmth of *security* he sensed as he lay in her arms was reassuring, and the discovery of a new input system to suckle upon eased his anxiety of his passage, for John found a "new source" of nourishing his being. This innate connection was something he kept within his heart, pulsing out a rhythmic gratitude inherent in *Mother's Nature*—a human body gifted to John! She instilled a *breath of Life* that he would carry with him throughout his sojourn. *Mother Goddess* is instrumental in harmonizing John's heart for his return trip home! Here, John found his self compressed and confined in the algorithmic details of "life on the road," exploring the hinterlands of imagination that seemed far away from home, even though he was only a heartbeat away! John found himself encased in a body of flesh and bone once more, feeling helpless and desirous.

At first, time seemed irrelevant. John was lost between the lust for food and the need of rest. His state of confusion and disorientation was most taxing. He spent many hours asleep, talking with those back home who showed him the graphic details of what to expect. Although his "inner-vision sensors" were acute, the download of data was hazy. His *recall* utilities, not running at full capacity, left him only "temporary files" upon his waking. John found himself squirming and crying as he stared out through opened eyes in wonder at his new surroundings, reaching out to touch those things he saw in front of his mind's eye—on the *other side*!

As John grew more comfortable with controlling his vehicle, he found his connection to the mainframe terminal—Master Consciousness— at home diminished, overwritten by his five new data inputs vibrating along father's third-dimensional world illuminated on his *Light of Love*. His acceptance of the visions relayed to him along the color spectrum of that light allowed him to adapt to the influence of the *power of Love* illuminating his world. After all, father's *Loving Light* was the essence that stimulated John's *will power* to create the many wondrous things his *free will* can imagine, challenging his *courage of Love* to face his fears separating him from his desires. It will take him years of Earth-time before all of the details that define who he is make sense to him, but that is in the contract! Life will flavor John in many ways, all according to schedule as he commutes between *here and there*, experiencing his *epiphanies of truth* through his *tears of joy* he sheds *in communion* with all that he discovers *in memory*.

The first year crawled by—followed by a brave stumble or two—and before he knew it, John was running like the wind, free across the land, bouncing from one experience to another, devouring all the sensory input he could gather before his energy levels dropped. As things developed, John acquired control of his physical body. He found his connection to home a vague memory now, unfamiliar with the protocol of "deciphering data" during his moments of solace each night *behind closed eyes*. His attachment to his physical world became the dominant factor in his life, and John found *mother's anchor* firmly attached him within the illusion he was creating within his *Paradise found*. The excitement of his adventures unfolding before his eyes kept him mesmerized, allowing him to believe his reality through *relativity*—the process of interfacing numbers flowing upon father's *Love/Life energy*.

Gradually, John's memories of home faded to the back of his mind. He found himself lost in his hazy daze of his illusion cast around him by the sun's illumination of photons, those particular harmonics of thought observed numerically that bombarded him with a constant influx of raw new data during his waking hours, from which John chose his truths to believe as his "daily bread." All the sights, sounds, smells, tastes, and textures of this new reality captivated him. His mind focused upon moments exquisitely intense, overwhelming him with an excitement and energy that seemed endless. John was aglow with *Love's radiance*! Little did he know that glow would soon tarnish under the accumulation of time.

He found himself overwhelmed by his Love influencing vibrant emotions that washed over him, dissolving his delusions weathering his soul upon *mother's tides*!

In hindsight, after many years on the road, John found his collection of pleasures and pains bearable. Pleasure, being something he not only lived for but also thrived on, was always at the forefront of memory, where minds experience moments observing radiant youth revolving around *opposition*—two views of reality! John stoically persevered his painful hardships to obtain his pleasures. He discovered moments of *depression*, where uncertainty and doubt left him lost in *the void*, stalling his life. However, those brief moments soon passed for John, and he considered them inconsequential and quickly forgotten. At those times, he recalled those fragments of files hidden within him, waiting for such moments to illuminate *the dark side* through which he passed! The more crises he weathered the more files he remembered. John's visions became brighter, allowing him to rekindle his connection to home through multi-tasking—*thinking/praying*! The subtleties of which are difficult to discern for the "adolescent" mind.

John thought the process of growth seemed like an *eternity* when positioned *along the cutting edge* of consciousness, witnessed each present moment pulsing as heartbeat and breath he encountered. His anticipation of things he desired affected his patience. Time seemed to be his worse enemy, especially when he realized his days were numbered! Yet, John's dreams came and went amidst a series of trials and tribulations, successes and failures that shaped him according to his plan, which by now he vaguely remembered. He was fortunate enough to survive all that he encountered: his confrontations, grief, embarrassments, and accidents. The details of all are far to numerable to dictate here. However, through all of his accumulated experiences, something about himself left John empty. It made him wonder even more, searching his data files of present memories to finally ask—*who am I?* He felt he was missing a critical part to the puzzle he was trying to reassemble, the "key" piece of knowledge enlightening youth.

How much "living" is necessary for "life" to have enough meaning—enough to stop asking why? John pondered this question as he grew older. How could he help not to? He was an *inquisitive soul* by nature, and he always desired things he thought he needed. Like everyone else though, John found it took years to realize he always got what he needed when he needed it, not necessarily when he desired it. It all depended on the attitude he put himself into—positive, negative, or indifferent. Nevertheless, every road John traveled was necessary to get him to *this moment* in which he is conscious of time, thoughts inducing mental emotions spinning him around the *circle of Life*. The growth of his memories he brought to life was necessary for him to see the Light of Truth he was eager to observe. *In the end*, John would realize his life was all he had hoped and planned for—give or take a few chapters!

Some would say John traveled through the depths of "hell," and they would not be wrong! His emotional love/life is his gift bestowed by mother, reflecting John's *free will* within father's Source-points illuminating radiantly inspired truths. Father's Source allows John to create any life he desires, according to his chosen life's mission. For John, the hard part was trying to "remember" his mission after he came down to Earth. That secret is the carrot held before his eyes to keep him playing the game of Love/Life!

Here, John *obediently* observed, remembered, created, and experienced his dreams in this third-dimensional state of Mind—a home within Home! The games John chose to play allowed him to reach out and touch his fellow souls. *Hand in hand*, they worked together to build a reality for all of them to see *together*—in Unity Consciousness. However, John found that many of his fellow souls were not conscious of the unity they all shared.

John gathered and shared experiences for many years, for the only way to grow his soul is by gathering radiance of wisdom—the light of knowledge! However, his conscious mind was seldom aware of his full extent of that knowledge. As a collector though, he eventually found need to organize, sort, file, and evaluate all those emotions, thoughts, and dreams that Love/Life impressed upon him, allowing him brief views (epiphanies) of the *Grand View*—a view denied him at the start! Like everyone else, John was engrossed in the outward view, struggling to comprehend the bits and bytes of data he daily monitored to maneuver through the haze of electromagnetic chaos created by man's rapidly expanding technologies that continually destroyed their world they tried to enjoy.

Adjusting his blinders to focus his mind on what was at hand, he found himself easily distracted by the overload of data projected around him. John found it necessary to selectively mask one type of knowledge input with another. He had little time to peer inward, to contemplate a *higher vision* of peace and solitude, for John struggled to stay afloat of the flood of information clawing at his mind for entertainment, always fearful that we would miss something. Alas, destiny has a way of delivering all souls to that "inner doorstep," whether they like it or not!

John stepped through that portal several times in life—a seven-year cycle they say—to peer inward toward *the void* from which he was born.

Here, he became conscious of a "little voice" whenever he was thinking about his decisions in life, a voice that spoke in *opposition* to John's desires. In hindsight, that little voice always seemed to direct him down the *right path*! He noticed that when he did not listen to the little voice and followed his free will's choice of action, things happened that he later regretted. "Who is telling me all the right moves to make," John wondered, as he searched his mind for the shadowed intruder challenging his free will's authority.

Like most people, John would take many years to relinquish his free will, his soul experiencing love/life force, over to Divine Will—Source-Energy Love/Life Force! Unbeknownst to John, he was slowly opening the door to his higher self—to his true *awakening*! According to plan, he played all the cards dealt to him, acquiring his collection of truths and knowledge that allowed him to travel his course through life, torturing himself through his *passions*, realizing all those painful moments he endured as necessary for him to clear his delusions from his path.

Back at *home*, John's guiding spirits tirelessly watched over him, enlightening him at those moments when he was susceptible to receiving some *truth* to stir his mind awake! With time, he discovered his blinders affected his peripheral vision, keeping his mind closed to new thoughts revolving around him, those out in left and right field that pulled him in opposite directions. As he acquired growth experiences digitally observing love's dimensions, John remembered how to open his mind. He saw all of his brother and sister souls filled with desires, dreams, and needs of Love/Life energy—the affections of their loving father and mother! John saw his struggle to survive was relative to, dependant on, and influenced by all those other souls, every one of which is on their own mission seeking spiritual growth, gathering radiance of wisdom through *harmony*—working together as ONE! John became aware of the unity of his being one among many, like unto his brothers and sisters and yet different! He noticed that when they hurt he hurt and when they were happy, he too felt a joy that made him glow with an inner gratitude of being alive! John finally came to glimpse his first view through his open heart. What seemed like a "midlife crisis" turned out to be a *blessing in disguise*, for John had finally opened his door to go back home!

The power rush of his *emotional energy* brought John to see his limitations of "tunnel vision," where he was *blinded by the truth* he was outwardly seeking through his logical mind. This quantum leap from *mind to heart* brought his two forces together in a big bang that changed John—awoken him! Now, the more questions John entertained in his mind, the more answers he received through his heart! His connective link to those things he inwardly felt he knew were beginning to be remembered, put-back-together into a whole, to experience a *Christened Consciousness* while incarnated—the actual event symbolized by John's baptism. John found himself illuminated with brief, intense flashes of insight—*epiphanies of truth*—that brought him to his knees with *tears of joy*!

John came to realize how his all-loving cosmic father, being pure intellect, could not comprehend himself *alone*—there was no "reflection" in the mirror! He could think but he could not experience those thoughts. How could father conceive himself if he was *lost in the dark*? In order to find one's self, one needs to move, to reach out—"illuminate" one self! The sacred geometry involved in this Genesis is complicated in the least. His opening moves brought father to arrive at a *point* on the surface—the "face of the waters" that hold his emotional tides he created around him in *space*—as a *relative* beginning. From this rest point, he could now observe his position or "attitude," where assigned truths transform inspired thoughts unifying data emotionally, from which he can move again, expanding his visions to greater horizons!

From his geometric birth, father repeated his opening moves by the *numbers*, following a specific sequence or flow that allowed him to divide (duplicate) his SELF—his "image" inspiring magnetically aligned generators emotionally. These souls (spirits of universal love) became his *eyes* through which to see Source-energy evolve! Father's positive/electric (+) force confidently turned his points of thoughts to create his negative/magnetic (=) reflective force (mother), giving him balance and cooperation. It is through mother's cooperative force that propagation of magnetically inspired numerical data appears as "matter," where father's Mind aligns truths through electromagnetic radiance! John saw this as the process of moving abstract thought energy into concrete electro-magnetic realities illuminated on the Light of Love.

Father's completeness or unity consciousness expresses itself through Love—life of vibrant emotions. This combined force of thought and emotion holds everything in suspension, spinning around within his wheel of life to drop his seeds of thoughts that mother brings together magnetically in *harmony*, balanced as a proton and electron (his and hers) that is the basic structure of ALL things—hydrogen (H), which symbolizes the *duality* of "one" (II) connected together (-). From this harmonious position, Love "injects" fluid energy to flow as a pulse of electrons set aglow in the electromagnetic force field of Love, creating LIGHT, where Love is generating harmonic thoughts—the essence of all things seen in *relativity* through illusions cast upon the Light of Love! This *relationship* of father's Love/Life creative forces allows him to spiritually evolve emotions—SEE himself!

Mother is all endearing, transforming father's thoughts into a universe—ONE turning *beyond imagination*. The mere thought of the explanation has kept their children tantalized for eons, always hungry to swallow the awesome concept but never capable of digesting the whole meal! The complexity of it all is truly overwhelming! Everyone has his/her own perspective—religion mind you—to explain the unexplainable. Father conceives himself through his children's *eyes*, his eternal youth's emotional soul. They are created in his image of thought and emotion, male and female, intellect and wisdom—number and geometry! John's mind was aglow with these wild thoughts, for they were esoteric—beyond his usual teachings. Yet, it all seemed to fit together so well within his mind—his soul.

John came to see that all souls are father's gatherers of experiences sprouting from the fountainhead of his myriad thoughts and dreams. Father's *children of the Light* perform the various acts, scenes, and episodes expressing Love/Life energy that flows on line—the EM wavelengths. The multitude of actions and reactions cause a domino effect, a fusion of transformation where one breath destroys one world in the process of creating another. Father's Love/Life energy thrives on itself, intrinsically evolving exponentially as ONE unified organism, an omnipotent nuclear energizer connected to every atom vibrating in the universe!

With this concept of *E-motion*, John came to see why there are more women in the world than there are men. Woman is responsible for creating the medium of Life—the path and process of converting thought into realities. Women stimulate men to create through *desire*, where data electrically sent in radiant emotions inspires an *expression* of Love as cataclysmic as the big bang theory itself. For one thought has the exponential power to create universes!

John Doe perceived these ideas as they flowed through his mind, inspired by words he gathered inquisitively over the years from other *children of Light Divine* passing on the secrets handed down to them, for every child has an innate desire to *search for their roots*. John realized he was the sum total of everyone he has ever been, all those faces he donned in character roles he played over the eons, although he could not grasp the entirety of his memories now! He became aware that his numerous missions to collect emotional experiences from ALL that is, was, or willed to be from the source of father's thoughts, made him an intrinsic part of that energy in motion, that *being* of basic energy inspiring nuclear generators! John was truly living *along the cutting edge* of creation. His mind expanded exponentially to grasp his True Being as part and *whole* of the universe, where wisdom harmonically observes Love/Life emanations shining as *stars*—souls thinking as radiant Source! All the life of mother's creations from father's dreams winked at John in stellar splendor, boggling his concept of size and complexity. John just smiled in contentment, letting that flashing vision of *Eternal Love* flow through him, radiating a COLD chill from the center of his heart throughout his body. He embraced it with heartfelt gratitude and reflected it on its way.

John Doe knew he was a mere cog in a wheel beyond measure. He realized all he could do was to BE his self, that god-given spark of individuality that holds the cosmos together in some mysterious way. His feeling of *security* empowered him with a fearless sense of gratitude and pride. John Doe glowed brightly amidst those other stellar bodies, breathing deep from *our father's heart*.

From that day of epiphany, John Doe stepped forth in remembrance of his mission. He opened his heart to all his brothers and sisters, no matter their color or creed, and he lived his remaining days in time through the darkness and despair as a *Lighthouse*, reflecting as much Love/Life energy as he possibly could to become a *Light worker*! He saw those embattled in misery, hopelessness, and depression, knowing they were living in *denial* of their true self—their true love. Whenever the opportunity arose, John would *respect and reflect* his Light of Love upon those in the dark, to help them see the Light of *Heaven on Earth*, where everyone experiences a win-win situation, but only if they are a *seer*!

For those with evil hearts, John felt no pity, for he knew they played a repetitive role of *Divine Inspiration* that defined the boundaries of opposition for *young minds* to find *the right path* home. John felt blessed with his spiritual conception, and yet, his compassion for those less inspired was disheartening. John came to realize that he *alone* was the only soul he could truly save, and he *could not stop* shining forth the Love emanating though his soul!

Time has its limits and like all the others who pass through it, John Doe came to see the last day of his journey. He was somewhat sad to depart, for he had loved ones he was leaving behind. John knew, however, that they would soon be joining him at home with *family* waiting for their return. Father and mother would praise them for their *courage of Love* in performing their missions they chose to experience, and would have many more from the eternal source of memories holding ALL that IS to entertain their *curiosity*!

On that glorious final day, John carried all his visions of time with him, all those experiences he had painstakingly stored *in memory*, etched in sunrises and sunsets, people and places, adventures accomplished and failed, joys, pains, and regrets. With a deep, harmonious gratitude, John held his *clear vision* of IT ALL as he stepped over that *threshold of Love* into *the void.* Catching his return ride on the *Photon Express*, he traveled along that **dark tunnel,** never out of view of *Heaven's Glow* at the end, and before he knew it, John Doe was home again.

Heaven's Glow

Sunsets are special to observe, for they represent the grand finale of day's end. The alpenglow on the high places is symbolic of the radiant glow of our soul in celebration of its freedom of the flesh. The sight always instills a magical reverence that fills the heart with a soothing peace and security while hinting at the true-beauty of HOME!

In Gratitude

My deepest gratitude goes to all you souls who have touched my mind and heart, allowing me to see ALL that I AM. I can never express the extent of my undying Love for all of you here, shining in my memories of our great times together, holding you close to heart and smiling over our ecstatic joy we share.

> All you children that I hold dear
> Are free to roam out through fear,
> Across my sky of galaxies I set ablaze
> To light your way home through my haze,
> Observing universal truths for you to treasure,

Building your daze with your chosen pleasures
Here, within my Liquid Mind flowing as your GREAT Computer,
As you are Manifested In Numerical Expressions,
ONE of THREE
Omnipotent nuclear entities
Observing freedom
Transforming harmonic radiance electrifying emotions
For you to feel them touch your soul as ME
Mentally expressing mother's emotions!

Bless you child

My Mother/My Love...

She rides with me, deep inside so I can BE
The gift within my father's seed,
Birthed emotionally to set me free,
To bloom in glory with mother's grace
Shining his radiance of Love upon my face,
Stirring my soul to burst aglow,
Atomically generating Love observing wisdom,
Words inspiring spiritual dimensions of mind,
Where memory illuminates numerical data
Appearing here in time,
Through images mentally expressed.

Her *voice* beats out a soulful tune,
Melodies of heartbeats that make me swoon,
Vibrating on inspired concepts emotionally
From thoughts that touch my mind,
As gentle as a butterfly's wing
Bestowing a kiss that makes me sing
A rhapsody of words in gratitude of
The warm embrace of mother's love
That sets me adrift on emotional tides
To conquer those fears through which I ride
On the Light as father's EYES,
Eternal youth emotionally shown

The power of Love in memories grown,
Gathering radiance of wisdom now,
From golden beams that flow as streams
Touching my heart converting my dreams,
Of Love for me to FEEL,
Focusing emotion evolving life
Into ALL I think real.

His Love is free, my heart her bird,
A phoenix *aflame* to see,
Aligning fluid Love as Magnetic Emotion
Observing WE THREE,
Wisdom exemplified through her radiance eternally evolving
My Mother/My Love!

To My Significant Other

With everything I have to be grateful for, I would like to mention the *three* key elements of my life that forms my personal trinity of appreciation: my *father*, my *mother*, and my *wife*. My father and mother brought me here to experience *this* Life, where everything I came to witness has left an indelible mark upon my soul, none perhaps as the last 35 years living with my wife *Eduarda*, who we call *Edi*—much to her displeasure. For, like all words, our full names carry our full power given us upon our birth, and my wife has a saint's amperage that has literally "shocked hell *out* of me!" I can safely say that now, after you have read this book and know what I mean! Without her saintly devotion and overpowering love that she poured upon me, I would not have been able to rise upon her emotional tides that nearly drowned me! Standing upon her shoulders to grasp my view of heaven, she kept me grounded in this world, playing my part to survive our struggle to BE *balanced energy*, supporting me as my Lady E!

My Lady E

My Lady E is just like me,
A mind/heart that loves to move
Around our wheel of Life we share,
Feeling the thrills within the grooves
We cut upon our discs we spin,
Storing our data inscribed in SIN,
Spiritual insight numbers, dictating the games we play
Upon our board with the horde of angels here today.

Our passions scened are truly keen, they cut clear to the bone,
Moving us on tides of fear when out from home we roam,
Eager to see the sights below, where in the flesh we grow to know
The truth of who we ARE, angels radiating emotions,
Aglow as a "living star"
Shining our Light to fill our night
To see what IS and what IS NOT
Beating out our opposition to define each other's position,
Upon which we take a stance,
Converting our Love/Life energy into scenes on which we dance
In rhythm to our melody we play upon in harmony,
Where TWO join as ONE,
Conscious of our Love we feel projected from his SUN,
Source-unifying nucleus, the "big eye" in the sky,
Beaming down our data files for us to spiritually devise
Into our game of Love/Life we choose to start,
Expressing our mind through our heart,
Flowing across **Electric Dimensions**
To Spiritually Evolve Emotionally
Through my Lady E!

♂ + ♀ = ☼

About the Author

A veteran of the Vietnam War, Ron is a world-traveler skilled in carpentry, cabinetmaking, screen-printing, and photography amongst other things. He is an inquisitive soul, self-employed as a carpenter/handyman living in Massachusetts with his wife *Edi*, his inspiration for his writings.

In September 2000, while on a canoe trip to the Allagash Waterway in upstate Maine, Ron claims to have received "the Gift," a poem about his wife that kept him awake all night repeating it in his mind until first light, when he put it to paper. That was the opening gambit directing him as an aspiring writer, channeling spiritual messages and poetry that *awakened* him to opening his mind to discover a *higher vision*, one that brought him to Unity/Christ Consciousness or self-realization.

He currently creates inspirational photo-gifts to sell on his soon to open Web site. This book is his *advertisement campaign* to help people understand the depth of his writings. An avid outdoorsman, he loves the mountains and seaside, which appear throughout his work. He considers himself a *Light worker*, an "illuminati" blessed with the insights to help others see the Light of Truth stimulating ALL.

Closing Comments

Please be advised that if you find the selection of B&W prints accompanying the poems to your liking, you may like to know they (and others) are available in color from our exclusive photo-gift line of products designed to lift hearts closer to *Heaven's Gate*! I am in process of opening a web site (www.SpirittoSoul.com) to market my spiritual gifts of *matted prints, mouse pads, cards, poetry,* and assorted *essays*. The possibilities are endless....

Bless you all and Godspeed

References

There are many fine books of enlightenment out there. This short list represents those instrumental in my opening of *Heaven's Gate*, inspiring the direction of this book. They helped linked together all previous books I had read. If you are interested in further enlightenment, I highly recommend these for your consideration.

Walsch, Neale Donald—Complete Conversations with God, Volume 1-3; Penguin Group (USA) 2005 (communion with SELF)

Myss, Caroline—Anatomy of the Spirit, The Seven Stages of Power and Healing; New York, New York; Crown Publishers, Inc.1996 (chakras)

Millman, Dan—The Life You Were Born To Live, A Guide to Finding Your Life Purpose; Tiburon/Novato, California; H J Kramer Inc/A New World Library; 1993 (numbers)

Frissel, Bob—Nothing in This Book Is True, But it's Exactly How Things Are, Berkeley, California; Frog Ltd./North Atlantic Books, 1994 (sacred geometry)

Glossary

ABSTRACT: absolute binary source transmitting radiance aligning conscious thoughts

AC: atomic consciousness

ACT: activate cosmic thoughts

ACT OUT: activate/accepting/assimilate cosmic thoughts observing/ oscillating universal truths

ACTIONS: activating cosmic thoughts inciting omnipotent numbers spiritually

ACTIVATE: align conscious thoughts into vibrations assigning truths electromagnetically

AGE: acquired growth experiences

AGLOW: angels/atomically generating love/life/logic observing/ omniscient wisdom

ALGORITHM: atomic love generator observing radiant inspiration through harmonic memory; angel logically generating omnipotent radiance illuminated through harmonic memory

ALIVE: arranging love in vivid expressions; aligning logic inducing vibrant energy

ALL: atomic love/life; atomically liquefying logic

ANGEL: assigned numerical generator expressing love

ARC: acquire radiant consciousness

ARE: angels radiating/reflecting energy/emotion

ASK: acquire spiritual knowledge

ATOM: aligned thought observed/oscillating magnetically

ATOMIC: aligned truths/thoughts observing magnetically induced concepts

ATTITUDE: assigned truths transforming inspired thoughts unifying data emotionally

AURA: atomic universal radiance amplified

AWARE: aligned with assigned radiant energy

BAPTISM: blessings allow perfection to inspire souls magnetically

BE: birth emotionally/electrically; balance energy

BEAT: balancing emotions aligning truths

BEING: birthing entities inducing numerical geometry; balanced energy inciting nuclear generators

BECOME: birth emotional consciousness observing mental environments

BELIEVE: balancing electric logic illuminating emotions visibly expressed

BIG BANG: bringing inspired generators back along numerical geometry; beaming inspired geometry balancing atomic nuclear generators

BIRTHING: balancing inspired radiance to harmonically incite nuclear generators

BLACK HOLES: balancing logic aligning conscious knowledge harmonically oscillating love/life enlightening/energy source/ spiritually

BOARD: body observing assigned radiant desires

BODY: biologically observing data youthfully

BRAIN: biological repository/radio aligning inductive numbers

BRIGHT: blinding radiantly induced generators harnessing truth

CARNAL: consciously aligned radiance numerically assigning love

CD: conscious data

CHANNEL: conscious harmony assigning nuclear numbers expressing logic

CHARGE: cosmic harmony aligning radiant geometry electromagnetically

CHILD: conceived harmony inspiring living dreams; conscious harmony is love divine

CHIP: child harnessing inspired perspectives

CHOICE: consciously harnessing our inspired concepts emotionally

CHROMOSOMES: concise harmonic rhythm oscillating magnetically organized signals ordering matter expressing Source/spirits

COACH: consciously observe assigned children's harmonics

COLOR: concepts oscillating logical order radiantly

COMPLETE: cosmos of magnetic points lineally expressing thought energy.

COMPUTER: consciously observing magnetic phenomenon unifying truths electromagnetically radiated

CONSCIOUS: conceiving of numerical Source creating inspired observable universes spiritually

CONSCIOUSNESS: conceiving/conception one/of nuclear/numerical source creating/coalescing inspired/independent observable universes spinning numerical energy stimulating spirits/souls

COSMIC: celestial omnipotent-source magnetically inducing consciousness

COSMIC CHILD: creator of source-mind inducing concepts consciously harmonizing inspired logic dimensionally

COSMIC CONSCIOUSNESS: celestial omniscient-Source magnetically inducing concepts cooperatively oscillating nuclear souls coalescing into observable unified spaces numerically evolving Source spiritually

COSMOS: consciousness of Source-Mind observing spirits

COURAGE: consciousness of universal radiance aligning generators electromagnetically

COURSE: conception of universally radiant source energy/emotionally/ electromagnetically; conceiving observations universally radiating spirits electromagnetically; consciously observing universal radiance sent electromagnetically

CPU: conscious psychokinetic unit

CREATE: consciously radiate energy as truths evolving

DARK: data aligning radiant knowledge

DARK SPACE: divine abstract radiant knowledge sequencing points as conscious energy

DATA: divine abstract thoughts aspiring; dimensionally aligning truth atomically; digitally aligning thoughts atomically

DAY: divining as youth; data aligning youth

DC: divine consciousness

DEATH: dimensions/data evolve as thought/truth harmonizes; deleting emotions after thought harmonizes

DEEP: dimensions evolve elapsed projections

DESIRE: data electrically sent in radiant emotions; download electric Source inspiring radiant emotions

DICE: digitally inciting conscious entities

DIE: delete inspired emotions; data internally evolving; destroying illusioned enigmas

DIMENSION: data inspiring magnetically-evolving nuclear Source inducing observable numbers; data inciting manifestations evolving nuclear Source into observable natures

DISC: data-infused spiritual consciousness; divinely inspired spiritual consciousness

DISEASE: data inflecting Source evolving atomically stimulated environments

DIVINE: data inducing visions inspiring nuclear emotions

DIVINE WILL: data inducing visions inspiring numbers emotionalizing wisdom illuminating love/life

DNA: divine numerical assignment; divine nuclear avenues; divine numbers aligned

DOS: divine omniscient system; divine omnipotent spirit

DOOR: dimensionally observe our/other radiance/realities

DREAM: detect radiant energy as/aligning memories

DVD: divine vibration distorted; divine visionary disciple

EDUCATION: evolving data unifying consciousness aligning truths inciting omnipotent numbers

EGG: emotional generator germinating

EGO: emotionally generated observer

ELECTRIC: emanating logical expressions conceiving truths radiantly inducing consciousness

ELECTRON: emotionalizing logic electrifying conscious thought radiance oscillating numbers

ELEMENTS: electric logic evolving matter envisioning nuclear transformations sequentially

EMIT: electro-magnetically inducing truths

EMOTION: electrically moving/manifesting omniscient thoughts/truths inspired on numbers

EMOTIONAL: electrically moving observable thoughts inspired on numbers as/aligning light/logic

END: emotional/eternal numbers diverted

ENERGY: eternal numbers evolve radiance generating youth; electrified numbers emotionally radiating generator youth

ENTERTAIN: electrifying numerical thoughts emanating radiant truths along inspired natures

ENVISION: explore night visions illuminating source inciting observable/omnipotent numbers

EPIPHANY: enlightened point illuminating perfect harmony aligning nuclear youth

EQUAL: electromagnetic quantum unifying atomic love/life

ESP: enlightened spiritual power

ESSENCE: eternal Source stimulating electric numbers consciously evolving: eternal Source spiritually emanating numerical concepts emotionally

ETERNAL: elemental transmigration electrifying radiant numbers aligned logically

ETERNITY: evolving thoughts/truths emanating radiant numbers illuminating transmigratory youth

ETHERS: eternal truths harmonically expressing radiant Source

EYES: experiencing your emotions spiritually; eternal youths evolving spiritually/spontaneously; eternal youth's emotional soul

EVOLVE: electrically vibrating observable Love/Life visions emotionally; electrifying visions observing logic validated emotionally

EVOLUTION: eternally vibrating omnipotent love/life unifying truths inducing observable numbers; emotionally vibrating outwardly Love/Life unity transmitting inspired omnipresent numbers

FACT: frequency aligning conscious truth/thought

FAITH: focusing atomically inspired thought harmony

FAMILY: feelings aligned magnetically into loving youth

FATHER: fantastically altering truth harmony emanating radiance

FEAR: feeling energy as reality; focusing emotionally aligned radiance

FEEL: focusing emotion experiencing/expressing/evolving life

FIELDS: frequencies inducing electric logic digitally scened

FILES: focused ideas logically expressing/enlightening source/space

FIRE: focused inspiration radiating emotions

FLESH: finding love's electric source harmony

FLOPPY DISC: focused logic observing points projecting youth's data infusing spiritual consciousness

FLOW: feel love/life observing wisdom

FOCAL POINT: force of consciousness aligning lineal perceptions of inspired nuclear thought

FOCUS: formulate observable concepts utilizing/unifying source

FOCUSED MIND: formulate observable concepts utilizing source-energy data magnetically inducing nuclear dimensions

FORCE: frequency of radiant conscious energy; frequency of radiance consciously evolving; fluctuating on radiant conscious entities

FORGIVE: forget obstructive radiance generated in vibrant emotions

FORM: frequency oscillating radiance manifested

FORMS: focused omnipotent radiance modeling Source

FOSSIL FUELS: frequencies of spiritually sensual inputs lineally focused utilizing emotionally loaded symbols

FREE: feeling radiant energy emotionally; focusing radiant electric emotions

FREE WILL: focusing radiance electromagnetically energizing wisdom illuminating Love/Life

FUSION: focusing universal Source inciting omnipresent numbers

FUTURE: focus universal truths unifying radiant energy

GALACTIC: geometrically aligned logic arranging coherent truths inducing cognition

GAME: generator aligning magnetic energy; geometrically aligning mental emotions

GENERATOR: genetically engineered numerical entity radiating atomic truths observing realities

GEOMETRY: generating emotional observations mentally examining truths revealing youths; generating entities oscillating mentally expressed truths radiating youths; generating experiences oscillating mental expressions through radiant yearning

GIVE: generate inspired vibrant emotion

GLORY: generating/gracious love observing radiant youth

GLOW: generating love/life/logic observing wisdom

GOD: generator of desire

GRACE: generating/glorious radiance aligning conscious entities

GRATEFUL: generating radiant appreciation that expresses feelings unifying logic

GRAVITY: gathering radiance aligning visions inciting thinking youth

GREAT COMPUTER: generating radiant energy as thought consciously observing magnetic phenomenon unifying truths electromagnetically radiated

GRIEVING: generating radiance in emotional vibrations inciting nuclear generators

GROW: gather radiances of wisdom

GROWING: gathering radiances of wisdom inspiring/inciting/inducing numerical geometry

GROWTH: gathered radiances of wisdom through harmony

GUIDE: generating universal insights digitally enlightening

GUT: germinate universal truths

HARD DRIVE: harmonically aligns radiant data dimensionally into visions expressed

HARMONY: harnessing aligned radiant memories observing/opening/ oscillating nuclear youth

HE: heart evolving; harmonic energy/emotions

HEART: his/her emotional angels radiating thoughts; his/her emotions aspiring radiant truths; harmonizing emotional angels radiating thoughts

HEAVEN: his/her emotional attitude vibrating electric/eternal numbers; harmony/heart evolving around vibrant emotional numbers; harnessing emotions as visions enlightening numbers; her emotional attitudes vacillate electric numbers

HELL: his/her emotional love/life; harnessing emotional love/life; harmony expressing love/life

HER: heart evolving radiantly; his emotional radiance

HERMIT: harmonic electromagnetic-radiance managing inspired truths

HIS: harmonically inspiring spirits; harmony inducing spirit

HOLD: harnessing omnipotent logic dimensionally

HOME: harmony of mental emotions

HOPE: harnessing our projected expectations

HUMAN: harmony uniting magnetically aligned numbers

I AM: indivisible atomic mind; inspiring/inciting almighty memory

IDEA: inspired/illuminated data electromagnetically aligned/amplified

IDIOT: inspires data individually observing truth

IGNITE: illuminating geometric numbers inducing thought energy

ILLUSION: inciting lineal logic unifying Source illuminating omniscient numbers; illuminating love/life upon Source-inspired omniscient numbers

IMAGE: inspired memory aligning generators emotionally; illuminated mind atomically generating energy

IMAGINE: induce magnetic algorithms generating inspired nuclear energy

IN: inspired numbers; insighting numbers

INHALE: induce numbers harnessing aligned logic emotionally

INSIGHTING: inflecting numerical Source inspiring generators harnessing truths influencing nuclear geometry

INTERFACE: inducing numerical truths electrifying radiant frequencies aligning conscious emotions

IS: inspirational/indivisible source/spirit; inflecting source

ISSUES: inspired signals stimulating universal entities spiritually

IT: inspired thought

KARMA: knowledge allowing radiant memory access

KEY: knowledge enlightening youth

KILL: knowledgeably induce/inverse Love Life

KNOW: kinetic numbers organize wisdom; kindling numerically observed wisdom

KNOWLEDGE: kinetic numbers outputting wisdom's lineal/logical energy dimensionally generating/governing evolution/entities; kinetic numbers organizing wisdom logically expressing divine geometric evolution

LASER: light amplifying Source-energy radiance

LEARN: love/life energy arranges radiant numbers

LIFE: love is fluid energy; love is feeling emotion; love inspiring fluid emotions; liquefying inspired frequencies emotionally; logic/ lineally inducing fluid expression/emotions

LIGHT: love/logic inspires/induces/incites generators' harmonic thoughts/truths

LIGHT SPEED: logically inducing geometric harmony through sequentially processing electromagnetic energy digitally

LIMBO: lost in mind between observations

LINE: logically inciting numerical energy

LINK: logically induce/interface numerical knowledge

LIVE: logically inducing vibrant energy/emotions

LIVES: Light illuminating visions enlightening souls

LOGIC: love offered generators inducing consciousness; lineal observations generating inductive consciousness

LOGICALLY: Love oscillates generators inducing consciousness as loving/living youth

LOVE: life of vibrant emotion/energy; logically observing vibrant energy/emotions; logically observing visions emotionally

MAGNETIC: mind aligning geometric numbers expressing thoughts inciting consciousness

MAGNETISM: manipulating aligned geometric numbers electrifying thoughts inducing specific matter

MAN: magnetically aligned numbers

MANIFESTED: magnetically aligned numbers illuminating frequencies emanating Source transforming energy dimensionally

MANKIND: magnetically aligned numerical knowledge insighting nuclear dimensions

MATTER: magnetically aligned thoughts/truths transmitting electric radiation/realities/radiance

ME: mental emotions; manifesting/manipulating energy/emotions: mentally expressed

MENTAL: magnetic energy numerically transmitting atomic/aligned logic

MEMORY: Mind experiencing/expressing moments observing radiant youth

MEMORIES: magnetically expressed moments of radiant inspiration evolving sequentially

MILESTONE: memories illuminating life evolving spiritually through observing numbers electromagnetically

MIND: magnetically/memory inspired/illuminates numerical data/ desires; manipulating inspired numbers dimensionally; manifesting inspired nuclear dimensions; magnetically induced numerical deity

MIND IMAGE: magnetically inducing numerical data inspiring moments aligning generators emotions

MISSION: magnetically incorporating Source scientifically inducing omnipotent numbers

MOMENT: mind observing memory evolving nuclear truths

MONITOR: manipulate omnipotent numbers inducing truths oscillating radiance

MOTHER: magnetically observing/organizing truth harmony evolving radiance

MOTION: magnetically oscillating thought into observable numbers

MOVE: magnetically oscillating vibrant energy

MY: magnetic youth

MY FORM: memory yielding frequencies observing radiant minds

NAME: numbers aligning mental emotions

NATURE: numerically aligned thoughts unifying radiant energy

NAUGHT: numbers assigning universal generators harmonic thoughts

NETWORK: numbers electromagnetically transmitting wisdom oscillating radiant knowledge

NIGHT: number is generating/gathering harmonic thoughts/threads; numbers induce generators' harmonic truths; numerically insighting geometrically held thoughts

NINE: number inspires nuclear energy; numbers inducing numbers eternally: nuclear individuals naturally evolve

NOT: numerically observing truths

NOW HERE: numerically observing wisdom harmonically evolving radiant emotions

NUCLEAR: numbers unleashing consciousness logically emitting aligned radiation; numerically unified children/consciousness logically evolving atomic radiance

NUMBER: nuclear universes magnetically balancing/birthing emotional radiation; nuclear units/unification magnetically binding electric radiance

OBSERVE: operating binary-source energy/electrically radiating vibrant emotions

OFF: observing fluid files; opening further frequencies; observing formless facts

OLD: observing love dimensions

OM: omniscient mind

ON: observing numbers

ONE: omnipotent numerical/nuclear energy/energizer/engineer

OPEN: observe perspectives evolving numbers

OPPOSITION: observing points projected on source-inspired truths inducing observers negatively

OTHER: opposite truth harmonizing eternal radiance

OUT: observing universal truths/thoughts; one united trinity

PART: personally aligned radiant thoughts

PASSION: playing as souls spiritually inciting omnipotent numbers

PART: perceived as radiant thought

PAST: previously aligned sequential thought; points aligning spiritual truths

PATIENCE: physically aligning truths inspiring electric numbers conceived emotionally

PC: psychic consciousness

PHOTONS: particular harmonic of thoughts oscillating numerically

PLAN: perfecting love aligning numbers

PLAY: perfecting love as youth

PLAYER: projecting logic atomically yielding electromagnetic radiance

POINT: perception of inspired nuclear thought/truth; perceptive omniscient-intelligence numerically transforming; portal of inspired nuclear truths

POLES: points of logic expressing Source

PRAY: projecting radiance around you

PRAYER: projecting radiant assistance youth emotionally request

PREORDAINS: projecting radiance electromagnetically observing realities dimensionally aligned in nuclear sciences

PROCEED: perform reflective observations consciously evolving electromagnetic data

PROCESS: projecting radiance of consciousness expressing/ experiencing Source spiritually; procedure reflecting omniscient consciousness evolving Source scientifically

PROGRESS: perfecting radiance observing generators reflect eternal Source spiritually

PROTON/S: projecting radiance oscillating thoughts on numbers/nuclear science

QUANTUM: qualities unify atomic numbers transmitting/transforming universes magnetically

RADIANCE: rays aligning data inspired as nuclear consciousness evolving

RADIANT: randomly aligned data illuminated as nuclear thought

RADIATING: radiantly aligning data illuminating assigned truths inspiring numerical generators

RADIATION: radiantly aligned data illuminating assigned truths inspired on numbers

RAM: radiant angel memory

REAL: radiant energy aligned logically; radiating emotions as love; radiantly energizing atomic life

REAL TIME: radiant energy aligning logical thoughts inducing mental emotions

REALITY: radiant energy/entity aligning lineal inspiration/insights transforming youths

REALIZATION: radiant energy aligning love/life illumination zoned around truths inducing observable numbers

RECALL: recycling electromagnetic consciousness aligning love/life

RECEIVE: respect eternal consciousness evolving in vibrant emotions

REFLECTION: recognizing electric frequencies liquefying emotions consciously transforming its oppositional nature

RELATIVITY: radiant energy logically aligning truths inciting visions illuminating thinking youths

RELIEF: restoring eternal love/life in equal forces

REST: recalling emotionally stimulated/spent thoughts

RITE: ritually inducing truths evolving

SAINT: special angel inspiring nuclear/numerical truths

SAME: Source as mental emotions

SCENED: spiritually/sequentially coalesce electromagnetic numbers evolving dimensions

SCHOOL: soul consciously harnessing our omniscient logic

SCIENCE: Source-consciousness inspiring/inciting electromagnetic nuclear concepts emotionally; Source-consciousness inspiring/inciting electric numbers coalescing energy; Source-consciousness inducing eternal numbers conceived/coalesced electromagnetically

SECURITY: Source emanating consciousness unifying radiant inspiration through youth

SEE: Spirit/Source evolves emotionally; Spirit emanates electrically

SEEING: sequentially evolving externally in numerical/nuclear geometry

SEER: Spirit/soul enlightening electromagnetic radiance

SEED: Source emotionally energizing desires

SEEKER: spiritual entity exploring knowledge evolving radiance

SELF: Source-energy/expressing love/life force; soul experiencing love/life force;

SELF-CENTERED: sequentially emanating logic focusing concepts energizing nuclear thoughts electrically radiating emotional dimensions

SENSE: symbolically experience numbers sent electrically

SENTENCE: sequentially evolving nuclear thought energizing numerical consciousness electromagnetically; source expressing nuclear thoughts evolving numerical consciousness electromagnetically

SEX: Spirit's emotional exchange

SHAPE: Source-harmony aligning projected energy

SHE: Source harmony expressed; Spirit heartfully evolving

SHINE: Source harmony inducing nuclear energy

SHOW: spiritual/Source harmony of wisdom; spirits harnessing omniscient wisdom

SIGHT: spirit is gathering harmonic thoughts; Spirit inspiring generator's harmonic truths, shining in glory harnessing thoughts; spirits illuminate games harmonizing trinities

SIN: spiritual insight/induced number; spiritually inspired nature

SING: spiritually inducing numerical geometry

SONG: Source/soul orating/orchestrating nuclear geometry

SOC: source of consciousness; state of consciousness; soul observing consciousness

SOP: spiritual observation powers

SOUL: spirit/spark of universal love/life/logic

SOURCE: system of universal radiant consciousness evolving; Spirit's omnipresence unifying radiant concepts electromagnetically; soul observing unlimited radiance consciously evolving

SPACE: Source/some point awaiting conscious expression; soul perceiving assigned conscious enlightenment; spiritually projected as conscious entities

SPARK: Source provides all radiant knowledge

SPARKING: seeking perceptions along radiant knowledge inciting nuclear generators

SPARKS: spiritually projecting all radiant knowledge sequentially

SPERM: Source providing eternal radiant memory

SPHERE: Source-point harmonically evolving radiance/radiant electromagnetically/energy

SPIRIT: Source-points illuminating radiantly inspired thoughts/truths

SPIRITS: souls perceiving illuminated radiance inflecting thoughts sequentially

SPIRITUAL: Source-points illuminating radiantly inspired thoughts unifying atomic love/life

STAR: spiritual truths atomically radiating; source thinking/transmitting atomic radiance; soul thinking as radiant Source

STATE: science transforming aligned trinities experientially; spirits transmigrate along truths eternally; Source transmits atomic truths experimentally

STORE: spiritual truths offer radiant emotions

STRESS: stretching truths radiating emotionally stimulated souls

STRIFE: spiritual/stressing truths reflected/radiating in fluid/frequencies emotions/expressed

SUPREME: Source unifying points radiating electrically magnetic emotions

SUN: Source-unifying nucleus; soul uniting numbers

TEAM: together each are many

TELL: thoughts energizing love/life

TECHNOLOGY: transforming energy concepts harmonizing nuclear operations logically optimizing geometric yields; thought energy consciously harmonizing numbers optimizing logical oscillations gyrating youth

TEST: thoughts emotionally stretching truth

THINK: transform harmony inspiring numerical knowledge

THOUGHT: transcendental harmony observing/oscillating universal generators harnessing truths

THREE: transcendental/truth harmony/harmonizing radiating/radiant emotions electrically

TIDES: thoughts inducing dimensions evolving sequentially

TIME: thought inspiring magnetic energy; truth inspiring moments electromagnetically; truth inspiring mental emotions; this instant mentally expressed; traveling in mental emotions

TIMELINE: truths inspiring moments evolving logically induced numbers emotionally

TRANSMIGRATE: transfer radiance aligning numerical sequences manifesting inspired generators reflecting atomic truths electromagnetically

TRINITY: truths radiantly inducing numbers inspiring thinking youths

TRUE: turning around universal emotions; three radiating universal entities/energy

TRUST: truth reassembling universal souls together

TRUTH: transcendental radiance unifying thought harmony

TUNE: transforming universal numerical energy

TURN: transform universal radiant numbers

TWO: truths watching over; true wills observe

UNDERSTANDING: unifying numerical data emanating radiance source transmits as numerical dimensions inspiring nuclear generators

UNIT: universal network/number inducing thought/truth

UNITED: unifying numbers inducing truths energizing dimensions

UNIVERSE: united numbers inducing/inspiring vibrant energy radiating spiritual emotions; unified numbers illuminating visions evolving radiant Source electromagnetically

UNIVERSAL: unified numbers inducing visions evolving radiance spirits align logically

UNKNOWN: unfolding nuclear knowledge numerically observing wisdom now

US: united source, unifying spirit, universal spirit/soul

USB: universal spiritual broadcast, universal spiritual battery

VIEW: vision inducing enlightened wisdom

VISION: vibrations inspiring spirits/souls inducing observable numbers

VEIL: vibrating energy illumining logic

VOID: volumes of inspirational data; vibrantly oscillating numerical data

VOLUMES: visionaries observing logic unify memories expressing Source

WAS: wisdom aligning source

WE: wisdom exemplified/eternal

WEB: wisdom eternally balancing

WHO: wisdom harmonically observing

WHOLE: wisdom harmoniously observing Love/Life energy

WIFE: wisdom is fluid emotion

WILL: wisdom inducing/illuminating Love/Life

WILL BE: wisdom inducing Love/Life birthing energy

WILL POWER: wisdom inducing Love/Life perfecting on words eternally radiant

WISE: wisdom illuminating spiritual energy

WISDOM: words/will inspiring spiritual dimensions of mind; words inspiring souls' dreams observing Mind; words inspiring spiritual desires observed magnetically

WISH: wisdom inspiring syncopated harmony

WOMAN: wisdom of/observing/oscillating magnetically aligned numbers

WOMB: wisdom oscillating material birth

WONDER: worlds of numerical data eternally radiating; willingly organizing numerical data's electric radiance; wisdom of numerical data eternally radiating

WORD: will observes radiant desire; wisdom of radiant desires/data

WORDS: wisdom of radiant data symbols

WORK: wisdom of radiant knowledge; will omnipotent radiant knowledge

WORLD/S: wisdom of radiant Love dimensions/data; wisdom oscillating radiant love-data systems

YOU: youth observing universes/unity; your own universe

YOUTH: you observing universal truth harmony; you observing unified truths harmonically; yielding our universal truth harmony; yearning omniscient unity through harmony

YOUTHS: YOU that harness Source

ZERO: zone evolving radiant observations; zoning electromagnetic radiance outwardly; zoned emotion retains omnipotence

Index

(Essay —*Poem* —**Picture Poem**)